Securing Sex

Morality and Repression in the
Making of Cold War Brazil

Benjamin A. Cowan

The University of North Carolina Press
Chapel Hill

Published with the assistance of the Authors Fund of the University of North
Carolina Press.

Set in Espinosa Nova and Alegreya Sans by Westchester Publishing Services
Manufactured in the United States of America

The paper in this book meets the guidelines for permanence and durability
of the Committee on Production Guidelines for Book Longevity of the Council on
Library Resources.

The University of North Carolina Press has been a member of the Green Press
Initiative since 2003.

Cover illustrations: Historical document censored by the Brazilian government's
Department of Censorship of Public Entertainment (photo by the author; source:
National Archive in Brasília); unzipped jeans, ©iStockphoto.com/numxyz.

Library of Congress Cataloging-in-Publication Data

Cowan, Benjamin A., author.
   Securing sex : morality and repression in the making of Cold War Brazil / Benjamin A.
Cowan.
        pages cm
   Includes bibliographical references and index.
      ISBN 978-1-4696-2750-2 (pbk : alk. paper)—ISBN 978-1-4696-2751-9 (ebook)
1. Brazil—Social conditions—1964–1985. 2. Brazil—Moral conditions. 3. Social
values—Brazil—History—20th century. 4. Cold War—Social aspects—Brazil.
5. Sexual ethics—Brazil—History—20th century. 6. Conservatism—Brazil—History—
20th century. I. Title.
   HN290.Z9M636 2016
   306.0981—dc23
2015031947

Contents

Figures

Acknowledgments

How strange: having found enough words to write a book, I am unable to find the words to express my brimming gratitude. Perhaps that is because I am so indebted. The completion of this book is a testament not so much to my own work as to the support of many wise, caring people and generous institutions. I simply can't thank them enough, but let this formal attempt be just one of many *agradecimentos*. First and foremost, there are the mentors who shepherded (or gently and expertly nudged) me at various points in this process: Robin Derby, Jim Green, and Jeff Lesser, indefatigably willing to counsel with kindness and to read with patience. Likewise, I am indebted to those sages who always responded when I needed their input, and whose brilliance shone into specific, unexpected, or neglected corners of my research and writing, sending me off in fruitful new directions: Ellen DuBois, Randal Johnson, Bill Summerhill, Andy Apter, Sueann Caulfield, Barbara Weinstein, Jerry Dávila, John French, Carlos Fico, Lessie Jo Frazier, Micol Seigel, and Celso Castro.

I would especially like to thank the friends who sustained me emotionally and intellectually through the last ten years—people on whom I have leaned for love and laughter, for stimulation, for relief, and for inspiration. These are my heroes, and their contributions to my life, not to mention my work, are infinite and ineffable. Natalie Carnes, perhaps the first person to think of me as a scholar, remains, these decades (!) later, the person who defines genius, empathy, and warmth for me; she is a born, as well as a trained, expert in humanity. Marianne Cook, Gabrielle Hunter-Rivera, Dan Droller, Spencer Rudey, and Roya Fohrer—I don't deserve you, and your support sustains me, every day. Several dear friends generously gave of their own brilliance, as rich in their affection and conviviality as in their intellectual virtuosity: Tobias Wofford (nurturer, listener, and wit extraordinaire), Christopher Tradowsky (intrepid hiking buddy, philosophical wonder, creative genius, and font of culture), Bibi Obler (empath, rock, inimitable interlocutor, stalwart spunner, fixer of hearts and more minor hitches), David Sartorius (who does everything well, makes it look easy, rightly charms all he encounters, and uses his powers entirely for good), Melanie Arias (whose passions seem always to make the world, and her communities, and her loved ones, better), and Julie Weise (a real-life superhero and also my academic sister, who has so often gone before and taught me everything I needed to know). These are my literati, my idols, and my tribe—I simply could never have imagined the privilege of basking in their warmth and wonderfulness. And who would have thought I would come to rest in Washington, D.C.—much less *Halifax?* I would not have managed the journey (not to mention traveled so pleasurably) without those boon companions who remained loyal, buoyant, and generally marvelous even when I pined insufferably for my ever-beloved LA: Radhika Natarajan, Paddy Riley, Bea Gurwitz, Chris Gregg and Chuck Cushman, Marcy Norton, Scott Larson, Siobhan Rigg, John Taht, and Megan Sokolowski.

Each of the institutions where I have been privileged to learn and (occasionally) to teach has furnished me with colleagues and friends who lent expertise, camaraderie, and companionship of all sorts. My fellow graduate students at UCLA endowed the craft of history with practicability and esprit de corps. Mir Yarfitz has so much to offer that I wonder at his patience in imparting some fraction of that wealth to me or any of his other admiring students. Zeb Tortorici, Dana Velasco, Xochitl Flores, Peter Villella, Liz Jones, Rob Sierakowski, and Molly Ball made for a cohort that provided everything from parties to sublets to tricks of the trade. At Occidental College, I had the honor of working alongside Lisa Sousa, who showed me how to be a teacher and a scholar, and Alex Puerto, whose friendship and company I even now think of as a gift. When I arrived in Nova Scotia, my colleagues took extra care to keep me from feeling lost—and I do not know where I might have ended up without Phil Zachernuk, Amal Ghazal, Shirley Tillotson, Justin Roberts, Ruth Bleasdale, and Krista Kesselring. At George Mason, I sometimes feel as though I have stumbled into academic Narnia. My colleagues are genuine, warm, supportive, and collegial beyond belief. I would especially like to thank Joan Bristol, Rob Decaroli, Jo-Marie Burt, Alison Landsberg, Meredith Lair, Matt Karush, Sumaiya Hamdani, Sam Lebovic, Zach Schrag, Randolph Scully, and Cindy Kierner for making my community at GMU such a welcoming place to teach, research, and, well, hang out.

Some who supported this project, at various stages, did so with their own natural magnanimity, as a matter of course. Several coconspirators helped make collegial, and communal, our plots to historicize sexuality, students, the Right, and counterculture: how to appreciate the solidarity, and the intellectual largesse, of Tori Langland, Margaret Power, Valeria Manzano, Pablo Ben, and Colin Snider? Each read, responded, appreciated, critiqued, with a judiciousness—and a repetitive willingness—that I cannot have deserved. Thank you, my friends and colleagues! Teo Ruiz, Stephen Bell, Kevin Terraciano, Michael Salman, and Geoff Robinson showed me the kind of scholarship to which I aspire; and Daryle Williams, Ken Serbin, Dain Borges, Ana Maria Goldani, George Chauncey, Gil Joseph, and Ramón Gutiérrez not only responded to my work (or to my requests) but showed me the path toward achieving that kind of scholarship. Christiane Jalles de Paula and Sandy Deutsch provided invaluable tips for navigating the study of the Right; and critical conversations with Jaime Delgado, Chris Dunn, and Renan Quinalha generated unlooked-for insights, for which I am ever grateful. I owe a special debt to those who helped create the space for the kinds of conversations that facilitated this book, fellow *brasilianistas* and other kindred spirits: Julio Capó, Ryan Jones, José Amador, Jason Ruiz, Nicole Guidotti-Hernández, and Margot Canaday.

In the field, I would have made no headway were it not for the aid of archivists and librarians who lent me expertise, patience, and sympathy. At the Arquivo Nacional's Brasília facility, Raynes Castro, Paulo Ramalho, Vera, Mariana, Daisy, and Pablo shared coffee, rides, and tips for wrestling with the ever-capricious *base*. I must offer particularly warm thanks to Silvana, to Sergeants Vidal and Wilber, to Regina and to Dona Cleide, pillars of the excellent team at the Escola Superior de Guerra. Then, too, I could not have understood what I was reading were it not for the magnanimous souls who allowed me to interview them in the Departamento de Estudos. At the ECEME library, Lieutenants Fernanda and Fabiana were always ready with a smile and a recommendation. I was consistently humbled by the personal radiance and professional capability of Dona Glória, sole proprietress, archivist, librarian, and staff member of the ADESG library. The entire *equipe* of the Arquivo Público do Estado do Rio de Janeiro could not have been more helpful. Many thanks to Renan Marinho de Castro for his friendliness—and his valiant support in my struggle with (against?) the CPDOC microfilm machines.

I am also deeply grateful to the staff of each institution to which I have belonged. At UCLA, at Occidental, at Dalhousie, and at George Mason, a support staff of patient, enterprising, and seemingly unflappable administrators never failed to respond to my incessant, sometimes ill-timed requests and masterfully managed my inexperience. Particular thanks to Hadley Porter, Jinny Oh, Lindsay Kovner, Nancy Dennis, Barbara Bernstein, Florine Tseu, Tina Jones, Valerie Peck, Carrie Grabo, Sara Duval, Nicole Roth, and Susie Leblanc.

This book would of course not have been possible without the generous support of institutions. They include the Social Sciences and Humanities Research Council, the American Philosophical Society, the Tinker Foundation, and the Andrew W. Mellon Foundation, as well as Dalhousie University, UCLA's Latin American Institute, Institute for Social Research, and the Pauley Fellowship. I am further indebted to the archives and libraries where I did my research, foremost among them the Biblioteca General Cordeiro de Farias at the Escola Superior de Guerra, the Biblioteca Nacional do Brasil, the Arquivo Nacional do Brasil, and the Arquivo Público do Estado do Rio de Janeiro.

First, last, and always, my most deeply felt thanks go to my family, the source of my joys, who always make me feel like anything is possible.

Acronyms

AAB	Aliança Anticomunista Brasileira (Brazilian Anticommunist Alliance)
ADESG	Associação dos Diplomados da Escola Superior de Guerra (ESG Alumni Association)
AIB	Ação Integralista Brasileira (Brazilian Integralist Action)
CAMDE	Campanha da Mulher Pela Democracia (Women's Campaign for Democracy)
CCC	Comando de Caça aos Comunistas (Command for Hunting Communists)
CFC	Conselho Federal da Cultura (Federal Council on Culture)
CFE	Conselho Federal da Educação (Federal Council on Education)
CENIMAR	Centro de Informações da Marinha (Navy Intelligence Service)
CIE	Centro de Informações do Exército (Army Intelligence Service)
CISA	Centro de Informações da Aeronáutica (Air Force Intelligence Service)
CNMC	Comissão Nacional de Moral e Civismo (National Commission on Morality and Civics)
CODI	Centro(s) de Operações de Defesa Interna (Internal Defense Operations Center/s)
CSC	Conselho Superior de Censura (Superior Council of Censors)

DCDP	Divisão de Censura de Diversões Públicas (Division of Censorship of Public Entertainment)
DOPS	Departamento de Ordem Política e Social (Department of Political and Social Order)
ECEME	Escola de Comando e Estado Maior do Exército (Command and General Staff College)
EMC	Educação Moral e Cívica (Moral and Civic Education)
ESG	Escola Superior de Guerra (Higher War College)
IBAD	Instituto Brasileiro de Ação Democrática (Brazilian Institute for Democratic Action)
IPES	Instituto de Pesquisas e Estudos Sociais (Institute for Social Research and Study)
LDN	Liga da Defesa Nacional (National Defense League)
MCI	Movimento Comunista Internacional (International Communist Movement)
PPGAR	Programa de Prevenção da Gravidez de Alto Risco (Program for the Prevention of High-Risk Pregnancy)
RM	Rearmamento Moral (Moral Re-Armament)
SNI	Serviço Nacional de Informações (National Intelligence Service)
TFP	Sociedade Brasileira de Defesa da Tradição, Família e Propriedade (Brazilian Society for the Defense of Tradition, Family, and Property)
UNE	União Nacional dos Estudantes (National Student Union)

Securing Sex

Introduction

That Is Communism Today: Envisioning the Internal Enemy

In 1974, Brazil commenced its tenth year of military government, a dictatorship marked by repressive campaigns to stamp out communist subversion. One afternoon that summer, Cristovam Breiner, a devoutly Catholic judge, former policeman, and decided supporter of the regime, boarded a public bus in Rio de Janeiro. There, to his shock and horror, he witnessed what he construed as an attack by the agents of subversion. These were not the (relatively few) armed revolutionaries whom, by that point, government forces had largely detained, exiled, or killed. Instead, Breiner recalled in an article written for the right-wing National Defense League, he had seated himself beside a "lady of modest and respectable aspect" when two students, aged "thirteen or fourteen at most," boarded the bus. It was then that the onslaught commenced, as "the pair of students . . . immediately began embracing passionately, and even started to caress each other, reaching the point of repeated kissing, as if they were in the most secluded hideaway." Appalled as he was, Breiner knew precisely how to interpret the scene before him. "*That,*" he explained to his readers, "is communism today, instigated by materialist subversives, as subversion lies implicitly . . . in that libidinous excess which is the greatest teacher of communist subversion [for which] it is necessary to instill libidinousness in the peoples of the world, to strip them of their character . . . that they may be more easily dominated."[1] Among the staunchest partisans of the dictatorship (which would last a total of twenty-one years, ending in 1985), Breiner rejoiced in the regime's repressive anticommunism. As he saw it, Brazilian society was pervaded by subversion, apparent in the rampant moral and sexual dissolution evinced by these two young "assailants." The situation, according to Breiner, necessitated authoritarian government, vigilance, and counterattack.

Breiner's testimony reveals a key element in his and other Cold Warriors' conjuring of enemy "subversives"—a way in which the Cold War could become "hot" via reimaginings of students, teachers, priests, artists, and other civilians as nefarious conspirators. Western Cold

Warriors' contemporary wisdom on vigilance against communism blurred the lines between combatants and noncombatants, making anyone—and sometimes, terrifyingly, everyone—a suspect and potential target. Military and intelligence experts throughout the Atlantic warned that the nebulous "internal enemy" would "disguise himself as priest or professor, student or peasant, vigilant defender of democracy or advanced intellectual . . . any role that he considers convenient to deceive, lie, and conquer the good faith of peoples of the West."[2] Breiner sought to penetrate these clever camouflages, to strip the "disguise" from enemy agents, foil their plans, and open them up to reprisal. To his mind, the face of the "enemy" materialized in moral and sexual deviance, especially where these intersected with youth or the public sphere. "*That*," as Breiner put it, "is communism today."

Breiner shared this vision of subversion and support for dictatorial violence with a cohort of outspoken and influential Brazilians. As early as May 1964, just weeks after the coup that inaugurated military rule, well-known journalist Gustavo Corção had advocated repression in similar terms. The need for the military's post-coup violence, wrote Corção, was obvious, particularly when it came to "young people linked with movements of the Left." Corção saw these young people as Breiner saw teenaged lovers—they "practiced, all at the same time, conspiracy and orgies. Sybaritism and Socialism." As Brazil muddled through the late 1960s and early 1970s (the darkest years of dictatorship, marked by armed conflict, torture, secret detention, and other civil and human rights violations), these views gained broad exposure and purchase. Corção spoke for those, in and beyond Brazil, who saw Western security threatened by a "worldwide revolution manifested in the growing dismantling of customs, the ascension of pornography, . . . and the downfall of the family." Such dissolution, in this view, was "not coincidental, [but] first and foremost a historical movement, directed by perverse minorities" of communist subversives.[3]

An intellectual and cultural history, this book excavates the ideology and activism of people like Breiner and Corção—representatives of a moralistic right wing that wielded critical ideological influence in mid–Cold War Brazil. I trace their perspective—which classified moral, cultural, and sexual ruptures as cornerstones of a subversive conspiracy—and its role in shaping dictatorial Brazil's security theory, policy, and practice. Anticommunist countersubversion, in Brazil and internationally, exceeded ideological opposition to Marxism and determinatively subsumed other, conflated anxieties—signally, as I demonstrate, anxieties about gender, sex, youth, and modernity. Brazilian authoritarianists' "modernizing" ethos has long elided the importance of supporters of dictatorship who, on the basis of those very anxieties, execrated modernization's consequences. For all its emphasis on the slogan "Security and Development" and much-heralded developmentalist technocracy, Brazil's military regime encompassed remarkable ambivalence when it came to the effects, real and perceived, of modernization. Indeed, a moral, sexual, and gendered "crisis of modernity," decried by far-right individuals and organizations, seemed increasingly palpable to powerful, conservative factions of Brazil's Cold Warriors in the 1960s and 1970s. This book treats of the endeavors of such rightists, their continuities with older and transnational iterations of conservative anticommunism, and the significance, as well as the limits, of their equation of subversion with moral disaster.

At its most potent, this right-wing sense of a cultural crisis lent coterminous structure to security theory and reactions against modernity, and helped elaborate the frameworks of authoritarian repression. Brazil's two decades of military government, of course, involved more than just panic about culture. Elements of the regime and its support base reacted strongly to perceived changes in (or threats to) traditional hierarchy and the nation's political and social economies. But just as technocrats directed the regime's economic, political, and social initiatives, a *moral* technocracy emerged to address vital concerns about moral dissolution and communist subversion. As this book shows, that moral technocracy gained considerable influence within the regime, especially as the power of right-leaning hard-liners waxed. This influence made antimodern moral panic a key component in the period's authoritarianism and anticommunism, and a compelling impetus to the deployment of dictatorial measures. As one former member of the regime later recalled, "There was talk of communism penetrating [Brazil] to do away with the structure of the family.... The plot was said to include things from the play *Hair*, which had a frontal nudity scene, to Chico Buarque's [play] *Roda viva*, where there were sacrileges that corrupted our Christian civilization."[4]

Brazil's military rule, technocratic restructuring, and extrajudicial state violence had regional counterparts across Latin America—a series of mid–Cold War, anticommunist autocracies that carved paths of terror, torture, disappearance, and death from Chihuahua to Tierra del Fuego. The lack of regard for the lives and liberties of civilians caught up in the fearsome machinery of these states has made Latin America's Cold War infamous. Survivors of military autocracy and paramilitary violence have attested to the Orwellian nature of this period in hemispheric history—often in stories that evoke the constant terror of potential repression, its seeming randomness, and the lives and livelihoods ended, ruined, or forever altered in single, relatively arbitrary moments. In Brazil alone, military governments held power for two decades, mandating draconian controls on civil and political liberties; murdered or "disappeared" hundreds of civilians; made torture standard procedure for those captured by the regime's political police; and created a culture of fear in which secret dungeons, government obfuscation, and impunity for atrocity perpetrators developed into long-term, institutional realities.[5]

This book recovers the lost stories of the repressive Right—reactionaries and extremists whose ideas about morality, sexuality, and modernity lent a certain animus and ideological structure to the authoritarianism and state violence that wracked the Americas in the decades after 1960. Though the rise and tenure of dictatorships have preoccupied scholars of Brazil and Spanish America for decades, recovering the stories of the Right remains crucial to understanding the ferocity of anticommunism in these contexts, the role of reactionary mobilizations in dictatorial Brazil and elsewhere in Latin America, and the apprehensions that informed and motivated hemispheric Cold Warriors. Where histories of the inter-American Cold War continue to foreground political, military, and diplomatic approaches (often with valuable insight), the cultural history of right-wing ideology and mobilization offers access to questions that have been sorely neglected.[6] What, we must ask, were the broader frameworks within which repression made sense to its rightist partisans and perpetrators? How did the devotees of counterrevolution talk about, envisage, and identify their enemies, especially in the context of military rule? How did Cold War countersubversion reach the volatile pitch exemplified by perspectives like Breiner's and Corção's—in which amorous, adolescent civilians became the focus of anticommunist vigilance and reaction?

To date, right-wing voices—especially those taking up the culture wars of their time—have been lost or ignored. This leaves us with shadowy and sometimes stereotypical profiles of authoritarianism and the contexts of violence—and in some cases, with rankling public debates about the nature of the military regimes, the responsibility for atrocity, and the extent and influence of extremist ideology. For decades, this has meant semantic deliberations about the application of the label "fascism" to Latin America's mid–Cold War autocrats, with relatively limited debate about the actual preoccupations shared by pre–and post–World War II rightists.[7] Then, too, we often hear the rote explanation that civil and human rights violations were the province of maniacal, ideologically autonomous underlings—unknown to and unsanctioned by the more urbane, presentable faces of the regimes in question.[8] In this book, I demonstrate that certain of the so-called excesses of dictatorship, often explained as the paranoias of the few, drew on an ideology that transcended regime hierarchies. Part of a larger framework of state violence and repression, moral, cultural, and gender concerns were championed by powerful sectors within and outside of the Brazilian state. These concerns gained strength across the vertical strata of Brazil's military regime, where they contributed to the intellectual and functional shape of Cold War countersubversion. Antimodern, reactionary moralisms (conspiracy theories, for example, that stigmatized sexually unconventional youth) formed an essential element of the anticommunism espoused by top members of the regime and their supporters. Moralistic anticommunism surfaced in high-level public debates and pronouncements, but also in classified and secret forums, in security theory, and in policing records, even when these did not take morality or culture as their principal subject matter or purpose. Disseminated by powerful right-wing activists, percolating among police and security forces, these moralisms reached (when they did not emanate from) the top echelons of anticommunist rule and reasoning. Recovering this history of the Right, then, illustrates neglected ways in which power and repression were invoked, deployed, and justified, and clarifies academic and public debates by illuminating key details of Cold Warriors' ideological armatures.

Reassessing Cold War Countersubversion: Getting to Know the Enemy

Securing Sex excavates a history of ideas essential to answering the above questions about Cold War countersubversion and, more importantly, about the transnational stories of anticommunism, cultural conservatism, and Cold War autocracy in the Americas. The project begins with a heuristic distillation, reducing those questions to a simpler, deceptively straightforward component: what *was* "subversion," in the minds of devoted countersubversives? The perceived threat of subversion lay at the heart of Cold War cultures of fear throughout the Americas and undergirded military ascendancy, prerogatives, and brutality. National security ideology, the doctrinal backbone of the armed forces' errands in government, combined economic modernization, nationalism, and a commitment to eradicating "internal enemies" classified as communist "subversives." Yet very little has emerged on how subversion was constructed and comprehended by those who sought to quell it. Scholars have rightly noted the conceptual ambiguity of subversion, its variable significations. Some, drawing on the language of military theorists themselves, have referred to subversion as a vague, fearsome "cultural broth" in which regime autocrats imagined the communist "virus" proliferating.[9] But what of the ingredients of this "broth"—what of the ways in which countersubversive actors *did* make their fears specific? How did right-wing militarists and their supporters conjure the ever-invoked menace of subversion—and what were the broader anxieties that facilitated such conjuring? Counterinsurgency and countersubversion, though they sometimes occasioned arbitrary violence, did not happen in an ideological or practical vacuum. Classificatory principles structured thinking about "the enemy" and made the battle against communism coherent to those who sought to eradicate it. If "subversion" could mean more than propagandizing, more than armed revolution, then what were the matrices that countersubversives, from anticommunist activists to military autocrats to security forces, drew on to comprehend their enemies?

These questions lead us to broader and deeper problems regarding the study of the Right more generally, beyond the frame of the nation-state. Latin American Cold Warriors' visions of their enemies continue to evade scholarly scrutiny because of a scarcity of research on the Right in the region.[10] In order to fully comprehend the roots, scope, and significance of Cold War authoritarianism and violence, we must interrogate the records left by Cold Warriors themselves. What do right-wing anticommunists have to tell us about this period and its disruptions? Though landmark studies have treated the early twentieth-century Right, we have yet to understand how to conceive of the latter-day Right—or Rights—and of countersubversives individually, organizationally, and as national and transnational actors. Moreover, the origins of these postwar right-wingers' worldviews remain inscrutable. This book investigates the ways in which their conservative visions transcended not only institutional and national boundaries, but also the temporal boundary of World War II and the demise of global fascism. What were the contours of countersubversive ideology among latter-day rightists? How did these ideas circulate—and how did they gain currency and power in the 1960s and 1970s?

These queries, of course, extend beyond Latin America and into the larger territory of the global Cold War. As I have begun to suggest, the transnational ways in which Western Cold Warriors at the height of their influence came to "know" their enemies remain ill understood. In the United States, innovative research has begun to unpack the ways in which conceptual "subversion" emerged from the raw material of everyday life, culture, and social behavior.[11] Where scholars of the North American security state have sought to counter traditional studies that "minimize moral and cultural concerns," this book expands the scope of culturally historicizing the Western Cold War.[12] The linkage of moral deviance and subversion—of, infamously, "communists and queers"—has often been presented as a North American story; in fact, it is a story about the construction of difference, extending far beyond the United States and even beyond the so-called Free World.[13] Recent scholarship hints tantalizingly at the hemispheric breadth with which Cold War and culture war intertwined: in 1966, as dictatorship descended on Argentina, a powerful military police official declared "pornographic magazines . . . the base of communist penetration"; Mexican conservatives made similar linkages in the late 1960s, claiming that—in the words of one letter to the president—student unrest in Mexico and beyond was "caused by the indiscreet baring of women's bodies when they wear miniskirts."[14] Here, I explore the ways in which countersubversion was transnationally and hemispherically articulated in quotidian terms that Cold Warriors could carry into "battle" against their perceived, culturally defined enemies—from "Lavender Lads" in Washington to "character weaknesses" in Toronto to the "degenerates" and "Pseudo-youths" whom we will encounter in the pantheon of Brazilian subversive icons.[15]

On levels broader still, this book takes up hemispheric stories not only about such "moral and cultural concerns," but about the Right itself. I demonstrate the need to widen the lens, to treat right-wing activism, anticommunism, and authoritarianism as Atlantic and/or Western phenomena. Insightful scholarship has considered such activism in the U.S.

national context, examining the mid- to late twentieth-century reactions and realignments and the centrality to them of gender and sexuality.[16] In this book I examine ways in which rightists from different parts of the West communicated with and influenced each other, building transnational networks of reactionary and countersubversive thought and identity.[17] These rightists collectively addressed the issues that are most of interest to us: the nature and manifestation of subversion, the ways in which it had to be combated, and its relationship with morality, culture, and modernity. The story of autocracy and repression in Brazil, as I demonstrate, is part of a larger, emerging, transnational story of reaction against perceived threats to tradition, family, gender, and moral standards, and conventional sexuality—a story, that is, of "culture wars."

Modernization, Moscow, and Moral Panic

> Pornography and obscenity are common currency. Sexual perversions are admitted and accepted without the slightest hesitation.... "Hippies" ... promote subversion as much by violence as by nonviolence.... The struggle against the dissolution of our customs, against the degradation of the family, against subversion, against the dissemination of drug addictions is ... essential to the sovereignty of the nation. The traffic in opium ... facilitates communist plotting. For this task, they recur to feminine wiles: girls of great beauty are chosen to seduce military men, high-level bureaucrats, and diplomats.[18]

This particular vision of subversion—riddled with sexually perverse "hippies," moral and familial decline, femmes fatales, seduction, and communist cloak-and-dagger tactics based in sex and pharmacology—will sound familiar to readers acquainted with the McCarthyite notion of "queers" as security risks and with the heterosexist "moral alert" of North America's Cold War.[19] Indeed, as noted above, the story of moral conservatism has gained increasing attention in scholarship on the rise of U.S. anticommunist and conservative movements. The passage above, however, comes from Brazilian Cold Warrior Dr. Antônio Carlos Pacheco e Silva, an influential psychiatrist whose anxieties I explore in chapter 3. Such anxieties lie at the heart of my investigation. This book focuses on Brazil—and certain North Atlantic interlocutors—to argue that Cold War countersubversion must be understood in cultural terms, as, in part, a reaction against the trappings of modernization. Counter-subversives operated within a universe of threatening possibilities—a sort of "broth." Yet that universe had essential organizing axes; and for the conservatives who gained influence in late 1960s Brazil, cultural, moral, and sexual reaction was a vital axis.

Cold War dictatorship in South America—and Brazil's dictatorship in particular—has traditionally been understood as an authoritarian gambit aimed, above all else, at modernization. This understanding is in many ways quite accurate—Brazilian military rulers, like their near neighbors, sought to economically awaken "*o país do futuro*" ("the country of the future") and to realize the potential encapsulated in the dictatorial slogans "No one can hold this country back now" and "Forward, Brazil!"[20] To a certain extent, the regime upheld a national tendency to celebrate industrial development and consumption itself as desirable, modern ruptures with a stagnant past.[21] Much of the animus behind the 1964 coup and its aftermath stemmed from ideological opposition to the reformism, labor politics, and radical nationalism of João Goulart's presidency (1961–64). The planners and partisans of the coup saw these elements of Goulart's regime as direct threats to plans for elite-led capitalist modernization. For many conservative authoritarianists, however, such modernization proved a mixed bag. Ongoing industrialization, increasing foreign investment, and an impressive—if poorly distributed—"Economic Miracle" (1967–73) generated significant transformations in Brazilian society and culture. Single motherhood, and the incidence of women working outside the home, increased markedly between 1960 and 1980; the explosion of television and of globalized communications brought new fashions, entertainment, and possibilities for consumption, particularly among young people, into Brazil's middle-class homes; and the availability of the Pill (1962) revolutionized the potential for birth control.[22] These transformations, as we shall see, were anathema to the Right, which did not hesitate to identify in them a "crisis of modernity."

If, then, we historicize Brazil's military rulers as (often ruthless) champions of modernization, we must also consider that their number, and certainly their supporters, included those who experienced modernity (including, ironically, the social and cultural ramifications of dictatorial policy) as a cataclysmic moral undoing. The accoutrements of the "modern," as I show in chapter 1, had long been the bugbears of the Brazilian Right—for whom these accoutrements, and by association modernity itself, meant changes in gender, sexual, and consumer behavior. Echoing the anxieties of generations past, moral panic regarding modernization and globalization drove a network of civilian and military rightists in Cold War Brazil—linked to international and transnational rightwing networks and organizations—to construct communist subversion as a moral and cultural threat, located in everyday life and social behavior. Hence the Cold War became more than a military struggle against rural guerrillas and urban terrorists; to moral technocrats, the battle had to be waged across sexual and bodily practice, clothing, music, art, mass media, and gender.

Moral and cultural anxieties vis-à-vis gender, sex, behavior, entertainment, and media served as a discursive fulcrum for the vitriol and violence directed against supposed subversives in mid–Cold War Brazil. I have chosen to illuminate this process using the term "moral panic"—a model that will be familiar to historians, though its origins lie more properly in sociologist Stanley Cohen's 1971 *Folk Devils and Moral Panics*. Theories of moral panic have blossomed and diversified in the decades since Cohen popularized this concept. For our purposes, moral panic will blend the original with more recent definitions, in which such panics generally involve (1) a reaction, often on the part of authorities or the press, to increased deviance—real or perceived—in social behavior or cultural production; (2) developments in media and communications technology or custom as a trigger for such reaction; (3) vehemence that outstrips the actual "threat"; (4) anxiety focused on young people, considered the principal locus of moral change; and (5) linkage of these anxieties with notions of degenerative sexual and bodily peril.[23]

My argument engages Brazilian politics, morality, sexuality, and popular culture at a time when these became the sites of significant upheavals—that is, a time when there were multiple arenas in which "crisis" (though not necessarily panic) emerged as a mode of understanding change. In addition to the broad demographic and technological changes enumerated above, the 1960s, 1970s, and 1980s saw the initiation and/or intensification of specific, critical debates about modernity and its societal ramifications in Brazil. In fact, certain cultural developments seemed to indicate an embrace of precisely what the moralist Right feared most. By the 1960s, there was broad discussion of "generational conflict" and the changing nature—and potential subvertibility—of youth. New fashions seemed to be emerging among middle- and upper-class young people at the very moment when these youths took to large-scale public activism—impressive protests commonly known as "the student move-ment." In partial consequence, Brazil's rightists focused their anxieties on young people of means and participated in the broader construction of youth as an emergent social, political, and cultural category in Latin America and elsewhere. This construction is critical to the problems taken up in this book, particularly given the overwhelming youthful-ness of countersubversion's victims.[24]

Upheaval touched other realms, too. The Catholic Church, riven by debates between progressive and conservative factions of the faithful, seemed weakened, even decadent.[25] Later, in the 1970s, *pornochanchadas*, a popular species of comedic soft pornography, became the most obvi-ous example of what President João Figueiredo called a "pornographic surge," part of a broadening of public conversations about sexuality that elicited both welcome and condemnation. As I demonstrate, alarm about pornography in particular created occasional and otherwise unlikely concurrences between Catholic progressives and the reactionary state—though moral panic tended to emerge on the Right, the politics of moral-ity and authoritarianism or antiauthoritarianism did not always neatly align.[26] Moreover, as redemocratization (a decade-long process, initi-ated in 1974) created a more permissive public sphere, gay and women's rights movements came into their own and grew increasingly vocal and visible.

Taken together, these issues and debates generated anxieties and bafflement among actors from across the political spectrum—but at a certain juncture in Brazil's Cold War, they facilitated the rise of an out-raged, empowered Right, politically and intellectually well-connected and based in Brazil's urban capitals. Taken apart, they demonstrate cer-tain subtle changes over time—between eras and across the course of dictatorship. Moralists held (and felt themselves to hold) more sway at the peak of their influence in the post-1964 dictatorship than they did during the regime of Getúlio Vargas (1930–45), itself often associated with right-wing Catholicism and waxing influence of conservatives. Yet even in the latter period, as my research demonstrates, moral conserva-tism and anticommunism experienced fluctuations of influence and vis-ibility. Right-wing culture warriors were not all-powerful; indeed, they were sometimes remarkably frustrated. They did, however, play a key ideological role. Their vision shaped notions doctrinal and practical about the workings of subversion—such that the idea of communism as a sexual, cultural, bodily- and art-borne plot percolated in the regime's most powerful quarters, among its exalted ideologues as well as its more humble functionaries.

Like many such categories, "the Right" proves a problematic and unwieldy container, a taxonomic conundrum with which scholars of right-wing movements have long struggled.[27] We shall, over the course of this book, encounter "rightists" who can only very loosely be grouped together and whose differences sometimes rivaled their similarities. In Brazil, hemispherically, and elsewhere, a single ideological or political category—the Right—can never uniformly subsume the many variants and instantiations to which the term is applied. What I refer to as the Right, in other words, did not comprise a monolithic bloc but was rather a shifting matrix of thinkers, activists, and sympathizers. These actors came from different class, national, and religious backgrounds, and they often had different priorities and strategies. What they shared was an ideological, often visceral orientation toward conservatism—the defense of hierarchy and of inequality as part of a more broadly conceived adherence to tradition and to validation of the past. Recent scholarship on right-wing mobilizations has shown that enmity and opposition cannot always define the Right.[28] As we shall see throughout this book, however, the Right referred to here *was* one united by a common enemy: communism—and the moral deterioration thought to be its corollary, helpmeet, and stratagem.

Given this diversity, I have sought the perspectives of rightists in a broad variety of sources, classified and public, state and non-state, private and published, and civilian as well as military, to name a few modes of divergence. Throughout the book, I draw on the documentary record left behind by key rightist individuals, institutions, and publications; on the broader journalistic and professional sources that contextualize the activities of these rightists; and, more occasionally, on the records of opposition figures and organizations. These rightist individuals include power brokers whose influence I demonstrate below—the likes of high-ranking generals Antônio Carlos da Silva Muricy and Moacir de Araújo Lopes; ministers of state such as Alfredo Buzaid and Ibrahim Abi-Ackel (both ministers of justice); and celebrated journalists Gustavo Corção and Lenildo Tabosa Pessoa. In the latter category (rightist institutions), I have consulted the records—often in disused archives and unexamined until now—of non-state organizations (conservative and anticommunist pressure groups) as well as the government's principal institutions of military learning and intellectual production, where moralistic ideas blossomed in the 1960s and 1970s. Brazil's Higher War College (Escola Superior de Guerra, or ESG), for example, "the authorized source of military ideology," which trained the regime's military and civilian elite, furnished me with much of the material for tracking the development of moral technocracy.[29] In the school's library, I gained access to decades' worth of academic research, reports, term papers (generally policy proposals of graduating students), and presentations left behind by students, professors, and guest experts who contributed to the formation of a national security consensus at this important think tank. My research on implementation led me to the ponderous collections of police and censorial records—intelligence assessments, interagency correspondence, surveillance reports, ideological and training memoranda, and procedural and official documentation on individual cases of censorship and/or other persecution. Some of these have only recently been declassified or reorganized for scholarly review. I have drawn on several species of periodicals, including major Brazilian newspapers and glossy magazines, the newsletters and bulletins of key rightist organizations, and the national military journals—particularly *A Defesa Nacional*—in which regime ideologues and officers or trainees worked out and reaffirmed their ideas about national security. Lastly, I carried out a series of interviews with five ESG staff members, who opted to talk with me largely according to their availability, and whose insights enriched my understandings of what I found in the documents.

Right-wing, censorial moralisms in midcentury North America dovetailed with what Whitney Strub has called the "newfound social capital of the expert"—a figure who updated, technocratized, and pathologized debates that had previously been conducted in "the language of sin."[30] In this book, I trace a similar process that took place somewhat earlier in Brazil: the coalescence of a self-appointed cadre of scientific and cultural authorities whom I call a moral technocracy. This process, I argue, created an influential core of moral technocrats who successfully brought their concerns about sex and subversion into national conversations (public as well as classified) about modernity, communism, culture, and security. Setting the tone of such conversations in critical forums within the state, they helped enable both authoritarianism and repression. Their interpretations, focusing on a categorical set of preoccupations (youth, global media, and gender), accompanied current events in Brazil and beyond, gaining purchase as political and cultural tensions increased—for example, in 1968 (when student protest exploded, nationally and abroad, and some linked it with cultural upheaval) and in the 1970s (when a sexualization of culture seemed undeniable, and the major work of countering armed guerrillas was finished). Moral technocrats' reaction was both proscriptive and prescriptive—beyond promoting repressive countersubversion, they focused their attentions on constructing an ideal, subversion-proof Brazilian subject, the dream of generations of rightists. Though women were among the principal loci of anxiety, this ideal subject was envisioned as male, quite in keeping with moralists' generally patriarchalist orientation.

To be clear, I do not mean to suggest that conservative ideas about sexuality and morality were the sole or the paramount reason that individuals were arrested, tortured, exiled, and murdered—as chapter 5 explains, the logics of police repression critically incorporated sexuality but also comprised other essential practices and paranoias. Yet such conservative ideas, as this book will show, were intimately, ineluctably bound up with countersubversive visions of the world and of the enemy. Anticommunists, from power brokers to police, came to envision a grand conspiracy emerging in sexual, moral, and cultural change. They interpreted these changes as evidence of a plot against the nation and against the West—a plot that implicated miniskirts alongside machine guns, gay rights alongside guerrillas, and pornography alongside propaganda.

Trajectories of Morality and Countersubversion

The seven chapters of this book consider ways in which Brazilian countersubversive actors and their Atlantic partners constructed subversion—how conservatives identified sexual and moral deviance as critical elements in a communist conspiracy to subvert national security, and how that identification impacted (and failed to impact) politics and repression. I examine right-wing ideology, policy, and practice, first among rightists in Brazil before 1945 and thereafter within Brazil's security forums and task forces in the period of military dictatorship.

Chapter 1 explores the heritage of right-wing activism across the twentieth century, beginning in the 1910s and continuing through the presidency (1930–37) and dictatorship (1937–45) of Getúlio Vargas. Responding to the changes they associated with modernization in the Vargas period, the radical (sometimes fascist) Right of early-twentieth-century and interwar Brazil developed certain key modes of reaction. Lamenting modernization itself, and hearkening back to a mythic, medieval European past, this Right linked anticommunism, antimodernism, and panic about morality and masculinity in ways that we will see resuscitated in the latter half of the century. Such panic encompassed seminal, patriarchalist reactions to urbanization, modern entertainment, and gender deviance (especially "new" womanhood, though moralists paradoxically lavished most of their amendatory energies on the nation's boys). This chapter shows that Getúlio Vargas tempered or coopted much of the reaction of these early moralists—the state in this period cooperated with conservatives only insofar as doing so was expedient, and privileged statist approaches to the critical issues of gender, reproduction, women's public roles, and education. Chapter 1, then, illustrates the peculiar dynamics of right-wing moralism in the Vargas years. It also begins to show that Cold War conservative authoritarianism cannot be understood without attention to the structures of difference, enmity, and national (in)viability developed by extreme rightists long before 1945. Though we think of post-1964 military authoritarianists as "modernizing conservatives," radical rightists' *anti*modernism, developed in the era of fascism, formed the core of a moralistic anticommunism that would gain ascendancy in dictatorial Brazil.[31]

Chapter 2 shifts the focus to the later period, contextualizing the right-wing mobilizations that linked countersubversion and moralization and demonstrating the panoply of narratives about morality and subversion. In one sense, this chapter explores what, precisely, rightists reacted against. Many Brazilians, responding to phenomena real and perceived, national and global, experienced the 1960s as a time of turmoil in culture, politics, and morality. I analyze linked cultural histories to uncover the ways in which emergent youth culture, sexual revolution, and radical politics were focal points for broad public debates in 1960s Brazil. Within those debates, right-wing reaction against changing gender and sexual norms represented only one of many publicly permissible viewpoints. The sheer diversity of these viewpoints makes clear several critical contextual factors. First, regardless of how drastically (or marginally) new gender and sexual patterns actually affected women, young people, students, or other demographics on which anxieties focused, moral panic was not the sole possible response to perceived changes in these realms. Second, though counterculture, political radicalism, and nonnormative sex each attracted considerable attention, narratives that conflated these categories did not monopolize public discourse—even those who feared or rejected moral and sexual change did not always associate it with subversion. Lastly, for all of the Right's insistence on this association, the regime's fiercest and most visible opponents never embraced sexual liberalization. Many were the voices who constructed "youth," "sexual revolution," and "subversion"—and not everyone, least of all those on the political Left, saw direct articulation between the three.

Chapter 3 lends greater attention to the transnational currents of right-wing ideology that influenced countersubversion. Here I exhume the long-overlooked priorities of right-wing activists in midcentury Brazil, revealing the centrality of moral panic and the legacy, in this milieu, of the rightists dealt with in chapter 1. I trace a network of right-wing individuals and organizations who achieved power and influence in the 1960s and 1970s. As tensions grew in the mid-1960s and especially between 1968 and 1974, rightists reacted to the idea that moral chaos (ranging from premarital sex to the advent of "waves"—ever the word of choice—of divorce, pornography, and abortion) had arrived. Though previous accounts have dismissed such rightists as marginal, I show that they successfully brought anxieties about youth, sexuality, and gender trouble into national debates about security, establishing these concerns as inherent in the struggle against subversion.[32] They did so, moreover, in transnational fashion—that is, in dialogue with anticommunist, "expert" informants from around the Atlantic, on whom Brazilian rightists would frequently draw to conceptually unite communism and deviance.

Chapter 4 traces the doctrinalization of this conceptual union, a key step in the process of operationalizing moral panic. In high-level forums on security and development, specific anxieties—about youthful behavior, global decadence, new media technology, and women in the workplace—became categorical pillars of national security strategy. Drawing on the records of students, professors, administrators, and government experts, I excavate the development of such strategy at the Escola Superior de Guerra. The most prestigious of Brazilian military think tanks, the ESG enjoyed an international reputation and epitomized Atlantic militaries' attempts to combine Cold War technocracy and counterinsurgency. Here, at the heart—or rather, the brain—of security planning, what I call a moral technocracy legitimated the conceptual slippage of "degeneracy" into "subversion" and the rationalization of biological, psychological, and sociological narratives of national viability. Thanks to this moral technocracy, pseudoscientific and governmental authority made the sexuality and morality of middle-class young people (a demographic fraught with anxiety for authoritarian developmentalists) a central Cold War battleground. This process, insistent on certain conflations that may seem unlikely, occurred via a species of intellectual myopia: a closed-circuit repetition and re-citation of ideas.

Chapter 5 investigates the impact of moral technocracy—the ways in which doctrinalized moral panic suffused security institutions and made inroads into repressive practice. Categorical alarm about youth, decadence, media, and working women manifested itself throughout Brazil's security establishment—in stock warnings about decadence; open letters to putatively deviant young people; cautionary parables about young women gone the way of sex and subversion; demands for moral censorship of putatively communist media; and even "studies" that technocratically affirmed sexual deviance as the path to youthful political subversion. These notions, moreover, did not merely percolate at the higher levels of government authority. Police and security forces on the ground, the foot soldiers of countersubversion, also bound sex and morality into their approaches to the "enemy." Intelligence and political police agents surveilled sexual deviance; the nation's spy agencies shared information about supposed orgies among leftist educators and their students; state representatives, from top-brass intellectuals to cops on a beat, wrung their hands over the "loss" of young people via sexualized subversion; and military and police guides to identifying and dealing with subversion outlined sexual seduction, "free love," and public eroticism as tactics of communist insurgency. The intensity of repression, like the reasons for arrest and atrocity, varied over time and in keeping with the multifarious suspicions of police; but the notion of sexual, gender, and moral deviance as a communist conspiracy framed police work in important ways.

Chapter 6 investigates the impact of this framework in a more public arena, via one of dictatorial moralists' successful forays, legislatively speaking, into quotidian moral countersubversion. Censorship and bloodshed were not the only weapons of which the empowered Right availed itself. The most strident moralists, introduced in chapters 3 and 4, devised a broad counterattack designed to reach each and every Brazilian via the nation's schools. Intended as a salve for anticommunist moral panic, Moral and Civic Education (EMC) sought to inculcate traditional moral, sexual, and gender precepts. It did so in concert with military service, further linking this program with a moral-hygienicist past in which its goals and methods were deeply rooted. That past also haunted the program's notable focus on men, with women included only insofar as they affected the anxiety-ridden reproduction and rearing of future, patriotic Brazilians. Translating their anachronistic anxieties not only into education policy but also into practice, moralists managed to influence the curricula of students across Brazil. As my survey of EMC textbooks demonstrates, classroom materials faithfully integrated conservatives' fusion of moralism and anticommunism. EMC sought to make countersubversion a daily moral imperative—to make students understand the putative link between subversion and immorality. This meant, as one textbook put it, inculcating "the self-discipline that will regulate your moral life, your social, emotional, and sexual behavior."[33]

Chapter 7 completes the arc of this story by analyzing the complexities of moralism's implementation and impact. Briefly put, rightist anxieties emerged strongly in the late 1960s and gained ground among police in the mid-1970s—even when, after 1974, those rightists and police found themselves in an increasingly embittered minority, marginalized by democratization. Problematizing the notion of a unitary authoritarian state imposing policy on culture and morality, I show that in these realms, as in others, the Brazilian regime often devolved into a confusing and contradictory array of agencies, factions, and prerogatives. If the unwieldy machinery of government closed ranks for some time around the hard-line, right-wing prerogatives of moralism and repression, the translation of reactionary ideology into repressive reality was not always seamless. The relative strength of these prerogatives faced challenges both in the uneven application of moralistic countersubversion and in the vicissitudes of rightists' power as the dictatorship dragged its way to a close in the late 1970s and 1980s. In other words, the story of moralistic countersubversion changed over time and in accordance with the contrasting fortunes of factions within the military regime. By the late 1970s, redemocratization and cultural pluralism waxed just as hard-line interests and the power of moralism waned—much to the consternation and alarm of rightists within and outside of the regime. Via the stories of Brazilian pornographic film and of debates over birth control, I demonstrate the ways in which moral concerns continued to motivate the regime's most repressive elements, in and out of power and favor.[34]

ATTEMPTS TO "regulate moral life...and behavior" stemmed from the sense of crisis animating the actors at the heart of this book. By the 1970s, sexuality had penetrated discussions of national security, from the lofty echelons of the National Security Council (CSN) itself to the surveillance and counterinsurgency operations of police and spy forces. While Breiner and Corção identified communist subversion in the caresses of young lovers and the supposed "conspiracy and orgies" of university students, the CSN—by law the country's supreme source for the "formulation and execution of national security policy"—fretted that morbid "social disorganization" had resulted from "the deterioration of customs [which] can be identified...in the high indices of criminality, in prostitution, in the proliferation of gambling, in homosexuality, and in exaggerated permissiveness." This deterioration, according to moral technocrats, was "crowned by the hedonistic notion according to which an ever-growing number of young people" concerned themselves with nothing but "sensual love." Sensual love, or unconventional sex and style of any kind, indicated subversion in the minds of these guardians of anticommunist national security.[35]

The result was a state of high moral alert and constant moral suspicion. Thus, when a São Paulo military police officer went fishing in August 1970 in a local lake, he was surprised to retrieve from the depths a smattering of books—surprised, and also wary. The motley assortment came from diverse owners, at least according to the names and addresses inscribed inside the covers. Nevertheless, military police knew just what to do with his unexpected haul. They identified those books deemed "subversive in nature" and forwarded them to Operation Bandeirantes (OBAN), the recently created (and soon infamously abusive) task force for combating left-wing subversion. Of the "49 books, two photos, and various personal letters and pamphlets apprehended," intelligence officials chose to focus on just six books and some scattered annotations. The names beneath the covers of books on Lenin or Stalin raised direct and obvious suspicion—but so, for these duty-bound Cold Warriors, did the volume *Sexual Education*, inscribed with the name of a certain "Mário." Mário's information was duly forwarded to the fearsome OBAN. In all likelihood those who abandoned these documents did so indiscriminately, fearing a police raid—and probably, like much of the organized Left, dismissed or disdained the idea of sexual revolution. The police who recovered the fisherman's haul, however, saw a conspiratorial method here, linking materials about sex with those about Stalin. This book explores why, and how, the sexual practice and moral politics of people like Mário came into the crosshairs of a hemispheric Cold War that located enemy machinations in sex, gender, and moral deviance.[36]

1

Only for the Cause of the *Pátria*

The Frustrations of Interwar Moralism

The place of youths, in this hour of decision, is not among the idle or the indifferent, the soft of spirit and body; it is at the vanguard, the first line of combatants, among the pioneers of constructive ideas. Thus I see you now, and with you, forming legions, all of Brazil's youths, dedicated to struggle and sacrifice, and exalted in the heroic cult of the *Pátria*.

—President Getúlio Vargas, "Salutation to the Youth of São Paulo" (speech), 24 November 1941

Many interwar rightists made common cause with the man who issued the above call to arms in 1941—Getúlio Vargas, savvy and storied ruler of Brazil from 1930 to 1945 and 1951 to 1954.[1] Vargas's first tenure comprised a heady decade and a half of state-led nationalism, industrialization, and centralization, accompanied by key developments in political culture: re-politicization of the Catholic Church, fervent imbrication of spirituality and nationalism, and flirtation with fascism and other international currents. Perceiving a world in economic, cultural, and political crisis, contemporary rightist reformers championed reaction and regeneration, the recuperation of a bygone world order; and they linked such reaction to moral conservatism and antimodernism. Indeed, at the heart of right-wing anticommunist activism in the 1930s lay a species of regressive idealism that we shall see emerge triumphant in later decades. The speech quoted above exhibits Vargas's noted stylistic sympathies with approaches favored by a variety of interwar rightists, including pro-natal eugenics, masculinization, militarization, the revitalization of youth, antiliberalism, and even fascism.[2]

Yet Vargas's speech also made a key omission: it did not mention church, God, or religious morality. Such an oversight—if, indeed, that is the word—reflected the ways in which Vargas selectively ignored and even alienated Brazil's most ardent reactionaries, many of whom would express frustration with the Estado Novo (the "New State," Vargas's

1937–45 dictatorship). Scholars of the period have elaborated the complicated institutional relationships of Vargas's rule, which saw state co-optation of support from several conservative strongholds—especially the national Catholic hierarchy and the fascist Integralist movement, or AIB—but which sometimes generated estrangement, if not hostility, between the government and the most traditionalist Catholics and conservatives.[3] In this chapter, I highlight a neglected aspect of this story, arguing that moralistic reactions to modernization formed a crucial node of divergence between the regime and rightist constituencies. Despite cooperation between the state and certain interest groups in this period, the Vargas regime generally marginalized the nostalgic, sometimes openly medieval reactions of right-wing moralists—what political scientist Scott Mainwaring, referring to the Vargas-era church, calls "atavistic" attempts to "halt secularization."[4] The most vocal and extreme of moralistic rightists (Catholic, fascist, or somewhere in between) championed an antimodern perspective for which the Vargas regime made little discursive and political space. Frictions emerged between these rightists and the state on the issues of modernization, morality, gender, sexuality, and youth.

Brazil's interwar rightists, like other constituencies ably managed by the Vargas regime's system of alliances, were forced to make sacrifices to adapt to and gain concessions from the wily Getúlio. The state generally gained the most from these bargains[5]—and in rightists' case, the sacrifice was often atavistic moralism. Conservatives disagreed among themselves, especially on how to confront (or accommodate) the Vargas state and how to relate to global fascism, yet the period's most outspoken rightists tended to coincide in making proposals based in moral and sometimes religious reaction to industrial modernity. By contrast, the Vargas government's statist nationalism, especially after 1937, privileged technical, developmentalist, and patriotic cultivation over the nostalgic, anti-industrial, antiurban morality promoted by conservatives.[6] As noted above, Brazil's interwar right-wing reformers did subscribe to some of the Vargas regime's core precepts. To these precepts, however, exponents of the Catholic and Integralist Right(s) added a strain of reactionary thought apotheosized by outright longing for the Middle Ages. This strain of thought decried a crisis of morality, based in modernization; took gender unconventionality, familial dissolution, and sexual deviance as the noxious trappings of modernity; denounced these trappings via pathologizing, eugenicist arguments; insisted that moral and civic instruction must redress these problems; and linked moral outrage to rightists' fervent anticommunism, yoking countersubversion to remoralization.

Here, then, we begin to trace a decades-long trajectory of moralism-as-countersubversion. Extant scholarship on Brazil, the interwar period, and the global Cold War suffers from a want of attention to the ways in which motifs of right-wing, authoritarian activism did or did not survive the historical and ideological shifts of the twentieth century. Despite the enduring attention that the Vargas period and the post-1960 dictatorships have received, little is known of the legacy of early-twentieth-century reactionaries in the rise and tenure of the Cold War's countersubversive repressions.[7] Yet this legacy holds keys to understanding the countersubversive fervor of the post-1964 military governments and their conservative supporters. What were the contours of right-wing moralisms in the 1930s, and how did they fare under Vargas? How did latter-day hard-liners' anticommunism descend and/or diverge from earlier incarnations?

This chapter explores certain eugenicist, antimodern, and fascist schools of thought and activism, delineating both their development and their relative marginality under Vargas's rule. Rightists reacted to modernity as a set of categories they execrated—principally, urban life and its modern diversions, secularization, putative changes in sexual and reproductive behavior, and the pathologized gender deviance of effeminate men and masculine (publicly visible and/or working) women. The state, meanwhile, did not fully share rightist reactions, and flirted with policies (especially the centralization and laicization of educational and family law) that generated moral outrage on the Right. This moral outrage, its categorical foci, and in some cases its individual proponents would outlive Vargas, survive the war, and influence the military regime and its supporters.[8] Moralism, operative across the decades in different political contexts and with different results, linked deviant sexual and gender practice with negative eugenic implications, communist infiltration, and national inviability.

In this regard, the right-wing agendas that took shape and gained vocal adherents in the years before 1945 presaged the moralistic concerns of the 1960s and 1970s with striking thematic faithfulness. Still, there were critical differences. Notably, early rightists reflected a global ideological milieu that was as antiliberal as it was anticommunist, predating the discrediting of fascism. They also maintained an external focus, tending to locate the communist moral scourge abroad—Soviet "Free Love," however baleful and menacing, remained *Soviet*, with less of the clear, present, and domestic danger it held for 1960s reactionaries. Finally, the early Right did not manage to parlay moralism-as-anticommunism into a central national security concern. The efforts of rightist activists and intellectuals of the Estado Novo period were tempered by the developmentalist practicality of Getúlio Vargas. An acknowledged agnostic (who named his sons "Luther" and "Calvin"), Vargas co-opted moralism and masculinization as engines of progress, availed himself of alliances and personal friendships with rightist and Catholic leaders, and yet did not fall in with rightist demands for antimodern "remoralization" and "re-Christianization."

Moral Crisis, Anticommunism, and the Early Right

The Vargas period saw dramatic movement in Brazilian and global politics and culture: the crisis of capitalism; the expansion of mass media (especially film) and avant-garde artistic forms; efforts at consolidation of secular, federal authority; the thriving of bohemia amid urbanization, industrialization, and increasingly contentious social relations. This was a Brazil in which state and non-state actors denounced liberal capitalism and dallied in corporatism and even fascism; in which bourgeois feminism struggled to gain ground; in which working women, visible in the labor force for decades, formed significant proportions of workers (a majority in some industries), even as their presence remained controversial; in which individuals like Patrícia Galvão (a noted feminist and political radical), Madame Satã (a celebrated transgender pimp, sex worker, performer, and convict), and Carmen Miranda cut notable figures in Rio, in São Paulo, and internationally; in which radio and cinema changed the face of diversion; and in which casinos, cabarets, and revues dominated an increasing segment of live and filmic entertainment. In this last vein, Brazilian films (the 1936 hit *Alô, alô, carnaval*, for example) debuted alongside and echoed Hollywood favorites like *Gold Diggers of 1933* and *The Jazz Singer.*[9]

Regarding these developments with hostility, the interwar Right coalesced around calls for remoralization, conflating communism and industrial modernity as chief causes of a multifarious moral crisis. The sense of such a crisis, or of a "crisis of decency," has been noted by excellent scholarship on this period's conservative institutions. As early as the 1910s, right-wing reformers had connected national viability with corporeal and spiritual socialization and masculinization (especially of youth), reflecting the early stirrings of an ideology that would link these categories not only with national security but with countersubversion and with morality as well. Early rightists brought together hygienicism, eugenics, militarism, patriotism, and national security, most conspicuously in the ideas of activist Olavo Bilac and his Liga de Defesa Nacional (National Defense League, LDN), a nationalist pressure group whose later exploits I explore in chapter 3. By the 1930s, when Getúlio Vargas dominated Brazil, the LDN had given way to a broad, if loose and fractious, coalition of conservative Catholics, fascists (the Brazilian Integralist Association, or AIB), and their sympathizers. These various elements of the Right united eugenics, masculinization, antimodern moral panic, and militant vigilance against communist subversion, laying the groundwork for decades of conflating immorality with communism.[10] Leading lights among these elements elaborated a set of concerns that they deemed indispensable—gender, public health, women's social roles (feminism and work), moral/sexual deviance, media (especially cinema), pedagogy, antimodernism, antiliberalism, and anticommunism.

This series of issues emerged clearly in rightists' reactions to the changes they saw in Vargas-era Brazil. In an exemplary 1936 speech reprinted in the aptly named *Encyclopedia of Integralism*, Belisário Penna—one of Brazil's foremost authorities on eugenics—linked subversion, somatic viability, gender, youth, and morality. Like nearly all of his contemporaries, Penna decried modern "moral anarchy" and traced it to the Right's two great political bugbears: global liberalism and communism. Penna insisted that communists' primary offensive lay in promoting hygienic, eugenic, and moral "degeneracy." "Subversive currents" of Marxism and liberalism, he claimed, would attempt to immolate the country in the flames of degenerative "moral weakening." Setting a long-term tone for anticommunist pseudoscience, Penna concluded that youth and women lay at the center of this subversive-degenerative plot, as—once abandoned by their gender-deviant, working mothers—"children are the preferred victims," among whom "syphilis and venereal maladies produce great devastation; prostitution gathers its victims before they reach puberty; in them alcoholism, dementia, and crime find refuge." Here, in what would become a rightist tenet, modernity and communism (and the associated evil of liberalism) portended a sexually and gender deviant, degenerative onslaught of moral dissolution.[11]

Plínio Salgado, the Integralists' founder and leader, epitomized the moralistic, masculinist, and antimodern orientation of his organization's anticommunism and protofascism.[12] Reflecting soon-to-be-familiar panic about youth and gender, Salgado's "Panorama of the Western World" lamented the emasculation of the entire Occident, an "absence of Man" manifested in massive "disorder" of sexual and "moral culture." Salgado blamed contemporary "isms" (communism and liberalism) for gender and sexual deviance that were bound up with modern media: disorder had reached "the point where young men are feminized into plastic displays of beach-going Ganymedes and young women masculinized in the Hollywoodesque development of girls of no morals." Typically, Salgado insisted that only proper moral and religious pedagogy could counteract moral and gender catastrophe, women's abandonment of the home, and sexual deviance, re-prioritizing moral manhood and domestic womanhood in what Salgado called "the global launch of the New Man of the New Times" or the "reconstruction of Man."[13]

A chorus of rightist voices echoed these themes, conflating—and bemoaning—subversion, modernity, degenerative emasculation, women's public lives, and sexual and moral dissipation. These concerns peaked in a specific and enduring antimodern motif: counter-Reformationist calls for a return to medieval social and sexual order. Openly longing for the Middle Ages, reactionaries traced the crisis of modernity from the Reformation—in the words of prominent Catholic activist and Integralist sympathizer Everardo Backeuser, "from Luther to Communism." An eminent engineer and professor of geography, Backeuser wrote with considerable technical authority, warning that "the moral perfections of the Middle Ages ... have been tragically dying" in increasing godlessness directed by the Kremlin. "Moscow," he warned, was no historical aberration, but a purposeful and millennial attempt to "annihilate the noble roots of the society that was built by the Catholic Church."[14] Those roots, he made clear, were the codes of moral, sexual, and gender behavior. Rome, with its fading medieval morality, represented "the Family" and "indissoluble marriage," whereas Moscow championed "divorce," the "extinction of the Family," "prostitution," and "Free Love."[15]

From Moscow to Madame Satã to the movies, rightists discerned such free love and immorality pervading modern life, and they responded with emphasis on eugenics and hygienicism, combining anticommunism, pathologization, and moral panic.[16] According to rightist thinkers, biological decadence, from decreasing birthrates to criminal senility, would accompany the moral dissolutions of modern society—dissolutions that rightists thought rampant in the culture and political economy of modernizing, urban, Vargas-era Brazil. The proponent par excellence of eugenic solutions to what he called the "Crisis of the Modern World," Father Leonel Franca has been called the "spiritual father" of Brazil's right-wing intelligentsia in this period.[17] An outspoken friend of Integralism, Franca played a prominent role in national debates about the biopolitics of birthrates and marriage; significantly, he emphasized that morality itself was the problem of "the most seriousness." Franca drew on the authoritarian and racist theories of North American psychologist G. Stanley Hall, agonized about the "degenerescence" of Brazilian young people, and blamed sexual and moral deviance. Lambasting Rousseau alongside Russia, Franca deemed it obvious that "we are passing through a grave moral crisis," composed of "criminality," "adulteries," "divorces," and "dissolution of the family." He blamed "biological factors," namely "alcoholism" and other "vices" that "vice-ridden fathers and mothers . . . transmitted to their children." These biological factors, he claimed, flourished in cities, which exposed the lower classes to "the fetid and drunken ambience of . . . cabarets," to "pornography," to "the street with all its licentious exhibitions," and to "theater and cinema [which] sum up in synthesis all the tempting forces of evil."[18] Franca shared this opposition to urban, industrial modernity (and to particular media) with other distinguished clergy and lay rightists, from Jackson de Figueiredo to Plínio Salgado, Alceu Amoroso Lima, and Archbishop Dom João Becker, who idealized rural "populations not contaminated by the modernism [of] life today, by the seductions of evil cinema and light-hearted diversions."[19]

Prominent rightists paired such antiurban, antimodern hygienicism with open admiration of European-style fascism. Nationally famed as a writer, politician, and sometime president of the Brazilian Academy of Letters, Gustavo Barroso represented Brazil's most extreme, fascist-inspired anti-Semitism.[20] His praise for Mussolini and denunciations of Jews revolved, however, around the very moral panic with which he and other rightists seminally contemplated communist revolutionary warfare: the sinful "excesses" of modern sexuality and gender, and their effects on young people. Jews, communists, and liberals merged in his reproofs of "prostitution," "homosexuality," and working women. Barroso, too, invoked the now-familiar theme of modern diversion, which "destroys the family, demoralizing customs by means of styles, luxury, cinema, literature, and divorce." Where 1960s theorists would fret over putative revolutionist exploitation of the nation's internal "antagonisms" (tensions between classes, races, and sexes), Barroso likewise accused "Judaic Marxism" of seeking to incite "civil wars," including "war between the sexes, fomented by means of the excesses of feminism."[21] Such gender trouble, Barroso argued, particularly affected young people, creating feminized, "so-called pretty boys," lost to the dissolutions of modernity: "youths who lose themselves in immoral theaters, indecent cinemas,...cabarets and casinos, in sensuality and in drugs." These he contrasted with the reconstructed men suggested by Salgado, masculine "Integralist youths, who pass their nights ready and waiting for the Communist attack, sleeping on the hard tiles of the floor."[22]

Demonization of "modern," extradomestic women featured centrally in such arguments, forming another long-term thematic pillar of moral countersubversive concern. As Sueann Caulfield has demonstrated, interwar Brazilian intellectuals of several stripes confronted "modern woman" and her attendant "crisis of morality." Where other reformers, more in line with the state's position, saw this crisis arising "not... from modernity itself, but from the Brazilian masses' unpreparedness," including "men's hyperstimulated sexual instinct," many on the Right "categorically declared modern women devoid of virtue."[23] Focusing (like reactionaries elsewhere) ferociously on the specter of "modern woman," rightists attributed her emergence to communism, and to industrial modernity. In the above-mentioned speech to fascist women, Belisário Penna struck notes of moral-hygienicist panic about modern women's increasingly public lives—what he called "licentiousness...and deviation of Woman," especially her "estrangement from the home," and the sexual deviance and degenerescence sure to follow therefrom.[24] Penna granted these maternalist ideas the weight of authority, especially within the Integralist milieu. Indeed, as sociologist Gilberto Vasconcellos has surmised, Integralists' slogan might have been something like, "Long Live the Mother! Down With Women!"[25] This attitude extended to rightists' patriarchalist remedies, which—as we shall see—tended to focus on boys. Pedagogical antimodernisms largely excluded girls, who presumably should confine themselves to the home and to stewardship of procreation and puericulture.

Yet Penna's notions typified a broader right-wing, anticommunist consensus that "modern woman" would spark moral and physical dé-

générescence.[26] As Father Álvaro Negromonte's staunchly anticommunist column in the conservative *Diário de Minas Gerais* explained, "one of the great evils that industrial life has brought to society is the separation of women from the hearth . . . The working woman abandons her household. The results . . . can only be deathly for her physical and moral health. Physical exhaustion, the restriction of births, . . . the lack of care and rearing of children, the weakening of the loving ties that strengthen home life, incidents bordering on conjugal infidelity, [and] moral decline."[27] Penna, too, traced the moral catastrophe of women's extradomestic work, media-borne "scenes of love and kissing," and "near-nudity" to the machinations of global communism, which—he argued—attacked the Integralists principally because communists wished to eliminate morality and premodern, domestic womanhood.[28] In Penna's view, both anticommunists and their enemies recognized traditional womanhood as a key terrain.[29]

When it came to uniting Catholicism, antimodernism, and moralistic anticommunism, however, few rightists could rival the anxious vitriol of two particular voices: *A Ordem*, the mouthpiece of the prominent conservative Catholic organization Centro Dom Vital; and Octávio de Faria, the quintessential representative of the ultramontane right.[30] Convening a constellation of Catholic reactionaries, *A Ordem*'s alarmism epitomized right-wing anticommunists' rejection of modernization, of women in the public sphere, and of any displacement of the church as a steward of public morality.[31] A 1937 treatise typified the magazine's moral panic vis-à-vis sex and gender behavior: "There is a moral crisis in modern society," it warned. "In the home . . . a weakening of customs invades. Heads of families . . . neglect their duties. . . . Women are no longer those figures full of dignity and respect. . . . And the children—ah! the children . . . today imbued with modern preconceptions . . . tragically violating the moral laws."[32] *A Ordem*'s contributors focused persistently on this perceived explosion of gender deviance, thought to affect men and women alike—what Alceu Amoroso Lima called the "spectacle of effeminate men . . . and the masculinization of woman." This gender-moral panic invariably attributed the putative crisis to modernity and to the "barbarous onslaught of communism." Proposed solutions stressed masculine moral renovation—a renewed, manly, "ardent youth," spearheaded by Catholic authorities.[33]

Octávio de Faria championed the most extreme of positions—but his ideas, rigidly moralistic as they were, gained the warm praise of prominent religious and social conservatives.[34] Tracing the modern crisis back beyond the French Revolution to the Renaissance—"essentially a loss of that equilibrium which the Middle Ages managed to maintain for centuries in Christian form"—Faria made sexual morality and masculinity key nodes of his plaint against modernity. "Immorality," "crime," and "sexual folly," he wrote, had reigned since the Renaissance. Indeed, Faria focused so exclusively on sexual dissolution that he felt compelled, near the end of his well-publicized *Machiavelli and Brazil*, to mention that "the loss of moral sense does not attack *only* in the terrain of sexuality. Every area is contaminated."[35] Even as he asserted that moral crisis went beyond sexuality, Faria resorted to the idiom of sexual and gender deviance to describe the intellectual and social ramifications of this crisis. For Faria, the essence of modernity was a loss of *manliness*, summed up in his lament that "the world has grown effeminate." In a passage that echoed the preoccupation with gender deviance that we have seen above, Faria conflated homosexuality, gender deviance, and global political and economic crisis: "Humanity proceeds, rich with the disorder that the cowardliness of those in power does not dare attack, . . . so as not to offend feminine susceptibilities. . . . Modern homosexuality exercises its action in the moral and intellectual terrain. We are witnessing . . . a great moment of intercommunication of the sexes that has resulted and continues to result in a general indistinctness. It has not been any particular man, but the world in general that has lost its virility . . . There is nothing more tragic in our days than that crisis of virility that accompanies the political and economic crisis."[36]

Despite their alarmism about moral decadence in general—and unlike the latter-day rightists who otherwise echoed their pathologizing, gendered, anticommunist reactions—the Octávio de Farias, Leonel Francas, and Everardo Backeusers of the 1930s and 1940s often approached the problem of *communist* moral subversion as one that remained abroad. A disastrously unsuccessful Brazilian communist uprising in 1935 created obvious exceptions to the interpretation of communism as a faraway menace. Yet early rightists often held that communists' attacks on moral and sexual convention were perpetrated by non-Brazilians, mostly outside Brazil. Even when it became clear that "communism is unfortunately no longer just an intellectual fiction among us [Brazilians]," many anticommunists continued to limit their condemnations to a few highly dangerous "foreigners."[37] This attitude would change quite dramatically by the 1960s, when the idea of an *internal*, homegrown "enemy" would dominate moral-countersubversive anxieties. *A Ordem* exemplified the earlier position, in that its bishops warned of "godless communism" as a moral scourge that threatened, but had not yet affected, Brazilian reproductive practice.[38] Even the most lurid of anticommunist propaganda presented itself as a prophylaxis against foreign communists' moral aggressions. The right-wing *A Offensiva*, for instance, described the "catastrophe" of Russian women's removal from their role as "moral and spiritual shelters of men" but presented this "as an *admonishment* to the Brazilian woman, at the mercy, *if she does not resist, of an identical fate, perpetrated by Soviet banditry.*"[39]

Indeed, the projection of moral laxity onto locales largely beyond Brazil's borders reflected a further distinction of 1930s and 1940s rightism—the tendency to condemn liberalism alongside communism as the source of global moral, sexual, and gender deviance. In accordance with international antimodern, antiliberal, and antidemocratic currents, Brazil's Right saw North Atlantic "materialism" and moral dissolution as twin harbingers of apocalypse. Integralists, in keeping with their fascistic appeal, demonized global liberalism and capitalism as coterminous deviations from a mythically moral antiquity. In *Integralism and Education*, for instance, Backeuser blamed "voracious democracy" for bearing "*women* to the workplace" such that "the traditional hearth ... is undone [and] mothers, forced to work outside the home, lose ... control of the moral and cultural rearing of their children."[40] Catholic detractors of liberalism singled out the "extreme licentiousness" rooted in North Americans' "practical materialism."[41] Writing in this vein, Father Álvaro Negromonte fretted about the "separation of women from the hearth" and blamed the "sensuality" of "liberals, who want liberty in everything."[42] Here, as throughout the complaints of Catholic and Integralist reactionaries in the 1930s, modernity seemed a sum of liberal excesses and communist incursions, both of which tended toward the dissolution of traditional gender and morality. While 1960s reactionaries, too, would condemn licentiousness in the United States, their censure paled in comparison with the ire of the 1930s.

The Estado Novo: Statist Masculinism, Statist Motherhood

Reflecting interwar ideological currents, the power brokers of the Estado Novo tended to concur with this antiliberalism. General Pedro de Góes Monteiro, sometime minister of war and an éminence grise of the

1930s security state, denounced the "Capitalist Nations" as a "threat [to] the fundaments of our Nation," and influential minister of education and health Gustavo Capanema, though a staunch anticommunist, identified "inveterate liberalism" as Brazil's "greatest adversary."[43] As the speech quoted at the outset of this chapter indicates, state concurrence with rightist positions extended into the arenas of masculinization and militarization, the hardening of "spirit and body." This included female bodies, as the state took an interest in promoting motherhood that was productive both within and outside of the home. Developmentalism and eugenics converged in the Estado Novo's concern with morality, gender, and sexuality, which was similar to the concern we have just seen; as Susan Besse, Joel Wolfe, Brodwyn Fischer, and Sueann Caulfield have shown, the Vargas regime was interested in policing women's sexuality and in promoting "links between centralized state power, national honor, and the 'traditional Brazilian family.'"[44] Yet the government's moralistic masculinism privileged the "centralized state power" in that formula; that is, it prioritized statist developmentalism, to the detriment of regressive or ultramontane religiosity, critically in the education and deployment of women. Rightists, in turn, reacted strongly, sometimes preemptively, to perceived dangers of state-driven coeducation and impingement on church-led pedagogy. To some, the Vargas regime signified "subversion of the natural hierarchy" in which the church predominated over other authorities (the family, followed by the state) when it came to morality, education, and culture.[45]

If rightists longed for the Middle Ages and linked moralism to countersubversion and socio-moral retrogression, regime power brokers explicitly disavowed this approach. Vargas cultivated cooperation from and friendship with the ecclesiastical hierarchy, especially as he consolidated power in the 1930s. Yet the Estado Novo's official preoccupation with bodies, sexuality, education, and morality revolved not around church prerogatives but around productivity, industrialization, and the regimentation of human resources on behalf of the state. This, then, was a complex and sometimes contradictory set of relationships, and at times the government's statism superseded rote moralism palpably enough that moralistic, countersubversive anxieties sparked objections to the regime. The state's inattention to the extreme Right rendered ineffectual the reactionary messages about communist moral crisis that would, in later years, influence state discourses, legislation, and repression vis-à-vis "subversion."[46]

The Vargas state's dissociation from right-wing moral extremism emerged among the regime's most powerful members. Leaders of the Estado Novo viewed the church not as an ideological partner but as an easily mobilized engine of support for programs whose moral and cultural orientation the *state* would determine without deferring to the religious Right.[47] Gustavo Capanema, himself a devout Catholic, wrote of "two Catholic currents": "the progressives," who were "in great sympathy" with the government, and "the conservatives," whom Capanema denigrated as "militants" and extremists obsessed with "the liquidation of communism." Capanema applied this devout-versus-extreme dichotomy precisely to "the politics of the family . . . and the politics of education"— insisting that "true Catholics," unlike the right-wing fringe, desired social and family politics that were free of "sectarian sentiments."[48]

In the 1940s, this disregard for right-wing antimodernism emerged in the government's staunch emphasis on developmentalism and productivity—even when that meant the frustration of right-wing agendas, and particularly when it came to remoralization, education, and reproduction. Aggravating rightist fears about an onslaught of centralized, secular coeducation, Capanema and Vargas insisted that the primary purpose of "ideal education" was not to promote morality, but to perfect male *and female* citizen-workers. Vargas's "politics of education" focused much more on a future, technically and physically fit labor force than on a morally reclaimed past. Schooling, he insisted, should serve "the development of productive activities," provide "professional preparation," and address "the most urgent aspect of the problem": the need for "the elements of work and production" to collaborate in "training those technicians that we so need." Inveighing against "hateful and parasitic intellectualism," Vargas promoted basic reading for the sake *first* of "economic propulsion" and "political culture"—with "moral progress" mentioned only as a last outcome.[49]

Capanema concurred, insisting that state-sponsored education favor technical over religious or moral training, and that it prepare "each individual for the service of the Nation" by fostering "discipline and efficiency, those two essential attributes of the citizen and the worker." Though "Moral Education" should form some vague part of the national program, Capanema's regime sought to "transform Brazil's upcoming youth into an *army of workers, useful to themselves and to the Nation*."[50] Outlining the goals of the government's physical education program, he directly opposed church hierarchs' prohibition on coeducation.[51] Capanema further envisioned a corps of bodies cultivated and mobilized on behalf of the state's developmentalist and modernizing errand. His 1942 educational reform, prompted by the need to streamline and update the scholastic framework, flew in the face of the moralistic right wing's prescriptions vis-à-vis gender and modernity—a particularly galling reversal given that the constitution of 1934 had accommodated Catholic demands on these very issues.[52] Despite the invective of extreme rightists against working women, Capanema limned a workforce that included men *and* women prepared for their duties within and outside of the home.[53] Masculinized "men of action" and appropriately feminine, working mothers would fulfill these duties, which revolved around service to the nation's material and productive progress: "Physical education [and] primary courses seek to provide students with a harmonious development of body and spirit, cooperating thus in the constitution of a man of action, physically and morally sound, happy and resolute, conscious of his value and his responsibilities; and in the preparation of woman for her mission in the home, *yet offering her the possibility of substituting men in work that is compatible with the feminine sex*; in the making of each and every Brazilian, of both sexes, apt for efficient contribution to the economy and defense of the Nation."[54]

With Capanema and Vargas at its helm, the Estado Novo's occlusion of church primacy in family, education, and sexuality extended into military, academic, and policy forums. The state and its agents emphasized masculinization and motherhood mobilized for the sake of productive citizenship, often at the expense of the moralistic and medievally nostalgic priorities of Catholic and/or Integralist right-wingers. In what one expert calls the "fascistization" of the Brazilian state, the regime aimed to "transform the worker into a soldier of work" and construct a "New Man," defined by his physical aptness, which the state itself would ensure. Government "preoccupation with the family," then, stemmed less from moral traditionalism than from a desire to spark "the material progress of the nation."[55] Certain religious and lay Catholic leaders found it expedient to seek approximation with the regime, but this "material progress" orientation countermanded much of the right-wing interest in promoting morality *per se*. Setting aside sexual or cultural remoralization, policy-makers looked forward to a time when physical, sexual, and civic training would perfect the Brazilian "race."

Figure 1 Milk advertisement featuring the "pride of our race"—children who competed in "robustness" pageants in São Paulo state, 1937. In *O Estado de S. Paulo*, 12 October 1937.

The Estado Novo years were replete with public, academic, and legislative displays of such state priorities, which coincided with global currents of eugenics and hygienicism. Government-promoted "Brazilian Race Day" celebrations featured military sporting competitions, parades "consecrated to the Ibero-American race," and "health processions" designed to simultaneously display and promote a regimented vision of bodily health in the name of "racial progress." During one such celebration, in 1937, an estimated 10,000 children (girls and boys) marched through the streets of São Paulo.[56] The parade coincided with the announcement of the winners of a "Robustness Contest" for children in the state of São Paulo, designed to identify and display "the robust child, the true pride of our race!"[57] The contest winners (see fig. 1) displayed the state's predilection for "robustness"—physical hardiness—in both girls and boys; while the regime spent much of its pedagogical energies on boys, it also (if less consistently) promoted physical education for girls, to the consternation of rightists.

Intellectuals and Estado Novo nabobs promoted such "robustness" as part of the state's production- and progress-centric vision of educational and family policy. The magazine *Cultura Política*, an official government mouthpiece, recruited the period's intellectuals to bring elites into Vargas's ideological fold. The magazine broadcast the government's cold shoulder toward theocratic moralism in favor of demography, productivity, and statism. In *Cultura Política*, Vargas partisans affirmed the primacy of the state in the "new era"—frustrating religious conservatives' hopes for dividing power between church and state.[58] The government, *Cultura Política* affirmed, trumped the church as arbiter of all things political and moral, including "sexual education, Eugenics, alcoholism, leisure time, and hygiene." Thus, while the Estado Novo was not wholly unconcerned with tradition, the regime shunned a reactionary "recuperation of the past" so prized by medieval-minded Catholic and Integralist militants.[59] Where, for instance, Catholic rightists mourned medieval religious and social traditionalism, a 1941 *Cultura Política* article favored "renovation" of "social relations" over the maintenance of "historical elements." The article disparaged the "medieval murkiness" and "struggle between ecclesiastical and temporal powers" ended by the "radiant onset of the Renaissance."[60]

If Octávio de Faria and the extreme Right disagreed with *Cultura Política* on the delights of the Middle Ages, they also faced a disappointment in the government's approach to the intertwined issues of modernity, gender, sexuality, and education. Forming something of a counterpoint to *A Ordem*, *Cultura Política* approached these topics from a perspective that emphasized morality, eugenics, and hygiene as *state* prerogatives, to be exploited for demographic and productive purposes. The evils of modernity, according to *Cultura Política*, lay less in cabarets and other dens of vice than in excessive capitalism and the deterioration of national unity and strength. The "current world crisis" stemmed from Rousseauean liberalism, but took the form of a crisis of masculinity and productivity. This crisis necessitated the recruitment of Capanema's "army of workers," the creation, by and for the Estado Novo, of what *Cultura Política* called the "New Man."[61] Dr. João Peregrino Junior, chief of endocrinology at Rio's general hospital, went so far as to decry a "national problem of the child and the adolescent"—but unlike moralists fretting about the "youth problem" in later decades, Peregrino identified a crisis entirely in terms of "biotypology" and eugenics. The principal challenge, wrote Peregrino, lay not in morality but in the "vitality of the race"—robust masculinity for boys and stolid future motherhood for girls. As such, he praised the Estado Novo for "addressing . . . the grave problem of the betterment of the eugenic conditions and the structuring of the Brazilian man ... strong of body, lucid of spirit, and pure of heart." The family, in this view, should be a source not of Catholic morality but of fertility and demographic power, a site for educating and generating "men of complete procreative virility." This language, foregrounding militarization and regimentation of "the Brazilian Man," included the state's reformation of women. Girls were to be trained both as workers and as republican mothers—their "robustness" in the service of the "race" would be marshaled for "eugenic" reproduction and the "security of the progeny."[62]

Military training, too, demonstrated the subordination of religious moralism to an ethics of state- and development-centered masculinism. In a 1939 speech at the Command and General Staff College (ECEME), distinguished pedagogue Manuel Bergström Lourenço Filho emphasized two principal "objectives" for education in the Estado Novo: the "strengthening of the race" and "training for work." The time for religious education, Lourenço Filho said, had passed: outdated pedagogy "had a different spirit: a religious one ... [but] education, as we understand it today, is dominated by the interests of the State."[63] The very textbooks of military training portrayed military service as a source of moral and civic instruction that would serve not the moralistic agendas of the Right but the productive and defensive ends of the state. Such instruction, according to military authorities, would convert potentially degenerate Brazilians (*homens rudes*) into civilized, civic-minded, and nationalist soldiers. "You are here," the Ministry of War's 1939 *Compendium of Moral and Civic Education for the Soldier* informed trainees, "to be transformed into citizen-soldiers, because the only citizen is he who makes himself able to defend the Pátria, that is, a man of discipline, strong of body ... apt for the rough work of the campaign, with his heart ennobled by the love of the Pátria."[64]

Among military pedagogues, even sex itself shed moral qualifiers in favor of eugenic ones. Unlike rightists, who saw and would continue to see abstinence as a weapon against communists' moral subversion, War Minister Góes Monteiro emphasized patriotic, hygienicist parameters. Soldiers must avoid "sexual excess" not for moral reasons but because "chastity" would protect their "indispensable robustness"—and hence the "greatness of the Pátria"—from sexually transmitted infection.[65]

"The Type of Man the Estado Novo Needs": Statist Policy-Making

This statist outlook shaped Estado Novo policy-making on the family, youth, and education. Early in his regime, shrewdly purchasing the support of church leaders, Vargas maintained the illegality of divorce and reinstituted religious education. Yet the regime's orientation toward progress and pragmatism jeopardized even these priorities. Vargas let it be known that he personally favored the legalization of divorce; and rightist Catholics remained dissatisfied even with the long-sought recuperation in 1931 of religious education, noting that its enactment by decree explicitly gave the state the power to revoke it at any time—yet another instantiation of wrongful state primacy.[66] The administration's 1939–40 debates on a new family code, for example, lit on fecundity and productivity as the code's central objectives. Proposed measures demonstrated the desire to encourage marriage for the sake of reproduction, via easy credit for couples, child health and welfare programs, and taxes on the unmarried and/or childless. As if to emphasize the focus on demographic concerns at the explicit expense of moral ones, the law featured proposals that enraged the moralistic Right and challenged its core precepts: premarital medical examinations (staunchly opposed by Catholic hierarchs) sought to eugenically ensure the health of future workers; civil marriage would replace religious marriage; and children born out of wedlock would receive legal recognition.[67]

Capanema defended the law in the most pragmatic of terms, arguing that family legislation must, above all, encourage "proliferation" for nationalist reasons. The objections that doomed this version of the family code came, in fact, not from Catholic right-wingers (many of whom could at least approve of its pro-natal provisions), but from members of the government who complained that the law still contained traces of religious moralism and did not focus enough on demography. "Encouraging the birthrate must mean encouraging national production," wrote one critic, "first and foremost [to] improve the quality of the population, making it stronger and more vigorous." The 1940 Code, as Schwartzman points out, eschewed "intransigent defenses of the traditional family" and—contrary to the proposals of reactionaries like Leonel Franca—even protected women's participation in the extradomestic labor force.[68]

Vargas's government sought to overhaul policies on education and youth, and here too privileged service to state and nation over moral concerns. The 1942 school reform included religious education as a balm for clerical authorities' displeasure but balked at rightist demands for the primacy of Moral and Civic Education (EMC). Rightists of the interwar period, as throughout the century, supported EMC as a fundament of anticommunist remoralization. In 1936, Everardo Backeuser called for moral and civic education as a complement to violent repression. Where repression "cuts the branches" of communism, he wrote, EMC would stamp out its "roots" by instilling faith and traditionalist behavior.[69] Yet the government did not share Backeuser's commitment to EMC—indeed, the 1942 law made moral and civic instruction the vehicle of yet more developmentalist training. EMC did not receive its own discipline, as right-wingers demanded. Instead, it would vaguely "suffuse other disciplines" and—thus blunted—seemed destined to promote *state*-centered moral prerogatives. The "essential elements of morality," according to the 1942 Secondary Education Law, had little to do with religious devotion, Catholic marriage, family, and/or sexuality. Rather, these elements were "the spirit of discipline," "responsibility," and "capacity for initiative and decision."[70]

This preoccupation with state-centered socialization reached an apogee in policy debates over extracurricular youth brigades, which explicitly sought the militarization and patriotic regimentation of all Brazilians, including military training for boys and "domestic education" for girls. In keeping with global trends tying nationalism to youth regimentation and masculinization, Estado Novo authorities enthusiastically explored options for nationalizing scouting (*escotismo*) and/or forming a Brazilian system of youth brigades.[71] Proponents of an officialized scout program endorsed it as a means of promoting masculine regiments steeped in a cult of statist and nationalist ascendancy. Government propaganda eschewed religion and spirituality in favor of the program's "principal value . . . to make the young man useful . . . turning him into a complete citizen . . . making him fight only for the cause of the Pátria."[72] Indeed, even when "moral" training did enter the scouting equation, enthusiasts linked it not to religion, but to the remasculinization they so admired in Robert Baden Powell, the British founder of scouting. "Moral education," read a 1939 government-published manual for scoutmasters, "is based on the laws of honor and virility." It must avoid, therefore, "vague theories and ideas" of doctrinal or religious training.[73] If scouting included moral education, it should engender "perseverance on the job," and "make [youths] resistant to . . . morbid infection and apt for continual work."[74] The omission of *bandeirantes* (girl scouts) from these state discussions reflects a broader focus on the training of boys—though as we shall see other state policy documents did manifest interest in marshaling both sexes.[75]

Scouting was not to have the grand destiny supporters imagined for it—precisely because, as an international "movement," it could never satisfy the statist and pro-regime needs of the Estado Novo. Instead, government planners focused on creating a coeducational, national breed of youth brigade—Brazilian Youth (Juventude Brasileira, or JB).[76] It is difficult to know what this grand plan for militarizing girls and boys would have looked like, as JB never amounted to much more than a parade-day pageant. Nevertheless, initial debates over the design of the organization reflected, again, the triumph of a state-centric focus on developmentalist militarization at the expense of rote moralization. On one—ultimately unsuccessful—side of this debate, right-wing moralists saw a government-sponsored youth organization as a potential avenue for atavistic remoralization. Integralist Gustavo Barroso, for example, wrote to Vargas that the youth brigades should deploy religious moralization to "immunize" young people against communism.[77] The most comprehensive proposal for a right-wing youth brigade came from General Francisco José Pinto, who outlined a National Youth Organization (Organização Nacional da Juventude, ONJ) that would respond to moral crisis above all else. Citing the rightist LDN's calls for moral masculinization, Pinto aimed to "stop the march of new generations toward moral decadence." He prescribed a new, moralistic Department of Youth Education, with special emphasis on total sex segregation. Moral education, Pinto insisted, must take precedence over patriotic education; only after guaranteeing the "moral and religious disposition of youth" could indoctrination hope to "awaken in the imagination the greatness of the *Pátria*." Coeducation was anathema here, and girls themselves an afterthought; Pinto intended the ONJ for the cultivation of boys, even if he acknowledged, on some level, that "girls, too," would need patriotic lessons, if only to "transmit them, later, to their offspring."[78]

The ONJ, however, never materialized as Pinto and Barroso envisioned it. Instead, government officials created the JB, focused much less on "moral decadence" or the "religious disposition of youth" than on crafting patriotic, loyal, and productive citizen-workers of both sexes. Supporters ignored religion, focusing instead on the statist goals of a patriotic youth brigade. The government should seek such characteristics as "the physical development of the race," "love of the Pátria," "cooperation," and "love of military duty, of discipline, and of hierarchy." Concerns about sexuality, where they did emerge, emphasized physical health and reproduction at the expense of moral restrictions. That is, youthful sexuality seemed dangerous only insofar as it might "squander the fonts of energy" among young Brazilians, diminishing their capacity for healthful reproduction. Indeed, despite the warnings of religious rightists against it, *Cultura Política* advocated a state-sponsored "healthful and conscientious orientation in sexual matters" through the newly created JB itself. The organization should further preserve young men's sexual and physical wholesomeness via "sports" and "life in the open air and the consequent preservation of health." Girls must also receive physical education, as the "physical development of the race" predominated over worries about "moral decadence."⁷⁹ Indeed, though JB proponents reaffirmed gender strictures, they were emphatic, at least, in their inclusion of girls. One enthusiast explained that the "primary difference" between scouting and the JB was that the latter would allow "mixing of the sexes," even as it would focus on girls' "mission ... as mothers of families."⁸⁰

Capanema's vision of the youth organization confirmed the predominance of developmentalism over morality and segregation of the sexes. His draft of the law creating the Juventude Brasileira excluded the moralistic proposals he had received from General Pinto. There was to be no reaction against "moral decadence," no mandatory elimination of coeducation. Instead, Capanema incorporated gender differences in ways meant to promote productive national citizenship. Boys were to receive military education, fostering physical vigor, while girls would take classes in "domestic education," becoming republican mothers. Both sexes would take part in physical education, an idea consonant with the regime's cultivation of hale mothers who would produce robust future generations. As the draft made clear, these measures aimed to create hardy, compliant, and cooperative citizens, imbued with "the habit of discipline, the love of initiative, intrepidness and perseverance in their actions."⁸¹ In a letter to Vargas, Capanema wrote that the projected youth organization would "provide an education that prepares the type of man that the Estado Novo needs to guarantee its survival, prestige and usefulness." A later draft indicated the primacy of the state's approach to gender over that of religious authorities—Capanema referred not to the "type of man" but to the "type of human" who would serve the Estado Novo above all else.[82] Boys and girls, then, could be marshaled into statist, patriotic service rather than remaining under the rigid, putatively watchful eyes of the church. Catholic indoctrination—a central preoccupation of church leaders—fell by the wayside in state proposals for the youth organization. Capanema's draft made no mention of catechism, and Minister of War Eurico Gaspar Dutra advised Capanema and Vargas against Catholic religious education in the program.[83]

Disappointment and the Early Right

The state's inattention to the moralistic preoccupations of rightists ranged from benign neglect to overt hamstringing of right-wing institutions like AIB and the Catholic Electoral League (both made moribund by the Estado Novo). Filinto Müller, the fearsome chief of Vargas's Federal Police and an erstwhile friend to Integralists (and Nazis), spearheaded the regime's 1937 move to crush AIB. Müller used "the same tactics employed against the communists" to hound AIB members, and when rightist clergy opposed the disbanding of their fascist, moralist ally, Müller, at Vargas's behest, moved to pressure these clerics into deferring to the regime. Despite his former closeness with the Integralists, Müller promoted the primacy of the state, looking with suspicion on cooperation between moralistic Integralists and the church.[84]

Whatever its nature and intensity, the regime's treatment of conservative moralist prerogatives was pronounced enough to generate objections and even outrage among some conservatives, precisely on issues of youth, gender, sexuality, and education. Vargas's rise to power in 1930 inaugurated a complex, ever-evolving shift in church-state relations. In some ways, the church—and especially certain hierarchs—renewed a cooperation with the state that had languished in the pre-Vargas decades; on the other hand, as detailed scholarship has noted, tension between the state and conservatives dated to the very beginning of the Vargas period.[85] Of key importance here, however, is the way in which such tension crystallized around issues of gender and morality.

Early in the Vargas regime, A Ordem's Heráclito Sobral Pinto roundly criticized Minister of Education Francisco Campos, alleging (despite Campos's reinstitution of religious instruction) that government educational reform represented a "Hegelian" aberration and a threat to "all values, moral, spiritual, and material." State relegation of Moral and Civic Education to secondary status was anti-Catholic, Marxist materialism at its most "daring and audacious," complained Sobral; it constituted a direct "affront to morality."[86] Exemplifying the perils of moralism in the Vargas years, Sobral bickered with powerful Catholic friends on these issues, deploring others' willingness to make compromises with the regime.[87] He would eventually abandon *A Ordem* and advocate democratic freedoms for victims of both of Brazil's twentieth-century dictatorships; yet anticommunist, Catholic moralism remained central to his thinking throughout his life.[88] Here, in 1931, he and others championed moralism as a direct security concern, in ways that suffused right-wing anticommunism across the decades in Brazil. Lamenting the lack of Catholic and Integralist influence on troops, Sobral argued that military discipline (and hence anticommunist national security) necessitated Catholic moralization of military circles. Without such moralization, "the Army's one specific finality—national defense—lies dead."[89]

Conservative Catholics mobilized to oppose any liberalization of education in the Estado Novo—in ways that explicitly conflated communism and immorality as central issues. The archconservative *O Legionário* warned in 1938 of the menace of "lay education," supposedly inspired by the excesses of liberalism and communism. This weekly was edited by Plínio Corrêa de Oliveira, whose medievalist group Tradition, Family, and Property (TFP) we shall explore at length below. According to *O Legionário*, Vargas's revolution of 1930 had brought "even more fatal consequences" for education, including coeducation: "That is why we say that, despite . . . the restoration of religious instruction, [education] seems to be even more disastrous than in the [secularist] regime installed in 1891."[90] Leonel Franca spoke out against the "laicization" of education, denouncing the "socialization of the child as a socialist or a communist." Tellingly, he identified the primary problem of such "communist" schooling: its purported tendency toward "sexual initiation," a symptom of the "disequilibrium . . . that modern society visibly demonstrates in questions of the sexual order." The only solution, Franca insisted, was "Catholic pedagogy, universal and comprehensive," without which "sexual education and the crisis of morality between the sexes, far from attenuating, will get worse." Franca cited a figure we will see influencing later moralists: "[G.] Stanley Hall, the prince of North American pedagogues," whose pathologizing moralisms had shaped child psychology in the fin de siècle United States.[91]

As the Vargas regime contemplated broad, centralizing educational reform in 1936, conservative Catholics gathered at the Centro Dom Vital to make "suggestions" for revising the new National Education Plan (PNE). Conservative Catholics felt threatened by the professionalization and secularization of education championed by reformers known as *escolanovistas* (literally, "new-schoolers"); the Right execrated these reformers as "communists" and eyed the state itself with "mistrust."[92] Accordingly, the Centro Dom Vital suggestions teemed with moral outrage about potential statism in pedagogy. The constitution of 1934, railed one critic, had allowed liberalism, socialism, bolshevism, and "Masonic Judaism" to "violate the natural rights of parents and the divine right of the Church" to inculcate morality. "The State," he grumbled, "does not grant Morality."[93] Another attendee alleged that statist education generated a "cosmopolitan" cesspool of moral and communist deviance: "Young men from other states who arrive . . . in Rio de Janeiro have encountered . . . a source of tremendous moral depravation. It is well known how among these students various communist cells have been formed, which will not have much difficulty in capturing the poor, inexperienced boys who come from remote places and are seduced by the enchantments and novelties of the great metropolis."[94] These complaints highlight the extremity of perspective here, as the constitution of 1934 had made crucial concessions to Catholic pressure groups led by Cardinal Dom Sebastião Leme. Even religious instruction in primary schools, reinstituted in 1931, did not mollify Catholics who sought a much broader goal: the restoration of the church as *principal* arbiter of culture and society, including pedagogy. The conservatives gathered at the Centro Dom Vital in 1936 viewed state-sponsored schooling— particularly the Vargas regime's guarantees of free, obligatory schooling, and even more so proposals for technical and professional programs—as threats that would harm rightists' paramount goals: religious, anticommunist, moralistic schools directed by the church. Pedagogical secularism, they sarcastically complained, would "disdain . . . the 'little problems of order and moralization.'"[95] A summary of the Centro's objections to the PNE written for *A Ordem* voiced opposition to government interference in "parochial schools" and "religious instruction." Anxieties about religious instruction and moral education took center stage among these Catholic intellectuals—state-controlled schooling provoked the *most* ire at the Centro Dom Vital meeting. Delegates, *A Ordem* reported, insisted on "integral Christian education, not as a specialization, but as a means of social defense."[96]

Secular "official schools" must be combated by a strong, universal program of church-led moral and religious education in schools. In the wake of the controversial 1942 educational reform (which, like earlier Vargas-era measures, preserved religious instruction as a carrot for Catholic authorities), Archbishop Jaime de Barros Câmara sent Capanema a "didactic regimen" for religious education developed by the church hierarchy, demonstrating the moral-cum-anticommunist goals of the bishopric. The "great finality" of church-led religious instruction, according to the archbishop, was to instill "Christian morality." Lessons must combine anti-Marxism with regulation of everyday moral, physical, and sexual behavior. The church leaders' proposal demanded control of instruction in the key areas of "Conscience and Sin," "Scandal and good example," "Diet, Clothing, and Entertainment," "Chastity," and "Abstinence." With particular emphasis on quotidian choices in style and recreation, the program called for a full unit of instruction on "The Young Person and Entertainment: (1) Happiness and Sin. (2) Wholesome diversions, Christian happiness. (3) Fashions and manners."[97]

Educational policy aside, conservatives took broader issue with the government—again on the grounds of sexuality, morality, and modern diversion. Alceu Amoroso Lima, in some ways a friend and supporter of the regime, criticized officials as "opportunists" bent on exploiting the church without advancing its moral agenda. His specific complaints surfaced in a letter to Capanema that demanded a better, state-led imbrication of anticommunism and moralism, as nationalist, conservative, and religious prerogatives. Blithely conflating anticommunism and moralism, Lima insisted that the Vargas state must "react firmly against the growing infiltration of communism in our midst"; that is, it must combat "communism . . . the epitome of all anti-spiritual and therefore anti-Catholic thinking" by "combating seriously the immorality of the cinemas and theaters with honest censorship."[98]

Sobral Pinto, an inveterate moralist and critic, objected to the Estado Novo in less diplomatic terms, accusing the government of irreligiousness, amorality, and communism. Enraged by Vargas's toleration of "vice," Sobral wrote to Capanema in 1944, affirming the need for censorship of "pornography and immorality." When an unconcerned Vargas government rejected an episcopal petition to end gambling (and prohibited the publication of pastoral letters on the subject), Sobral railed against moral dissipation at the Urca, Atlantico, and Copacabana

Casinos—all examples, according to Sobral, of the ways that the state usurped church power in "establishing the rules that govern . . . morality and customs." Sobral insisted that government tolerance of libertinism constituted a moral threat as serious as that confronted by "the Christians of the first few centuries." Beset by liberalism on the one hand and communists on the other, the church faced government pressure to "forget its mission as Chief Censor of public and private custom and Intransigent Defender of the dignity of the person." Sobral branded government officials "enemies of the Christian Faith, whether hidden or undisguised."[99]

Rightist, Catholic reaction to Estado Novo statism was so enduring that many years later Plínio Corrêa de Oliveira, founder of the medievalist Catholic sect Tradition, Family, and Property (TFP), would remember the Vargas period in terms of the very moral strife described by Sobral. Interviewed decades after Vargas's demise, once TFP had become an important outlet for right-wing, moralistic anticommunism, Oliveira recalled the Vargas-era struggle to keep Brazil on the path of righteousness. Referring to the conflicts of the 1930s, Oliveira indicated that only the agitation of Catholic reformers like himself had maintained the moral prerogatives of religious education, prohibition of divorce, and religious marriage. Conservatives, he held, had single-handedly defended these moral and sexual bulwarks, threatened by Vargas's reorganization of government and society.[100]

Conclusion

Vargas's dictatorship ended in 1945, inaugurating nineteen years of tenuous democracy in Brazil. For many of the rightists we have met here, however, the return of democracy did not augur the remoralization they sought. The Integralists, disbanded in 1937, reemerged as a registered political party, the Popular Representation Party (PRP), in 1945. True to form, ex-Integralists retained the antimodern patriarchalism of AIB and other Vargas-era moralists. As Gilberto Calil has argued, they did so in specific reaction to moral and cultural changes they associated with modernity: modifications in women's extradomestic roles, the "libidinousness" of youth, new media, and the emergent schism between progressive and conservative Catholics.[101] One party member summarized the "principal projects of PRP activism" as follows:

to combat the sexual depravation divulged by all the . . . vehicles of social communication, . . . the cause of all the evils and illnesses; to defend and incentivize belief in God, Brazilian nationalism, conjugal fidelity, indissoluble marriage . . . and love of the Pátria among the youth in schools and in church; to combat homosexuality, abortion, contraceptives, caesarian sections . . . and other unnecessary filth; to control sex, utilizing it only when necessary between a faithful, married man and woman; to end prostitution, which ruins woman; . . . woman should return to the home to save her abandoned children and to regenerate humanity, to recuperate her dignity and save herself.[102]

The following chapters demonstrate that this moralistic agenda, propounded in the Vargas-era disarray of the Right, could have emanated from key national security forums in the post-1964 dictatorship. In its focus on women, on marriage, on media, on youth, on religiosity, on sex, and on morality, this litany of moral, sexual, and gender troubles prefigures the particular concerns of 1960s and 1970s rightists, just as it echoes the concerns of the rightists we have briefly met in this chapter. Like the 1930s Right, the PRP dealt in crisis, and conflated immorality, communism, and modernization; leaders presented their organization as the party of "re-Christianization." Yet—also like its predecessors—the party experienced relative powerlessness and frustration with the ruling authorities. Even as the PRP grew and achieved some electoral success, Plínio Salgado and other exponents of reaction continued to feel politically "small" and "impotent."[103]

In its frustrated, antimodern moralism, the PRP can be seen as an extension of the kinds of right-wing consternation we have examined in the face of the Estado Novo. Interwar rightist agendas held only selective weight in a Brazilian government dominated by the eminently savvy Getúlio Vargas. His regime concurred with many right-wing reformers when it came to calls for masculinization and regeneration—but the state also diverged from moralists in this period on the issues of morality, religiosity, and modernity. Vargas, to be sure, made some shrewd concessions on moral issues—including marriage and religious education—but only when these meant "another victory for the state," which ultimately co-opted masculinization and pedagogy as parts of an agenda that doomed the very pastoral, medieval order that moralists prized.[104] Interested far more in creating an "army of workers" than a vanguard of neo-medieval Catholicism, the Estado Novo often ignored the concerns of the far Right. Looking *forward* to a state-centered, industrialized future of masculinized, ideal citizens, Vargas and his administration neglected—or outright stymied—the nostalgic, antimodern moralism of people like Octávio de Faria. In policy and practice, then, the Estado Novo's notions of countersubversion differed substantially from those we shall encounter in the post-1964 period—when reaction to moral, cultural, and gender change gained prime discursive spaces within the state and became important, formal parts of the framework for considering subversion and the parameters of authoritarian government and repression.

In the rest of this book, we shall explore the complaints of rightists in the 1960s and 1970s, who built on the anxieties we have encountered thus far, constructing and conflating subversion, morality, gender, and sexuality. Indeed, some of the conservatives active in the 1930s continued to agitate for moral and antimodern reform throughout those later decades. We shall reencounter Jaime de Barros Câmara, Plínio Corrêa de Oliveira, Plínio Salgado, Álvaro Negromonte, Octávio de Faria, TFP, and the LDN, again associated with laments about the moral cataclysms of modernity, particularly in terms of sexual and gender dissipation, corrupted young people, and working women. The legacies were, at times, quite specific: moralistic pedagogues in the 1960s would continue to use texts authored by Olavo Bilac; echoing Leonel Franca, later pathologizing moralists would draw on G. Stanley Hall (and on Franca himself) and promote scouting as, in Franca's words, "a flower that to reach the full splendor of its beauty must be cultivated in the gardens of the Church." Gustavo Capanema, himself a devout Catholic, dismissed Catholic archconservatives in 1937 and continued to denigrate them well into the 1960s, when he criticized Gustavo Corção and other anticommunist moralists as latter-day variants of the 1930s fringe.[105]

The reactions of Jaime de Barros Câmara and especially of Plínio Corrêa de Oliveira suggest a possible causal link here. We can speculate that moralistic rightists, active but frustrated in the Vargas years and afterward, honed a set of concerns—gender, sexual morality, education, media—which they addressed more successfully in the more turbulent and (in some ways) more authoritarian years following 1964. Spurred by Vargas-era defeats or not, the 1960s Right replicated the complaints of its 1930s predecessors with remarkable thematic precision, decrying contemporary media, pathologized sexual and gender deviance, women's public roles, and the loss of the medieval socioreligious order as communist machinations and, hence, national security concerns. Rightists' struggle against modernization itself would, of course, remain largely futile; but their ideas about gender, morality, subversion, and young people would intensify—and gain traction within the state—as Brazil moved deeper into industrial modernity and into the Cold War.

2

Sexual Revolution?

Contexts of Countersubversive Moralism

We were militants, soldiers of the revolution, and soldiers don't
have sex!

—Sonia, ex-militant, interviewed in 1977

Horrified, the Colonel examined a copy of a quiz that a teacher had
given to third-grade students in a local Brasília school: *Who is
Guevara?... Have you heard of Régis Debray?... Where does Ho Chi
Minh live and what does he do?... What is napalm?... Is virginity important
in marriage?* The Colonel, on the eve of promotion to general, has
been given the task of managing student affairs, and he is making a
somewhat intense and secretive job of it. He has shown that singular
quiz to various colleagues. And from one of those colleagues, a
member of the so-called "hard line" who presently commands a key
unit on the southern border, he got the following response: "Why
hasn't this teacher been shot?"

—*Manchete* (newsmagazine), 6 April 1968

Sex, war, revolution, and the classroom—a heady combination under
any circumstances, this cluster of issues had particularly explosive salience in the stark worldview of Brazil's late-1960s military rulers. In
Brazil, as elsewhere, this moment focused much attention on such
topics—as in the passage above, from the splashy newsmagazine *Manchete*, Brazil's leading weekly at the time. To many contemporary and
later observers, 1968 was a focal year—in Brazilian cities, massive student and middle-class protests began in March and culminated in the
26 June "March of the 100,000," rocking civil society and generating a
repressive backlash.[1] Lived experience and historical memory of these
years have proven very difficult to parse, as has the precise importance
of 1968 itself.[2] Nevertheless, it is clear that Brazilians of diverse stripes
saw broad transformations afoot. As several historians have speculated,
these broader transformations were much talked about and sometimes
little enacted—to say the least, the relationships between sexuality, poli-

tics, and popular and youth culture were shifting and complex terrain. Rock music and Che Guevara made commercial splashes, while translations of Herbert Marcuse's inflammatory *Eros and Civilization* did not sell very well in Brazil; some former students later recalled that they talked of sexual liberation but only "acted like" they "put out"; still others experienced more permissive sexual relations after 1968. Certainly as the 1960s came to a close, many Brazilians had observed changes in morality, sexuality, and gender, at least at the level of discourse; and in the 1970s, there was a notable increase in the amount of sex in public imagery and popular culture.[3]

As the above epigraph suggests, some hard-line military men experienced even discursive changes as cataclysm, perceiving direct links between transgressions against sexual/moral traditions (those concerning virginity), geopolitical nonconformity (attention to Guevara and Debray), a suspect and unwholesome exposure of young students to these issues, and the violence (in this case, summary execution) needed to combat subversion. The fate of the teacher in question remains unknown—but undoubtedly many Brazilians *did* face the kind of violence suggested here. Within a few days of its March 1964 coup d'état, the new, authoritarian regime made a drastically polarized vision of society—divided, for political and policing purposes, into ordinary civilians and "subversive" enemies—the basis for the first of many waves of repressive violence. Rounding up thousands of suspected subversives, Operação Limpeza (Operation Cleanup) enshrined countersubversive, anticommunist national security as the military government's primary, justificatory responsibility. For two decades, such national security underpinned the dictatorship's openly declared war on subversives thought to lurk throughout Brazil. In the darkest, most violent years of dictatorship, this repression drove some activists—drawn largely from the ranks of middle- and upper-class students—into clandestinity. As the 1960s came to a close, the large-scale demonstrations of what had come to be called "the student movement" gave way to more pointed bloodshed; the most dedicated demonstrators became guerrillas, locked in a devastating armed struggle with security forces. Over the course of the dictatorship, Brazil saw thousands of political arrests; institutionalized torture so widespread it became something of a public secret; and the death or "disappearance" of at least 434 people at the hands of the state.[4]

Transatlantic military doctrine laid the ideological and tactical foundations of this kind of war, stressing hypermasculine counterinsurgency theory—itself rigidly moralistic—as the fundament of Cold War de-fense.[5] Atlantic military theorists had constructed *guerra revolucionária* (the doctrinal name for putative, communist revolutionary warfare) as something of a bugaboo—a totalizing, global, moral, and millenarian battle between Good/West/Capitalism and Evil/East/Communism. In Brazil, however, in the 1960s and 1970s, this battle took on quotidian reality. To some, the devil appeared to walk abroad, trailing cultural and moral chaos in his wake. Disturbing changes mingled the structural and economic with the cultural and the commercial: women left the home for the workplace; single motherhood proliferated; middle-class young people talked openly about premarital sex; the Pill expanded the possibilities for non-procreative sex; and the consumer-based "economic miracle" made troubling new entertainment and fashion available to a generation of middle- and upper-class Brazilians. Some perceived a sex-ual revolution, in the making or well under way. Interpreting this chaos as the handiwork of communists, an increasingly influential segment of the Brazilian Right envisioned morality and culture as preferred spheres of subversive attack. This attack appeared tangible in the frightening accoutrements of modernity mentioned above—specifically in gender and sexual unconventionality. As I have indicated, analysis of how sub-version was thus visibly and specifically conjured, as a category binding together violence, revolution, sex, and customs, has evaded all but a few accounts.[6] In this chapter and those that follow, I excavate "subversion" and its cultural contexts, exploring the ways in which specific, anti-modern anxieties united and galvanized countersubversives in several contexts.

This chapter sets up that excavation by examining the sociocultural context within which rightists constructed their brave, new, moralistic world. Rightist moral anxieties were framed by socially and culturally fraught processes in Brazilian and, more broadly, American (hemi-spheric) history—especially in two related areas, under-researched and ill understood to date: youth, youth culture, and government reactions to youth, on the one hand; and the relationships (real and imagined) between sexuality, revolution, armed resistance, and young people, on the other. Such inattention takes on particular urgency in Brazil, where human rights abuses, including torture, had a disproportionate effect on young people, especially those under thirty years of age—and where, as we shall see, authoritarian technocrats grew increasingly concerned about what they called "The Youth Problem." A related and equally pertinent neglect plagues the study of relationships between gender, sexuality, and subversive revolution in this, a period famed then and now for its youth-led sexual and cultural upheavals. Tellingly, we know little about whether, when, and to what extent a "sexual revolution," if indeed such contemporary terminology remains applicable, actually affected sexual and gender practice, particularly on the Left.[7]

In 1960s Brazil, perceptions of such changes extended well beyond right-wing observers. This chapter opens my discussion of rightist preoccupations with a contextualization: an analysis of the ways in which youth, sexuality, and morality were at the center of public debates in Brazil's 1960s. These debates' very existence makes clear that conservative, anticommunist moralisms were only one of several possible responses to perceived changes; I demonstrate the wide variety of publicly assumed perspectives on these issues, from the reactionary to the radical. Significantly, the latter position in this complex matrix did *not* necessarily correspond to the political Left. From militant anti-monogamists to relative moderates and even some conservatives, observers exhibited multifarious viewpoints with a common denominator of crucial significance: regardless of how much nonnormative sex young people were or were not actually having, a generalized moral and countersubversive panic did not monopolize public discourses on the issue. In other words, there were several, vocal, highly visible points of view that did not conflate counterculture, radical politics, and subversive sexuality. Moreover, though a few left-wing groups did eventually advocate sexual revolution, the most eminent progressive forums opposed it on politically or religiously doctrinal grounds. Within this matrix of broad possibilities, however, rightist reactionaries made an influential case for sexualizing subversion, endorsing—as the following chapters show—the idea that moral-cum-political apocalypse had arrived in Brazil.

The political polarization that underlay the coup and structured the years of repression that followed echoed and coincided with cultural and moral polarizations that had reached a somewhat feverish intensity in the 1960s—culture wars, or the tensions between conservative moralists and those who putatively favored liberalization of moral, sexual, and aesthetic customs. Indeed, certain of the changes that preoccupied the Right were very real, and quite palpable to other observers. Much research remains to be done on the extent of gender, moral, and sexual "revolution" in this period—but at the very least, as noted above, broad changes transpired between 1960 and 1980. Women went to work—and young, middle-class women went to university—in greater numbers; new technology revolutionized communication and advertising, most patently through the proliferation of television; the church underwent a very public schism; the Pill became available after 1962. Ironically— given the traditionalism we shall encounter among right-wing regime members and supporters—many of these changes stemmed from the economic policies of the authoritarian government itself, and particularly from the multivalent consequences of the "economic miracle." Where, for instance, economic restructuring spurred white-collar employment opportunities for increasingly educated middle- and upper-class women, it created concomitant hardships for the popular classes, effectively forcing nonelite women into the extradomestic labor force.[8] Middle-class families—and, significantly, their middle-class children—benefited most from the consumption-driven growth of the miracle, gaining further access to television and to the consumer goods promoted by a globalizing popular culture. By 1967, "All You Need Is Love," alongside images of the Beatles, had burst across Brazilian airwaves with a passion and a revolutionary message that, for some, epitomized the ethos of a new generation. Miniskirts, long hair, "extravagant" clothing, and *os hippies* had become recognized signifiers of apparently unprecedented moral and cultural paradigm shifts, which appeared to affect youth in particular and to encompass public, political, sexual, moral, and aesthetic revolution. In Brazil, as in other parts of the world, young people seemed to inhabit the forefront of an attack (or a series of attacks) on traditional religious, political, cultural, and moral customs; and such attacks, to many of their critics, represented a "weakening" of moral standards and of the social fabric.[9]

Yet the question of just how deeply (and even whether) such weakening—that is, rapid and widespread reformation of reproductive, moral, artistic, and psychopharmacological practices—actually affected Brazil (and particularly the disparate elements of the Brazilian Left) in this period remains a source of controversy and an impetus to more exacting investigation. As early as 1988, journalist Zuenir Ventura began questioning the legendary sexual liberalization of the 1960s. "Sexual Revolution" was "more an appearance than anything else," he reflected, and "sex was probably written and talked about more than it was actually had."[10] Ventura suggested what recent scholarship confirms: that connections between the political Left and sexual revolution were often apocryphal, the figment of contemporary imaginations and romantic memoirs. The landscape of sexual and moral practice shifted—perhaps rather rapidly—by the late 1970s, but to some extent sexual liberation during Brazil's most repressive period was more the terrain of sensationalistic reporting and popular perception than of actual practice.[11] In this regard, Brazil's sexual revolution both reflected local awareness of debates about sexuality abroad and conformed to the trend identified by historians of sexual revolution—a trend wherein changes in practice and perception sprang from multiple fonts (not necessarily revolutionary) and revolved around the relative publicity of sex, particularly extramarital sex.[12]

Subsequent parsing of sexually revolutionary theory versus practice notwithstanding, public discourse in 1960s Brazil demonstrated a marked interest in these issues, suggesting at the very least widespread perception of the potential for moral-cultural change. Indeed, a survey of the period's mainstream press, particularly broadsheets like *Realidade* and *Manchete*, shows hippies and homosexuality, "sin" and sexual revolution, abortion and adultery on the tip of Brazilian tongues. Though such publications were only purchased and read by a small portion of the public (literate and able to afford such extravagances), broadsheets were a widely consumed form of print capital, their glossy, largely image-based allure intended to capture even nonreaders' attention.[13] Hence many Brazilians who were not inclined to discuss changing standards of modesty, homosex, prostitution, or sex before marriage would have been at least tangentially exposed to these debates.

And debates there were. By the end of the 1960s (notably, both before and after the watershed events of 1968), the "new" morality was being openly discussed, in tones that ranged from condemnatory to approving and even exultant. If some associated cultural and sexual radicalism with communism, student militancy with both communism and sexual deviance, others denied and even derided such associations. So if sexual revolution was more a rhetorical than a physical phenomenon, it nevertheless garnered public attention and inspired a full range of reactions, from the celebratory to the horrified. The ruptures of the late 1960s wore into further openness, in some circles, in the 1970s—yet public and academic discussions of the ideas of sexual revolution and moral change did not universally condemn either, nor inevitably link such phenomena to political subversion, real or imagined. In short, the moral panic that we shall encounter in certain quarters was matched by radical approbation in others.

"Inhumane and Stupid Virginity":
Public Discourses on Sexual Liberalization

Among the most radical of those who publicly called for sexual revolution, psychiatrist José Ângelo Gaiarsa staked his career on denouncing traditional marriage, advocating polygamy, and championing liberalized sexuality through sex education—the last of these touching, significantly, on a political maelstrom with youth, sex, and education at its center. Gaiarsa's general critiques ranged from the novel (masturbation did not, in fact, do irreparable physical harm) to the sensational (monogamy was a mistake, virginity "inhumane and stupid") and, at times, the polemical (sexual conservatives were "old, ignorant psychopaths"). In his highly publicized *Young People Confront Sex* (1967), Gaiarsa surveyed middle- and upper-class Brazilian youth, concluding that "our group proved very conservative, barely or not at all different from the youth of 30 years ago." Gaiarsa openly bemoaned this sexual conservatism, exhorting a "round, incisive and definitive 'NO!'" to traditional valorizations of virginity and monogamy. Published by a major Brazilian press, Gaiarsa's book showed that conservative positions on sex, marriage, virginity, and youth did not enjoy hegemony in public debates. All of these issues, and particularly those bearing on youth's sexual attitudes and education, would come to obsess right-wing cultural warriors, but for Gaiarsa and other prominent health and education professionals, sex education and sexual reform were steps toward societal health. Joined by fellow psychiatrists, sexologists, and education specialists, Gaiarsa entered what the popular magazine *Realidade* called the "great debate" over the legitimacy of sex education.[14]

Champions of sexual liberalization and of the introduction of sexual education in primary and secondary schools included esteemed psychiatry and public health professionals. Throughout the late 1960s and 1970s, editorial staff and repeat contributors to the academic journal *Arquivos Brasileiros de Psicotécnica Aplicada* (*Brazilian Annals of Applied Psychotechnique*) railed against "preconceived notions of sexual behavior," deriding authoritarian moralism and opposition to sexual education.[15] Psychiatrist Euridice Freitas warned that "exaggerated repressions of the impulses," such as the stigmatization of masturbation, would *harm* the family; and a 1975 *Arquivos* book review consonantly trilled that "the sexual revolution has arrived to liberate men and women."[16] Medical experts often took the relatively moderate position that sexual education should seek to heteronormatively "prepare the human being for normal sexuality" and wean young Brazilians away from "natural," if undesirable, habits like masturbation and homosexuality.[17] Even here, however, advocacy of sexual education represented—to reactionaries—radicalism in and of itself.

Promotion—radical or more moderate—of sexual liberalization and of sexual education in fact came from a variety of sectors and appeared in wide-ranging media. *Paz e Terra*, a liberal Catholic journal, sought to divulge progressive ideas to an intellectual, Christian readership of 20,000 until it folded in the face of repression.[18] The magazine devoted an entire 1967 issue to the subject of sexuality, sex education, and sex in the media. Here, Catholic priest Eliseu Lopes joined educational psychologist Maria Helena Kühner and literature professor Maria Luiza Cesar in calling for sexual liberation and even—in the latter cases—toleration of nontraditional sexual and family relationships, including homosexuality. Lopes took a tack more moderate than that of Kühner and Cesar, further demonstrating the multiplicity of publicly permissible positions on sexuality—and the divorceability of advocacy for sexual education from sexual revolution and from the political Left. The priest attacked "Moralists" whose "essentialist" approach divided human consciousness into "animality" and "rationality," with "sex ... bound to animality." This rigid perspective, according to Lopes, made for a "dehumanizing and mutilating formative process," causing the rash of divorce, marital infidelity, and dissipation that he identified as a contemporary problem. By no means a sexual radical, Lopes grouped "so-called free love" together with prostitution as evils that a liberalized conversation about sexuality would redress. Nonetheless, his support for sex education and for the destigmatization of sexuality-as-sin demonstrates the diversity of public advocacy for sexual liberalization.[19]

Moderation, however, did not determine publishability. Lopes's middle-ground approach appeared quite literally alongside the more extreme positions of Kühner and Cesar, whose inclusions reflected public discourses' extensive tolerance of unorthodoxy—a tolerance so marked that overt sexual radicalism appeared in mainstream magazines. The striking explosion of sexuality and sexual unconventionality into mainstream media in fact inspired a *Paz e Terra* study on the topic. Sociologist B. Peres referred to an "eruption of the sexual problem in Brazilian magazines" and to the ways that major, nationally influential broadsheets like *Realidade*, *Manchete*, and *Claudia* had taken, if anything, a publicly favorable stance on sexual liberalization.[20] Certainly the work of sexual radicals appeared in these forums. By 1968, both *Realidade* and *Claudia* published pieces by feminist journalist Carmem da Silva, whose long-running column The Art of Being a Woman championed birth control, divorce, and women's extradomestic employment, militating against sexual convention and "that old story of 'men don't do this and women don't do that.'"[21] Gaiarsa himself was a repeat contributor to *Realidade*, whose regular staff reporters referred to the radical sexologist as an expert on everything from virginity to adultery—the latter, according to Gaiarsa, a deed performed for the "benefit of mankind."[22] In 1968 alone, the magazine included articles on adultery, homosexuality, free love, sexual education, and sexually progressive schooling. Tellingly, the articles both predated and postdated the critical events of March–June 1968, indicating that authors and editors did not necessarily link massive protest with an explosion of sexuality.

More tellingly still, *Realidade* sought and published readers' *responses* to the discussion of sex and sexuality—responses that demonstrated overwhelming public interest and a panoply of perspectives. Between 1966 and 1968, of 264 letters to the editor, 114 (43 percent) dealt with sex and sexuality. Opinions ranged from angry reaction to frank sexual revolutionism in a relatively even split.[23] Ronaldo Harari, a reader from São Paulo, wrote of his great admiration for the techniques of Britain's Summerhill School, but complained that "given that the greatest revolution in ideas at Summerhill has been in the realm of sex, morality, and religion, I was disappointed to see the relatively small space devoted to these topics" by *Realidade*—this despite the magazine's devotion of a discrete section to Summerhill's revolutionary approaches. (Subheadings in this section included "Love," "Delinquency," "Hygiene," "Homosexuality," "Inversion," "Virginity," "Menstruation," "Masturbation," "Morality," and "Nudity.") Respondents to articles on homosexuality, adultery, divorce, and hippies likewise mingled enthusiasm, toleration, and indignation, demonstrating the variance in public opinion on these topics.[24]

Disarticulating Sex, Counterculture, and Subversion: Youth as "Noisy, but Obedient"

The buzz of interest in sexual liberalization and moral change did not unilaterally promote logics of repression in which gender, sexual, or moral radicalism automatically articulated with political unorthodoxy. In insightful research on student mobilizations and their repercussions, historian Victoria Langland has observed that certain media evoked an image of sexually edgy, politically left-wing femmes fatales.[25] Yet mainstream sources did not universally or predominantly connect young people's political activism and unconventional style with putative sexual misconduct, or vice versa. Indeed, in 1969, as debates raged about censorship and sexual subversion, *Veja* published a positive review of *Hair*, even joking that "like good 'hippies,' these actors demand to travel for free"; and a year later the magazine, musing about "sexual revolution" contemplated reaction to that revolution philosophically, with the placidity of Arnold Toynbee: "as much in its communist as in its fascist version, the petit-bourgeois reaction to 'permissive' society risks being intolerant and anti-intellectual."[26]

As the 1960s wound to a close (both before and after the massive protests of 1968) *Realidade* confronted the issue of sexual-political radicalism among students head-on. Designed as a series of portraits of young people (a demographic, some suggested, in crisis), the 1967 article "The College Youth" sought to investigate the veracity of a general notion that students had grown subversive in a way that implicated left-wing politics, religion, and sex. The article focused on a motley (and revelatory) assortment of issues—student protests, anti-Americanism, miniskirts, female virginity, and fornication—and concluded that students were by no means sexually radical and only barely politically radical. Anticipating Zuenir Ventura by some twenty-one years, "The College Youth" asserted that even those students who *did* propose sex before marriage "don't always make these theories realities."[27]

Other observers recognized sexual and gender unorthodoxy, but disavowed a connection with political leftism and/or communist subversion. Mylton Severiano da Silva sought to explain counterculture—"shirts in loud colors, tight pants, shoes full of holes, extravagant jewels, weird bracelets, long hair, short skirts, and a careless attitude toward everything." Silva built on overwhelming, phenomenological concern: "Our cities," he wrote, "are seeing more and more of this type of youth each day." At the core of such concern lay gender trouble, evident in Silva's repeated descriptions of young men in jewels, bright colors, tight pants, and long hair. Acknowledging alarm at the fact that "boys are wearing tight pants, loud shirts, and *women's bracelets*," Silva dramatized the growing and perplexing visibility of such trouble—yet his report made no reference to political radicalism. In fact, the article exemplified the ways in which press coverage conspicuously did *not* make the conflations of which it has been accused. This trend continued during and after 1968—an article from July of that year on radicalized student protest described the political commitment of the students, with no reference to sexual revolutionism. Indeed, even when the journalist noted that coed occupiers slept in mixed dormitories, he affirmed that this derived not from lasciviousness but "from pure lack of space."[28]

Beyond showing that it was possible to discuss long-haired boys and miniskirted girls without reference to their politics, journalists also drew on psychological experts who debunked the notion that such young people were dangerously rebellious or subversive in a fashion that united gender and sexual radicalism with communism and the political Left. Quoting prominent psychologist Haim Grünspum, Silva argued that these aesthetically and behaviorally disaffected young people represented nothing more than the physical manifestation of growing pains. Grünspum attributed the new, gender-troubled fashions to adolescents' biologically determined discomfort with their own bodies: "Their arms and legs are growing at an accelerated rate . . . and [teenagers] find themselves ungainly." Marialice Forrachi, a pioneer of youth sociology and an expert in the field, echoed Grünspum, assuring readers that unorthodox young people were not "irresponsible" but were in fact "inoffensive." In short, aesthetic counterculture and its gender and sexual components were not only no cause for concern—they were unrelated to deeper, political subversion so threatening to anticommunists.[29]

Such "experts," of course, tended to dismiss young people's protests and stylistic innovation as childish, hormonal, and inconsequential. Yet there were also those who treated student activism not only as isolated from moral dissolution but also worthy of serious political consideration, motivated by rational, legitimate disquietude. The weekly *Manchete*, though rather staid and conservative in comparison to *Realidade*, epitomized coverage of youth, protest, and counterculture that engaged neither in moral panic nor in infantilization and trivialization. In 1968 alone, *Manchete*'s coverage included articles with titles like "The Universal Youth Rebellion," "Why the Students Rebel," "Marcuse: All Power to the Students," and "The Beatles in the Age of Reason," as well as pieces on (and pop references to) subversion and ongoing guerrilla operations in Brazil.[30] Significantly, *Manchete*'s approach was measured or ambivalent, when not altogether positive, on the issues of student protest and cultural unorthodoxy. Student protest and moral-cultural unorthodoxy appeared as global phenomena, present in communist as well as in capitalist countries. In the fall of 1968, as student protest in Brazil took on new and (to many) surprising intensity, *Manchete* doubted that young people in the West, no matter their clothing or sexual choices, really served as fodder for communist conspiracies. As "The Universal Rebellion of Youth" reasoned, "the Italian press affirms that neither the Communist Party, nor the Trotskyites, nor the Maoists, have been able to co-opt [rebellious] young people."[31] Domestic youth, meanwhile, received *Manchete*'s decided support. Neither sexualized nor pathologized, such students did not represent the onset of communist moral subversion; instead—as the magazine emphasized with a bold-faced block quote—"the students demonstrate great maturity and lucidity in confronting their problems and seeking solutions."[32] Even Marcuse, whom—as we shall see—anticommunist extremists and moral panickers limned as the godfather of a worldwide sexual conspiracy, appeared in *Manchete* as a respected intellectual and outspoken opponent of the Soviet Union.[33]

Abstention from moral, anticommunist panic characterized even moral traditionalists, including Rui Martins, a columnist for the conservative *O Estado de S. Paulo*. In 1966, pop sensation Roberto Carlos topped the charts with his controversial "Quero que vá tudo pro inferno" ("To Hell with Everything"), causing a national firestorm with his fledgling countercultural style and *iê-iê-iê* music. (The name mimicked English-language rock's "yeah, yeah, yeah.") Martins, in turn, wrote a short exposé of the Jovem Guarda (Young Guard) musical movement to which Carlos belonged. No champion of sexual or cultural liberalization, Martins fretted over faltering patriarchy and gender distinctions as women entered the workforce and "acquired short heels, short hair, and pants." Nevertheless, his book treated young and countercultural Brazilians with remarkable detachment and lack of moral panic. Martins saw Carlos, *iê-iê-iê*, and youth rebellion as generally innocuous and certainly not politically revolutionary. The moral problems of Brazil— "disaggregation of the family," divorce, and homosexuality—could hardly be blamed on a group of young people who had little to do with these problems and even less to do with communism. Responding to charges about the "supposed liberality" of Carlos, Martins insisted, correctly, that the "youth leader" eschewed (indeed, ignored) radicalism and believed in "well-behaved young women who get married as virgins." In fact, Martins suggested, bourgeois adults, including those most opposed to communism and to the deposed government of ex-president João Goulart, equally enjoyed the "go to hell" sauciness of a Roberto Carlos. If Carlos was at the center of a culture of protest, its "escape valve" included *anti*communist and moral, middle-class, non-youth protest. Carlos, in short, represented his generation's harmlessness: "Youth is becoming, quite simply, noisy but obedient."[34]

Those who might have joined this "noisy but obedient" youth tend to remember their experiences in a predictably motley assortment of ways. For some, counterculture and political radicalism cannot be classified in stark terms as articulated or disarticulated, as the idea of dissidence was *itself* a question of style, without inevitable substance. Fred, a sometime student activist who spent his teenage years in Bahia in the early 1970s, alternated between the strict aesthetic discipline of military school and his desire to emulate the long-haired, lavish style that some associated with counterculture. As a student of thirteen or fourteen, Fred "hated" the military government, but remembers this attitude itself as a matter of style and even conformity. "Everyone was talking about it," he recalls, mentioning hairstyle and opposition to the government in one breath: "The style was to have long hair, and the . . . dictatorship was also a hot topic." Fred participated in some minor, spontaneous acts of protest, even walking out from the military school his father had obliged him to attend. These episodes, however, had much to do with youthful rebellion and what was "cool," and little deeply political substance. Where Fred remembers some vague discussion of socialism, he insists it was surface-level and relatively unimportant; what *did* matter was "not cutting your hair," a choice that was more about promoting "disorder" in the context of military school than it was about political subversion. For Fred, both he and his teachers understood his activities and those of his comrades as youthful acting out, with little political import: "The reason [I resisted] military school was freedom. Not political freedom, which I didn't really understand, but freedom to express myself, freedom of movement, freedom to wear what I wanted."[35]

Where Martins implicitly critiqued reading young people like Fred and Roberto Carlos as radical, others openly countered rightist inclinations to connect sex and subversion. Even relatively conservative commentators who acknowledged troublesome changes in sexual culture—liberalizing customs, sexuality's increasing public visibility—ridiculed right-wing and government tendencies to blame such changes on communist subversion. Notably, these tendencies had grown so conspicuous by 1970 as to elicit open criticism, including that of *O Estado de S. Paulo* editor Oliveiros S. Ferreira. As the 1960s wore into the 1970s, more and more commentators seemed interested in the putative links between sexual and political radicalism; yet even those who noted real and imagined changes in moral behavior did not assume the validity of those links. Concerned, like Martins, with the "problem of the corruption" of gender and sexual tradition, Ferreira nevertheless dismissed the idea that such corruption could be the work of communists, and lampooned the prevalence of this idea among policy-makers: "In all of the official pronouncements ... the corruption of customs is associated ... with a subversive campaign to destroy the conscience of the Brazilian Nation. Faced with this campaign—in which the word assumes the symbolic importance of Mao Tse-tung's ideology—it seems there is only one way for the State to guarantee national security: ... establish new punishments for ... the exploitation of eroticism." Insisting that sexual and moral "transformations happen independently of subversion," Ferreira presciently blamed the structural and economic changes taking place under military rule. Journalist Flávio Galvão likewise posited a "sexual revolution" occurring in Brazil and beyond—but the government's attempts to police sexuality as international communism at work, he said, "arrived at the limits of the ridiculous, the laughable."[36]

This message—mistrustful or dismissive of putative links between subversives, counterculture, and sexual revolution—endures even in the memories of members of the military establishment. An informant at the ESG, who was a junior officer in the 1970s, recalled this as a decade in which style, sexuality, and politics were easily, and sometimes mistakenly, confused. Though he did suggest a reliable connection between armed subversion and "the hippie movement" in Brazil, this officer also mused that radical clothing, music, and other consumption choices did not automatically extend into revolutionary politics. Dismissing countercultural youth as lost in ridiculous, vague dreams of "peace and love," he recalled, "The hippie kid ... was basically Americanized. He wasn't worried about fighting for communism. He was for peace and love. He was for smoking his pot ... The youth from the hippie movement ... wasn't going to get involved. He didn't want to carry out assaults ... he wanted to make peace and love. He didn't want to throw bombs anywhere ... much less to kidnap an ambassador, for whatever reason."[37]

"A Liberal Militant Is Just as Bad as a Scared Militant": Left-Wing Sexual Conservatism

Media unwillingness to take up the morally crusading mantle of sexual-izing subversion reflected the very real rejection of sexual liberalization by contemporary representatives of the political Left, from the old guard to the vanguard. Communist parties the world over had, of course, long abandoned any traces of Bolshevik sexual and moral experimenta-tion. As early as the 1930s, Stalinism legally discouraged divorce, banned publications with references to extramarital sex, and re-criminalized sodomy in the Soviet Union; revolutionary doctrines from Mao to Fi-del followed suit to varying extents, placing traditional family morality at the center of models for state and society.[38] Accordingly, many of Brazil's young radicals, Leninist, Maoist, and Castroist, refused (with rather uncharacteristic unity) even to countenance the idea of sexual revolution, dismissing it as decadent and bourgeois. Far from embrac-ing sexual anarchy, some oppositional student groups denounced the "cheap sex" and "pornography" creating a "crisis" in the world of Bra-zilian art and culture.[39] Yet more tellingly, protest and revolutionary groups—both largely composed, by 1970, of middle-class and wealthy students and ex-students—explicitly disavowed unconventional gender and sexual behavior. A political directive from the leadership of the Na-tional Student Union (UNE) instructed militants to avoid "lack of re-straint in sexual relations," holding that a sexually "'liberal' militant" was quite as counterrevolutionary as a "scared militant." The guerrilla group POLOP, meanwhile, warned participants that "disorderly habits [or] sexual life" would result in termination from the organization and from the armed struggle.[40]

More generally, the political Left viewed the reputed cultural, moral, and sexual (mis)adventures of middle-class youth with profound dis-dain. Shifting cultural terrain complicated this picture, as some young Brazilians responded simultaneously to counterculture and radical politics.[41] Still, for many on the Left, politics trumped "bourgeois" ex-perimentation; Roberto Carlos, iê-iê-iê, Tropicalismo, drugs, sex, gender-bending, and even feminism remained frivolous diversions, when not taboos. This was so much the case that when Fernando Gabeira (exiled for his role in the 1969 kidnapping of the U.S. ambassador) returned to Brazil in 1979, his drift toward support for feminism and gay rights—not to mention an infamously slight bikini he wore on Ipanema beach—

earned him the rejection of many former comrades.[42] Noting leftist leader Leonel Brizola's outright homophobia, Zuenir Ventura evocatively observed that "the Left—even the radical left, which dreamed of a generalized Revolution—looked upon [counterculture and sexual revolution] with the impatience of someone who is interrupted in the middle of a serious activity by the inopportune appearance of an obscene act. This left exhibited a sober disdain for the behavioral transgressions of the generation."[43]

Such behavioral transgressions—or the notion of them—were dismissed, when not condemned, by leftists of several stripes. *Paz e Terra*'s B. Peres wrote of sexual radicalism *and* countercultural style as trifling distractions, an irresponsible flight from the basic, structural problems of the day. Even the more sexually progressive Maria Helena Kühner, who considered sex a fundamental "dimension of human liberty," saw contemporary youths' putative experimentations as decidedly counterrevolutionary. Kühner condemned rightist moral panic ("the terror of Victorian-style moralists"), but noted that Maoist and Marxist-Leninist groups just as vehemently opposed sexual liberalization. Channeling Bolshevik sexual radicals, Kühner prized liberalization as a means of achieving women's freedom. Still, she had nothing but studied contempt for counterculture and the supposed revolution of 1960s youth. "The young, *iê-iê-iê* generation's revolt," she wrote, was a mere escape from social justice and gender equality problems. This escape failed to challenge the "structures of domination" that true revolution would have to address.[44] (Notwithstanding the nuance of her position, intelligence agents surveilled Kühner and labeled her a nefarious source of politically and morally objectionable "pornography" in Brazilian theater.)[45]

In the tumultuous years surrounding 1970, some left-wing attitudes did change, but at the time of Kühner's writing (late 1967), traditional structures of domination remained evident at the level of gender, where leftists, particularly guerrillas, participated in a masculinist, Guevara-inspired culture that prized left-wing, moralistic masculinity and overtly repudiated gender and sexual transformation. The hero worship accorded Che Guevara by young would-be and actual revolutionaries in 1960s Brazil made myth, legend, and beloved martyr of the bearded warrior, an image around which a new, revolutionary masculinity could coalesce—often at the expense of sexual and gender liberalization. In 1987, recalling his encounters with women Communist Party activists two decades before, film director Luiz Carlos Lacerda compared them to "nuns" in terms of gender and sexual traditionalism, bound by "submission" and "insecurity." As historian Victoria Langland reveals, this traditionalism reached the level of retrograde patriarchy—for example, in an incident where male student dissidents "returned" a female comrade (suspected of collaboration with police forces) to "her parents' custody."[46] The Left, at its most doctrinal and dedicated core(s), thus rejected sexual and gender liberalization, with a firmness rivaling that of moralists on the far Right.

If guerrillas and Old Left ideologues saw sexuality and/or counterculture as an "inopportune" distraction, leftist Catholics championed their own brand of moralism. Ironically, given the sexualized demonization of progressive Catholics we shall presently witness, social justice–oriented clerical voices went well beyond "sober disdain" for sexual liberalization. In the early 1970s, just as the progressive clergy were facing accusations of sexual impropriety and as discussions of celibacy and of broader sexual liberalization intensified (regardless of the realities of sexual activity), left-wing Catholic clerics spoke out against sexual immorality. Like their counterparts on the Right, progressives were concerned with a gamut of issues, encompassing priestly sexuality, but extending to more general moral and sexual changes.[47] These progressives, however, did not link socialism, sexuality, and subversion—quite the opposite. Increasingly a font of human-rights-based opposition to the regime, the Archdiocese of São Paulo published *O São Paulo*, which took the military to task on economic and social justice issues—but joined conservatives when it came to moral-sexual reaction. The paper expressed alarm about "the nudist wave, which has women and men disrobing in public, in a free 'strep tease' [*sic*] . . . a materialistic civilization, eroticized, drunk with sex, wasted and impoverished." Combining traditionalist prudishness with misogyny, *O São Paulo* affirmed that this degradation could be traced to "moral pollution" in magazines and television programs, but also to "the frivolity of woman's psychology . . . which seems to suffocate the most profound anxieties of her soul and her being, which is naturally religious and good."[48]

Support for censorship and for a strong stand against abortion and birth control—twin "evils" of modern womanhood—appeared regularly amid progressive Catholic calls to arms about social justice. In a revelatory twist, progressives tended to blame capitalism and industrial mass culture for the "wave of eroticism" and the disintegration of Brazilian families. A council of bishops wrote to morally conservative Minister of

Justice Alfredo Buzaid, applauding moves to control "the abuse of certain means of mass communication" but insisting that the problem lay deeper, in a "society . . . completely turned toward profit, exploitation of women and materialism." *O São Paulo*, meanwhile, clamored against structural poverty and hunger in Brazil, all the while commending government censorship of "magazines . . . dedicated to the exploitation of sex." As late as 1980, Father Carlos Strabelli summarized the "problems of the family in Brazil," blaming "false moral values (free love . . . sex . . . abortion, divorce)" on profit-driven mass communication. More tellingly still, he nominally supported women's struggle against "authoritarianism or machismo" but complained about women in the public workplace: "If the mother leaves to go to work, with whom are the children left?"[49]

Left-wing Catholics upheld the traditional family and the suppression of eroticism, even as they denounced the government's (mis)measure of subversion, sex, and progressive politics. A 1972 diatribe against the magazine *Ele Ela* ridiculed government censorship efforts as ineffective at all but impeding social justice. The magazine, this critic alleged, "continues distributing sex and exalting the erotic." Playing on the government conceptualization of actionable subversion, the author wrote that "such a magazine, and others like it, are the maximum 'subversion' of values." The piece implicitly called for a complication of the government view, in which publications supporting "Social Justice and Fraternity" were deemed part of the same subversion as this "pornographic magazine." In reality, the critique suggested, such subversion—that is, anything "in the service of eroticism"—should be suppressed, not to combat socialism but to morally protect the "youth of our Fatherland." Moreover, progressive pressure to address inequality and hunger must not be lumped together with the "unraveling" of national values in a generalized, rightist vision of left-wing subversion.[50]

The Catholic Left's most vocal and visible exponents likewise insisted on parsing sexual liberalization, progressive politics, and communist subversion. Prominent progressives like Alceu Amoroso Lima, Dom Hélder Câmara, and Dom Lucas Moreira Neves exhibited a distinct brand of family-centric moralism that rebutted right-wing assumptions of a link between these categories. Lima maintained a characteristic moral conservatism, railing against "hippies," consumerism and "generalized abortion" in early 1973. He blamed this moral crisis, however, on inequality, "poverty, malnutrition, and unemployment," and execrated those reactionaries (like Gustavo Corção) who conflated social justice activism, moral transgression, and "complicity with subversion."[51]

Dom Lucas's unimpeachable moral credentials made him the only Brazilian named to the Vatican's Pontifical Commission on the Family, convened to address papal anxiety vis-à-vis abortion, divorce, and contraception. With Dom Waldyr Calheiros—whom military police would accuse of permitting the subversive, sexual bankruptcy of clergy in his diocese[52]—Dom Lucas anchored the Christian Family Movement, a Catholic pro-family group. Yet, like other progressives, Dom Lucas tempered his public championing of traditional, family morality with rebuttal of right-wing attempts to link *progressismo*, immorality, and subversion. When right-wing critics (including officers from the Army Intelligence Service) decried sexual subversion in the performance of a play at the Church of Our Lady of Consolation, Dom Lucas argued in support of the play and of Dom Paulo Evaristo Arns, who had permitted it. Rejecting the putative link between sexuality, communist subversion, and the progressive church, Dom Lucas affirmed that the play had "an evangelical message" and "religious and literary value."[53]

This is not to say that there were no sexual revolutionaries on the political Left. As we have seen, Maria Kühner, even if she dismissed contemporary Maoists, Leninists, and members of the *esquerda festiva* (the "party Left," a derogatory term referring vaguely to countercultural youth), did advocate for greater sexual and gender freedom in the progressive forum *Paz e Terra*. Notably, Kühner wrote in 1967—in the decade that followed, especially in the later 1970s, some on the Left would drift toward a politics of sexual and gender inclusion. Indeed, documents from police archives indicate that security forces' fears about links between political and sexual radicalism were occasionally confirmed. Surveillance teams reported with alarm, for example, that the group Revolutionary Marxist Organization-Socialist Democracy (ORM-DS) called for state-sponsored abortion and an end to "the repression of pleasure." Intelligence agents seized the organization's newsletters and redistributed them to other security forces—complete with highlighting of the most objectionable sections. Characteristically, the apprehending agents focused on a passage in which ORM-DS argued that "it is necessary to create, defend, and amplify spaces in which [to] freely exercise . . . sexuality and pleasure. Hence it is necessary to combat machismo and violence against women, . . . demanding legal abortion, free and guaranteed by the state."[54] A manifesto of the Trotskyist Revolutionary Workers Party, obtained by agents of the Air Force Intelligence Service (CISA), likewise rang moralist alarm bells. The manifesto called for the "legalization of abortion" and "distribution of contraceptive methods that do not put women's health at risk."[55] Incidents like these, however, in which security forces found the sexualized left-wing conspiracy they sought, seem to have been few and far between. Moreover, both of these examples come from rather late in the dictatorial period (1983 and 1978, respectively)—which suggests that radicalization on sexual issues lagged behind other political radicalizations, sometimes by years or even decades.[56]

Conclusion

In the late 1960s and early 1970s, the spectrum of public perspectives on morality and politics ranged from the radical to the conservative. Emblematic of this spectrum's complexity, celebrity journalist and playwright Nelson Rodrigues combined moralistic hand-wringing, vocal anticommunism, his own brand of cultural radicalism, and a refusal to attribute moral crisis to the nefarious work of communists. A committed Catholic and regular critic of progressives, Rodrigues constantly bemoaned the state of Brazilian society, the "deterioration of Brazilian goodness."[57] Indeed, he agonized about the liberalization of sexuality, denouncing "free love" and the increasingly revealing fashions on Rio's beaches.[58] Communists, especially those of Brazil's traditional party, Rodrigues simply called "rotten." Yet Rodrigues did not unilaterally blame leftist politics for moral change. And how could he, when—despite his eloquent moral plaints—he himself authored certain of the period's most controversial works of theater? Rodrigues's scripts (in)famously skewered the very moral and familial institutions that he so ardently defended in his prose. A sometime friend and ultimate ally of Gustavo Corção in the so-called "good fight" for anticommunist Catholic values in Brazil, Rodrigues nevertheless did not share Corção's views when it came to linking immorality and subversion—what Corção, as we have seen, called "conspiracy and orgies" (see introduction)—nor Corção's enthusiasm for censorship. So risqué were Rodrigues's works that several of them—to the author's incessant frustration—fell victim to moral censors. *Casamento*, a novela commissioned—ironically—by ex-putschist Carlos Lacerda, was banned by the Justice Ministry for "demoralization of marriage and ... of the family," tantamount to "subversion of our

Christian and democratic way of life." Indeed, General Antônio Bandeira, whose censorial efforts we shall further witness in chapter 7, considered Rodrigues's artistic innovations not only morally but politically suspect. Petitioned with proofs of Rodrigues's anticommunism, the general replied, "That Nelson Rodrigues still hasn't convinced me."[59] Security forces in fact saw Rodrigues as part of a plot against Western morality that went beyond Brazil. By 1969, secret police in Rio de Janeiro were complaining about Rodrigues's translations of U.S. author Harold Robbins's *The Carpetbaggers* and *The Adventurers*, which, intelligence agents claimed, brought moral subversion from abroad into the very heart of Brazilian popular readership.[60]

While Bandeira, the minister of justice, the military and political police, Gustavo Corção, and, indeed, Rodrigues himself fretted over the fate of Brazilian morality and tradition, Euridice Freitas inhabited another point on the spectrum. Freitas fully endorsed putative changes in sexual and moral behavior. She acknowledged that "techno-scientific development," including new forms of entertainment media, had created entirely new parameters for the family, morality, and sexuality—but she argued that this development was a force for good, for discarding "old standards" and adapting sex, style, and relationships to the "current conditions of life." The "crisis" of the family, to Freitas, was no cause for panic—it reflected desirable evolution, and certainly had no connection with communist subversion. If, as Freitas put it, "to many, we are seeing the path to disintegration itself" because of "the high frequency of divorces . . . and separations, the decline of birthrates, the weakening of customs," she meant to tell such moral panickers, basically, to relax and accept the new "sociocultural changes."[61]

As we have seen, Freitas was not alone—neither in her liberal perspective on perceived moral, sexual, and cultural transformation, nor, more generally, in speaking out on these issues. Sex, to reiterate Zuenir Ventura's formulation, may or may not have been "written and talked about more than it was actually had"—but the writing and talk surrounding sex, youth, and morality reveal broad matrices of public concern and permissible viewpoints. These matrices expanded in the years surrounding 1970—in the space of a few years, sex was more and more talked about, with little consensus on what new sexual patterns (real and imagined) meant, politically speaking. Responses to the idea of sexual revolution included radical celebrations like that of José Gaiarsa; radical frustrations like those of Maria Kühner; tepid dismissals, like those that appeared in mainstream magazines and among moderate conservatives; and condemnations from Catholic progressives and the armed Left. Participants in the public debates about sexual and moral behavior, moreover, recognized rightists' theoretical linkage of sexual deviance, counterculture, and subversion—and many of those participants, progressive or not, rejected that linkage or outright ridiculed it, as in the case of Flávio Galvão. In sum, the right-wingers whom we shall soon encounter inserted themselves into a much broader field of possible interpretations; within this field, they adhered to a perspective bound by specific nodes of moral panic. For the Right, "subversion"—a shadowy, monolithic menace—meant an upheaval simultaneously political, cultural, sexual, and moral, exemplified by groups like ORM-DS or the Trotskyist Revolutionary Workers Party.

3

Sexual Revolution!

Moral Panic and the Repressive Right

A sense of cultural tumult, then, broadly (and variably) accompanied the political upheavals of Brazil's 1960s. The dictatorship institutionalized and endured until the mid-1980s, when Brazil once again stood on the verge of regime change. By 1983, nineteen years after the coup, fifteen years after the regime's 1968 "hardening," and nine years after the beginning of *abertura*, or redemocratization, the hard line was losing its battle to maintain authoritarian control. In October, Air Force Intelligence Service (CISA) officers distributed a report to peers at the army, navy, Federal Police, and national intelligence services. Mingling triumph, vindication, disgust, and apprehension, the report accompanied a copy of a newsletter apprehended from Marxist revolutionary group ORM-DS. As noted above, CISA agents had highlighted passages from the newsletter dealing with sex—but they also described the publication as typical of a sexualized subversion, by this point familiar. "In the attached newsletter," they wrote, "ORM-DS presents a platform ... Among the 'demands of the students' are ... spaces in which they might '*freely exercise their sexuality and pleasure*,' which can be understood as the transformation of the University into a brothel. The demands of the students, again according to ... ORM-DS, are also '*legalized abortion, free and guaranteed by the state*.' ... It is obvious that, aside from the mere existence of this organized and active Trotskyist group ... the material published herein, presented as 'demands of the students' ... constitutes grave attacks on national security, punishable under the National Security Law."[1]

In the eyes of these agents, sexual liberalization constituted a punishable offense against national security. The newsletter's championing of sexuality led agents to identify it as an attack, and they were not alone in considering this—to use their word—"obvious." This idea of the Left—a Left in which abortion and the liberation of "pleasure" took precedence—mobilized exponents of the moralist Right and gained a place of distinction in countersubversive and anticommunist efforts. Though, as we have seen, Marxism and moral-sexual radicalism did not necessarily, or even often, coincide in Brazil, rightists commingled them with theoretical abandon, and with considerable influence. Indeed, by the time of the CISA report above, that influence had in some ways begun to falter (a process we shall explore in chapter 7). This might explain some of the outrage of the CISA officers here, who may have been as frustrated with redemocratization (begun in 1974 by President-General Ernesto Geisel) as they were with students' "exercise of sexuality and pleasure," or who, like moralist hard-liners, may have conflated the unraveling of dictatorship with just this kind of dissipation.

The year 1983, then, was late in the game—a point at which the turmoil of the 1960s and 1970s, combined with rightist anxiety about democratization, had long since led hard-liners across institutions, within and outside the regime, to conflate sex and subversion. In the 1960s, however, democratization remained distant. Brazilian military and governmental elites had come to see national society not as a complex whole, but as a mass divided between "men of worth" and "others."[2] Countersubversive rightists, meanwhile, had made this Manichaean distinction for decades, defining enemy "others" in moralistic terms. After 1960, key sectors of the Right updated earlier moralisms and conservatisms and successfully disseminated their sense of communist subversion as a palpable, domestic (at-home in both national and household senses) reality—with moral, cultural, and sexual upheaval among its foundations. These Cold War moralisms both antedated and responded to the growing sense of cultural crisis that emerged, if not precisely in 1968, then across the so-called "years of lead"—1968–74, when discussion of counterculture, armed revolution, and sexual and political change gained visibility in Brazil and around the world.

By the mid-1960s, a network of intellectually and institutionally intimate power brokers and activists construed contemporary youth's putative follies as perilous, even apocalyptic. This morally panicked narrative conflated communist subversion and armed resistance with sexual radicalism, delinquency, and degeneracy. The most right-wing, pro-regime, and pro-repression of organizations, public as well as private, relied on this moralist nucleus to prioritize cultural antimodernism in national conversations on countersubversion. As these exponents of moral anticommunism saw it, subversives had weaponized sexuality, morality, and gender by corrupting young people; indeed, moralists perceived this as one of communists' chief stratagems. After 1960, and especially in the later 1960s and 1970s, rightists saw such corruption all around them—in mass media (particularly television), in women's extradomestic work, in the public schism within the church, and in the behavior and consumption patterns of middle-class youth—and responded with moral panic.

As we saw in chapter 1, anxieties like these had long animated anticommunism in Brazil, particularly in the revilement of materialism and sexual anarchy in the Soviet homeland. Compared to their moralist precursors of decades before, however, 1960s rightists—and the institutions to which they and their ideas pertained—enjoyed greater sympathy and intervention in Brazil's power centers, at least for a time. In the context outlined in chapter 2, of much-ballyhooed cultural and political dissent, the latter-day rightists we shall meet in this chapter secured the ascendancy of moralism as a national, authoritarian, and anticommunist priority through the harshest, hard-line years of the dictatorship. The moralizing anticommunism that appeared in putschist and pro-authoritarian forums like the National Defense League (LDN), the Institute for Social Research and Study (IPES) and the Brazilian Institute for Democratic Action (IBAD), Tradition, Family, and Property (TFP), and Moral Re-Armament (Brazil's Movimento de Rearmamento Moral, or RM) would make its way into the mainstream of state-sponsored security ideology at the ESG and beyond. There—as chapter 4 demonstrates—communist subversion became a conceptual successor to the "degeneracy" that had been vilified by generations of moralistic and eugenicist reformers.

The reactionary moralisms of the 1960s, 1970s, and 1980s drew on and even included some of these morally and biologically reformist predecessors, but the moral panic of latter days achieved formal state sanction and influence, and won policy goals in the name of moralism itself. Moreover, this later moralism was characterized by increased urgency, a sense that where the Leonel Francas and Octávio de Farias of the 1930s had warned vaguely against foreign dissolution into amorality/communism, by the 1960s the nightmare had come true at home in Brazil, with communists successfully, visibly subverting national sexuality and national security. At the heart of subversion, as right-wing moralists saw it, lay the family, young people, sexuality, and the church itself, all targeted by a perverse conspiracy. These moralists responded to a peculiar configuration of alarming events, emerging and evolving across the course of the 1960s and 1970s—the extreme anticommunism, locally and abroad, of the early 1960s, apotheosized in Brazil by civilian demand for a coup and by the military takeover itself; the strengthening of social justice–oriented factions within the church and the resultant schism; increasing public debate over sexuality, discussed above; the flood of consumer goods and entertainment associated with the economic "miracle"; international commotion about the "generation gap"; and the visible protests of Brazilian students and youth.

Toward Presentist Moral Panic: "Philosophies that Exalt the Erotic and the Perverse"

Ever a paragon of moral countersubversion, Dom Geraldo Proença Sigaud (Archbishop of Diamantina) had championed extreme-right, Catholic anticommunism and moralism since before World War II. Rooted in that activist past, Sigaud's 1962 *Anticommunist Catechism* foreshadowed moralism to come—to which Sigaud would lend support.[3] Where earlier warnings had denounced the machinations of indistinct communists in the distant East, *Catechism* argued that sinful, sexual conspiracy had at last breached Brazil's defenses. Here, then, lay the stirrings of a presentist right-wing moralism that would last, with waxing and then waning influence, the length of the military regime. Sigaud's chapter "The Materialism of the West Is Preparing the Way for Communism" held dire warnings for failed Christians who gave in to "materialism, sensuality, and pride" and thereby "create[d] the cultural broth in which the communist virus proliferates." Sigaud listed transgressors whose "materialism" and "sensuality" were "preparing the victory of communism": "those who revel in the pleasures of this life," "who . . . dress sensually, without modesty," "who dance the modern dances," "who read obscene or sensual magazines," and/or "who frequent immoral movies and television."[4] Here Sigaud highlighted what was to become a classic combination of concerns, connecting communism with a putative conspiracy of sinful sexuality—one that ranged from pornography to pleasure to the latest dances. Moreover, Sigaud located the problem in the here and now. Visible sensuality and sexual culture (borne, notably, via new mass media) demonstrated communists' success at subverting Brazil and the Occident.

Other high-profile conservatives shared Sigaud's perspective in the early to mid-1960s, the years encompassing both Brazil's experiment with reform under President João Goulart and the doom of that experiment in the 1964 coup and its aftermath. Indeed, the most famed and influential pressure groups in Brazil expounded presentist, moralistic anticommunism. These groups included behind-the-scenes coup plotters as well as the agitators who organized the (in)famous "March of the Family, with God, for Freedom," publicly advocating a coup in 1964. Among the latter, the Women's Campaign for Democracy (CAMDE) has become a focus of scholarship and historical memory; yet the group's oft-forgotten emphasis on moral sanitization brought full circle the links between anticommunism and moralism. CAMDE, like Sigaud, argued early on that communist immorality had already arrived in Brazil. The group sought "remoralization"—particularly in education and mass media—as a balm for moral-cum-communist subversion. Throughout 1964 and 1965, as the military regime took shape, representatives of CAMDE sought to eradicate "the enemy" (communism), which they saw "on the radio, at rallies, on television, right in front us all ... Machiavellianly trying to destroy all democratic forces." The group's Elisabetta Martinelli, ideologically and personally linked (through her marriage) to the regime's most repressive elements, served as head of CAMDE's Student Sector, which sponsored a new youth club in Rio. CAMDE must, Martinelli insisted, respond to the moral catastrophe of "wayward youth," in order to "guarantee the indispensable liberty of Christian Democracy [and] the essential values of Christian Society." The club would therefore stress "religious and family education"; "moralization of radio, television, film, and theater programming"; "centers of civic duty"; "health, physical education, and sports"; "instruction in home economy."[5]

CAMDE played a critical role in the anti-Goulart movement, but its members' influence paled in comparison with that of the putschist Institute for Social Research and Study (IPES) and its propaganda arm, the Brazilian Institute for Democratic Action (IBAD). Founded in 1961 by a consortium of business, military, and political nabobs, IPES drew support from United States government agencies (including the CIA) to achieve its primary goals of combating "ideological warfare," "inspiring a deep terror of communism," and ending the Goulart government. The group's campaign to galvanize the Brazilian middle class and defame Goulart as antidemocratic, communist, and un-Brazilian drew together the top minds that would plan the putsch of 1964. Such connections between IPES and Brazil's business, political, and military elite are well known—as is the rise of IPES conspirators to post-coup positions of power.[6] While acknowledging IPES's and IBAD's multifaceted assault on public opinion, however, discussions of their role in bringing military government to Brazil have tended to neglect the actual content of this assault—and hence the ways in which moral panic suffused the publications of this instrumental cabal.[7]

While IPES itself made policy proposals marked by reform and moderation, its public relations operations conflated moral and political dissolution—and IBAD's notoriously propagandistic campaigns depended on gender and moral panic as anticommunist fodder. Much of this production occurred in the early 1960s, before the more acute upheavals of the 1968–74 period. In its early days, IPES concerns about students, sexuality, and protest do not seem to have maintained quite the presentism of Sigaud, CAMDE, and the moralists we shall discuss below—but the organization's consistent preoccupation with these issues did lead to publications and propaganda that connected student demonstrations and Catholic progressivism with attacks on the traditions of church, family, and sexual morality. As early as 1962, the IPES monthly newsletter (Noticiário) denounced student protest as "Communist agitation" and called on "mothers to protect their children . . . from an impious and well-organized [communist] minority."[8]

Well before the fateful 1964 coup, IPES developed propaganda that showcased moral panic as a mode of anticommunism. By the Noticiário's estimate, IPES's anticommunist film series—the jewel in the organization's public relations crown—had reached 100,000 Brazilian viewers within three months of its release.[9] The pedagogical potential of moral panic surfaced quite clearly in the third installment of the series, Raising Free Men (1962). This "documentary" highlighted IPES anxieties, warning of impending moral-sexual disaster among young Brazilians. Opening (like all the films) with an image of Pope John XXIII's Mater et magistra, the film quickly moved to frighten viewers with a montage of delinquency and sexual deviance: young people drinking, smoking, and playing cards as the narrator asked, "On whom will we count, if their vitality is corrupted?"; a newspaper headline—"Problem of Wayward Youth Preoccupies the Nation"—flashing across the screen, followed by images of a teenage boy and girl kissing passionately, surrounded by other teenagers dancing wildly between tables covered with liquor bottles; a young man smoking and contemplating the graphic novel Gang Girl, whose cover features a scantily clad blonde, as the narrator queried, "And in our rich families, are we not seeing grave moral maladjustments?" The disturbing images continued until the film's climax, at which point the script abruptly changed. "Solution!" announced the narrator as the frame shifted to a stable image of a Catholic church. The subsequent images, presented as examples of "education for good voting," showed a boy and girl riding bicycles at a chaste distance from one another; well-heeled schoolchildren in uniform; and multiple shots of placid school yards. The film's final scene, a man coming home and embracing his waiting, apron-stringed wife, accompanied the film's didactic conclusion: "NO to disorder and demagoguery!"[10]

The film's suggestions, befitting its propagandistic nature, were obvious: moral-sexual cataclysm imminently threatened Brazil's youth, among whom smoking, drinking, dancing, and uncontrolled sexuality ran rampant. The future, if Goulart-style "demagoguery" and "disorder" were allowed to continue, would include none of the traditional values enshrined in the film's final images of chaste teenagers, obedient children, and appropriately gendered husbandly homecoming. Instead, the government targeted by the film series would continue to foster a youth population sexually, morally, and culturally unfit for a democratic future. Notably, the film seemed to indicate there was still time to stave off the youth morality crisis—but future warnings would wax more urgent. Indeed, by 1968, the *Noticiário* reacted to the "contagion" of the global "student problem," praising the response of moralist par excellence Pacheco e Silva, discussed below; IPES stocked and distributed the books and pamphlets of moralists national and international, including Pacheco e Silva himself, Gustavo Corção, Admiral Carlos Penna Botto (leader of the fanatical Brazilian Anticommunist Crusade), and North American Fred Schwarz; and an IPES "educational forum" featured Fernando Bastos de Ávila holding forth on the "crisis of youth" and its fundamentally moral roots.[11]

More indicative, in 1963, of the here-and-now moral panic to come was IPES's book-length attack on the National Student Union (UNE). Published with covert assistance from the United States, distributed without attribution and at no cost to readers, *UNE: Tool of Subversion* portrayed a student population tainted both sexually and politically. Sonia Seganfreddo, a former student at the prestigious (and notoriously activist) National College of Philosophy (FNFi), penned the book as a memoir. Seganfreddo described the process by which, matriculating at FNFi, she had encountered "Marxist proselytizing mixed with the most complete immorality." The book recounted her nightmarish navigation of FNFi's sex- and communism-ridden halls, clarifying that the "complete immorality" was sexual and constituted UNE's primary subversive weapon. "The Catechists" of UNE, she warned, brought unwitting co-eds into the communist fold via a "coup by romance" (*golpe do namôro*). Further, such "conversion" had a central, "moral component" in which "family, society, marriage, are things to be abolished. The literature offered as proof is pornographic, but is labeled cutting-edge." Driving home this point, Seganfreddo concluded, "It must be said that pornographic magazines are obligatory at all of these student gatherings; and not just the magazines—also the practices."[12]

Sexual subversion, according to the book, also targeted male students, as femmes fatales were a key part of the Marxist strategy. "The leftist, female student," wrote Seganfreddo, "is of great importance at school to the work of [Marxist] indoctrination. When she is beautiful, she attracts the guys by means of masculine attitudes of absolute independence, granting them every concession and leading an exciting nightlife." Here *Tool of Subversion* highlighted concerns about young men's susceptibility to sexual subversion, but also the importance of gender deviance in the construction of these communized, sexually bankrupt young seductresses—masculinized by their scandalous "attitudes of absolute independence," they had not the least of sexual or moral scruples.[13]

Public "education" pieces like *Raising Free Men* and *Tool of Subversion* thus placed the powerful, putschist IPES squarely within the realm of anticommunist moral panic—but IPES was a complex organization, with varied subgroups ranging from public relations to planning to data collection. IBAD, on the other hand, pursued its propaganda agenda rather more single-mindedly, publishing posters, films, advertisements, and the newsletter *Ação Democrática* (*Democratic Action*). Linked institutionally and personally to right-wing Catholicism through Dom Jaime de Barros Câmara, Gustavo Corção, and the resurrected Centro Dom Vital, IBAD's Cold War moral panic was perhaps overdetermined.[14] Showcasing its attentiveness to gender and to youth, IBAD cultivated connections with anti-Goulart groups catering to these issues: CAMDE and the rightist youth organizations Patriotic Action Group (GAP) and Democratic Youth Front (FJD).[15] *Ação Democrática* stepped unhesitatingly into the terrain of moral crisis, lambasting communism as a moral, gender, and sexual conspiracy to destroy Brazilian families. This material ranged from the playful to the truly terrifying—from denunciations of the Eastern Bloc as a genderless realm where a dowdy Mrs. Khrushchev, clad in mannish *sapatões* (large, unflattering shoes), presided over hordes

Moral Panic and the Repressive Right   79

of desexed female workers to accusations of communist plots to kidnap Brazilian children and plunge Brazil into an inferno of sex and drugs.[16]

Ação Democrática brimmed with stories of communists abducting children and destroying traditional families—though, like *Raising Free Men*, some of IBAD's early-1960s sensationalism leaned more toward warnings about a potential future. The 1962 article "Where They'll Take Brazilian Children" featured text superimposed on a garish image of a soldier tearing a child from the grip of its mother (see fig. 3); and the magazine's feature on "The Family in Russia" alleged that communism's "revolutionary sexual morality" had "confused liberty with libertinism, with licentiousness" to such an extent that traditional morality had disappeared. "The more liberally a woman gives away her body," warned the article, "the more 'sincerely communist' she is considered."[17] Yet if attacks on Soviet womanhood and family morality were old hat, dating back at least to the pre-Stalin era of sexual and familial experimentation, *Ação Democrática* extended its allegations to the present, linking communism and political radicalism to alarming contemporary sexual and moral changes. Divorce, free love, drug abuse, and rock 'n' roll appeared in *Ação Democrática* as newsworthy, disturbing signs of the times—and the magazine implicated the Left in the spread of these phenomena to Brazil. The May 1962 issue suggested that young women were literally seduced into revolutionary struggle, in what the magazine called *"guerrilha por amor"*—"guerrilla warfare in the name of love."[18]

If, in 1962 and 1963, *Ação Democrática* and Sonia Seganfreddo had only just begun sounding the alarm about clear and present moral-sexual subversion, this trend would grow even stronger in subsequent years. Over the course of the decade, and intensifying in the years surrounding 1970, a sense of urgency manifested itself in complaints of varying provenance. As we shall see, these complaints emanated from influential rightists like Gustavo Corção and the archconservative thinkers of the magazine *Catolicismo*—but they also came from a broader public, a chorus of moralists contesting perceived liberality with moral panic about sex, youth, and education. As mentioned in chapter 2, public opinion encompassed counter-positions, including significant support for moral change; but there were also signs of dissatisfaction, from the eminent as well as the humble. Conservative reactions to notions of homosexuality, hippies, divorce, drugs, and free love focused their outrage on the abrupt advent in Brazil of these phenomena, especially among young Brazilians. One reader, for example, wrote in 1968 to blast *Realidade* for reporting

Figure 2 The February 1962 cover of *Ação Democrática*. The issue featured Miss Universe 1961, East German native Marlene Schmidt. "She too," reads the caption, "fled from the communist paradise." The accompanying article suggested that Schmidt's feminine beauty—"of which we needn't speak, because it's already been shown by the cover of our magazine"—pertained to a free world marked by respect for gender and sexual tradition, whereas Soviet communism damned women to dowdiness and masculine drudgery. Photo by author; original courtesy of Arquivo Nacional do Brasil.

Figure 3 The 1962 *Ação Democrática* article "Where They'll Take Brazilian Children." The superimposed image purported to depict a Castroist soldier tearing a child from the arms of its mother. Photo by author; original courtesy of Arquivo Nacional do Brasil.

on hippies, whose "vulgar, dirty appearance" and "immoral habits" portended disaster for Brazil's "hale and disciplined" youth; another lumped together sexual and political radicalism, a moral and sexual crisis destroying Brazilian young people via "homosexuality, masturbation, delinquency, crime, nudity, swearing, free sexual life, etc."[19] The notion of a national morality besieged by communist plotting pervaded a similar letter written in 1969 to prominent reactionary General Antônio Carlos da Silva Muricy. Homemaker Lúcia de Noronha Guarany complained of a communist "conspiracy" of "dangerous philosophies that exalt the erotic and the perverse." Guarany begged Muricy for moral-countersubversive action. "Our young people," she concluded, "are being Communized, perverted, and turned against their parents, even in the [Catholic] schools and Churches."[20]

In some circles, such thinking spanned the decades between 1960 and 1980. Indeed, in the latter year, long after CAMDE's debut and Sigaud's *Catechism*, General Oswaldo Cordeiro de Farias, a veteran putschist, would reaffirm the centrality of Catholic "good customs" (*bons costumes*, here shorthand for sexual and religious morality) as the most important of the nation's needed reforms, one that brought national security and morality together in a central set of concerns, which, according to Cordeiro de Farias himself, had preoccupied right-wing government officials since the days of the 1964 coup. In a speech to the Federal Council on Culture (CFC), Cordeiro reiterated that "the global crisis is, *above all, moral.*" He equated "moral education" with national security, affirming that remoralization was "much more important" than other concerns. Like Sigaud and Guarany years earlier, Cordeiro focused on the ways that destabilizing moral dissolution had already advanced upon Brazil's bodies politic and social. Condemning the "plague" of immoral television and radio, he lamented widespread "errors" that "have caused our youth . . . to take up . . . sexual permissiveness [and] to stop believing in the family."[21] The general's speech is notable, too, for its relative lateness; certain eminent rightists championed this brand of anticommunism throughout the dictatorship—despite well-known fluctuations in the "hardness" of the regime and even in policy toward the family, marriage, and the church.[22] Decades after the advent of military rule, national security and morality remained intertwined in a way that specifically implicated young people, mass media, sex, and the family—categories that moralists, from *Realidade* readers to Lúcia Guarany to General Cordeiro de Farias, saw deteriorating before their very eyes.

Moralist Champions: Gustavo Corção and Antônio Pacheco e Silva

As the involvement of Cordeiro de Farias, IPES, and CAMDE indicates, however, these were not random, isolated, or uninfluential reactions. By the early 1960s, prominent anticommunist individuals and organizations had begun to create a network of ideological and political connections between countersubversion, moral reaction, and support for military authoritarianism, as well as for violent repression. The military regime enabled the approximation to power of key individuals and groups championing moralistic reaction—and (as chapter 4 demonstrates) their ideas met with marked success in a Cold War moment when closed ideological circuits facilitated an unprecedented doctrinalization of ideas about sexual subversion. Important members of Brazil's national political elite featured among these individuals and within their organizations—distinguished public figures, politicians, and power brokers close to (when not *at*) the centers of government authority.

The CFC, for instance, created as part of what Randal Johnson has called "a virtual cultural offensive by the military government," included, from its earliest incarnation, moralists old and new.[23] In fact, this body represented something of a triumph for rightists and even fascists whose agendas had been frustrated in the 1930s. President Castelo Branco appointed several rightists of stature to the council, including former Integralists and sympathizers, as well as Octávio de Faria, the ultra-moralist reformer whom we met in chapter 1.[24] Cordeiro de Farias noted not only the moral conservatives on the council's roster but the long-standing preoccupation of its members (especially Gustavo Corção) with the moral concerns that Cordeiro himself reaffirmed. "The great and unforgettable Gustavo Corção, among other eminent councilors," Cordeiro recalled, had already warned the council of Brazilian youths' putative "sexual permissiveness" and its political implications.[25]

No one individual managed to make subversion and countersubversion so explicitly about sexual morality, youth, and progressive Catholicism with quite the influence and national visibility of Corção, who emerged as the ultra Right's fieriest representative. A nationally prominent intellectual and journalist—he published more than a dozen books, authored a column that appeared in many of the country's major dailies, and eventually had a street named after him in Rio de Janeiro—Gustavo Corção spent decades at the forefront of conservative Catholicism and anticommunism. He shared much ideological ground with the security theorists we shall encounter at the ESG (where, indeed, he claimed to have instructed President Castelo Branco),[26] but he enjoyed the broader support of a range of moralists, from the Old Right likes of Octávio de Faria to contemporaries including Djacir Menezes, Nelson Rodrigues, and Hélio Fraga.[27] Indeed, it was precisely his preoccupation with morality and sexuality that defined Corção's perspective, his representation of the Right, and his national influence—a fact that has eluded extant accounts of his life and work.[28]

Corção's exemplary vision of moral-sexual conspiracy materialized in its most sensational form as part of his epic battle against the emerging, progressive faction of Brazilian Catholics. Issues of reform, human rights, and social justice split the Brazilian church in the 1950s and 1960s, causing alarm among many Catholics, but especially those of the traditionalist Right, for whom Corção emerged as champion. In 1964, he led right-wing Catholics in a dramatic desertion of the preeminent lay organization Centro Dom Vital, prompting its near collapse.[29] Though national debates raged over income redistribution and agrarian reform, Corção's critique of reformist Catholicism, from the early 1960s onward, revolved around youth, sex, culture, and morality. Throughout these years, but especially in the turbulent years after 1968, he regularly condemned progressives (*"progressistas"*) as sexual deviants conspiring to subject Brazil to divorce, communism, free love, sexually educated (and hence sexually bankrupt) youth, and general moral dissolution— phenomena whose interconnectedness Corção presumed without question. His focus on youth and sexuality surfaced most clearly in denunciations of Catholic schools and churches as places where devious nuns and priests initiated the scions of Brazilian patriots into the coterminous mysteries of sex and communism.

Like Lúcia Guarany, Corção suspected the progressive clergy of using sex to lure children into subversion. His admonitions on this score spanned the sixties (as we shall see below), but reached exemplary heights of vitriol in 1971; as moralism and repression crescendoed, he authored a series of essays presenting communist subversion, sexual and familial dissolution, and progressive Catholicism as inextricable parts of "a worldwide revolution" led by "perverted minorities." This organized "movement," according to Corção, used Catholic pedagogical institutions to sexually and politically corrupt young students. In Corção's estimation, progressive priests had gone beyond mere indoctrination of Catholic youth—they had turned "communion" into "communitarian orgasm."[30] Sex education, he said, ranked among the chief crimes of "the Catholic Left, perverter of youths," which worked to effect the "communization of young people"; communist corruption of the schools meant that "many young ladies from the Colégio Sion [a Catholic girls' school] are coming out transformed into guerrillas"; and activist nuns habitually "propagate[d] their seminars on sex."[31] Corção accused progressives of promoting communism via inappropriate contact between youths of opposite sexes, as well as "degenerated bacchanals" and "pornography and bestiality."[32] This sex-and-subversion-in-the-schools approach dominated Corção's public criticisms. For example, of the twenty-five columns he published in the last quarter of 1971, more than half (thirteen) dealt with putatively subversive sexuality; an equal proportion excoriated the progressive clergy; and youth and education cropped up in nearly a third (eight and seven, respectively).

Corção's vigilance vis-à-vis youth sexuality was more than just propaganda or grandstanding; he also engaged in vigorous private correspondence on the subject. Moralism even fueled his highly divisive tête-à-tête with Cardinal Eugênio Sales, by the 1970s one of Brazil's most important Catholic leaders. The breakdown in relations between the cleric and the columnist—which grew so bitter that in 1973 Sales would publicly brand Corção the "destroyer of the Church"—stemmed directly from the sexual critique launched by the latter. Their verbal and political sparring touched less on religion and doctrine than on children, sexuality, and education.

This conflict was already under way in 1971, when Sales wrote to Corção to complain about the latter's allegations of "communitarian orgasm." In a series of letters, the cardinal criticized Corção's "preoccupation with . . . communism," specifically objecting to Corção's characterizations of Catholic schools, authors, and officials as "perverted."[33] Corção's response bespoke his vision of a sexually corrupt progressive church that he himself had to halt in its tracks. His primary object, he wrote, lay in protecting unsuspecting parents from submitting their children to the sexual and political subversions of the church. He particularly meant to warn military "officers . . . who have daughters in this school of so-called 'nuns,'" and swore to "continue to struggle and cry out when I see that the wave of aberrations in the Catholic schools only grows stronger, [and that] in addition to the libidinous excesses, children are conditioned to rise up against their parents." He even sought to advise the cardinal, warning that such revolutionist "conditioning"—a reference to the idea that Soviet children were encouraged to turn against their parents—went hand in hand with the "pornography" and "sex" that Corção discerned in church classrooms.[34]

In this moment of perceived threat to millennia of church history, Corção represented those who saw *any* challenge to Catholic traditionalism as a symptom of sexual-cum-Marxist revolution. Initiatives to end priestly celibacy, he argued, were merely another tactic of the "anti-Church," whose nefarious agents continued to promote "revolutionary anarchy."[35] Kenneth Serbin's history of the Brazilian church expertly investigates the ways in which celibacy featured in ecclesiastical debates of the 1960s and 1970s; yet rightists' focus on sexuality, morality, and gender extended far beyond celibacy, as Corção's oeuvre demonstrates.[36] Corção's more general concerns were echoed by conservatives who, by the late 1960s, fixated on abortion, homosexuality, and the putative gender deviance of nuns, relegating celibacy to just one issue in a constellation of panic-inducing moral transgressions.[37]

Where, for example, Corção fretted generally about "sybaritism and socialism" making coterminous inroads among youth, the reactionary magazine *Catolicismo* focused less on priestly celibacy than on women's fashion and sexuality as key, contemporary threats both to the church and to Western anticommunist defenses. In the mid-1960s, as Corção led the exodus of conservative Catholics from the Centro Dom Vital, *Catolicismo* (founded in 1951 by TFP leader Plínio Corrêa de Oliveira and other veterans of *O Legionário*) likewise denounced conflated threats of progressivism, divorce, communism, and gender change. In 1969, under the headline "Shadowy Groups Plot Subversion in the Church," the magazine showed images intended to prove a linked conspiracy of communism, women's sexual and gender deviance, and irreligiousness. A nun in contemporary dress—that is, not in full habit—came under fire as the locus of gender trouble and sexual suspicion. The caption to an image of "Sister Germaine" (fig. 4) asked, "Is she married or single? . . . Nothing [about her appearance] makes it clear. She's just a functionary like any other. This is the 'new look' of female religious orders . . . the ideal of desacralization."[38] This image was juxtaposed with that of "an authentic religious woman," in full habit and surrounded by the schoolchildren who were her proper charges. A wedding photo drove home the point that "desacralization" indicated sympathy with communists and centered on moral and aesthetic changes. The caption took issue with the style of the mass and, signally, with the bride's clothing. "In another photo," *Catolicismo* informed, "one can see that the bride is wearing a miniskirt." This, it seemed, was "just a timid step" in the gender-sexual conspiracy plotted by leftists, aimed "at desecration and the new morality that they wish to implant."[39]

Corção stationed himself at the forefront of this mode of reaction, which took on special significance in the years surrounding 1970, as

Figure 4 "Sister Germaine." In *Catolicismo*, April/May 1969.

public discussion of these issues intensified. Yet Corção's opposition to sexual subversion antedated the watershed events of 1968. By the time he denounced "communitarian orgasm," such attacks had made him "the symbol of 'integral' Catholicism in Brazil," representing a community of traditionalist thinkers bent on "moral revolution."[40] Indeed, Corção's correspondents and friends included staunch allies in the fight against communism, *progressismo*, and moral dissolution: powerful conservative clerics—Cardinal Jaime de Barros Câmara, Archbishop Geraldo Sigaud, and Cardinal Vicente Scherer (with whom Corção commiserated about communist-inspired moral dissolution via *iê-iê-iê*)—as well as conservative laypeople.[41] Internationally, Corção's connections included Thomas Molnar, archconservative author of *The Pagan Temptation* and *The Counter-Revolution*, and General Francisco Franco.[42] In concert and correspondence with his Brazilian allies, Corção agitated throughout the 1960s against sundry, conflated threats: progressivism, divorce, abortion, premarital sex, and communism. As he put it in a 1966 letter to Scherer, the "wave of overwhelming modernism" in behavior constituted "the gravest error of our times"—and it manifested itself most visibly in "the youth and the priests" whose progressive Catholicism encompassed the linked deviations of rock music, counterculture, and communism.[43]

As debate and violence grew more heated in 1968, 1969, and the 1970s, Corção's outbursts against progressive Catholics grew so fierce as to earn him the wary admonitions of his publisher (who pled for temperance), the censure of fellow Catholics, the enmity of church officials, and even the threat of excommunication. São Paulo Cardinal Paulo Evaristo Arns reputedly called for a boycott of the daily *O Estado de S. Paulo* if it did not stop publishing Corção's column, and Bishop Benedito Ulhoa went so far as to suggest that Corção should be preemptively denied funeral mass.[44] Progressives, unsurprisingly, dismissed Corção and his ilk as reactionaries complicit with (when not supportive of) a violent and illegitimate regime.[45] Even the relatively moderate Gustavo Capanema, in a demonstration of just how distant such reaction lay from the statist moralism of the Estado Novo, had written off Corção's outlook as the "simplistic" approach of entrenched "conservative sectors."[46]

Corção's extremism, though it distanced him from prominent Catholics and from the church's hierarchy, fell far short of alienating him more generally. As I have indicated, Corção served as a respected, even revered, representative of the outraged Right. In the thick of his public conflict with Cardinal Sales, rightist supporters—led by Hélio Fraga, head of the prestigious Federal University of Rio de Janeiro, who himself spoke at the ESG against "permissiveness" and the "deformation of youth"—lodged a public protest against Sales's denunciation of Corção. In a petition published in *O Globo*, these self-described "friends and admirers" defended Corção's "stalwart culture, piety, intrepid faith, and indefatigable work in divulging the Good Word." Support for Corção as just such a representative of the moralistic Right, however, went far beyond these petitioners. Though the petition included prominent signatories (professors, minor government officials, and fellow moralists), Corção's influence ranged from general popularity to the very top levels of government.[47] By his own count, Corção had a weekly readership of over two million souls throughout Brazil, his column appearing in *O Globo*, *O Estado de S. Paulo*, *O Correio do Povo*, *A Gazeta do Povo*, *A Tarde*, and other major dailies.[48] Perhaps more importantly, he enjoyed honors from and influence on nationally powerful officials, including those with jurisdiction over his pet concerns of youth, education, and subversion. Between 1968 and 1974, Corção's crusade against progressive education earned him the National Order of Educative Merit from Minister of Education and Culture Jarbas Passarinho; his colleagues on the CFC lauded his "medieval crusade" for morality; Minister of Education Suplicy de Lacerda (famous for his cooperation with USAID and his denunciation of the "virus" of communism among students) wrote to Corção to praise his solidarity in the fight against communist infestation of churches and universities; in 1974, the conservative legislature of Minas Gerais decorated Corção for his service to God and country; and Hernani de Aguiar, chief of the Special Agency for Public Relations (AERP, the government public image outfit), invited Corção to write on the church's behalf to commemorate the fifth anniversary of the 1964 coup—making Corção the regime's voice of the faithful.[49]

Even the presidency proved susceptible to Corção's charms: in addition to receiving an Order of Military Merit from President Arthur da Costa e Silva, Corção enjoyed direct political influence with the military regime's conservative (and ultimately repressive) second head of state. Two moments in 1968 illustrate this influence. Wishing to obtain an appointment to the Federal Education Council (CFE, Conselho Federal da Educação) for his friend and fellow moralist Gladstone Chaves de Mello, Corção wrote a note praising Mello as a "fervent Catholic." The note contained a testament from Corção's powerful longtime friend Cardinal Jaime de Barros Câmara, and it was carried to the president's desk by none other than (future president) General Emilio Garrastazu Médici.[50] When it came to the critical issues of youth, education, and student protest, Corção's line to the president proved unmitigated—Costa e Silva turned to Corção during the protest crisis of May 1968, requesting a private advisory meeting. Afterward, Corção triumphantly announced that he and the president held the same views on students, liberalism, protest, and repression: "I had the satisfaction of knowing that our preoccupations are the same, and I had the comfort of conveying to the President the satisfaction that I have—when I consider that Brazil, as much in 1964 as now, has known how to deal with student crises provoked by agitators better than the more advanced European countries, who have so much criticized us."[51] Here Corção referred to Europe's own student uprisings of 1968—and responded to Europeans' outspoken opposition to authoritarian repression in Brazil.

Corção implied that while the "more advanced" countries had mishandled 1968, Brazil's hard-line military rulers could easily take matters in hand.

Indeed, though Corção initially acknowledged that some "abuses" might have "accidentally" occurred at the hands of the regime, he sanctioned the repressive tactics systematized by these hard-line rulers.[52] As protest and (talk of) counterculture grew more visible and the regime more entrenched, Corção and like-minded moralists responded with increasing support for violent repression. By July of 1968, as open battles raged between students and security forces, Corção would proclaim that "we are not against violence. There is good violence. There is sacred violence. God loves the violent and rejects the timid."[53] Throughout the rest of that tumultuous year, Corção wholeheartedly endorsed government violence, particularly against activist students, who "ought to be punished, ought to be mercifully castigated."[54] Indeed, Corção sometimes criticized the regime's supposed leniency, and he heartily approved of the restrictive Institutional Act No. 5 (AI-5), which laid the legal groundwork for government-sponsored torture.[55] His concurrence with friends in the military-governmental hierarchy, then, made Corção's "medieval crusade" as violent as it was moralistic.

Sharing the moral-cultural Right with top members of Brazil's military government, Corção also enjoyed the company of other dedicated, extra-governmental reactionaries whose activism helped pressure the regime (and its think tanks) to commit to moral anticommunism. Among the most nationally prominent of these (though perhaps lacking Corção's household-level name recognition), Antônio Carlos Pacheco e Silva had by the 1960s already established himself as a leading exponent of São Paulo's psychiatric community—he was director of the venerable Juqueri psychiatric hospital, chair of the Psychiatry Department at the prestigious University of São Paulo medical school, and president of the Brazilian Psychiatric Association. Pacheco e Silva had built his professional reputation on an association with degeneracy and racial hygiene theories, participating—with Renato Kehl, perhaps Brazil's most famous eugenicist—in the First Brazilian Eugenics Conference (1929) and committing himself to the battle for "racial hygiene" and against *dégénérescence*.[56]

Pacheco e Silva's moral-hygienicist anticommunism changed with the times. In the context of the Cold War, Pacheco e Silva transformed this 1930s concern with "racial perfection" into a national security issue, speaking out against what he saw as a nefarious communist design to subvert Brazil via moral, cultural, mental, and somatic degeneration. In two widely read books on communist strategy—*Subversive Warfare on the March* (1959) and *Hippies, Drugs, Sex, Pollution* (1973)—Pacheco e Silva sought to alert fellow psychiatrists and Brazilians in general to the prurient perils of revolution. The former broadcast generalized warnings about modern (that is, "subversive") warfare's use of culture and exploitation of women and youth for its nefarious ends. Fourteen years later, Pacheco e Silva responded—as the latter title suggests—to the set of conflated issues that acutely alarmed Corção: sex and communism as imminent, intertwined menaces. Inscribing hippies into a centuries-old struggle between good/restraint/morality and evil/instinct/dissolution, *Hippies, Drugs, Sex, Pollution* presented deviance, particularly sexual and psychopharmacological deviance, as a political, moral, and biological attack on Western Christendom, a degenerative trigger that would facilitate communist victory in the Cold War. The book limned the titular ills as a "Maoist offensive," part of a "Revolutionary Apparatus." This apparatus, according to Pacheco e Silva, combined the "dissolution of customs" with the "degradation of the family" according to the dictates of communists' "modern warfare, which seeks not only the . . . conquest of enemy territory, but above all, the annihilation of enemy morality."[57]

The book exhibited hallmarks of moral panic and, in doing so, revealed specific tensions underlying rightist cries of moral subversion. Pacheco e Silva linked the onslaught of moral "annihilation" to particular, recent developments: the rise of mass media, the advent of birth control ("above all, the Pill"), the execrable "emancipation . . . of women who work," and, of course, the titular hippies themselves, a word that had but recently splashed across Brazilian and global lexicons. Pacheco e Silva and his colleagues on the Right viewed these current developments as part of the "one movement" described by Corção—the legacy of a near-timeless process of ungodly revolutionism, represented in the 1960s and 1970s by communist subversion. Accordingly, Pacheco e Silva condemned media (particularly television), contraceptives, drugs, and working women as part of a larger plot against the family, perpetrated by a shadowy "activist minority" in the employ of "the Revolutionary Apparatus." These alarming phenomena, warned Pacheco e Silva, targeted young people, who exhibited communist-inspired moral and physical "decadence." He closed with a rallying cry to Western psychiatrists: "transcultural psychiatry," he insisted, must turn its "highest attention" to "the instinctive deviations, above all the sexual ones" at the root of "human decadence."[58]

Pacheco e Silva's fusion of psychiatry, eugenics, and moralism fell on highly receptive ears in Brazil's primary national security forums; moreover, the psychiatrist enjoyed recognition from and cooperation with the military regime itself and its hardiest supporters. Invited on multiple occasions to lecture for IPES, Pacheco e Silva rubbed shoulders with—and, indeed, instructed—the very architects of Brazil's 1964 coup. (The organization, in turn, published and distributed Pacheco e Silva's books.) In his memoirs, Pacheco e Silva would recall the friendship that blossomed between him and future president Humberto Alencar de Castelo Branco when the two encountered each other at the ESG in the late 1950s. Pacheco e Silva described the friendship as formative for both parties, as he "had long discussions with [Castelo Branco], who was very interested in the study of psychological problems, given the importance that they had in the Cold War." More strikingly, Pacheco e Silva recalled a like closeness with Alfredo Buzaid, Brazil's reactionary justice minister from 1969 to 1974. "With [Buzaid]," Pacheco e Silva wrote, "I came to be on the most intimate terms. . . . I gave him my modest collaboration in investigating and analyzing the diverse psychosocial factors shaping the disturbed spirits of those interested in upsetting the life of our Country."[59] On a mission to rescue Brazil's deteriorating human rights reputation, Pacheco e Silva traveled to the United States in 1971, dispatching a series of reports to Buzaid and his security team in Brasília. The reports demonstrated the intrusion of anticommunist moralism into official government business, bemoaning a North American moral crisis as serious as the perceived Brazilian one. The United States, like Brazil, suffered from what Pacheco e Silva called the "diabolical techniques of the communists," in the form of "youth gone astray" and "perverted sexuality, pornography, rebelliousness, disintegration of the family."[60]

That Corção and Pacheco e Silva could bask in the public backing of conservative allies, call on friends in high places, and identify with ministers and presidents when it came to anticommunist, youth-focused, and anti-student moralism is consonant with *moralistas'* influential penetration of Brazil's power centers. As chapter 4 demonstrates, the ESG formed a nucleus for the confluence and dissemination of high-powered moralisms, whose exponents included important government insiders: powerful ministers of state, high-ranking members of the military, prominent intellectuals, and presidents themselves, particularly those of the "years of lead" (1968–74), when Brazil's Cold War grew hottest.

Networks of Moralism: Organizations of the Anticommunist Right

Such individuals, however—even such powerful individuals—could not stand alone as the bastions of anticommunist moralism. Instead, they participated, as members or supporters, in a series of organizations that performed moralism's logistical legwork, linking rightist thinkers across Brazil with national and international currents of ultramontane, moralist, anticommunist, and authoritarian thought. By the 1960s and 1970s, Brazil's most virulently and influentially anticommunist organizations, established as well as emergent, shared a tendency toward moralistic agendas that highlighted traditional morality and sexuality as cornerstones of the country's struggle against subversion. In this sense, IPES/IBAD (analyzed above), the National Defense League (LDN), Moral Re-Armament (RM), Tradition, Family, and Property (TFP), and even terrorist organizations like the Brazilian Anticommunist Alliance (AAB) both disseminated moralistic anticommunist extremisms (Brazilian and international) and institutionally linked them to powerful individuals and centers of governing authority.

Originally founded in 1917 by revered patriot Olavo Bilac, the LDN had appeared in Brazil decades before the advent of counterculture, Cold War military government, or sexual revolution—and had disappeared in the 1920s, to resurface intermittently thereafter.[61] Nevertheless, the League's roots in hygienicism and eugenics may have predetermined its 1960s plunge into pro-coup, hard-line moralism.[62] The post-1960 League publicized its anticommunist agenda through radio and television programs, ultimately sponsoring a national educational television project focused on the hallowed precepts of family, authority, and patriotism.[63] It was in the monthly *Boletim* (bulletin) of the LDN's national directorate, however, that moral panic emerged most forcefully, envisioning moral outrages—particularly gender deviance and the sexual corruption of youth—as the central tactic of an insidious, communist-inspired conspiracy against Brazil. Indeed, moral panic in the *Boletim* ranged from general alarmism about moral dissolution to specific accusations of communists' deplorable immorality. Denunciation of moral decadence came from nationally prominent authorities, including Djacir Menezes (vice-rector of the Federal University of Rio de Janeiro, ESG lecturer, CFC member, and friend and supporter of Gustavo Corção) and Bahian Cardinal Augusto Alvaro da Silva, who, in the January 1964 *Boletim*, described communists' impending plot to "destroy convents, rape nuns . . . and attack families."[64]

The cardinal's sensational images of outrages to come, however, barely matched the moral panic of less star-powered contributions to the *Boletim*. As early as 1962, an anonymous "Appeal to the Brazilian Woman" worried that women would abandon their domestic posts as "guardian angels of the hearth," rendering "the family, society, and the Pátria" vulnerable to "the global character of communism and its multiple tactics."[65] By the 1970s, these fears had developed into full-blown panic at the LDN. Cristovam Breiner—sometime president of the League—published the 1974 "Causes of Decadence," affirming from the outset the "blatantly obvious" fact of "grave moral decadence," indicating youth sexuality as the epicenter of such decadence, and locating its roots in the onslaught of communist subversion. Breiner, whose denunciation of amorous teenagers on a public bus we saw in this book's introduction, blamed moral dissolution on "libidinous excess, which is the *greatest* teacher of communist subversion," and which would facilitate the "domination" of "the peoples of the world." Breiner underscored the centrality of moralism to this anticommunist worldview, where moral dissolution constituted the most representative part of a communist conspiracy, the very face of subversion. As Breiner put it, "*That is communism today*, instigated by subversive materialists."[66]

Intimately bound up with sexual morality, gender formed an essential part not only of the "Appeal" to anticommunist domesticity, but of responses like Breiner's. Careful to affirm the gender-moral conventionality of his co-passenger, the "lady of *modest* and *respectable* aspect," Breiner condemned the amorous young woman much more emphatically than her companion. Indeed, Breiner mused that while the incident might provide a testament to the boy's gender conformity, a "demonstration of his masculinity," the girl could derive nothing but disgrace. "For the young woman," he wrote, "it is a dishonor to be seen so intertwined with her companion." Breiner's parsing of responsibilities and proportional shame suggests a double standard of sexualized subversion, where female sexuality lent itself much more easily to interpretation as moral-cum-political destabilization and subversion.[67]

Rightists did not, however, apply this double standard universally; instead, they fretted that gender and sexual unconventionality linked both young women *and* young men to communist subversion—putting masculinity itself at risk. As the 1960s drew to a close, LDN rightists reacted typically to apparent changes in fashion and presumed changes in sexual behavior. A member of the LDN secretariat and regular contributor to the *Boletim*, Colonel Sylvestre Travassos Soares crafted the League's official "line of action"—and in a 1969 article on "Morality and Communism," he laid out the League's concerns vis-à-vis sexual and moral subversion. Drawing on the parables of Sodom and Gomorrah, Soares cited long-haired young men and miniskirted young women as evidence that a communist-inspired moral apocalypse was at hand, facilitated by subversive mass media:

> No nation can survive moral collapse, and we can see the example of this in . . . Sodom and Gomorrah. . . . *This is how Communism, . . . operating through moral collapse, is always present,* . . . and through its assaults makes men and women lose their sense of . . . modesty [*pudor*]. So we see young men letting their beards and hair grow long, not grooming as they ought, . . . arm-in-arm with young women who run around half-naked (some even showing their unmentionables). . . . All of this is the result of television programs that have reached a terrible degree of depravity, *resulting from communist infiltration.* [As for] the allegation that in the old days men had long hair and wore handkerchiefs in their cuffs, this doesn't hold water because . . . *they weren't effeminate, they knew how to be masculine* and they knew the precepts of hygiene, which the [long-haired boys] of today have forgotten.[68]

As we saw in chapter 2, by 1969 miniskirts and long hair garnered the attention of many Brazilians. Yet Soares's denunciations, like those of Corção and Pacheco e Silva, reaffirmed the centrality of gender and sexual deviance to rightists' moralist vision of acute communist subversion. Communist-engineered "moral collapse" functioned through new media technology intended to recreate Sodom and Gomorrah; young men's poor grooming aroused not only Soares's vaguely hygienicist distaste, but his concern that traditional masculinity itself was under attack.

Like the "Appeal to the Brazilian Woman," Soares approximated the gender preoccupations of earlier rightists, who had similarly fretted about the attenuation of female domesticity and the decline of national manhood.[69] "Morality and Communism" explicitly posited long-haired young men as the "effeminate" companions of scantily clad women, whose gender deviance indicated communist conspiracy enveloping both sexes. Such concerns resonated with broader, hemispheric concerns about long-haired, flamboyant, and/or unmasculine youth—that is, countersubversives across the Americas connected gender, sexual, and political deviance among young men. Much research remains to be done in this vein, but such attitudes emerged in Argentina and Mexico— as when, in 1974, President Luis Echeverría dismissed urban guerrillas not only as criminals but as young people "with a propensity for sexual promiscuity and high incidences of female and male homosexuality."[70]

The LDN, like other forums of its kind, revealed a correlation between the most committed moralists and those who favored hard-line repression, even before the escalation of hostilities in 1968. Indeed, Corção himself led the charge to discredit and repress activist youth— and the LDN *Boletim* broadcast his outcry. Corção's article "Cultural Terrorism" appeared in the May 1964 issue, denouncing those who sympathized with student protesters and dismissing criticism of the regime's response to them. As noted above, Corção favored repression of "leftist" youth based on its putative penchant for "conspiracy and orgies. Sybaritism and Socialism."[71] Repression, then, was merited by the inextricably moral, sexual, and political misdeeds of wayward youths. Corção's friend and fellow moralist Cardinal Jaime de Barros Câmara waxed even more extreme, speaking out in the immediate aftermath of the 1964 coup. As military police rounded up thousands of people, amid rampant rumors of torture and even execution, a *Boletim* article announced Câmara's defense of the state's repression. Government "tolerance," the cardinal affirmed, "would promote the audacity to do evil." He urged staunch support for the violence: "Don't . . . be swayed, dear listener, by any false sense of mercy. He who owes must pay."[72]

The LDN's connection to like-minded rightists as well as to prominent exponents of military rule and repression stretched beyond Corção and Câmara to other centers of moralistic thinking and the highest levels of national government. Members of the League included ranking statesmen, generals, intellectuals, and ministers, illustrious both for their fame and their influence.[73] The LDN itself, especially in the later

1960s and 1970s, enjoyed influence in the military government and its central ideological and policy-making organs. In 1973 the *Boletim* rejoiced at the inclusion in Médici's cabinet of LDN sympathizer Colonel Octávio Costa as director of AERP, the government propaganda agency; and in 1977 the League collaborated with the ESG to sponsor a symposium on national security and "Brazilian Realities." Indeed, the LDN enjoyed working relationships with Médici himself and with Costa e Silva, the military regime's two most notoriously hard-line presidents. Direct meetings with both presidents reflected the League's advisory capacity: conferring with the moralistic Colonel Soares, Costa e Silva commissioned an LDN study of the state of "ideological warfare" in Brazil, and Médici openly welcomed LDN collaboration from the beginning of his presidency.[74] Even to the hidden agents of government surveillance and repression, the LDN seemed a righteous ally of the regime and of repression. For example, a report from the National Intelligence Service (SNI, the government's internal spy agency) complained of uncensored press articles on "sex, losing weight, and conjugal life." The report denounced these sexual "tenets of the left" as attacks on the League (unmentioned in the actual articles), alongside "the great majority of the military, the [post-1964] Governments . . . [and] the ESG."[75]

Though not so prominent and influential as IPES/IBAD or even the LDN, smaller organizations like Moral Rearmament, the Brazilian Anticommunist Alliance, and Tradition, Family, and Property linked into the network of authoritarian power brokering via right-wing moralism itself. TFP, perhaps the most theatrical of the organizations in Brazil's moral-conservative network, explicitly inscribed the country's struggle against communism into a Western, Christian struggle against evil dating back to the Middle Ages. Indeed, Brazilian TFP members took to the streets in medieval garb, bearing chivalric standards in demonstrations of their commitment to the legacy of the Crusades. The flagship of an international network of TFPs that attempted to reconstruct Western Christendom functionally as well as ideologically, Brazil's TFP inspired those of more than a dozen other countries, including France, the United States, neighbors in Latin America, and Portugal, whose chapter venerated medieval Christianity via its name: the Reconquest Cultural Center. In 1959, TFP founder and leader Plínio Corrêa de Oliveira had defined revolution, generally, as an evil heritage of modernity, with communism its latest manifestation. "Revolution," Oliveira insisted, "is a process already in its fifth century, ... destroying Christianity since the decline of the Middle Ages." The signs and symptoms of this millennial process, for Oliveira and other TFP spokespeople, were—according to the group's own institutional history—"principally moral and religious," concentrated in the moral and sexual quandaries of abortion, divorce, and traditional families. Hence Brazil's TFP, always very presentist in its denunciations, dedicated itself to combating a wave of communist-inspired moral-sexual aberrations, especially after 1964 and increasingly through the 1960s and 1970s. In a memorandum presented to the minister of justice in 1972, TFP's leadership decried an explosive rise in abortion, divorce, and "nudism"—all of which constituted "subversion and barbarism," part of that "universal revolutionary process (communism, terrorism, subversion)" dating back to the Middle Ages. If the government did not take action against such moral-cum-political subversion, TFP warned, it would "lend an enormous hand to the designs of international Communism on our Homeland."[76]

Such pronouncements lent TFP anticommunism the notes of moralism that animated Corção and like-minded rightists at the LDN, IPES, IBAD, and elsewhere. TFP support for dictatorship as the solution to the combined crises of communist subversion and moral cataclysm reinforced this commonality. These crises, to TFP eyes, had already arrived in Brazil. In perhaps its most well-publicized public endeavor, TFP waged a years-long campaign, beginning in 1966, against the legalization of divorce in Brazil. When Senator Nelson Carneiro once again tried to pass a divorce bill, TFP reached out to a wide swath of Brazil's public, collecting over one million signatures for an anti-divorce petition, and presented the maintenance of traditional morality and marriage as the military government's primary mission. TFP's reaction bespoke the anticommunism, militarism, and moralism of this moment. Denouncing "communo-progressivism" in church and society, the organization associated divorce with the "communist" government of João Goulart and "applauded" Castello Branco's intervention to quash the "*divorcistas*." The petition blamed "*janguismo*" (a deprecatory reference to support for Goulart) for the divorce bill, a measure whose "characteristic leftist hallmark" lay in its attempt to destroy "the Brazilian family ... in favor of concubinage and illegitimate offspring." From TFP's perspective, this was an "inexplicable" turn of events, given that the "Revolution of March 31" was to have "banished" this "ideological milieu ... from our country."[77]

For the rightists of TFP, the "Revolution" of 1964—for so supporters referred to the coup—was to be a *moral* revolution, ever more necessary in the late 1960s and early 1970s. And TFP's calls for moral rearmament did not go unheeded. Though it could not claim the same favor as the more prominent LDN or IPES, TFP did have allies in key government positions, including the presidency. In a 1967 letter to General Castelo Branco, TFP patriarch Plínio Corrêa de Oliveira called for regulation that would "repress licentiousness"; within two weeks, Oliveira and TFP's national directorate were received by the president at his office for consultation. Then, as tensions swelled in late 1968, Archbishop Sigaud himself met with President Costa e Silva to promote, via their friendship, TFP's campaign to block divorce and "evade communism." Nearly a decade later, when hard-line fortunes had changed and TFP extremism tarnished its public image, a thousand ESG students and alums came to the organization's defense, denouncing a supposed communist plot to besmirch TFP. The organization expanded its reach to include powerful international supporters; in 1982, TFP's newsletter proudly reported that Ronald Reagan himself had thanked TFP for its struggle against "socialism" and "the abandonment of our traditional ideas."[78]

TFP's moralistic anticommunism garnered popularity among the state's repressive apparatus, the front lines of countersubversion, especially in the "years of lead" and indeed throughout the 1970s and 1980s. In 1970, federal police deputies in Paraná praised TFP for "combating subversion and other elements that attack the morality of society." Top agents at the secretive SNI, meanwhile, corroborated the opinion of intelligence and security officials from the Ministry of Justice and the federal police—all of whom lauded TFP as an ally in countersubversion. "Leftists," a classified report complained, were orchestrating an insidious campaign against TFP, which ought, instead, to receive commendation for "defending Christian civilization" against the twin enemies of communism and divorce. SNI agents called for more regime support of TFP, whose goals coincided precisely with "those of the government."[79] Some former members of the repressive apparatus allege even closer links between TFP and atrocity perpetrators. As ex-DOPS (Department of Political and Social Order, the federalized political police) officer Cláudio Guerra recalls, TFP lent money, property, and support to secret countersubversive operations in the early 1970s—and "all of the colonels of the hard line" were linked with the Catholic reactionary group.[80]

Similarly transnational in scope, the Moral Re-Armament movement (MRA) also linked Brazilian power brokers to international visions of moral decadence, limning anticommunism as a struggle against sexual and cultural revolution. Founded in 1938 by British Reverend Frank Buchman, MRA fused Christian morality and anticommunism. Buchman denounced "sin," "materialism," and "decadence" as the fodder of communism and built Moral Re-Armament around a belief that the twentieth century's global "crisis is fundamentally a moral one," for which "the nations must re-arm morally."[81] Worldwide, the movement deployed armies of Buchmanite supporters, described by *Time* magazine as "apple-cheeked, athletic Britons," who "descended en masse upon communities, distributing literature, staging M.R.A. morality plays," and encouraging people to "get square with God" through large-scale public confessionals.[82]

Such foot soldiers, like Buchman himself, were received warmly in Brazil, where the Movimento de Rearmamento Moral (RM) took root with all the force of morally reactionary anticommunism. A Brazilian synthesis of the movement's ideals, titled *On Global Crisis*, showcased the national variant's (now-familiar) moral panic. Denouncing the current "epoch of licentiousness," *On Global Crisis* quoted Buchman himself on the ways in which the Cold War was "a combat between Christ and Antichrist," and reiterated the warning of Buchman's successor Peter Howard on the most dire problem of the age—those "pretend Christians, who acquiesce on divorce, on sexual questions, alcohol, gambling, and communism."[83] Brazilian Buchmanites, like their counterparts worldwide, located the Cold War's battlegrounds in the spaces of everyday moral, sexual, and cultural choices—and their vision gained ground in various national power centers. Rodrigo Motta has noted Marshall Juárez Távora's avid support, which led to an editorial in *O Estado de S. Paulo* on RM as the "final solution" to the anticommunist struggle. While Motta slightly modifies Dreifuss's dismissal of RM's crusaders as marginal "extremists of the right," neither account fully explores the group's connections or its activities after 1962.[84]

RM's influence in authoritarian Brazil stretched beyond Juarez Távora and well beyond the installation of the military government. In 1966, the movement would find a national advocate in Justice Minister Juracy Magalhães, who pressed President Castelo Branco to patronize the group's youth rearmament program.[85] Magalhães had even addressed the organization's international conference at Mackinac Island, Michigan, in 1964, waxing emotional: "On my very first contact with Moral Re-Armament," he recalled, "I sensed that I had found a new message for my troubled spirit."[86] RM's influence blossomed in the 1960s and 1970s as other top military moralists joined the organization's outspoken and nationally prominent supporters.[87] Security forces followed suit, a secret 1981 SNI report detailing the "innumerable praises" that rightfully pertained to RM then leader Hermes Guimarães.[88] Fellow rightist institutions shared this appreciation for RM. IBAD's *Ação Democrática* reported favorably on its presence in Brazil and internationally, and as late as 1984, the right-wing National Commission on Morality and Civics (a government body established to address the perceived moral crisis via education) invited Rearmamento Moral's collaboration on the implementation of moral education in primary schools.[89]

Dismissal of moralistic anticommunists, even those of the ultraconservative Right, as uninfluential extremists thus fails to take into account their access to and influence on the centers of power in Brazil's authoritarian government. Moralism, moreover, was more than just an ideological agenda. As the commentaries of Corção and Breiner, TFP's anti-divorce petition, and Paula Couto's defense of TFP demonstrate, moralism's proponents made it a principal justification for the "Revolution of 1964" and for visiting upon opponents the "repression they deserve[d]." This connection between moralism, the anticommunist hard line, repression, and even violence emerged spectacularly in the outraged pronouncements of the Brazilian Anticommunist Alliance (AAB), one of several anticommunist militant organizations whose terrorist attacks within Brazil spiked after the end of the most intense years of government repression. Reactionary indignation roiled throughout the late 1960s and 1970s and only grew as right-wingers felt their influence (and authoritarianism in general) slipping after 1974. Incensed at the prospective end of the regime's most brutal measures and the beginning of *distensão* (President Ernesto Geisel's relaxing of authoritarian strictures), these groups—likely with the collaboration of intransigent government security forces—responded with bombings, threats, and kidnappings.[90] The Alliance claimed responsibility for the sensational 1976 bombing of the Brazilian Press Association's headquarters, as well as for the kidnapping and beating of the Bishop of Nova Iguaçu, Dom Adriano Hipólito. While the dictatorship gradually relaxed its grip, hard-liners and moralists—who continued to see Brazil under attack by sexually unscrupulous subversives—felt themselves in an increasingly desperate position. As AAB's own proclamations explained, the violence emerged in response to *distensão* and to the moral cataclysm represented by re-democratization.

Calling themselves the "true revolutionaries of 1964," AAB members printed leaflets characterizing their actions as authentically patriotic. Their agenda, they claimed, reflected that for which conservatives had struggled in 1964, and it revolved around twin axes: support for hard-line repression and denunciation of communist sexual deviance and treachery. AAB manifestoes expressed particular outrage at the repeal of the dictatorship's most repressive legal measures (AI-5 and Decree-Law 477, used to muzzle and/or punish those university denizens suspected of "organization of subversive movements") as well as at the general amnesty granted to victims of political persecution. These acts, suggested the group's fliers, were the work of a group of gender and sexual miscreants who had hijacked the "Revolution" of 1964 and were now installing a "COMMUNIST pre-Revolution." AAB pamphlets released on the twelfth anniversary of the coup charged that those in the government who favored democratization had engaged in "orgies" and "concubin[age]," and were guilty of "compromising . . . morality."[91]

AAB painted dissidents and activists, meanwhile, as unbridled sexual deviants, whose moral and political transgressions went hand in hand. Claiming that Bishop Hipólito maintained a young male lover named Fernando, AAB further alleged that the cleric cunningly presented the youth as his nephew. (Fernando Leal Webering, Hipólito's nephew in point of fact, was kidnapped along with him; Webering's fiancée witnessed the abduction.) "AAB," the missive insisted, "combats the communists . . . like D. Adriano Hipólito, a vice-ridden, repugnant specimen, whose amorous entanglements with his 'beloved nephew' appear in the deposition of Fernando at the DOPS, where he confessed that he is not [D. Adriano's] nephew but actually his 'little friend,' living in the parish house with him and maintaining 'intimate relations.'" Such moral transgressions, the proclamation declared, had led AAB to kidnap and beat Bishop Hipólito, then "abandon [him] naked, in a public street."[92] The violence did not end there; for years after this incident, rightist graffiti accused the bishop of combining "pederasty" and "communism." In 1979, disgruntled conservatives spray-painted "Faggot Bishop," "This Is the Headquarters of the PCB," and "Communist Bishop" on the walls of Bishop Hipólito's church; while doing so, they shot and killed a dog.[93] AAB spuriously accused Dom Ivo Lorshceiter, too, of sexual misconduct (in this case with female lovers), calling him "an example of the depths of . . . moral depravation in the lives that these communists . . . lead."[94]

Like AAB, the downright notorious Command for Hunting Communists (CCC) made morality a prominent node of its violent anticommunism. Famous for acts of vandalism, intimidation, and terrorism (especially its 1968 attacks on performers of the risqué play *Roda viva* and 1969 assassination of a well-known progressive priest), the CCC joined forces with other rightist groups, calling themselves the New Fatherland Phalange and the Moralist Brigades, to fight pornography and communism. These groups claimed responsibility for bombings of newsstands in several Brazilian cities, combining denunciation of leftist publications with that of pornographic magazines.[95] CCC operatives made their motives clear with pamphlets accusing publishers and sellers of acting as "useful innocents of the immoral reds!" As one such pamphlet, addressed and distributed to "distributers and booksellers" in Santos, São Paulo, put it, "You have been collaborating with the augmentation of communist propaganda and erotico-pornographic literature in our country, distributing or selling to the population of this city (which once upon a time demonstrated freedom and charity to the Fatherland) obscene and Marxist-Leninist magazines."[96]

From *Hippies, Drugs, and Promiscuity* to *Hippies, drogas, sexo, poluição*: Transnational Rightist Visions

As the years of lead slowly gave way to democratization after 1974, terrorists reacted violently, adhering to a nationalist, anticommunist narrative in which sexual and gender order corresponded to political order; the supposed "moral depravation in the lives that these communists" led demanded retaliation by "true" patriots. The other right-wing organizations that we have discussed, however, were wont to appeal to a much more international narrative, drawing throughout the mid to late Cold War on the "expertise" of a cadre of prominent anticommunists from around the Western world. The scope of TFP and RM, of course, made such transnational connections institutional—but references to many of the same right-wing security theoreticians (indeed, to the same books) demonstrate the familiarity with which these ideologues figured in discourses of Brazilian moral panic. Just as an Atlantic military community had furnished the masculinist and moralistic foundations of counterinsurgency theory, so an Atlantic cohort of anticommunist "experts" doggedly cropped up in the ideological bedrock of moral-cultural rightism.[97] As we shall see, the international informants keeping IPES, IBAD, TFP, RM, and LDN up-to-date on communist moral conspiracy coincided almost exactly with those who appeared in references and bibliographies within Brazil's military-pedagogic and security institutions (ESG, ECEME, *A Defesa Nacional*). They included the famous (George Orwell), the infamous (J. Edgar Hoover), and many others whose stars waned after the Cold War: Fred Schwarz, Suzanne Labin, Jan Kozak, George Cronyn, Leslie C. Stevens, Peter Howard, Frank Buchman, Richard M. Ketchum, Douglas Hyde, J. Bernard Hutton, and John Strachey. These authors' books and articles appeared in the library and on the distribution lists of IPES; quotes from their works underpinned the warnings of *Ação Democrática* and the LDN's *Boletim*; and their varying degrees of celebrity in the Atlantic world matched the regularity with which they were cited by Brazil's community of moralistic security theorists.

Fred Schwarz's 1960 *You Can Trust the Communists (. . . to Do Exactly as They Say!)*, translated in 1963 as *Você pode confiar nos comunistas (eles são comunistas mesmos!)*, became a smash hit among Brazilian anticommunists, appearing in nearly every forum of right-wing and authoritarian thought (see fig. 5). In 1953, Schwarz founded the Christian Anticommunist Crusade, an Iowa-based (later California-based) fundamentalist campaign whose stated goals as of 2015 included continuing Schwarz's lifelong battle against the "very mask of Satan . . . the ideas of Marxism, Freudianism, evolution and postmodernism."[98] The best-selling *You Can Trust the Communists* pioneered this crusade, reverberating with moral panic; citing HUAC (the notorious U.S. House Un-American Activities Committee, for which he served as an expert witness), Schwarz described Soviet sexual crimes as the epitome of "Communist love"; he argued that communists saw love and sexuality ruled by hormones rather than religious morality and that, animated by this mindset, communists preyed on university youth, such that "Communism has completely reversed the meaning of our basic moral terms."[99] Schwarz's characterization of communists as instinctive and hormonal closely resembled LDN denunciations of Brazilian communists' "zoological" sexuality—a logical coincidence, given the prevalence of references to Schwarz and to *You Can Trust the Communists* among Brazil's moral panic–driven, right-wing

OVER 750,000 COPIES IN PRINT!

a **P.H.**
paperback
50¢

You Can Trust the Communists

(to be Communists)

Find out why "you can trust the Communists to be Communists" in this fascinating, forceful history that gives you the inside facts on how Communism affects you . . . and tells you what to do about it.

by Dr. Fred Schwarz

Figure 5 The cover of Fred Schwarz's best-selling *You Can Trust the Communists (to Be Communists).* Used by permission of Christian Anti-Communist Crusade.

anticommunists. Among the influential rightist organizations we have examined here, Schwarz's work made inroads emblematic of the importance of such foreign moralisms: the LDN *Boletim* published an entire section of Schwarz's book in its June 1963 edition; IPES, in turn, not only stocked the book in its library for consultation by members but actually bought and distributed copies, so efficiently that a 1963 inventory reported the organization's "stock depleted."[100] The depleted stock did not go unread, at least not in certain circles—as we shall see in the next chapter, references to Schwarz at the ESG and other centers of national security doctrine reached near-hagiographic levels.

Schwarz, however, was far from alone. Other foreign theoreticians helped form a constellation of moral anticommunist celebrities, at whose forefront stood French political scientist Suzanne Labin. Labin's résumé boasted a report on Soviet propaganda commissioned by the United States Congress; some thirty-three books in French; and translations in at least eleven languages, with eighteen editions in English, twelve in Spanish, and seven in Portuguese. Her colorfully titled repertoire—including *Embassies of Subversion* (1964), *Red Foxes in the Chicken Coop* (1966), and *Hippies, Drugs, and Promiscuity* (1968)—lived up to the alarmist promise of its book jackets. *Hippies, Drugs, and Promiscuity* exemplified Labin-style anticommunist moral panic. Like her followers in Brazil, the author reacted to the cultural and political developments of the mid to late 1960s, describing a world in which communist moral degradation had forged a counterculture-fueled, apocalyptic Western decadence. Labin bemoaned a "softening already detectable in the fiber of American youth," a "soak in the hippie-drug culture" that doomed "the nation [to] end in decay"; she predicted that "the whole West will follow America's decline."[101] Labin acknowledged the developing culture war, waxing resentful of sixties backlash against her own brand of extreme anticommunism. She was quick to affirm that this "decay," this "softening in the fiber" of youth, stemmed from communists' best-laid (and most devious) plans:

> When conservatives declare that pornography, which is spreading everywhere today among Western youth, is an insidious weapon being used to undermine society, the left sniggers at them, acting as if they were backward puritans who see witches everywhere. The "liberals" assure us that nudity, eroticism, even homosexuality and pornography, are forms of art or modes of expression in

themselves. . . . But the Communists, expert in the art of moving the masses, skillful alchemists of passion and commitment, know better. They know that extreme carnality [or] the revolt of the flesh quickly has its effects in the political domain . . . precipitating the downfall of our political system, which is founded on the family. . . . [Communists] use every instrument at hand to weaken the fiber of the Western world.[102]

Such alarmism appeared throughout Labin's oeuvre, replete with admonitions about Western moral decadence.[103] *Em cima da hora*, the widely cited Brazilian translation of Labin's *Il est moins cinq: Propagande et infiltration soviétiques*, opened with an emblematic warning: "The days of life or death, for Western Civilization, have arrived."[104]

This championing of doomsday, anticommunist moralism earned Labin international recognition as an anti-Soviet heroine. In Europe, she headlined conferences to help lay the groundwork for the notorious World Anti-Communist League, whose French chapter she led. In the United States, Senator Thomas J. Dodd described her as a pen-wielding "Joan of Arc of Freedom," and according to *Time*, her "rare feminine eloquence" proved that "Liberty Is a Lady." The magazine lauded her as a vivacious, feminine exponent of hawkish resistance to communism's covert, amoral infiltrations: "Suzanne Labin writes with a hatpin. This young (thirtyish) French political scientist impales totalitarian myths and neutralist delusions, prods lukewarm intellectuals who rarely rise to the defense of democracy."[105]

Brazil's anticommunist Right matched these heights of gushing praise. Pacheco e Silva's *Hippies, Sex, Drugs, Pollution* cited the "plentiful authority" of Labin's *Hippies, Drugs, and Promiscuity*.[106] Famed coup supporter Carlos Lacerda translated *Em cima da hora*, hailing Labin's contribution to "the glory and prestige of France" and limning her work as anticommunist gospel—"a guide in the midst of chaos, an antidote to the venom of inertia."[107] Lacerda met Labin in 1948 and greeted her as a fan and friend when she traveled to Rio de Janeiro in 1963—a trip that underscored her early-1960s connections with Brazil's anticommunist right, as it formed part of a junket of lectures she delivered as a featured guest of IPES.[108]

Indeed, IPES and the rightist organizations we have thus far encountered displayed a marked affinity for the "Joan of Arc of freedom." Beyond sponsoring Labin's lecture series, IPES stocked and distributed her books and pamphlets (some of which had been printed and disseminated by the CIA) and allocated funds to publish eight thousand copies of *Em cima da hora*.[109] IBAD followed suit, block-quoting Labin and referring to her as a source of crusading inspiration.[110] TFP, meanwhile, incorporated Labin into its medievalist support for repression. Facing, after 1975, denunciation and ridicule as an ally of the increasingly unpopular dictatorship, TFP's defenders portrayed themselves as modern-day Cassandras, citing Labin's admonition that "the primary condition for the success of a [communist] conspiracy is the discrediting of those who denounce it."[111] Labin herself praised the international Moral Re-Armament Movement as a prominent source of what she called "Missionaries of Liberty"—her vision for an all-encompassing, peace-corps-cum-crusades errand into the developing world, a "new breed of . . . economic, political, and cultural . . . apostleship" that would send hale young men to carry the Western, Christian way of life into vulnerable Asia and Africa. Strikingly, she linked the success of the mission to the familial morality of the missionaries themselves. Their traditionally gendered family structure and Spartan sturdiness must serve as an anticommunist bulwark. Equipped with nothing but "a jeep, a modest house with water, light, and a radio," she mused, these latter-day crusaders would live "surrounded by a wife and children."[112]

Conclusion

By the early 1960s, Schwarz and Labin—like Strachey, Kozak, Hutton, Hoover, and other extreme-right peddlers of anticommunist paranoia—had brought a touch of transnational solidarity to the notes of moral panic sounded by the reactionary, extra-governmental organizations and individuals we have encountered in this chapter. As we shall see in the chapters that follow, citation of such international authorities also informed authoritarian, anticommunist moralism *within* the official fonts and policy-making outlets of Brazilian national security doctrine—the prestigious and foundational ESG, other institutions of military learning, and security forces like the SNI and DOPS. These official forums notwithstanding, we have seen how the reactionary worldview of firebrands like Corção and Sigaud enjoyed considerable political influence, in part through organizations like IPES, IBAD, LDN, RM, and TFP. This worldview involved a focus on moral and sexual deviance (the effects of what Corção and Scherer called "overwhelming modernism" on family, media, the church, and youth) as both symptom and tactic of communist subversion—and hence as justification for state-sanctioned or -led violence. Indeed, in the 1970s, as state-sponsored repression gave way to violent outbursts of paramilitary, right-wing terrorism, the moralism of the extreme Right turned even on the military regime itself, which hard-liners perceived as traitorous to the original, morally reactionary agenda that had cemented their support for the coup and its authoritarian aftermath. This agenda predated 1968, but intensified during and after the years of lead, when Gustavo Corção criticized the regime's "leniency" toward "sybaritism and socialism"; when terrorist groups condemned redemocratization as the work of moral degenerates who had hijacked the "Revolution" of 1964; and when TFP continued to blame communists for threats to God, family, and property, demanding tougher government stances against progressive Catholicism, abortion, and divorce. Sex and revolution, twinned concerns, animated the spectacular anxieties of rightist extremists and underlay their advocacy of repression and violence.

4

Drugs, Anarchism, and Eroticism

Moral Technocracy and the Military Regime

The government's principal concern consists in banning from the market obscene publications . . . and prohibiting permanently the attempts of the agents of international communism to use radio and television to exercise subliminal influence in the bosom of our families by means of insidious programming.

—Alfredo Buzaid, Minister of Justice, 1970

WHEREAS, the Constitution of the Republic, in Article 153, Paragraph 8, determines that publications and exhibitions contrary to morality and to good customs will not be tolerated;

WHEREAS, this regulation seeks to protect the institution of the Family, to preserve its ethical values and assure the rearing of hale and honorable youth;

WHEREAS, moreover, some magazines produce obscene publications and some television channels broadcast programs offensive to morality and good customs;

WHEREAS, the distribution of books that directly offend common morality has become widespread;

WHEREAS, such publications and exhibitions stimulate permissiveness, insinuate Free Love, and threaten to destroy the moral values of Brazilian society;

WHEREAS, the implementation of these means of communication is subordinate to a subversive plan, that puts National Security at risk . . .

—Decree-Law 1077, 26 January 1970

By 1970, moral countersubversion had a visible impact on the military-authoritarian agenda. Absent the national legislature, President Médici institutionalized preemptive censorship via Decree-Law 1077, whose preamble appears above.[1] As the final lines made clear, a conservative vision of links between "permissiveness," obscenity, "Free Love," morality, and national security had hereby gained the weight and force of law. The decree operationalized Article 153 of the authoritarian constitution of 1967, which made "publications and exhibitions contrary to morality and good customs" an exception to otherwise guaranteed freedom of expression. Justice Minister Alfredo Buzaid explained the legislative reasoning behind such a measure in no uncertain terms: "pornographic publications" and similar "assaults on morality" were "as much an attack on national security as the propaganda of War, as the subversion of order."[2] Here subversion acquired legal-conceptual substance—in national security legislation designed to reinforce the nation's moral and sexual customs against patent communist machinations.

The moralizing legislation took effect against a backdrop of volatile national and international politics. After 1968, intra-regime rivalries in Brazil left hard-line advocates of authoritarianism and repression in power for six years. While civil society retreated beneath the weight of the draconian AI-5 and subsequent oppression, rightists inside and outside of the regime went on the offensive against subversion. As we saw in the previous chapter's examination of moralist activism, this offensive had begun before 1968, but intensified amid late-1960s and early-1970s cultural and political tumult (real and perceived) in Brazil and beyond. As historian Victoria Langland has demonstrated, Brazil's policing in the years of lead was deeply affected by immediate memories of 1968; security forces assumed that student protesters and armed guerrillas were one and the same.[3] Indeed, memories and interpretations of protests and cultural changes in, before, and after 1968 became the fodder for moralistic hand-wringing within the regime's intellectual and policy-producing centers, particularly in the 1970s.

Buzaid's explanation of Decree-Law 1077 reflected the perspective of the men and women who, like the minister himself, enabled such juridical codification of anticommunist moral panic. A cadre of "experts," both civilian and uniformed, flooded the military state's centers of national security planning with ruminations on moral crisis and with detailed theories of the ways in which moral dissolution, as a tool of communist subversion, posed physical, cultural, psychological, and social threats to Brazil and Brazilians. Morality, in other words, became a focal and *formal* national security concern, such that the government's countersubversive struggle approximated the remoralization demanded by the right-wing actors we encountered in chapter 3. If, as we have seen, a pantheon of morally reactionary, anticommunist individuals and organizations made moral panic about youth sexuality a central node in their own visions of countersubversion, this arrangement increasingly took on official and technocratic weight in national planning institutions—particularly the Escola Superior de Guerra (ESG), where political heavyweights, security nabobs, and professional consultants rubbed shoulders in a colloquium of influential military and civilian minds. Together, they shaped and disseminated a national security doctrine with moral concerns among its cornerstones.

This chapter explores the ways in which moralism came to suffuse anticommunist security ideology and policy (elaboration of national security doctrine, interpretation of the "Revolution" of 1964, rationales for dictatorial measures) *within* the state apparatus. Focusing on the ESG—the technocratic institution par excellence, where a military-civilian coalition laid the foundations for the 1964 coup and generated policy recommendations for the governments that ruled thereafter—I argue that a profound sense of moral crisis led security theorists, many of them nationally prominent authorities, to posit a national security-based revitalization of traditional gender and sexual morality as a crucial regime mandate. Indeed, the most sensitive nodes of this perceived crisis made it rather a classic moral panic. Here, at the heart of "conservative modernization," rightist anxieties repudiated modernity itself. Technocrats—the ESG's peculiar mix of military and civilian experts and power brokers, some already illustrious and some soon to be so—agonized about youth consumption patterns, global and national decadence, new media, and changing gender roles, doctrinalizing these realms as a volatile sphere of subversives' conspiracy.

The molding of these specific anxieties into a semiofficial code of government priorities occurred via what I call a *moral technocracy*, of considerable influence at the ESG and beyond. The ESG, founded in 1949, was in some ways the ideal place for such a technocracy to take shape. A Cold War brainchild of officers influenced by experiences in the United States, the school aimed to foment what political scientist Alfred Stepan termed a "new professionalism"—a broadened military role in issues of development and internal security. By 1963, the ESG's seven departments—including "political affairs," "psycho-social," and "economic" alongside "military" and "intelligence-counterintelligence"— had become redoubts of authoritarian thinking, "socializing" (to borrow Stepan's terminology) military leaders and civilian experts in the tenets of developmentalist national security, sloganized as "Security and

Development."[4] Military officers studied, taught, and did research alongside civilian scientific, medical, clerical, sociological, and juridical authorities, usually in a one-to-one military-to-civilian proportion. Together, ESG students and researchers brought the Brazilian government's quasi-positivist, technocratic approach (enshrined in the collaborative, military-civilian space of the ESG) squarely into the arenas of morality and sexuality. Like the Right of the 1930s, and like the activists we encountered in chapter 3, these specialists envisioned modernity as a troubling onslaught of what they called "fundamental changes." Introducing pseudoscience to national conversations about security, ESG moralists drew on linked religious, moral, and public health concerns with roots in the previous century. Hearkening back to late-nineteenth- and early-twentieth-century ideas about public health, bodies (biological and social), and "civilization," the ESG's brain trust substituted 1960s-era communist subversion for the "degeneracy" and "decadence" eugenicists had feared. Pathologizing subversion as a "biopsychosociological" threat, these moral technocrats helped establish what would become a morally conservative, elite-level national consensus, bearing (as chapter 5 demonstrates) the standard of moralism-as-anticommunism into the heart of important security institutions and forums ranging from military schools and journals to police and intelligence organizations. Authoritarian, even violent countersubversion, according to this consensus, must focus on preventing the erosion of Brazil's moral fiber— must, as Secretary of Social Communications Said Farhat told an audience at the ESG, "safeguard . . . custom and morality, as well as exhort civic behavior and the cultivation of the history and traditions that form the base of society itself."[5]

This chapter takes up the story of this moral technocracy and demonstrates how its reactionary perspective evolved and gained traction in the 1960s and 1970s. The first section of the chapter draws on the efflorescence of ESG intellectual production on moral anticommunism (blossoming in the late 1960s and into the 1970s) to identify the specific changes to which conservatives responded—namely, middle-class youth consumption patterns, modernizing and globalizing media, and new gender and family patterns. Perceiving what they called "fundamental changes" in these realms, ESG moralists classified their concerns in a particular set of categories: "the youth problem," the "global village," "women's liberation," and the "disaggregation of the family." More importantly, they doctrinalized these categories as canonical theaters of guerra revolucionária. The second section of the chapter traces the roots of this doctrinalization not only in the rightist anxieties of the moment but in a species of intellectual myopia—the ideologically closed circuits in which moral technocrats' self-circumscription allowed for the replication and confirmation of their brand of countersubversion.

Moral Crisis: Youth, Women, and Decadence in ESG Anticommunism

In a 1976 essay entitled "Strengthening the Family," written for the ESG's research unit, Judge Maurício Gonçalves de Oliveira denounced pornography, hippies, homosexuality, "moral collapse," and public sex—then affirmed that the 1964 coup had arisen precisely to deal with these problems, to sanitize Brazil against communists' "corruption of customs and of morality." Oliveira explained that a prime "objective" of the "Revolution of 1964 . . . was to combat corruption in all its forms and to elevate the moral standards of the Brazilian people. . . . The counter-objective lies in communist strategy: weakening by corruption the customs and morality of the Brazilian people . . . and among them, the FAMILY, first and foremost."[6] Beginning in the mid-1960s and increasing after 1970, a host of fellow *esguianos* (affiliates of the ESG) joined Oliveira in positing the 1964 coup as the inaugural sally in a war pitting righteous, military-led "middle-class moralism" against the twin foes of communism and sin.[7] Well-known ESG technocrats limned military authoritarianism as a moral endeavor. In a 1973 excursus on national security and censorship, Antônio de Arruda—the school's principal historian and one of its most hallowed thinkers—bemoaned past failures to regulate "public morality and good customs." Confirming that the primary aim of the "revolutionary process" (that is, military strictures) was to preserve such morality, Arruda hailed the repressive AI-5, Article 153, and Decree-Law 1077 as "restorations" of that process. Only *after* serving their chief purpose of ensuring moral rectitude, Arruda wrote, could censors turn to "other aspects," more narrowly political.[8]

Esguianos' inclusion of this moralistic core in the military government's putative mandate stemmed from the conviction that a communist-promoted moral crisis had taken hold of Brazil. Perceptions of moral crisis had dogged Brazilian intellectuals for decades, in the form of subtly racialized class prejudice by which elites "explained" national problems in terms of the supposed indolence and unfitness of nonelites.[9]

In midcentury Brazil, however, putative crisis took on new urgency and profound influence. The traditional focus on—to use Carlos Fico's formulation—"ethical comportment" and civic "solidarity" did not disappear, but the security-theory variant of moral crisis honed this focus into a vision of modernity as cataclysm. Many Brazilians, as noted above, observed transformations in national and international society and culture; in the face of changes in youth behavior, women's public roles, and entertainment, security theorists proposed remoralization, a rescuing of traditional sexual, family, and gender strictures. If vague and varied notions of moral crisis had long been a part of Brazilian intellectual life, they took very specific form at the ESG, where security ideologues officially and authoritatively accused communists of hatching a sexual, moral, "psychosocial," and biological plot against the West—a plot whose results had grown alarmingly apparent.

In the late 1960s and early 1970s, ESG research, conference speeches, and term papers (generally policy proposals written by graduating students, individually or in working groups) brimmed with direct references to such a crisis, putatively epidemic in proportion and manifestation. Increasingly frequent admonitions waxed simultaneously apocalyptic and technocratic, often drawing on "studies" and on "experts" to justify assertions of widespread "moral collapse gripping the modern world"—what one group of students called "the gravest problem of all . . . hedonism and pleasure at any price."[10] These assertions, some of them dating back to the 1950s, linked such crisis to a laundry list of sins, ranging from divorce to "free love" to birth control and general laxity, and connected the whole with communism and national security. "Permissiveness," "weakening of customs," "modernism," "degradation of women," "pornography," "drugs," and "exotic, imported customs"—all key, recurrent terms in ESG parlance—populated this litany of moral collapse, which reports blamed directly on the so-called International Communist Movement (MCI, shorthand for a putative global conspiracy), whose "strategy of guerra revolucionária is a massive attack on feminine honor and morality."[11]

Such notions of moral crisis as psycho-social warfare reached into the most authoritative of ESG forums, the core of ESG thought on subversion. An ESG permanent staff member and ideological architect, General Antônio Carlos da Silva Muricy designed key portions of the institution's curriculum, including the doctrinalization of guerra revolucionária.[12] Muricy located Catholic morality at the center of his storied, lifelong crusade against communism and insurgency. In a characteristic 1969 speech, he confirmed the "cultural and social base" of communist guerra revolucionária—whose effects, he claimed, were manifest in the moral-cultural upheaval of the day: "We are witnessing, at the moment, the attempt to destroy moral principles, particularly in the heart of our youth, by means of dangerous philosophies that exalt the erotic and the perverse."[13] The ESG's commandants similarly weighed in to condemn guerra revolucionária as primarily moral and focused on youth. As early as 1965, celebrated general Aurélio de Lyra Tavares (ESG commandant, 1966–67) penned *National Security: Current Problems*, an influential denunciation of the worrisome, media-fueled "moral decadence" attenuating young people's and families' "resistance to the forces of subversion and destruction."[14] By 1975, even the ESG's *Basic Manual* (the school's primary textbook and doctrinal compendium) insisted, in an oft-quoted passage, that "it is in the moral and spiritual realm that the most profound crisis of the modern world resides, the greatest reason for generalized insecurity.... We are living ... in an age of protest, that includes generational, class, and ideological conflict."[15]

These declamations of moral crisis saturated ESG reports in the 1970s, reflecting spiraling preoccupation with a precise series of issues. Many esguianos experienced modernization itself as that "profound crisis of the modern world," most manifest in the problems specified by the examples above: youth behavior, familial dissolution, pornography and media, and women's changing roles. In other words, despite the seemingly indiscriminate alarmism of prognostications on the "universal climate of eroticism" and communists' supposed "propagation of ... the exaltation of sex," ESG conflations of communist subversion with the issues of youth culture, family structure, media, and gender did not emerge in a structural vacuum.[16] In keeping with the technocratic and formal nature of their enterprise, esguianos systematized and categorized their notions of moral crisis. They addressed these problems as semiofficial, doctrinal categories: "the Youth Problem" (*Problemática da Juventude*), "Disaggregation of the Family" (*Desagregação da Família*), modern media ("Means of Social Communication" or *Meios de Comunicação Social*), and "Women's Liberation" (*Liberação da Mulher*). The focus of decades' worth of attention at the ESG, these categories (invariably noted by the above descriptors) lent structure to the moral and sexual anxieties that informed countersubversion here, at the ideological nerve center of state security planning. As we shall see below, the institutional entrenchment of these anxieties developed via a moral-technocratic core of ESG thinkers, whose contributions granted the weight of professional expertise to an ideology that highlighted youth sexuality, globalized entertainment culture, and changing gender roles as front lines in guerra revolucionária.

The Youth Problem

The anxieties of ESG discussants, from ordinary students to celebrated specialists, revolved agonizingly around young people and the so-called youth problem, or *problemática da juventude* (sometimes capitalized, as a title or for emphasis). Esguianos historicized youth dissent and delinquency as problems for the ages; indeed, as if to demonstrate institutional uniformity of perspective, the bulk of essays on youth cited the same four examples of ancient preoccupation with youth disorderliness (Socrates, Hesiod, a nameless Egyptian priest, and a Babylonian inscription from 3000 BCE). Nevertheless, these essays stressed the unmatched extremity of the contemporary "youth problem." If a bit vague on precise chronology, most at the ESG dated this new severity to the 1960s, when communist agents purportedly succeeded in sexually infiltrating Brazilian (and, more broadly, Western) youth. Where one general claimed that the problems dated to "1963 . . . with particular worsening after 1967," a 1972 paper tellingly observed that "the youth problem has grown worse in recent years for reasons known to us all" (an apparent reference to counterculture and to street protests). A 1974 report, meanwhile, bemoaned the crescendo of youth "nonconformity" unthinkable even "a decade ago," before "young people's . . . indifference toward timeless values" created "a cultural broth in which the germs of subversion, planted clandestinely by agents of foreign ideologies, might ferment." In the late 1960s, this paper argued, the problem had grown so grave that "the physiognomy of subversion [had become] multiform: here it caters to the base instincts of youths, justifying all sorts of permissiveness in the moral arena; . . . there a pessimistic philosophy opens the doors to all species of eroticism."[17]

As these passages suggest, esguianos interpreted changes (real and perceived) in moral, social, and cultural behavior as threats to national security. Those at the ESG who wrote and spoke about young people saw a paroxysm of moral-sexual dissolution gripping Brazilian youth—and agreed that communists had engineered this catastrophe. This conviction permeates the documentary record at the ESG; a sample of those items whose topic included "youth" illustrates the pervasiveness of such ideas. In the period 1960–80 (with particular concentration in 1969–76), the overwhelming majority of such essays and speeches (88 percent) concerned themselves with perceived moral and/or sexual dissipation, and nearly nine out of ten of the documents in that majority explicitly blamed a communist conspiracy for the onslaught of such dissipation. The term "youth problem" itself became something of a catchall for conflations of delinquency, drug abuse, sex deviance, and capitulation to communism. Such conflations blamed the "active presence of communist ideology" for a range of youth-related issues, typically listed together and without distinction: "suicide, the use of drugs, alcoholism, delinquency, prostitution, subversion, and a . . . generalized protest against our moral and ethical values."[18]

It was in this last, "generalized" form of protest that ESG moral panic found its most tenacious—and most visible—inspiration. National security theorists referred to a vague notion of counterculture as the "fundamental problem of the Western world and of Brazil." This notion lumped together subversion, violence, guerrilla warfare, and even "terrorism" with counter- or "hippie" culture that visually represented subversive moral deterioration. If some specialists could denounce subversion, prostitution, delinquency, drug abuse, and generalized protest in one breath, many ESG theorists went further, citing specific, visual examples of counterculture—long hair, beards, loud music, unconventional style—as hard evidence of youth-based national security threats. From this vantage point, young people's style, music, and grooming could serve as cues for identifying "subversion on the march." As we have seen, militant Leftist youth largely rejected counterculture, harshly disciplining "disorderly habits" in "sexual life." Nevertheless, one group of ESG students summarized what they called the "concrete threat to National Security itself" as a dubious amalgam: "a dangerous protest that takes various forms . . . from hypothetical hippie pacifism to urban terrorism [*guerrilha*], from . . . [unconventional] ways of dressing and styling the hair to the individual and collective delirium of pop music, from the experiences of free love and collective family to hallucinatory visions and psychedelic flights."[19]

An esguiano veteran whom I interviewed in 2008 remembered this relationship in rather more specific detail, clarifying, at least in memory, the relationship between moral and aesthetic choices, subversion, and youth. Not all hippies, he claimed, entered the armed struggle, but the contrapositive *was* true: "all subversive or communist young people were hippies" at some point. "Many of those hippies," he added, "moved on and went into the movement" against the government. Another informant was more straightforward: "In the vision of the [ESG], the counterculture was not something to be controlled, but to be combated." Direct, physical assaults on the state (terrorism, for instance) thus joined changing modes of dress, music, sexuality, and substance abuse in an overarching category of security-sapping "subversive activity," whose trappings included "hippie" philosophy, pop music, free love, jeans, headbands, and sandals.[20]

Here, esguianos responded to a very specific aspect of the "modernity" that so troubled them: the consumption patterns of middle-class youth, newly enabled by the confluence of an emergent international youth culture, novel advertising platforms, and the "economic miracle" of 1967–73. At the ESG, excursus on youth focused on the *consumer* trappings of counterculture (clothing, jewelry, music, and fashion)— items whose socioeconomically circumscribed use reflected the classed nature of the ESG-theorized youth problem.[21] As anticommunist moral panic gained both lexicon and official weight in esguianos' reports, it centered explicitly on the sexuality and morality of youth of means. Indeed, though Cecilia Coimbra has rightly pointed out ways in which countersubversion retained legacies of prejudice against the "dangerous classes," these classes were not at the heart of ESG concerns about subversion. Instead, esguiano technocrats focused on the middle class as "the bedrock of the nation's equilibrium" and the place where weakened family structure and "promiscuous sexual relations" mattered most."[22] Denouncing a "behavioral explosion among today's youth, condemning, contesting, in a complete break with socio-moral-religious standards," experts at the ESG made clear that lower-class youth did not factor into this explosion; presumed to be more likely to commit petty theft or assault, they did not inspire the same alarm as delinquent scions of the middle and upper classes.

The latter, on the other hand, plainly showed the "disaggregating influence of Marxism." According to one 1978 report, "In the middle and upper economic groups, ... youths have a propensity for sexual crimes.... Influenced by communists, ... and anarchists, youth has been involved in crimes of a political nature. There are the riots in the streets, the attacks on authorities, kidnappings ... assaults [which are all parts of] guerra revolucionária. And there's sex in the antisocial form that has very much compromised female youth. In Brazil today, three great problems compromise our youth: drugs, alcohol and sexual libertinism."[23] "Our youth," then—the youth so threatened by sexual subversion—meant urban, elite young people, from student movement protesters to urban guerrillas to those engaging in "antisocial sex." Such young people dominated this category of anxious, anti-Marxist conflations. One esguiano even complained of the doctrinal entrenchment of this class exclusivity. The "topic of the *youth problem*," wrote Antônio Pedro de Souza Campos, "now so incorporated into the pedagogical, psychological, and sociological lexicon," entirely neglected lower-class youth demographics.[24]

The focus on middle- and upper-class youth lent the ESG's anticommunist moralism a resemblance to the similarly classed, decades-old tradition of positivist, hygienicist, and even eugenicist thinking on *dégénérescence*—a tradition with which, as we shall see below, the ESG's moral technocrats shared not only penchants for antimodernism and pathologization, but direct intellectual heritage. Brazilian forays into hygienicism, eugenics, and degeneration theory had long made explicit their exclusive concern with elites, whom turn-of-the-century sanitization and moralization campaigns sought to quarantine from the inevitably degenerative "dangerous classes."[25] The theoretical bounding of the 1960s "youth problem" by like class distinctions, however, was just one of multiple ways that youth-focused subversion emerged as a successor to the degeneration envisioned by previous generations of elite social thinkers and reformers. Just as nineteenth-century European narratives of *dégénérescence* had described a moral and "socio-biological" progression ending in "general enfeeblement, depravity . . . insanity . . . lost virility . . . and impotence"—and just as Foucault's bourgeois Victorians "deployed sexuality" in the service of class interests involving "the body, vigor, longevity, progeniture, and descent"—so Brazilian eugenicists and hygienicists of the early twentieth century had linked class, public health, morality, sexuality, social behavior, physical viability, and evolutionary biology to "progress" and the advancement (or regression) of civilization.[26]

ESG discussants adapted such thinking to their perceptions of Cold War geopolitics, conceptually melding the subversive, the perverse, and the degenerative into a single "sociobiological" process in which unconventional moral, sexual, and social behavior had consequences at once psychological, physiological, sociological, political, and military. These consequences amounted to the mental and physical enfeeblement of Brazil's middle- and upper-class youth, who would thereby become pliant fodder for communists' conspiratorial designs.[27] In fact, ESG discussants alluded to juvenile subversion's classically degenerative nature in the very modifiers—"sociobiological," "psychosocial," "biopsychosociological," and "psychopathological"—with which they described the youth problem. Moral authority and sometime regime favorite Fernando Bastos de Ávila, for instance, spoke at the ESG in 1974 on the "psychosocial problem" of sexual "permissiveness" and "perversion" in pedagogy and socialization. "Perverted" education, by Ávila's account, threatened to visit physical and psychological degeneration on young Brazilians, making them "prematurely old," exposing them to "ideological problems," and transforming them into subversion-prone shells of the robust youngsters they should have been.[28]

This type of pathologization became so prevalent that ESG reports on contemporary youth tended to begin with a uniform, obligatory introduction. Often dubbed "the Sociobiological Problem of Youth," these introductions defined "youth" in terms of vulnerability to subversion, determined biologically and sociologically by age-driven "psychological aspects," the "explosion of puberty," and youth's "instinctive sexual impulsiveness."[29] Between 1960 and 1980, nearly six of every ten ESG documents (58 percent) on youth began with such introductions. In part, this uniformity of perspective was nationally based, derived from tightly closed ideological circuits (discussed below). Yet there was also undoubtedly something supranational at work here. Beyond Brazil, too, such psychopathological, sexualized constructions of contemporary youth became common in the mid–Cold War, with examples from Canada to Argentina to Europe.[30]

Decadence and the "Global Village"

Alarmists at the ESG who denounced the wave of sexualized subversion among Brazilian young people not only decried the moral crisis, but sought to fully chart its roots and significance. In the process, they broached related, component apprehensions, likewise rooted in reaction against the "modern world." As in other moral panics, new media and technology generated particular apprehension. Esguianos saw television, movies, and music transcending the local and promoting unprecedented, materialistic decadence. Beginning in the 1960s and intensifying in the 1970s, these thinkers experienced modernity as a time of troubling, "fundamental changes" in local and global lifeways—and they identified the most shocking and detrimental changes in the realm of mass culture, or "means of social communications." If young people had succumbed to a massive communist conspiracy, that conspiracy worked most effectively through a technological and media revolution—what esguianos called the "bombardment" of youth with messages about consumption, sex, drugs, and other topics deleterious to the maintenance of "good customs."

ESG students, teachers, and guest speakers regularly bemoaned the pace of global modernization, engaging in something of a panic about the "crisis" of globalization itself. Such lamentations accompanied hopeful envisionings of television as a means of national unification— esguianos had generated the 1962 Brazilian Television Code, which sought to harness the problematic powers of new media technology in the *service* of national security and development.[31] Harnessable or not, telecommunications formed a principal node of concern about modernization, particularly notable in ESG intellectual production after 1970; many ESG reports cited Marshall McLuhan, such that the term "global village" decisively entered the institutional lexicon.[32] The phrase "fundamental changes" and the very word *mudança* ("change") also became standards of the school's literature, couched in somber assertions that "we have entered an era of history . . . when rapid change is a constant," and that this era began "after the fifties . . . when society set aside its traditionalist conception of life and entered the epoch of change."[33]

For esguianos, the "epoch of change," like the global village itself, was a concept defined by its moral and sexual implications. In the 1970s, Brazil's national film and television industries did, in fact, produce remarkably more sexual material—a phenomenon we shall discuss further in chapter 7—but esguianos responded to the "wave of pornography" (real and imagined) by blaming a global media-borne sexual conspiracy. Alongside denunciations of "modern technology" and the "exponential rhythm of our days," ESG ideologues decried unprecedented "permissiveness," "sexual exacerbation," "homosexuality," "pornography," "sexual anarchy," and "eroticism." Anxieties about this sexual crisis generated volumes of ESG work on media ("means of social communication"). These invariably identified the "global village" as the primary conduit for sexual corruption benefiting (when not designed by) international communism, the insidious "MCI." Sexual dissipation, such documents made plain, dominated a nexus of concerns about youth, subversion, globalization, and media technology. In a 1980 lecture, famed sociologist and writer Marcos Almir Madeira denounced "comic books," "pornography," and "eroticism" as threats to "public safety," alleging that social "communication . . . has become, therefore, *antisocial* communication . . . it inverts, perverts, and subverts."[34] Another report traced national "vulnerability" to pornography and an explosion of "permissiveness . . . in our communications media. 'Babylonian' society could be said to be nearly universal. Lesbianism and many other social deviancies, nudism, immodest feminine fashions and even immodest male fashions have become commonplace."[35] These perceptions of an acute, media-generated moral crisis typified the interpretive mood at the ESG. For example, of the reports on media written between 1960 and 1980, most (70 percent) argued that communications media were promoting sexual and moral dissipation.[36] These reports were well received, garnering the approval of ESG authorities and (as we shall see below) the respect and citation of other ESG students and guests.

Such reports often envisioned a generalized—indeed, "Babylonian"— moral crisis, rooted in the media but "nearly universal" by the mid-1970s. Yet almost all coincided in their emphasis on two specific elements: the targeted menace that modern media posed to youth and the surety of communist plotting behind the media-fueled attack on sexual morality. In keeping with the preeminence of the putative youth problem and with the more general notion—common to moral panic—that media disproportionately corrupted young people, ESG documents on mass communications insisted that such media had Brazil's children and young adults, more than any other group, in their sights. Prosecutor and social critic Darley de Lima Ferreira, for instance, worried that pornography sought to affect, above all, "a portion of our youth"; an ESG team lamented in 1981 that "popular, erotic magazines" were a "favorite" of youth; and Air Force Brigadier Paulo Gurgel de Siqueira pointed to a "study" that "found that 75 percentof the education of our youth is accomplished through vehicles of social communication," such that youth was being "violated" by media "themes like sex, sadism, crime, violence, and scandal."[37]

Communist psychological warfare, esguianos argued, was the source of such "violation." While a handful of texts at the ESG casually indicted the United States and Western democratic cultures as sources of immorality (from the Beatles to James Bond), even these texts blamed moral crisis on communists' use of media as an insidious weapon.[38] A typical 1973 term paper warned, "It is imperative that we recognize that humanity is, in fact, involved in a grand-scale psychological war, . . . characterized by the constancy and strength of its effects—the degradation of customs, the use of drugs, the revolt of young people, the absence of moral values, and social agitation for different causes—all stimulated, inflated, and exploited by . . . international communism for the achievement of its designs."[39] This perspective grew remarkably entrenched at the ESG. The claim that Lenin himself sought to "launch youth . . . into eroticism" became a commonplace, alongside the dubious imputation that a global communist "strategy [of moral dissolution] comes from Lenin: 'Demoralize the youth of a country and the Revolution is won.'"[40] Accordingly, nearly half (45 percent) of the studies on communications between 1960 and 1980 explicitly blamed international communism for the media-borne moral crisis. Moreover, policy-makers linked with the ESG demonstrated the extension of this thinking into channels of direct governance. In a 1980 ESG lecture, communications czar Said Farhat called the media/morality crisis "a cruel form of conquest." "I'm afraid," he warned his audience, "that all of this is part of a larger plan to corrupt society in order to more easily dominate it."[41]

This central, pervasive idea has weathered the years for some at the ESG. Navy official Paulo, a professor at the school, used the language of decades gone by to describe to me the use of mass media in revolutionary warfare. "There were a lot of useful innocents," he insisted, alleging that musical celebrities served communists' nefarious designs—"Caetano [Veloso] and [Gilberto] Gil definitely served as useful innocents." Paulo remains convinced that music and television, in particular, made ideal weapons for communist subversion. "Music, I am sure that it was used a lot," he says, whereas subversives "used [telenovelas] to call attention to the breakdown of values . . . and if you attack [values], you are attacking National Security." Mass media, then, was a minefield of "communist infiltration" via immorality.[42]

In the category "social communications," esguianos thus found a forum ideal for applying Cold War geopolitics to anxieties about traditional morality. Concurring, then, with classic elements of media- and youth-focused moral panic, esguianos turned to a tried-and-true stratagem for countering such panic: censorship. Exercising one of the regime's most controversial and pervasive means of social control, government censors, like moralistic members of the public, displayed overwhelming concern with obscenity.[43] Accounts of the dictatorship, however, have tended not to elucidate (and in some cases even obscured) the fact that architects and supporters of censorship in Brazil did not conceptually isolate antiobscenity from anticommunist intervention. Far from mutual exclusivity, censorship of pornography and censorship in the name of anticommunism were in many ways one and the same.[44]

Obscenity censorship, then, long a part of Brazil's cultural and political landscape, was not a by-product or afterthought—those at the ESG who called for censorship of materials "prejudicial to morals" sought to reinvigorate this stricture as a central part of their plan to safeguard national security against communism.[45] ESG thinkers maintained that atomic warfare had negated the possibility of direct military confrontation and led communists to resort to subtler tactics—namely, revolutionary war-by-pornography. Just as counterinsurgency theory called for a new Western Warrior, endowed with counterguerrilla prowess, so censorship's proponents demanded a reinvigorated Cold Warrior—an expert censor—for the cultural front. "The impossibility of a direct [atomic] confrontation between Marxist-Leninist Communism and Western Democracy," wrote ESG student José Tavares, led "the promoters of subversive, global guerra revolucionária [to] take advantage of . . . Social Communication as a way to systematically destroy the morality and good customs of the nation." To counter the "erotic appeal" and "immorality" supposedly fostered by revolutionaries, Tavares suggested a warrior developed specifically for the censorial offensive—a "man of censorship" who should be "biologically, intellectually, socially, and morally prepared . . . to elevate" national publications, "avoiding the divulgation of . . . eroticism."[46] Censorship thus targeted immorality *as subversion*, in a context where pornography and communism were indistinct parts of the same whole. Rather than envisioning an offensive against "information that was viewed as a threat to national security *or* prejudicial to morals," esguianos—led, as we have seen, by Justice Minister Buzaid—saw media immorality itself as a subversive national security threat.[47]

These ideas had direct policy impact, as lawmakers drew on the sex-as-subversion narrative to craft national security measures. This conspiracy theory informed not only Buzaid's championing of Decree-Law 1077 but also the law's reaffirmation by senatorial committee. As notoriously autocratic committee chair Eurico Resende put it in 1970, "It is well known, and beyond unquestionable that an agency of international pornography and eroticism has installed itself in this country, operating at full capacity, in a blatant process of polluting and contaminating our children and youth."[48] Where previous ESG voices had called for precisely this kind of measure, the early 1970s saw esguianos' celebration of AI-5, Decree-Law 1077, and other authoritarian measures as policy victories and key tools for ESG-style cultural countersubversion.

Yet more strikingly in terms of impact, policy implementation took this form of cultural countersubversion as its point of departure. Influenced, that is, by the kind of thinking laid out at the ESG, political and military police on the street, at the cinema, and in theaters saw censorship as a tool for combating moral-cum-political subversion.[49] As chief of staff of the federal police, for example, esguiano Raul Lopes Munhoz stood on the front lines of censorial war on subversion. Munhoz applied his powers of censorship to many late-sixties works of art and theater, embodying the "man of censorship" who must, according to ESG prescriptions, combat pornographic guerra revolucionária. Perhaps the most sensational of these works was Chico Buarque's 1967 play Roda viva, which blurred the lines between the sacred and the profane. Debuted in Rio in 1968, the production faced a barrage of legal and extralegal violence. In São Paulo and Porto Alegre, performances were interrupted by right-wing paramilitaries from the Command for Hunting Communists (CCC) who attacked the cast and destroyed sets and equipment. Director José Celso Martínez Corrêa was later arrested, accused of links with guerrilla groups, and tortured. Many have written of Roda viva as a touchstone of anti-regime artistic expression, as an "edgy," innovative watershed in Brazilian theater, and as an example of political censorship (because the play ridiculed the military).[50]

The play's avant-garde sexual themes, however, did more than shock audiences—sex, above other concerns, gained Roda viva the suspicion and enmity of countersubversives, as the chief censors themselves focused *primarily* on the play's sexually subversive potential. Munhoz, writing a security brief to Air Force Minister Márcio Mello (a fellow ESG alum), could not sufficiently emphasize the sexual and moral nature of the production's threat. "Subversive, pornographic, and obscene," he argued, "the truly depraved show" abounded with "libidinous acts," the "unmistakable sexual act," and "scenes of 'women with women' and 'men with men.'" Munhoz justified censorship precisely because

Moral Technocracy and the Military Regime   127

such material was evidence of clandestine communist plotting: "Prohibiting public exhibition [of *Roda viva*], this Office . . . has taken a firm decision against irresponsible artists, bound up with groups that secretly try to undermine the government and democracy via the great weapon of mass communication."[51] By 1968, then, "mass communication" could already be assumed to be a "weapon." Subversive, immoral use of social communications, the bugbear of ESG theories of cultural Cold War, seemed realized in works like *Roda viva*—and government and paragovernment forces responded accordingly.

Modernity and *Mulheres*

Inhabiting a third, essential nexus in the ESG web of concerns relating anticommunist security theory and moral panic, "women's liberation" (*liberação da mulher*) and the "disintegration of the family" (*desintegração da família*) represented categorical anxieties that, if not as prevalent as worries about "the youth problem" and "means of social communication," nevertheless cropped up regularly as foci of morally and culturally countersubversive attention. In general terms, the maintenance of the family as a "Western, Christian value" formed a recurrent node of concern in national security doctrines.[52] To many thinkers at the ESG, the destruction of traditional family structure formed part of the communist-inspired moral crisis wrought upon the West. The repeated claim that "the family, today, is the principal target of the Marxist-Leninists" accompanied the near-constant ESG mention of the "disaggregation" or "disintegration" of the family, a phenomenon presumed to result from a Marxist strategy to doom Western civilization.[53] As Dr. Mário Altenfelder (the esteemed president of the government's child-welfare program) wrote in his 1966 ESG paper, "Communism assaults the Christian family because it is such an enormous source of resistance against materialism and . . . atheism. Communism [does] everything it can to destroy the family."[54]

Anxieties about "the Brazilian family" had, of course, animated notions of moral crisis and, indeed, of anticommunism long before the 1960s.[55] Security theorists at the ESG, however, moved beyond the vague accusations of yesteryear—namely, that foreign and faraway communists were dismantling traditional family structure in their own societies. Inscribing familial anxieties into their particular vision of Cold War geopolitics and cultural crisis, esguianos claimed that such dismantling had already arrived, to catastrophic effect, in Brazil. The Brazilian family, according to such thinking, now faced utter and ultimate undoing, thanks to the insidious plots of international communism. To achieve this undoing, ESG thinkers argued, the subversive authors of these plots had launched two related and devastating offensives against the Brazilian family: women's liberation and women's work outside of the home.

Sanctioned by no less an authority than the ESG's basic training manual (*Manual Básico*), the idea that "women working outside the home has . . . contributed to the weakening of [the family]" permeated ESG analyses in the late 1960s and 1970s.[56] Here esguianos responded to what was in some ways a very palpable phenomenon: dramatic late-twentieth-century proportional and numerical growth in Brazilian women's extra-domestic employment. By some estimates, women participating in the labor market increased from 14 percent in 1950 to 20 percent in 1970, and then doubled (to over 40 percent) by 1990; and the sheer number of working women doubled between 1970 and 1980 alone.[57] As noted above, these developments resulted, at least in part, from the hardships imposed by "authoritarian modernization" after 1964. Ironically, however, ESG reports and assignments habitually blamed communist subversion for perceived familial dissolution—triggered, to esguiano minds, by the specific mechanisms of women's political liberation and increased participation in public economy. One 1976 report traced the so-called youth problem itself to the incidence of working mothers and (consequently) dysfunctional families. As author Antonio Carlos de Seixas Telles—then a sitting member of the powerful Supreme Military Tribunal—explained, "The deficient attention of the mother to her children, . . . because she is so often obligated to work outside the home" had directly enabled young people's "contaminat[ion] by the aggressive movements, all of them subversive in nature, inspired by the nefarious doctrine of Marxism-Leninism."[58] Scholars have shown that regulation of motherhood (from "smothering" to neglect) took on special significance in Cold War cultures from Argentina to the United States.[59] Here, among Brazil's moral technocrats, absent mothers were charged with abandoning Brazil's future generations, exposing them to communist "contamination."

Other reports more overtly indicted working and/or "liberated" women, referring less to mothers "obligated to work outside the home" than to women taken in by the troubling forces of political and economic emancipation. These ideas replicated, with neat precision, the discourses of the 1930s antimodern proponents of a "third way"—including Brazil's fascist Integralists, who bemoaned the deleterious effects of communism and liberalism on traditional womanhood. At the ESG, Pastor Daltro Keidann's essay on pornography and national vulnerability yearned for yesteryear's "stable . . . patriarchal family [in which] the woman was dependent." To Keidann's chagrined alarm, "society [was] transforming," with "more and more independence for women, even in the voting booth," such that "the instability of the modern family" formed the foundation for the "moral crises to which its members are now subjected."[60] Yet more straightforward in terms of his excoriation of modern woman, university professor Antônio Joaquim Coelho compared feminism to "Free Love"—each, to his mind, a cover for global communist warfare: "The most flagrant example of this strategy of revolutionary warfare [guerra revolucionária] is the massive attack against the honor and morality of Woman, seeking to degrade her by means of any and all artifices. . . . It is well known that the woman (mother) is the anchor of the home and the cornerstone of the family. This is the reason for the campaigns conjured against her. . . . The International Communist Movement [and] the enemies of society hide behind . . . standards like 'women's liberation,' 'feminism,' and others . . . like 'Free Love.'"[61] The doctrine of modern woman (and the "modern family" that her liberties created) as an agent of guerra revolucionária grew so ingrained at the ESG that at least one female ESG student denounced women's extradomestic labor as the fodder of communist subversion. Iraci Schmidlin—the education secretary of the city of Joinville, whose venture out of *her* home into policy work and ESG course work, we must presume, remained above suspicion—wrote in 1976 that "the work of Woman outside the home" and the related "modern family" had "facilitated . . . the implantation of Guerra Revolucionária."[62]

Here, too, the specters of pathologization and the pseudomedical, hygienicist, and eugenicist traditions of decades past reared their heads. If references to the absence of working mothers from the helm of child-rearing obliquely recalled earlier theories about republican motherhood and public health, some at the ESG made these connections more directly.[63] Rio de Janeiro–based criminal judge David Mussa epitomized this pathologization in a 1972 study commissioned at the ESG. He listed "women's extradomestic work"—alongside adultery, divorce, and "the widespread acceptance of sexual perversions"—as a "psychopolitical method of mental implantation, with revolutionary objectives of ruin-ing the basic social institutions, [used by] Marxist-Leninist ideology."[64] Mussa's sense of why these "psychopolitical methods" had achieved such success revolved around pseudomedical expertise on the "role of Woman." Defining this role according to the gendered prescriptions of generations of public health professionals, Mussa echoed the concerns of state planners in Brazil (as elsewhere in Latin America) who had long railed against the "modernization" of families, arguing that work-ing women posed a physical, moral, and psychological danger to national "stock."[65] He held that pregnant women who worked would endanger their unborn children; that "biological love" should make "the mother . . . the great guarantor of the future soundness of her child"; that "psycholo-gists know all too well the disastrous results" of faulty mothering; and that women who worked would leave their children with a "psychic hunger" disastrous to national viability.[66] Typically, these ESG anxieties about women brought gender to the forefront of cold war and culture war; yet, as in earlier concerns about gender change, women mattered only insofar as their role as procreators and puericultors was concerned, so prescriptions for remedying the culture remained focused, some-what paradoxically, on men. Accordingly, even the military regime's of-ficial propaganda, attempting to promote traditional values alongside modernization, featured women in very limited quantities and only in domestic roles.[67]

Mussa, alongside other experts, revealed another key aspect of cul-tural countersubversion here, promoting technocratic management of public morality. To him, as to other authorities, the moral and cultural disaster threatening the Western world stemmed from the masses' lack of ESG-style technical knowledge about issues like maternal and public health. Hence Western decadence, vulnerability, and "social disorgani-zation," he concluded, could be traced to public "lack of comprehension of the function of Woman, as a mother, who plays such an important role in the construction and reconstruction of societies."

Moral Technocrats and (Trans)National Reaction

Mussa's reference to such time-honored pathologizations, to the "sci-ence" of family structure and child-rearing, may appear anachronistic and even—coupled with his allegations of communist conspiracy—ridiculous to contemporary readers. The logics that Mussa exemplified, however, made perfect sense in the technocratic context of ESG policy planning. As noted above, the ESG represented something of an ultimate think tank, staffed by an elite of scientific and professional authorities. The school institutionalized what Guillermo O'Donnell described as the bureaucratic-authoritarian mission: "to 'depoliticize' social issues by dealing with them in terms of the supposedly neutral and objective criteria of technical rationality."[68] To this end, the ESG brought together specialists from a wide variety of fields: psychology, law, academe, journalism, medicine, engineering, pedagogy, economics, the clergy, and—of course—military science.

Indeed, these experts are the key to explaining the rise of moral panic at the ESG, the extremity of perspective in the "brain" of top government. The moral panic that we have witnessed thus far developed at the ESG with integral assistance from what I call a moral technocracy, some of whose members have already appeared in these pages. Composed primarily of psychiatric, clerical, juridical, and military professionals, this core group of consultants generated, justified, and legitimized ESG moral panic. Working in a transnationally conceived context, moral technocrats facilitated theoretical interpretations of moral transformation, counterculture, and sexual revolution as part of a gendered, global conspiracy. Their work posited and reiterated notions of "the youth problem," "means of social communication," and "disaggregation of the family" as subversive plots—providing source material and a stamp of collective, technocratic approval for the bio- and gender-laden moral panic that infused excursus like those we have been exploring.

The importance of these technocrats and their ideas at the ESG—and beyond—helps to explain just how morality and countersubversion grew so powerfully intertwined in official channels. Bound to reactionary moralism by a certain intellectual myopia (recurrence to a very limited and often antiquated canon of scholarly resources), these men and women enjoyed considerable sway in esguianos' discussions of the issues of sexuality, public health, and subversion—and they linked the main currents of such discussion not only to earlier periods of anticommunist reaction, but to an influential national and even international coterie of moralistic rightists.

Indeed, ESG moral technocrats themselves could be said to form such a coterie, at least in national terms. We have already heard from some of these leading lights—Supreme Military Tribunal justice Seixas Telles, for example, and pediatric nabob Mário Altenfelder. As these men's participation suggests, the ESG brought together an influential collection of ranking and renowned moral experts. These ranged from prominent psychiatrists like José Leme Lopes (cofounder of the Brazilian Psychiatric Association and its first president, known as the "father of modern Brazilian psychiatry") to clerical celebrities Fernando Bastos de Ávila and Francisco Leme Lopes; from jurists to academic venerables (among them Tarcísio Padilha, department chair at the State University of Rio de Janeiro, former president of the Centro Dom Vital's Brazilian Society of Catholic Philosophers, and a member of the government's secret commission for negotiating with the church, among other illustrious positions); and from high civilian officials (communications czar Said Farhat, for example) to military-bureaucratic bigwigs, including Antônio Carlos da Silva Muricy, Juarez Távora, Jorge Boaventura de Souza e Silva, and Carlos de Meira Mattos.[69]

These moral technocrats led the charge at the ESG to connect sin, sex, and subversion, making the national conversation about morality and sexuality coterminous with that about national security. The trend toward conflating sex with subversion and counterculture with communism thus emerged under the aegis of a specific competence and authority; a generation of ESG "experts," representing a broad spectrum of professional backgrounds, decisively equated unconventional sexuality and/or substance abuse with communist warfare. One such authority, university chancellor Guilardo Martins Alves, coauthored a 1974, ESG-commissioned study denouncing the designs of "Bolshevik politics" on young people. Communists' "deliberate ... psychological warfare and psychopolitical techniques," the study warned, sought to use the "exploitation of drugs and eroticism ... [to achieve] the destruction of society."[70] Martins, like other experts, affirmed authoritarian measures as the solution to the problem of sexual subversion. As noted priest, author, and government educational consultant Francisco Leme Lopes put it, communists had sought to inspire "bad taste, shameless pornography and class hatred" via the National Student Union (UNE). The 1964 coup, he wrote in 1967, had "put off the communist threat," though "communist brainwashing continues to act, largely camouflaged" in the smuttily subversive media of youth publications.[71] Looking back on the influence of such experts, one ESG veteran told me that their technocratic undergirding of moral countersubversion "did not *obligate* anyone to think a certain way," but it did "valorize" a moralistic and religious approach to anticommunism.[72] As we shall see below, such valorization mattered in an ESG ideological world where limited citations were the rule.

Where such theories envisioned moral and sexual unconventionality as a threat to national security and to the "Revolution" of 1964, policy soon followed. Esguiano literati threw their support decisively behind repressive government measures, justifying intrusive state security as a necessary response to sexualized subversion, especially in the years of lead. In an ESG speech given at the height of government repression, Tarcísio Padilha (enjoying, by this point, not only considerable academic prestige but also membership on the Federal Education Council and the Federal Council on Culture) recalled the massive protests of 1968 with undisguised outrage and lauded AI-5 as the "natural fruit" of what he described as a monolithic wave of youthful protest, amorality, and "terrorism." Padilha located the roots of this wave in the ever-maligned "means of social communication," through which subversive "propaganda . . . disburses sex in increasing doses," leading to social, moral, and familial "dissolution."[73] As noted at the outset of this chapter, Justice Minister Alfredo Buzaid (likewise a former Integralist, whose juridical clout earned him the chancellorship of the University of São Paulo and a seat on Brazil's Supreme Court) also argued that government national security measures, which he helped to craft and implement, must address manifestations of sexualized subversion. Like Padilha, Buzaid referred to the upheavals of 1968 as part of a global communist conspiracy to draw youth into "sexual revolution." Defending the regime's censorship laws, Buzaid made the sexuality-security connection with impeccable clarity: "The attempts at sexual liberation and the resistance to laws that restrict pornographic publications constitute *a plan of revolutionary action that corresponds to the proposals of Marxist-Leninist agitation.* . . . In an era when the democratic State has to defend itself against the agents of international communism, the Brazilian Constitution considers as enemies of the Pátria those who promote the propaganda of war, of the subversion of order, of religious, ethnic, or class prejudice, *as well as those who create publications or exhibitions contrary to morality and good customs.* And thus, decidedly, [the constitution] prohibits [such publications or exhibitions] *in the name of national security.*" Indeed, Buzaid went so far as to emphasize that the *primary* goal of the censorial Decree-Law 1077 was "not, therefore, to establish general censorship . . . but to block erotic publications" sponsored by "international communism."[74] Echoing fellow experts at the ESG and, by this time, the school's *Basic Manual* itself, Buzaid prepared a memorandum for President Médici promoting the measure. "Everyone knows," he warned the president, of the communist plot at the root of sexually explicit cultural production. Tellingly, Buzaid sought legislative support for the measure from his friend and former Integralist comrade-in-arms Plínio Salgado.[75]

If moral technocratic justifications for military repression lent credence to general ideas of the Cold War as a culture war, these justifications rested on the familiar ideological bedrock of pathologization. Minister Buzaid and General Muricy justified moralization-as-national-security with references to "professional medicine" and the "neurosis" that facilitated subversion via sexual revolution, and celebrated psychiatrists and clerics lent their imprimatur to this medicalization of communist subversion as a sexual, physiological, and psychological pathology.[76] These professionals argued that juvenile sexual development (puberty and adolescence, or "the Sociobiological Problem of Youth") naturally predisposed young people to subversion and that communist plots used corrosive sexuality and amorality to physically and psychologically maim the young. Eminent psychiatrist Noemi da Silveira Rudolfer blamed the "Crisis of Modern Adolescence," the root of Brazil's subversive problem, on a range of putative congenital, developmental, and moral ailments, from "weakness" to "inadequacy," "somatic insufficiency," "low muscle tone," "homosexual orientation," and even—with rather anachronistic flair—"neurasthenia" and "excessive or insufficient vapors."[77] José Leme Lopes, meanwhile, explained that Marxists found easy prey in the immature sexuality of those who had only recently gained "reproductive function"; indeed, "functionality in the role of a heterosexual adult" provided the only safeguard against communist subversion.[78]

Yet even as they pathologized youth sexuality, psychology, and physiology as "natural" sources of political vulnerability, these psychiatric professionals envisioned the process itself of subversion as a psychopathological, sex-fueled descent into mental and emotional instability. José Leme Lopes exemplified this trend, claiming in an early (1965) ESG speech that moral and sexual liberalization—the "relaxation of customs" at Brazilian universities—constituted a Marxist plot designed to psychologically destabilize students. Citing Sonia Seganfreddo (whose account of students' subversive "pornography" we encountered in chapter 3), Leme Lopes held that the blurring of moral conventions sought to "attack the foundations of the personalities of students of both sexes, so as to immediately, and more easily, implement Marxist lines of attack, in a definitive coordination with the Communist party." Further establishing his commitment to the theory of subversion-as-pathology, Leme Lopes proposed a treatment for those affected by the menace of communist moral dissolution: "psychotherapy," designed to "return this politicized minority to the path of righteousness."[79] Massive psychotherapy aside, Leme Lopes supported other repressive options. He praised AI-5 as a warranted response to rampant subversion among young people—subversion that, Leme Lopes reaffirmed, resulted from the "deviant sexual conduct," the "climate of permissiveness," the "promiscuity," and—worst of all—the "homosexuality" that had produced what he called "personal and social psychopathology" in contemporary youth.[80]

The dogmatism of such moral-technocratic opinion—its persistent, "expert" insistence on sexuality-as-subversion—coupled with the apparent anachronism of direct references to neurasthenia and oblique references to degeneration, begs questions about the provenance of such ideas among moral technocrats. What explains their unilateral visions of subversion as a degenerative, endocrinologically enabled, sexual and moral plot? Why, well into the 1970s and even 1980s, did such dated perspectives persist among recognized and influential authorities? In fact, the sources on which moral technocrats themselves drew provide substantive clues about the roots of their views. A species of intellectual myopia—recurrence to the same eclectic, often antiquated coterie of resources—appears to have underpinned ESG authorities' sense of moral crisis and conviction that communist-inspired moral and sexual warfare had targeted Brazilians. The footnotes and bibliographies of the moral technocratic corpus at the ESG reveal a worldview informed by a specific and circumscribed set of interlocutors. These interlocutors' principal characteristics included pertinence to previous generations of pathologization, moralization, and anticommunism and/or membership in something of a transnational, Western cohort of "experts" on the subjects near and dear to ESG moral technocrats: morality, media, sexuality, and subversion.

Rudolfer, with her concern about neurasthenia and insalubrious vapors, provides a prime example of just how intellectual and bibliographic myopia could inform these perspectives. Published as early as 1938, Rudolfer herself belonged to a bygone generation, both professionally and in terms of moralist activism. In the 1940s, she had volunteered as commandant of a "University Women's Battalion" marshaled to "police" public entertainment—a service for which she received an honorary medal from the Ministry of War.[81] Her psychiatric training, accomplished in Brazil and in the United States during the 1920s and 1930s, furnished her with an unswerving academic faith in her "mentors," among whom she listed various notables of early twentieth-century—when not nineteenth-century—psychiatry and pedagogy: Brazilian educational pioneer Manuel Bergström Lourenço Filho, erstwhile American Psychological Association president Gardner Murphy (b. 1895), and educational philosopher W. H. Kilpatrick (b. 1871), among others.

By the time she spoke at the ESG, then, Rudolfer had enjoyed a career spanning at least four decades—and she continued to rely on intellectual informants of pre-midcentury vogue. In her 1938 *Introduction to Educational Psychology*, Rudolfer venerated famed eugenicist Francis Galton (who, she wrote, developed ways to "accurately study individual differences") alongside G. Stanley Hall (who decried "overcivilized male passionlessness" and the decline of masculinity in the fin de siècle United States; Rudolfer lauded the "perfection" that Hall had "brought . . . to the study of children").[82] When she spoke at the ESG in the 1970s, Rudolfer's reliance on the old masters persisted: she cited Hall to shore up her claims that "homosexual defense mechanisms" and the "oedipal complex" underlay what she called the "Crisis of Modern Adolescence." Indeed, her bibliography recurred not only to Hall but to a menagerie of pre-midcentury theorists of childhood, sexuality, psychology, and sociology: Eduard Spranger (b. 1882), German author of the 1914 treatise *Types of Men*; pediatric psychoanalysis celebrities Anna Freud (b. 1895), Helen Deutsch (b. 1884), and Melanie Klein (b. 1882); Margaret Meade (Rudolfer's references were limited to Meade's 1930s publications); and group psychotherapy pioneer Paul Schilder (b. 1886), among others.[83] The average date of the works cited for this speech was 1947, three decades before Rudolfer's appearances at the ESG. The bibliographies of her further ESG contributions reflected similar (when not identical) references, such that when Rudolfer spoke of neurasthenia, she did so on the authority of the antiquated texts that had informed her own professional development.

Rudolfer's temporally limited source base matched that of other moral technocrats like Leme Lopes and Guilardo Martins Alves, who shared Rudolfer's predilection for Spranger and Hall; both, in fact, cited Hall to undergird their pathologizing definitions of youth as endocrinologically disposed to subversion.[84] Indeed, not a few esguianos reached over a century into the past to cite French social psychologist Gustave Le Bon (b. 1841), whose theories on mass behavior conflated racial and sexual endocrinology with sociology and social pathology. Among esguianos, Le Bon's work served to extend the pathologization of subvertibility beyond youth to lower-class, nonwhite, and theoretically feminine subjects.[85] But ESG thinkers tended to hearken back to bygone predecessors in realms other than psychiatry and sociology; many connected their struggle with an earlier period of moralistic anticommunism, referring to celebrities of the 1930s-era Catholic right. These included Leonel Franca (cited by esguianos for his adamant opposition to birth control and divorce) and Plínio Salgado (the leader of Brazil's 1930s fascist movement, the Integralists).[86] In an ESG-commissioned study on the "psychosocial problem" of divorce, law professor Othongildo Rocha denounced the "universal climate of eroticism" and hailed Franca's *Divorce*, then in its forty-fifth year, as the foremost authority on the subject: "The most perfect study on the issue was realized by the wise Jesuit Leonel Franca, in his book *Divorce*, which meticulously refutes those ... who seek to support divorce."[87] Another member of Rocha's working group referred directly to Plínio Salgado's "How to Exterminate a People," replete with the ex-Integralist's admonitions that "sexual revolution" and "birth control" lay at the heart of subversives' "cold and cruel war" against the West.[88]

Not all of the informants on whom ESG technocrats drew predated 1950; in fact, professional authorities at the school developed a penchant for citing members of a relatively contemporary—if ideologically circumscribed—transnational menagerie of "experts" on morality, mass media, anticommunism, and subversion. Locally, such experts included referents whose perspectives we have already discussed: conservative Archbishop Dom Geraldo Proença Sigaud, right-wing journalist Gustavo Corção, and even the reactionary Tradition, Family and Property (TFP), for instance, surfaced in ESG documents and bibliographies as sources of moralistic countersubversion. Warnings about "free love" drew liberally on Corção, and one group of esguianos even interviewed him for their report on the 1966 Tricontinental Conference in Havana. Unsurprisingly, the report concluded that the "fanatic cult" of Marxism had brought a strategic combination of activism and sexual impropriety (they specifically mentioned conspiratorial, "miniskirted nuns") to Brazil.[89]

Marshall McLuhan, as noted above, served as a preferred referent for esguianos who argued that the "global village" forged by mass media was in fact a conduit for sexualized communist plotting—but moral technocrats padded their claims about sexual subversion and cultural dissolution with other, often more vitriolic sources from across the Caribbean and/or the Atlantic. The favorites included those countersubversive celebrities whom we encountered in chapter 3: Suzanne Labin and Fred Schwarz, whose books cropped up in many an ESG bibliography. Indeed, by the mid-1970s the latter had become so familiar that esguianos could refer to him simply as "Schwarz," without even a bibliographical clarification. The ESG audience of initiates apparently did not need further identification of this moral anticommunist standard.[90] Other such celebrated right-wing referents included Peter Howard (of Moral Re-Armament fame), Charles Stickley (a shadowy contributor to *Brain Washing: A Synthesis of the Russian Textbook on Psychopolitics*), Paul Johnson (*Enemies of Society*), J. Edgar Hoover, the Reverend Charles McFadden (*The Philosophy of Communism*), and erstwhile Marxist (turned Ronald Reagan Medal of Freedom honoree) Sidney Hook.[91]

Some esguiano excursus became little more than regurgitations of one alarmist or conservative treatise after another. Adolpho João de Paula Couto, a rising ESG star in the 1970s, made reference in each of his published essays to a standard coterie of right-wing North Atlantic thinkers, in many cases printing block quote upon block quote of moral panic. In pages that often contained more extracted material than original text, Paula Couto borrowed liberally from Suzanne Labin, Fred Schwarz, J. Bernard Hutton (*Subverters of Liberty*), Douglas Hyde (*Peaceful Assault: The Pattern of Subversion*), J. Edgar Hoover (*Masters of Deceit*), Ronald M. Schneider (author of *Communism in Guatemala* and a contributor to *The Anatomy of Communist Takeovers*), James D. Atkinson (*The Politics of Struggle: The Communist Front and Political Warfare*), Paul Wilkinson (*Political Terrorism*), Jules Monnerot (*Démarxiser l'université*), and Jacques Bergier (*La troisième guerre mondiale est commencée*), among many others.[92] The quoted material—repeated in each of Paula Couto's tracts—included warnings about communist-inspired "moral disintegration" (Atkinson), "middle class morality . . . under attack" (Johnson), "immorality and what we might call dissolution of customs" (Roger Mucchielli), and "moral and civic decadence of the young" (Monnerot). Each reference served to buttress Paula Couto's own, equally unambiguous conclusions about the stratagems of communist subversion: "Through widespread exploitation of eroticism and drugs," he wrote, "a dangerous moral deterioration is being developed in the heart of Western society. This weakening of customs, whose principal target is youth, constitutes yet another manifestation of the complex political war to which we are subject and of which the majority of us is unaware."[93]

I do not mean to suggest that esguianos as a group merely accepted the "wisdom" of extremists like Hutton, Howard, and Schwarz—indeed, the interpretive agency of ESG technocrats emerges with undeniable force in their incorporation of more centrist international thinkers, from McLuhan to Arnold Toynbee, Raymond Aron, Jacques Maritain, and Serge Tchakhotine.[94] Even when they referred to internationally renowned minds that were not expressly right-wing, esguiano moral technocrats inscribed these authorities into the constellation of reactionaries that informed ESG thinking. Ruy Vieira da Cunha, for instance, drew both on Toynbee and on Aron to deplore the subversive potentialities of eroticized mass media and the "sex, drugs, and rejection . . . of morality" into which such media had plunged contemporary youth. Whereas Aron—quoted in Cunha—warned that "democracies are perpetually threatened by the decadence that anonymous power, mediocre leaders, and passive, soulless multitudes muster," Cunha placed the French philosopher's words in the context of presumed, media-driven moral catastrophe in the West: "And this," Cunha added after the passage from Aron, "in a world desacralized, a . . . 'technologized civilization.' "[95] Famed decentralization theorist Peter Drucker met similar treatment at the hands of esguiano moralists, who largely ignored Drucker's principal arguments about industrialization in favor of his alarm about an era of "hasty marriages and excessive divorce."[96] Even Theodore Roszak's rather dispassionate—when not overtly sympathetic—appraisal of "Counter Culture" appeared to legitimate ESG condemnation of *contracultura* as sexual subversion. In a 1972 speech, former education Minister Cândido Motta Filho argued—citing Roszak—that television and mass communication supplemented the influence of controversial philosopher Herbert Marcuse, "forming, *in toto*, an exotic factory of pathogenic behavior produced by drugs, anarchism, and eroticism . . . a cult of pornography."[97]

Such pathologizing, angst-ridden mantras about sexual subversion gained the force of dogma at the ESG via reference to transnational right-wing authorities combined with the *internal* significance and apparent persuasiveness of ESG moral technocrats. The latter were not, in other words, a lunatic fringe, but impactful arbiters of institutional ideology. As noted early in this chapter, moral panic and putative connections between guerra revolucionária and moral crisis emerged even at the highest levels of ESG authority, among the school's commandants and in its basic handbook. This range of effectiveness reflected the intra-institutional influence wielded by key ESG moral technocrats, whose works and ideas tended to appear and reappear in the speeches, term papers, and reports of their fellow esguianos. The pages of ESG documents from this period brim with direct references to moralists whose own speeches and reports clearly held sway among subsequent ESG students and scholars. Fernando Bastos de Ávila, Noemi da Silveira Rudolfer, José Leme Lopes, Guilardo Martins Alves, Tarcísio Padilha, and Ruy Vieira da Cunha, whose ESG studies in moralism, hygienicism, and pathologization we have already witnessed, cropped up in the bibliographies of many a term paper or commissioned study—often alongside other moral technocrats whose individual oeuvres we have not the space to consider.[98] Within two years of his speech on the "Youth Problem," for instance, references to José Leme Lopes appeared in at least seven ESG research projects.[99] Guilardo Martins Alves, Pacheco e Silva, Father Bastos de Ávila, and, above all, Noemi Rudolfer experienced similar vogues—Ávila even appeared in an ESG textbook, a compendium of course readings on "Moral Ethics."[100] Perhaps more impressively, esguianos writing about youth, sexuality, and subversion began to cite the psychosocial authorities on whom Rudolfer and Leme Lopes had themselves drawn. Rudolfer appears to have been the first to mention G. Stanley Hall at the ESG, but in the aftermath of her speeches, as well as Leme Lopes's and Alves's, references to Hall, Spranger, and Anna Freud became commonplace in documents that sought to "biophysically" define young people as susceptible to subversion.[101]

When they were not citing technocratic authorities of Rudolfer's, Leme Lopes's, or Ávila's luster (or, by extension, Spranger's or Freud's), less well-known esguianos nevertheless quoted from *each other* to reinforce theories of sexualized subversion. That is, the intellectual closed circuit at the ESG comprised a sort of combining and recombining of reactionary ideas, passed on from one term paper or speech to the next via direct citation. The ESG by the late 1970s had become a bastion of intractably antidemocratic sentiment in a military establishment inching toward *distensão*, or "decompression" of the authoritarian state.[102] This retrograde attitude, among esguianos, may have derived from the very recombinant tendencies that characterized the discourse on morality and subversion. For example, a 1978 report denounced—despite the lateness of the hour—"free love" and "women's liberation" as coequal disguises for Marxist moral warfare. The report's arguments on this score drew on a pool of fellow esguiano sources: Décio Diaz's 1976 "Strengthening the Family," in which decadent "moral failure" made the family Marxism's "principal target"; Mário Altenfelder's 1966 admonition against the Marxist "eroticization of society"; Antônio de Almeida's identification of "eroticism" as a "psychopolitical technique"; and the *Basic Manual* itself, complete with its dire assessment of the "moral crisis" facing the contemporary West.[103]

Conclusion

By 1975, "fundamental changes" in youth, sexual, and gender behavior seemed overwhelming to many at the ESG. In a ten-year plan submitted to the school's "psychosocial" unit, education specialist Antônio Rafael de Menezes captured the ways in which these changes preoccupied esguianos. With families, the church, and popular culture in "crisis," he reported, young people had descended into a stultifying rhythm of sex, drugs, and rock 'n' roll. Contemporary youth were thus "deformed," "antisocial," "maladjusted," bedeviled by "permissiveness of gestures and clothes," and actively engaged in "protest . . . against everything and everyone." Restricting his concerns to youth of means, Menezes referred specifically to university students and ridiculed such young people's "patently ridiculous form of showing solidarity with the less fortunate," since the rich rebels' countercultural clothes were "bought in boutiques at high prices." Moreover, his anxious appraisal engaged in familiar pathologizations. In a section titled "biotypology of youth," he clarified that the perturbing moral and cultural characteristics to which he had referred were part of a "social pathology," "social illness," or "physical, metabolic illness, . . . born of cultural conflict." This "psychosomatosis" had launched young people into "drugs, aggressiveness, hippie libertinism, protests, abortion, crime, the destruction of values, loud music, parasitism, pseudo-suicide in high-speed cars, subversion, and the destruction of all that is apparently normal."[104]

The conflations patent in Menezes's 1975 account categorically corresponded with the moral anxieties that we have explored in this chapter. By the mid-1970s, esguiano treatises regularly mingled assessments of youth, popular culture, family and sexual morality, public health and pathology, "subversion," and the shadowy "International Communist Movement." Such assessments tended to focus on the specific anxieties percolating in Menezes's report: young people's consumerism and departure from cultural norms; familial dissolution (particularly via women's liberation); and pop cultural media that putatively adulterated *brasilidade*, moral fiber, and resistance to communism. As we have seen, thinkers at the ESG gathered these anxieties into categorical topics, specifying "the Youth Problem," "Means of Social Communication," and "Women's Liberation" as issues that simultaneously threatened national morality, public health, and national security. In many ways, this codification of anxiety—its dogmatism, apparent persuasiveness, and longevity— derived from the authority of a group of expert, often illustrious, moral technocrats at the ESG. Psychiatrists, clerics, sociologists, juridical professionals, academics, and government officials lent the weight of authority to schematics in which communists putatively utilized sexual dissolution to corrupt, enervate, and consequentially subvert Brazil's future generations. Indeed, Menezes himself depended on a canon of ESG technocratic moralism, his citations including José Leme Lopes and Guilardo Martins Alves, among others.[105] Though he did not cite G. Stanley Hall, Francis Galton, or Gustave Le Bon—whom ESG moralists continued to venerate into the 1970s—Menezes did demonstrate familiarity with other nabobs of the institution's international canon (Arnold Toynbee, Jacques Maritain, and Ortega y Gasset), suggesting once again the ways in which a transnational coterie of intellectuals, read and cited through the prism of ESG moralism, served to justify and legitimate such thinking.

This school of countersubversive thought, which we have here explored within the ESG's confines, would extend far beyond that institution into other fonts of national security ideology and, perhaps more importantly, into certain practical applications. If esguiano moralists, including Justice Minister Buzaid himself, supported and in some cases designed censorial and other repressive legislation, these moralists managed to bring these forces to bear outside of the ESG, in (as the next chapter explores) other security forums and even among police and intelligence services, as well as in legislation designed to morally reinvigorate youth in the very name of anticommunism and national security.

5

Young Ladies Seduced and Carried Off by Terrorists

Secrets, Spies, and Anticommunist Moral Panic

In June of 1969, local police in São Sebastião, a coastal city in São Paulo, detained a driver whose license and documents did not appear to be in order.[1] The incident seemed routine—until officers discovered incriminating materials in the car. Their suspicions aroused by the owner's employment with a major press outfit, police searched the vehicle and discovered enough evidence of subversion to merit the involvement of the military. They surrendered the case, and the car itself, to a local air force commanding officer for further investigation. The name and personal information of the driver were handed over to the São Paulo DOPS, the political police. What, then, were the offending materials that suggested involvement with the "internal enemy"? As a classified air force memorandum later informed the DOPS, "The motive of the apprehension . . . was that in the interior of the vehicle were found ample pornographic materials—offensive to morality—which can be considered subversive on account of being used in the moral degradation of the community." It is possible that the political police and intelligence agents who eventually handled this case had other reasons for desiring the driver's detention; perhaps he had some involvement with left-wing protest or armed resistance groups. Remarkably, however, the arrest, detention, and intelligence records omitted any mention of such involvement.[2]

Decades later, Colonel Carlos Brilhante Ustra—by this time infamous as the first military officer convicted of kidnapping and torture on behalf of the dictatorship—revealed the longevity of ideas about the moral and cultural dimensions of countersubversive "war." Ustra helped orchestrate repression at the height of the regime's violent war on subversion (real and perceived), in the now-familiar period surrounding 1970. Recalling his days as a foot soldier of anticommunism, the colonel framed his former career as a crusade to recuperate traditional sexuality and gender—a crusade in which subversive deviance and moral unorthodoxy went hand in hand. Ustra quoted from documentation he claimed to have retained from 1971, making reference to the conflated political and cultural disorder of that time. A letter from August of that year, he said, told the story of a militant arrested with what the letter indicated were the aesthetic cues of the subversive: "a fiery girl, with unkempt hair, without makeup, who refused to get a manicure, who only wore 'blue-jeans,' who refused to get new clothes and shoes." According to Ustra, the letter described how he helped restore her to the life of a "mature young woman, adult, tranquil, with her hair done and her nails painted, though not extravagantly, who argues with the seamstress when her dress does not come out right, who is demanding in her choice of new shoes, and who has returned to her old boyfriend and will get engaged in the next few months."

This retelling, like any such narrative, is a complex one, mediated in this case by nearly forty years and by Ustra's attempts to exonerate himself publicly. The colonel's recollections seem dubious on several fronts. How could he or other state agents have accurately identified subversives based on unkemptness and "inflammation" if, at the height of the armed struggle, militant groups were striving to live clandestinely, to *avoid* standing out? Likewise, what did it mean to associate engagement and marriage with political conformity when, of course, many leftists were married? Nevertheless, it is worth noting that Ustra, and the 1971 letter, resorted to moral, gender, and stylistic terms to describe the distinction between combatant and noncombatant in revolutionary "war": grooming, clothing, attention to femininity, sexual convention, willingness to marry, "lack of exaggeration"—in the late 1960s and early 1970s, these were constructed as cues that might identify the minions of the enemy to the state's spies and enforcers (like Ustra).[3]

Moral technocrats, as we have seen, lent this vision of subversion the weight of authority at the ESG, which became a state-sanctioned lightning rod for the moralistic anticommunisms gripping Brazil's right-wing sectors in the middle Cold War. The incident in São Sebastião, however, like Ustra's framing of the work of repression, indicates such ideas had an impact in other arenas of national security—here, the arena of everyday policing, literally on the street. The government's repressive apparatus focused its sights on, and ultimately decimated, shadowy networks of clandestine, largely young militants—including those who indeed took up arms against the government. Yet the archives of police and intelligence agents reveal that morality was also a key discursive frame for the forces of repression. Indeed, the notion of a total war, in which morality (compartmentalized in gender roles, sexuality, youth behavior, and mass media) served as an important battleground, spread far beyond the ESG, into other security forums and into the state's governing and enforcement apparatuses themselves. This spread, notable in references to moral and cultural "war," was palpable—and in some cases quantifiable—by the end of the 1960s and certainly in the early 1970s, when presidents, police, think tanks, and strategy publications made their moral preoccupations patent.

As the regime hardened and violence increased, police could thus construct pornography, blue jeans, and especially the gender and sexual unconventionality of young, middle-class women as component parts of a much larger, deviant whole. In this chapter we shall explore the ways in which moral panic—the sense of overwhelming, cynically engineered moral degeneracy, targeting the nation's youth—affected countersubversion in the various redoubts of the security establishment, from illustrious theoreticians to on-the-ground security agents. Such panic gained new vehemence among prominent state authorities, institutions of military learning and philosophy, and active security forces, who developed and operationalized stock warnings about depraved young men and sexually wayward young women. Prominent right-wingers and their moralistic message enjoyed the enthusiastic support of policy-makers and countersubversive police forces. Sexual suspicions even cropped up in the day-to-day work of state surveillance and repression, particularly when it came to expressing anxieties about the uncontrolled sexuality of bourgeois women. This kind of moralism appeared in public and private forums (where it could not have been merely an appeal to popular morality), and it characterized security and policing records that did not have an overtly moral purpose, reflecting generalized presumptions of the connection between sexual, gender, and political deviance.

Esguianos Abroad

A cohort of national power brokers, whose moral authority had been recognized in appearances at the ESG, helped nationalize the moralizing anticommunism that had emerged at the Escola. What esguiano moral technocracy had sanctioned, these men carried into the halls of more direct government. Indeed, the very predominance of ESG moralists (some of whom we have already met) within the regime is so striking that space prohibits a full enumeration of them here. If, for example, Said Farhat ruminated at the ESG about immoral media as a "cruel form of conquest," he soon found himself in a position to directly counteract such conquest when he became the president's Secretary of Social Communications. From Farhat's secretariat to the powerful Justice Ministry (headed by Alfredo Buzaid), and from the presidential Press Secretary to the Ministry of Education, key government positions came under the sway of the moral panic gestated at the ESG. Amid the political and cultural tension of 1968 and the surrounding years, sex, morality, and the language of "pornography," "libertinism," and "psychosocial maladjustments" as crucial security risks moved into the heart of government.[4]

By the 1970s, while some Brazilians contemplated changes in sexual and moral behavior (with responses ranging from apathy to celebration), moralistic reaction had gone all the way to the top echelons of government. It was a mantle assumed by two relatively different presidents: Emilio Garrastazu Médici (1969–74) and João Baptista de Oliveira Figueiredo (1979–85)—fellow ESG alums, despite the hard-line affiliation of the former and the comparative moderation of the latter.[5] Figueiredo and Médici had different approaches to the wielding and maintenance of authoritarian power—yet their shared ideas about morality and national security demonstrate the ascension of countersubversive moralism to the heights of national authority, in this case despite the factionalism that divided the military regime. Having created the alarmist Secretariat of Social Communications, Figueiredo endorsed—and sponsored the broadcasting of—the "Crusade for Morality" led by evangelical pastor (and fellow esguiano) Nilson Fanini.[6] To the president, the faltering of heterosexual, family-based morality was both a symptom and a cause of national security failures. A former head of the fearsome SNI, Figueiredo emphasized his face-to-face experience with the "internal enemy"—and used that experience to promulgate the idea of a causal link between the subversion of youth and the "decadence" of traditional families and morals. In a 1980 interview, Figueiredo recounted a conversation with a captured militant, and suggested that young subversives—especially women—were characterized by their loss of faith in marriage and family morality.[7] Médici, meanwhile, brought reactionism full circle, preaching moral rearmament to a new generation of esguianos in his speech at the opening of the school's 1970 academic program. Denouncing the "liberation of instincts" promoted by communist subversion, Médici promised to combat it by giving "special care . . . to the family and to . . . moral and civic upbringing."[8]

General Antônio Carlos da Silva Muricy, however, provided the most spectacular example of ESG moralism gone viral. Long a symbol of military conservatism and intransigence, Muricy epitomized the ascendancy of a moralistic Right rooted in the militarism and extremism of the interwar years. Derided as a reactionary and a putschist well before the coup that brought the generals to power, Muricy made no secret of his sympathies for fascist Integralism. He shared close friendship and ideology with Integralists and found, among the works of their supreme leader Plínio Salgado, "one of the greatest books I have ever read."[9] A graduate and permanent staff member of the ESG—a key author, in fact, of the school's doctrine of guerra revolucionária—Muricy championed Catholic traditionalism in several high-level capacities, including his positions as army chief of staff and leader of the secret Bipartite Commission, charged with mediations between the church and the repressive Médici government. Muricy consistently sought to maintain public and state attention on moral anticommunism. In 1968, for example, he wrote a public treatise on "Warfare Today," which appeared in the *Jornal do Brasil*'s Sunday edition and directly responded to the recent student protests. Tracing communist revolutionary warfare to Bukharin and maintaining that its conspiracies were principally cultural, Muricy wrung his hands about the "moral disaggregation" wrought by communists. "Only the blind," he wrote, "do not see . . . [that conspirators] are working to destroy what they call 'bourgeois morality,' to prepare the way for the advent of communism."[10]

In the following years, Muricy became a gold standard for vetting morality (and, consequently, relative subversiveness) even in the shadowy channels of state security and intelligence. As a top-secret report from the Air Force Intelligence Service (CISA) opined, certain candidates for positions in the National Film Institute must surely be "good names"—that is, neither leftist nor pornographic—because they had been indicated by that venerable cultural Cold Warrior, Muricy.[11] Muricy's authority had emerged quite publicly in 1970, when he spearheaded an inquest into just how young people were being "enticed" into subversion. As army chief of staff, Muricy ordered teams of psychologists and security officers to carry out examinations and interviews designed to create "psychological profiles of subversives" detained in prisons across Brazil.[12] In a series of public pronouncements in 1970–71, Muricy alleged that these profiles had uncovered the "essential causes of entice-ment" into subversion—among which he listed "social maladjustment," parental divorce, and sexual seduction. According to Muricy, young women tempted by communist agitators were "ruined" and forced into a life of clandestinity, promiscuity, and subversion: "The entrance of young women in the terrorist system is accomplished, many times, by means of romance with subversive youths, who are schooled in this technique. Once the pernicious influence is consolidated, the young lady is betrayed. From then on, she keeps away from home and has no means by which to return."[13]

Muricy's comments reflected a double standard whereby putatively subversive women often suffered more sexual stigma than their male counterparts—indeed, Muricy quoted an Army Ministry report's con-clusion that "the majority of [recently subverted] young women live with young men whom they barely know. Many contract venereal dis-eases and some become pregnant."[14] This sexism ironically coincided with that of the Left, noted above. Yet Muricy also saw male youth as potential targets in this model of sexual subversion (that is, seduction). In fact, he provided a general description of the process of subversion, emphasizing the way that, "as a rule," this process mingled sexual with ideological seduction: "If possible, sex appeal is utilized, and the tech-nique of flirtation [*namoro*] is employed. . . . In these meetings and conversations a systematic campaign is unleashed against the family, re-ligion, and extant morality. The stimulus of sex is achieved by means of pornographic literatures presented as advanced works . . . and by means of the conveniences that promiscuity provides."[15]

As I discuss below, this focus on women (Muricy referred to the "moral degradation of youth, especially young ladies"), with the inclu-sion, albeit secondary, of potential male seducees, formed something of a pattern in the countersubversive imaginary. To make his case, Muricy relied on scandalous anecdotes—like the "case of a young lady who went to reside in São Luis Gonzaga Street, there found a young man whom she had never seen before," and emerged fifteen days later a ruined woman—but he also sought to portray sexual subversion as a scientifically demonstrable phenomenon. The studies he had commissioned, in other words, epitomized the attempt to bring the moral-technocratic, "expert"-based approach into the public sphere. To that end, Muricy quoted from reports that included graphs and diagrams intended to map sexual subversion. In his November 1971 speech to the Brazilian Educational

Association, the general referred listeners to a "Figure 1" in which he had listed the psychological antecedents that could lead to "entrance into subversion"—the "family situation" of the prisoner-respondents, Muricy's report contended, could predetermine their subvertibility, particularly if they suffered from "separated parents" or a "lack of affection in the family." A separate illustration (Muricy's "Figure 3") likewise attempted to quantify the "Means and Reasons for Being Enticed" into subversion, including "amorous ties to leftist elements." To further link his conclusions with the authority of countersubversive technocracy, Muricy publicly appealed to renowned, international anticommunist expertise. Muricy's exposé of youth subversion featured ESG favorite Fred Schwarz himself, who, Muricy reminded his listeners, had traced the ways in which communists urged their young victims to "accept any debased morality, taking amorality and immorality as the norm."[16]

"Against Revolutionary Warfare": Moralism and Military Learning

Individuals like Muricy, Buzaid, Farhat, and many others bore the standard of moral technocracy into public, policy-making, and even presidential spheres, but ideas about the putative connection between youth, changing moral and sexual standards, and cataclysmic subversion also met with significant success in security and military institutions beyond the ESG. One such institution was the school's alumni and outreach organization, the Association of ESG Alumni (ADESG). Founded in 1951, the ADESG bore responsibility not only for maintaining a permanent ideological network among alumni, but for "disseminating doctrinal concepts related to Security and Development, in accordance with the methods . . . and studies of the ESG." This dissemination was wideranging, as the ADESG's audience extended beyond former students to include the thousands of attendees of conferences and study programs designed by chapters in various cities.[17] The ESG's "doctrinal concepts," as interpreted by core and influential ADESG members, emphasized the moralistic tendencies of the institution's security theory—an emphasis consistent with the presence in the ADESG hierarchy of strict moralists whom we have already encountered. Indeed, Tarcísio Padilha— who had complained, at the ESG, of subversive "works that attack morality"—served as director of ADESG outreach courses, and Muricy as ADESG president. Beyond such in-house moralists, the ADESG reached out to international exponents of moral anticommunism. In January 1965, less than a year after the coup that had brought many esguianos into government, ADESG members arranged for a private address from Peter Howard. Leader of the international Moral Re-Armament movement, Howard had come to Brazil to strengthen links with local moralists and anticommunists—many of whom he found at the ADESG.[18]

Segurança e Desenvolvimento (*Security and Development*, the ADESG magazine distributed nationwide to alums both of the ESG itself and of separate ADESG programming) perhaps best reflected the morally reactionary bent of the association's central leadership. A glossy journal of national security research and thought, the magazine had by the early 1970s surpassed printing ten thousand copies per year—and become the dominion of prominent moralists. The habitual moral panic of these men pervaded the magazine, bringing to a national platform, nearly verbatim, the themes of moral technocrats at the ESG. Renowned priest, Catholic University president, and moral authority Fernando Bastos de Ávila warned of descent into degeneracy and barbarism based on youthful affinity for Herbert Marcuse. Justice Minister Alfredo Buzaid, meanwhile, published three contributions in *Segurança e Desenvolvimento* in a single year (1971–72), each bringing the moral technocracy's familiar blend of antimodern concerns (youth, media, morality, and Marxist subversion) to a national platform. Hailing the 1964 coup as an errand in remoralization, Buzaid condemned sexual revolution, counterculture, liberalism, and even the French Revolution, identifying—with a nod to medievalism—the Renaissance as the "first mistake" in an execrable "cultural revolution." Typically faithful to the trends we have discussed in the context of the ESG proper, Buzaid cited decades-old right-wing antecedents (Leonel Franca, for example) on the evils of the Renaissance. "Communism," Buzaid told readers nationwide, relied on a cultural process of revolutionary warfare—it "destroys the family by means of wild propaganda of sex, Free Love, and obscenity," relying on mass media to "destroy the fiber of youth."[19]

If institutional proximity destined the ADESG for ESG-style moral anticommunism, physical proximity might have played a like role in the curricular development of the Command and General Staff College (ECEME), located about a kilometer's walk around the edge of the Sugar Loaf from the ESG. Admission to and academic achievement in the ECEME constituted a prerequisite for advancement to high rank for Brazilian military officers in the postwar period—and by the late

1960s, the ECEME, like its nearby sibling institution, had become a focal point for steeping the officer corps in the tenets of National Security Doctrine.[20] Such doctrine, at the ECEME, also featured the anticommunist moralism so present among esguianos and their international co-reactionaries. ECEME textbooks, curricula, and student term papers showed the same preoccupations with morality and sexuality as focal points for guerra revolucionária—demonstrating, in fact, that these preoccupations extended up the chain of command to the Army General Staff (EME) itself, the army's supreme executive and the final word on doctrines and curricula. Indeed, the General Staff published a series of lectures that served as a textbook at the ECEME, under the title *Educative Action against Revolutionary Warfare*. This text combined the work of Brazil's ESG-, French-, and U.S.-trained security theorists, whose citations of international anticommunist experts undergirded the notion that subversion functioned through moral dissolution, "creating new standards of judgment and conduct," appealing always to "the sexual interests," and "exploiting sexual appetites."[21] Citations in *Educative Action* included a smattering of ESG publications, as well as references to national and international moralists, some of whom we have already encountered at the ESG: Suzanne Labin, Murillo Vasco do Valle Silva, Antônio Carlos Pacheco e Silva, and Aurélio de Lyra Tavares.[22] These ideas were deployed in the classroom: an EME-approved class outline for the ECEME's 1963 course on guerra revolucionária drew directly on the ESG canon, defining subversion as a "psychological" and "spiritual" attack on a target population, designed to trigger "decadence and the demise of the moral compass."[23]

ECEME students who studied this curriculum likewise reflected the sorts of moralism so rampant at the ESG. In keeping with the nature of the ECEME's mission, assignments there tended to focus on basic operational tactics rather than on geopolitical strategy or philosophy—what to eat on a counterguerrilla campaign, for instance, as opposed to the (im)moral nature of the enemy. Nevertheless, moralism crept into the lexicon even here. Infantry Major Hélio Gama Capistrano's "Psychological Operations of the Internal Enemy" exhibited a familiar focus on "works by communist and socialist authors," which wrought "destruction of national morality" and "negative influence . . . on youth." A pamphlet annexed to Capistrano's report denounced Brazil's progressive Catholics, lampooning liberation theology as "Libertine Theology" and depicting a bejeweled, purse-carrying, gender-troubled prelate (see fig. 6).[24]

Figure 6 The cartoon "Libertine Theology," from an anonymous pamphlet appended to an ECEME report, lampooned liberation theology. In Helio Gama Capistrano, "Operações psicológicas do inimigo interno" (1979), Biblioteca 31 de Março MO 1336. Photo by author; original courtesy of Biblioteca 31 de Março.

"Why Young People Are Embracing Subversion": Military Journals

Despite the centrality of the ESG and ECEME to military career advancement, not everyone could study there. Yet Brazil's military journals—particularly the nationally important *A Defesa Nacional*—provided a forum in which anticommunist moral panic could gain further, national exposure. Founded in 1913, long controlled by an exclusive, fixed board of editors, and written by and for military officers, *A Defesa Nacional* constituted a critical military-intellectual outlet, intended to "forge a military mentality."[25] The magazine enjoyed the Army Ministry's official endorsement, as well as significant financial subsidy.[26] By the early 1960s, that subsidy underwrote a redoubt of putschist hard-liners, many of whom both edited and contributed to the magazine. A 1961 issue, for example, expressed gratitude to and solidarity with soon-to-be coup plotters. Decidedly pro-authoritarian, the magazine's editors in fact framed the coup in terms of morality, eulogizing the "Regenerative Movement of 31 March" as a "moral transformation."[27] Moralists and extremists numbered among *A Defesa Nacional* editors themselves, ranging from Carlos de Meira Mattos (later of the moralizing Meira Mattos Commission) to Army Intelligence Service (CIE) founder Adyr Fiuza de Castro, who would defend torture as a regime strategy as late as the 1990s, to Germano Seidl Vidal, who authored an ESG class reader urging "moral cleansing" along the lines of the "Moral Re-Armament [movement] led by Peter Howard."[28] The magazine, as a rhetorical home for both putschists and those who conflated countersubversion with moral "cleansing," not only served as a mouthpiece for moralistic countersubversion, but also underscored connections between moral reaction and the military-authoritarian hard line.

By the early 1970s, moral concerns suffused the pages of *A Defesa Nacional*. In the 1950s and 1960s, contributors to the magazine had engaged in a transatlantic conversation among military men about the "new," revolutionary warfare—a topic that took up morality, modernity, and gender in significant ways, but did not necessarily entail moral panic of the kind we have witnessed at the ESG and elsewhere.[29] Such discussion of guerra revolucionária monopolized a significant proportion of *A Defesa Nacional* articles (as many as one out of three in some issues) through the 1960s. As that decade wore on, however, new topical foci crept into the magazine's corpus. Gustavo Corção himself surfaced as a contributor in 1969, lauding authoritarianism and signposting a turn toward concern for subversion's "moral apparatuses."[30] By 1970, more general attention to guerra revolucionária had given way to anxious excursus on youth, education, and moral subversion—topics that grew predominant in the magazine's approach to countersubversion. Of the twenty-seven *A Defesa Nacional* articles on communist warfare in 1970 (a peak repressive year), a majority (59 percent) addressed education or youth as areas of anticommunist anxiety, whereas fewer than half (41 percent) treated other theoretical aspects (unrelated to morality, youth, and education) of guerra revolucionária.

Illustrating the intensity of such concerns, *A Defesa Nacional* stressed the "crisis" brought on by "the proselytizers of subversion and perversion." Contributors from across the spectrum of military rank and authority demonstrated the pervasiveness of moral panic, fretting about communist-inspired "degenerescence" and a generation of sexually "poisoned" young people who "want not Brazil, but Cuba."[31] As at the ESG, nationally powerful figures weighed in, showing the prevalence of these ideas at top levels of government. In some sense the government's principal spokesperson, Lieutenant Colonel Octávio Pereira da Costa was the architect and manager of the official government propaganda and public relations organ (AERP)—and in *A Defesa Nacional* he characterized the post-coup regime as an errand in "moral renovation," whose challenges lay in the pornographic detritus of "provocative headlines" and "immoral leaflets."[32] In 1973, reflecting the increased anxiety of the years of lead, Attorney General (and ADESG alum) José Fernandes Dantas waxed more dramatic, his essay complaining that "political-ideological conditioning" had led young people to an alarming "cultural retrocession" that threatened national viability and security. As a result, these young people "simply abandon themselves to the experiences of Free Love, without any fear of . . . consequences that would insist on the protection of virginity, devalued by the abandonment of modesty [*pudor*] and by the sexual stimulus of contraceptives!"[33]

It was from esguianos themselves, however, that the most virulent moral anticommunisms of *A Defesa Nacional* emanated, especially during the peak repressive years. Key ESG personages—including commandants and influential ideologues—brought the school's perspective to the magazine and emerged as its most morally and culturally reactionary countersubversives. The magazine celebrated the unyielding cultural conservatism of General Muricy ("one of our most distinguished associates"), General Jorge Boaventura, and General Moacir de Araújo Lopes, who affirmed that revolutionaries waged their battles across the moral and behavioral topography of the nation's young. In 1969, following Muricy, the editorial board went so far as to conclude that guerra revolucionária was "basically cultural and social."[34] Lopes, an influential ESG alum who played a determinative role in the development of Moral and Civic Education (the focus of chapter 6), demonstrated the explicitness with which powerful moral technocrats made their case. In a late-1968 diatribe against his nemesis, Herbert Marcuse, Lopes bemoaned an explosion of "homosexuality," "fellatio," and even "anal eroticism," which would "lead to the *communist paradise.*"[35]

Fittingly, given its imbrication with esguiano thought, moralism in *A Defesa Nacional* introduced (or reinforced) for its readership a moral panic centering on precisely the themes we have seen emphasized at the ESG: focus on youth and women; pathologization of the perceived threat; preoccupation with media and "social communication"; and a tendency to reach out transnationally to anticommunist allies in the "good fight." Of these, anxiety about youth was unquestionably the most pronounced. As the magazine's guide to "Getting to Know the Internal Enemy" put it in 1978, "There is currently no problem more serious . . . than the insidious penetration of communist subversion in the bosom of our youth."[36] *A Defesa Nacional's* editors had in fact voiced these very concerns more than a decade earlier, commissioning a 1966–68 series of articles topically dedicated to youth, morality, and subversion.[37] The series complained of "Youth in Crisis" due to pop songs, "art that is directed intentionally toward the sordid," sexual profligacy, and women's liberation. "Women's evolution," as one author called it, ranked among communist stratagems for subverting youth, as the emergence of women's rights had led to "weakening of family ties," to "instability in the home," and to the resultant "abandonment in which a significant part of our children and youth are living."[38]

As the 1960s drew to a close, a spate of open letters cropped up in *A Defesa Nacional*, linked by their common format and theme—all were cards to figurative youth, lamenting the advanced state of moral/cultural degradation and warning against communist subversion concealed therein. The letters showed the ways in which these concerns, in military-intellectual forums, had grown so entrenched as to become formulaic, and indicated once again that young men's sexuality (and conflated subvertibility) pertained to national security. In 1970, for instance,

Lieutenant Colonel Jonas Correia Neto—then a student at the ESG—penned "Letter to a Student at Military School," an exercise in avuncular moralizing. "Son," Correia Neto warned, "now is the time . . . of the exacerbation of many bad instincts, of the exploitation of many weaknesses," ranging from "ridicule of parents" to "devaluation of marriage" to "rejection of moral rules ('sexual freedom'), dissemination of drug abuse, and neglect of bodily hygiene and physical health." Correia Neto insisted that such moral, cultural, and physical disaster derived from "the proselytizers of subversion and of perversion," their sole aim "to leave . . . moral and corporeal degenerescence where there were moral and human values and mental and physical haleness."[39] Later that same year, *A Defesa Nacional* published similar letters—including "Notes for a Cadet" and "Letter to a Young Brother." The latter, subtitled "What a Man of Sixty Has to Say in 1969," lamented the figurative addressee's predilection for "a type of liberty that results in libertinism." Sexuality and mass media featured front and center in the author's alarmism, where "supervaluation of sex, always and in everything" had blossomed via "the broadcasting of television harmful to your [the 'young brother's'] moral upbringing."[40]

Where young men's sexual subvertibility generated these morose, moralistic open letters, anxieties about young women's uncontrolled sexuality generated a veritable outpouring of grief and rage at *A Defesa Nacional*. A different genre of article addressed the salacious strategies that communists putatively designed for young women. *A Defesa Nacional* contributors often recurred to something akin to fables of fallen womanhood—cautionary rumors and tales much like those publicized by General Muricy, in which university-age women, seduced both sexually and politically, faced personal ruin. In *A Defesa Nacional*, of course, these parables would reach a military audience, but they were not entirely unknown in the popular press—a 1968 *Realidade* article, for example, recounted the sad story of a female university entrant who, unchaperoned for the first time in her life, began "living in a student colony." Here she began to "doubt religion . . . family . . . and social conventions," until she decided that "being a virgin was 'silly'" and had sex "not because she was in love with the guy, but 'to be more authentic.'"[41] The *Realidade* article presented this story in the context of a variety of perspectives on sexual liberation (see chapter 2), but at *A Defesa Nacional* tales like that of this *moça perdida* ("fallen" or "lost" girl) inevitably appeared as warnings against the ways that communists used sex to "ruin" young women. At the National College of Philosophy (FNFi), one article explained, communist agents had created a virtual army of female foot soldiers via seduction and sexual defilement: "Thirty female students, of the thirty-two enrolled in a particular course, suffered sexual violation at the hands of male students; under the threat of public scandal, these girls were forced down the errant path of Marxism by dint of ideological blackmail. . . . How many of those girls, now teachers, might currently be teaching in elementary schools?!"[42] Seduction, rape, and sexual blackmail, in this view, thus signified more than mechanisms for youthful perdition and the loss of innocence—here were conscious tools of Marxist subversion, deliberately employed to combine political with moral and sexual ruin. Once deflowered, the young women in this account lay beyond help—indeed, they posed a danger to the schoolchildren over whom they might one day preside.

The series "Getting to Know the Internal Enemy" provided two consecutive examples of the deeply classed nature of these parables, which emphasized girls from "good families" going bad—smoking, drinking, and sinning their way into communist-wrought disgrace. The stories, significantly, opened a section titled "Why Young People Are Embracing Subversion" and were presented as the primary examples of what the author called "factors that drive youth into subversion." Echoing General Muricy's technocratic conclusion that seduction and sexual betrayal lay at the heart of Marxist designs on university-age women, *A Defesa Nacional*'s guide to the "internal enemy" charged putative communist agents with deliberate creation of an environment in which even the most stolidly moral of young women could not fail to give in to temptation and thereby to subversion. The first story, recounted in the voice of a repentant victim herself, emphasized that she had come from a middle-class, religious family and had—until her encounter with a skillful Marxist seducer—herself been quite "retrograde," at least when it came to morality and tradition. "I was raised," her story began, "in a good family."

> Our family could be classified as a family of traditional standards: respect for and obedience toward elders, religious education with obligatory attendance at mass, avoidance of new fads (long hair, extravagant clothes), rigid personal habits and schedules. I entered the university very early, at seventeen. I was totally bewildered by the environment that I found there. I didn't understand the slang of my classmates, and I was reluctant to accept habits like collective

smoking, to permit certain licentious liberties, to go out with the boys, to use certain kinds of dress, etc. My colleagues called me "square" and "retrograde," among other epithets. They avoided my company.... That was when a certain young comrade (I don't need to tell you that he was a subversive) seemed to take pity on me and began courting me. I was so excited about that! And thus he began to teach me, that is, to indoctrinate me, into a new reality.[43]

The narrative did not go into further details about this new "reality," but the suggestion was clear: subversives had transformed Brazilian universities into dens of the most offensive, "licentious liberties," especially when it came to relations between the sexes ("going out with the boys"). Given the moral-cum-political turpitude into which communists had plunged student life, even the most well-bred of middle-class young ladies might find themselves seduced by smooth-talking subversives.

Such stories played on longstanding preoccupations with privacy, stewardship, and female sexuality. In his landmark *The House and the Street*, Roberto da Matta explored the deep roots in Brazil of a binary division between home—a space of morality, privacy, safety, and proper chaperonage of women—and street, a public arena where class status and sexual purity might melt away in an instant. For bourgeois families, "nothing could be worse" than such a loss of traditional class- and gender-based identity.[44] The *moça perdida* parables dramatized this nightmare in a narrative that specifically addressed bourgeois women ("from good families" in both Matta's and *A Defesa Nacional*'s lexicons) and subsumed sexual loss of respectability and capitulation to communism. Young women, the stories presumed, once released into unchaperoned university life, would capitulate to seduction and to indoctrination and would, with their families, suffer the resultant disgrace and stigma. Just as Cold War moral panic updated the moral-hygienic, public health concerns of earlier decades, so—via these parables of errant womanhood—it inscribed traditional anxieties about public, private, and the cloistering of female family members into the theoretical struggle for Brazil's soul, a struggle that pitted righteous traditionalism against the inextricable forces of communism, sin, and chaos.

The cultural weightiness of this construction lent it power—and longevity. An esguiano informant, relating his recollections of the "war" on subversion to me in 2012, affirmed the potency of the putative seduction-as-recruitment scheme. Apparently unaware of the far Left's rejection of unconventional sexuality, my informant remembered a version of women's entrance into subversion that reproduced Muricy's tales of fallen women. Young women, sexually seduced, would join the enemies of the state, in a formulaic chain of events: "A young woman who was 'ahead' of her time, who did not worry about virginity. . . . She would find refuge among subversives, because there she wouldn't be censured. There . . . she would be perfectly within the limits of normality. She'd be easy prey [*presa fácil*] for subversives." Reverting to the terminology (*presa fácil*) of bygone decades, this esguiano attested the persistence of the idea that the route to subverting young women led through their virginity. The theoretical linkage of moral and political revolution, regardless of its pertinence to the lived experience of the armed Left, remains potent.[45]

A Defesa Nacional essays about youthful subversion took on a now-familiar transnational scope in that they included the same, extreme-right national and international references that had characterized similar contributions to the ESG canon. As we have seen elsewhere, these references sought to lend the weight of transnational authority to contentions about communist-style warfare's moral and unconventional nature. The domestic network of right-wing moralists whom we encountered in chapter 3 peppered the pages of *A Defesa Nacional*, as editors and authors cited, quoted, and reprinted Corção, Pacheco e Silva, and even TFP founder Plínio Correia de Oliveira.[46] International "experts" featured even more prominently. Suzanne Labin, for instance, cropped up in various contexts at *A Defesa Nacional*, confirming "amorality"—alongside "guerrilla" and "psychological warfare"—as a critical element of communist *guerra revolucionária*.[47] Journal contributors cited Labin, Fred Schwarz, Douglas Hyde, and J. Bernard Hutton, among others, expressly to justify constructions of communist warfare as an insidious, clandestine form of attack—with sexualized mass media among its core weapons.[48]

Monitoring "Subversive Activities": Intelligence and Police Forces

In the pages of national military journals, as at the ESG and among civilian right-wingers, anxieties about communist subversion fused with those about moral and cultural soundness, especially of Brazilian youth. If (as we shall see in chapter 6) such moralistic anticommunism generated not only censorship policy but also a national educational offensive; and if (as we have already established) many of the moralists who spoke and wrote at the ESG and in other forums held positions of national power and influence, countersubversives of less celebrity also engaged in a species of Cold War moral panic. Indeed, the primary foot soldiers of Brazil's war on subversion found themselves far removed, by rank and privilege, from the lofty retreats of the era's Alfredo Buzaids, Antônio Carlos Muricys, and Gustavo Corçãos. Police and intelligence work, the quotidian theater of war on the "internal enemy," constitutes another essential arena for investigating the meanings and definitions of (counter)subversion. Research in this realm presents, of course, challenges above and beyond the stumbling blocks in the sources with which we have dealt thus far. Surviving records tend to be partial, only marginally organized, and cryptic even when fully available. Nevertheless, my inquiry into reports generated by various police and intelligence agencies—the National Intelligence Service (SNI), the Department of Political and Social Order (DOPS, a federal political police force), the Army Intelligence Service (CIE), the Naval Intelligence Service (CENIMAR), the Air Force Intelligence Service (CISA), the federal police (DPF), and various components of Rio de Janeiro's civil police—demonstrates that the theory of sexualized subversion had, by the late 1960s, seeped into the framework of policing and spying. Increasingly, the security forces charged with securing the ideological frontiers of dictatorial Brazil saw those frontiers as congruent with the moral and cultural condition of the nation. Though paranoia about subversion led such warriors of national security to define subversion and subversives in the most wide-ranging of terms, there emerged a distinct tendency to interpret perceived moral and cultural deviance as "cryptocommunism."[49] When the state's shadowiest agents set out to do the work of violence, they were well attuned to the sexual, gender, and moral practice of suspected "internal enemies." Some went so far as to outline cultural cues for identifying subversives, implying that nonconformity could justify repression—an ironic, and certainly not very effective, approach to policing a Left that likewise eschewed sexual and stylistic unconventionality.

The reports left behind by these agencies show, on the one hand, that intelligence and police officials could classify nearly anything as subversion, from the most banal political conversation to mild social criticism, pamphleteering, graffiti, student activism, and even, in at least one case, complaints about public transit woes.[50] Indeed, a survey of reports from political police and intelligence services shows a notable, rather predictable focus on vaguely leftist speech, publications, and public demonstrations—but also an overwhelming, somewhat baffling concern with even the most seemingly insignificant of perceived infractions.

Such variation and seeming arbitrariness complicate, of course, the task of ascribing comprehensibility to police and intelligence workers' sense of their enemy. Nevertheless, certain trends do emerge, particularly in the records of the SNI and the military intelligence branches, where the doctrine of sexual and moral subversion had made significant headway by 1970. In patterns that reflected the countersubversive moral panic we have thus far witnessed, morality, culture, religion, and student activism—linked concerns, in the minds of intelligence officers—drew these agencies' attentions. Though it is sometimes difficult to gauge how low-ranking officials and operatives interpreted the moralistic admonitions of their superiors, the records show national and regional intelligence authorities' predilection for disseminating moralism among the guardians of their precincts. For example, of the SNI "Summary Evaluation" reports (distributed by the agency's national headquarters) from 1974, half dealt generally with the student movement, and half highlighted subversive sexuality and/or drug abuse. The report covering the period 15–24 June 1974 is illustrative in this regard. Its lexicon of "global" conspiracies, "psychosocial strategy," "professional leftists," and "target-public," like its focus on young people, mass media, the family, pornography, sexuality, and drugs, mimicked the discourse of moral technocrats discussed above. As the SNI's regional outposts learned from this report, "the diffusion—through the means of social communication—of sexual, erotic, and pornographic material is growing. In this picture we must include the evil deeds of professional leftists infiltrated in the different means of communication. Within our psychosocial strategy we must prevent the progressive capitulation of the target-public (Brazilian youth as a whole and the family in particular) in the face of this systematized and global aggression."[51] "Professional leftists," thus insinuated into the heart of public media, lay behind the progressive corruption of such media, a "psychosocial" catastrophe that linked communist subversion, drugs, criminal activity, and the "descent" into erotic deviance. Moreover, by the mid-1970s—as the tone of the above paragraph indicates—this argument had become routine among security forces. An army intelligence report, circulated between all the major spying and policing agencies in 1975, resorted to doctrinal, familiar terms: "It is well known that, in the communist scheme to conquer a people, there is . . . first and foremost the perversion of social and moral norms, . . . which is achieved by the exploitation of sex."[52]

Intelligence officials envisioned this sexually subversive campaign targeting youth not only through diffuse communications media, but through specific agents disguised as pedagogues. In fact, SNI and military intelligence accounts of subversive activity at Brazil's universities echoed the charges we have seen leveled by Sonia Seganfreddo, Pacheco e Silva, and the moralists of *A Defesa Nacional*, who depicted Marxist agents using sex and seduction to recruit unsuspecting young students. A special missive shared between the SNI, the Air Force Intelligence Service (CISA), and the Internal Security Division of the Ministry of Justice sought to enlighten state agents on "Faculty Activities Promoting Leftism Among Brazil's Student Population." At this point, after 1974, security forces' campaign of torture, disappearance, and counter-guerrilla maneuvering had virtually eradicated an armed Left once thousands strong. Yet this particular memo made no mention of the ideology and activity of those rebels, save a lone allusion to "nationalization of the economy." Instead, the report focused on a sort of origin myth for such revolutionaries, their creation via other "important themes" of "subversive action"—themes like "the family," "sex," and "drugs," which were presented as critical recruitment devices. SNI officials held that devious faculty were promoting dissolute moral attitudes vis-à-vis drugs, homosexuality, and the family, and using sex, drugs, and orgiastic parties to swell the ranks of student Marxists. Just as Muricy had accused university-level subversives of employing the "stimulus of sex," the report waxed explicit in describing the process by which innocent students might become Marxist dupes:

The professors propose the adoption of a "natural" and "realistic" attitude . . . toward the consumption of drugs, homosexuality, the disintegration of the family, and the principle of authority, etc. In practice, these professors . . . participate in get-togethers, impromptu parties [*festinhas*], etc., where homosexuality and the ingestion of drugs and hallucinogenics occur, and they [the professors] seek to demonstrate the absolute naturalness of these things, so as to corroborate what they have said in the classroom and, at the same time, gain the confidence of the students, decisive factors in the success of their work in recruitment.[53]

Drug-fueled homosexual orgies, then, ranked among the seductive tactics of the operatives that intelligence workers envisioned lying in wait for Brazil's youth. These *festinhas*, combined with in-class indoctrination, would function quite like the pornography, seduction, and general dissolution that Muricy, Pacheco e Silva, Seganfreddo, and a host of others had decried as the tools of subversion in the universities.

Internal security monitors' moral anxieties, however, extended far beyond the reaches of universities. The documents left behind by the SNI, CIE, DOPS, and other surveillance and enforcement organizations abound with conflations of political conspiracy and moral dissolution. The gender, sexual, and cultural issues that had garnered attention in other security forums—women's social roles, middle-class youth, communications media, family morality—tended here, too, to structure such conflations. Throughout the 1970s, intelligence officers' readings of Brazil's national security barometer were suffused with vague accusations about "communist infiltration in the means of communication," fomenting a "chronic problem" of pornography, with its "negative influence on the rearing of Youth."[54] Demonstrating the impact of these ideas not only on particular agencies but on the security apparatus as a whole, such documents were constantly shared and re-shared between military and civil police forces, operationalizing morally countersubversive theory in each of the nation's most powerful and impactful redoubts of state surveillance and violence. According to a 1972 report, distributed to all the regional SNI headquarters, the government public relations outfit, the National Security Council, and the country's principal military and ministerial intelligence agents, "an eroticist movement . . . a true sexolatry" demonstrated the presence of a Marxist plot, supported by Khrushchev and "in accordance with the quote from Lenin: *'demoralize the youth of a country and the Revolution is won.'*"[55]

Focusing on middle-class youth, intelligence agencies internally disseminated and shared shrill warnings about "*Hipies*" [sic], young people "mostly descended from traditional families" who sought to live in the most morally dissolute, "complete liberty"—and whose "apparent simplicity" disguised the "subversive character and tendencies" of this phenomenon. Indeed, a 1973 CIE memorandum warned that behind the "cover story" of hippie pacifism lay "another type of element, much more dangerous," calculatedly seeking to "contravene National Security itself."[56] DOPS and federal police officials, corroborating the conclusions of their military intelligence colleagues, saw hippies as a manifestation of the communist threat to young people. A 1970 memorandum shared between federal police from the Justice Department and the DOPS hierarchy in Rio de Janeiro traced the spread of hippies across the West, describing their tendency to corrupt young people. "'Hippies' have proliferated," the memo warned, "obtaining publicity in color photos in magazines, smoking marijuana, tainting the consciousness of the immature, and contributing to the destruction of youth's moral fiber." The police authors of this report strongly suspected a direct link between hippies and an international communist conspiracy, but they seemed unconcerned with proving such a link, given that hippies' putative moral deviance made their activities tantamount, a priori, to communist subversion. In fact, it was precisely hippies' departure from moral custom that made them so portentous to security workers. As the report concluded, "The 'Movement of Hippies' cannot be directly linked to the International Communist Movement, but [it can be linked] indirectly, because, [being] contrary to good customs and healthy social traditions, it benefits [the MCI] based on its ... dissolute character."[57] Thus, even if police and spies could not find any direct linkage between conspiratorial communists and hippies, they could *presume* such linkage existed, on the basis of moral deviance. The major work of countersubversion lay in fighting flesh-and-blood guerrillas in the Amazon and in Brazil's cities—and yet in 1970, at the height of repression, police construed counter- and hippie culture as parts of the selfsame "International Communist Movement" that motivated armed militants.

Indeed, general suspicion of counterculture among intelligence and police officials led them to denounce *contracultura* as such. Political police were particularly alarmed at the thought of a transnational "Countercultural Movement" linking Brazilian musicians and youths with like-minded, bohemian leftists in Argentina and Chile. Unsurprised army intelligence officers reported with derision on suspected leftists and exiles who adopted "extravagant clothing," unkempt hair or beards, communal or bohemian living, "the most complete sexual promiscuity," or, in one case, "long, blond hair, in the 'hippie' style; gold-rimmed glasses, in the 'hippie' style; extravagant and unbuttoned clothing, in the 'hippie' style."[58]

Moral and cultural unconventionality, thus equated with opposition to military national security, could be nowhere more apparent than in the increasing visibility of male homosexuality, something intelligence operatives saw as a subversive plot. Police had long associated sex between men with susceptibility to subversion—but as identitarian gay rights emerged in the late 1970s, these concerns evolved and grew more acute. To security forces, the *movimento gay*, or gay rights movement, and media attention to it, seemed part of a communist attempt to "normalize" same-sex desire. From this perspective, open gay rights represented a Marxist routinization of depravity, with the ultimate goal of concomitantly debilitating national sexuality and national security. Indeed, as James Green has pointed out, authorities during the dictatorship seemed most concerned with the *publicity* of male homosex.[59] The evidence in police archives indicates this concern emanated from the fear that such publicity reflected a moral component of guerra revolucionária. Hence reports denouncing "communist infiltration" of the media blamed such infiltration for coverage of the "*Movimento Gay*, which is nothing more than the *promotion of homosexuality*." For SNI-, CISA- and CIE-based evaluators of national security, the mass-media appearance of "*homosexual* or effeminate hairstylists, dressmakers, and social columnists" derived directly from communist plots against morality. The family, "mother cell of resistance" to the "spurious ideologies [and] activity of the MCI [International Communist Movement]," was under attack by gay-friendly media.[60]

Because of the publicity granted to sex and/or gender deviance by "hairstylists" and activists alike, the visibility of both was seen as an active Marxist campaign to subvert national morality. As one CIE report tendentiously put it—revealing the depth of implicit, presumed links— "the investment of communists in this proselytism *can well be imagined*." Those responsible for orchestrating Brazil's repressive agencies, then, operated under the assumption that moral and sexual change meant communist infiltration. According to one SNI report, communist-ridden "press organizations have begun to exploit, in a systematic way, the manifestation of such elements in Brazil. In this way, the 'Gay Movement,' which basically seeks the social recognition of homosexuals, has come to have a significant presence in our country, constituting [a] *threat* to the institution of the *family* and to *morality*, the very anchors of society."[61]

Generalized outrage about counterculture, gay rights, or other morality trouble led to accusations against individual targets of state surveillance and repression, fueling persecutions of people and organizations that had little or no connection to the clandestine Left. Artists, especially popular musicians appealing to young audiences, raised the hackles of agents from across the gamut of security forces. Stars like Nara Leão, Chico Buarque de Holanda, Egberto Gismonti, Ney Matogrosso, and Vinicius de Morães were accused of culturally disruptive "proselytism" in the service of an international conspiracy of communist youth.[62] SNI assessments identified celebrated actress Ruth Escobar as the subversive agent behind "the so-called 'Feminist Movement'" whose attempts to undermine Brazilian families, per the SNI, stemmed from the "special attention" granted this tactic by the "International Communist Movement."[63] As discussed above, Chico Buarque's play *Roda viva* drew the ire of censors and the violence of paramilitaries because its sexual subject matter was thought to threaten democracy. Buarque himself elected to leave for exile in 1970. Imprisoned and then banished the previous year, Caetano Veloso and Gilberto Gil (the singers who had pioneered Brazil's *Tropicália*, or Tropicalism, aesthetic in the 1960s) never received definitive explanation for their persecution. Yet Veloso, at the very least, had been on the radar of security forces because of his gender deviance—which CISA officials interpreted as *homossexualismo*.[64]

SNI higher-ups also denounced moral subversion in organizations, publications, and the most unlikely of cultural phenomena. Such was the case with several television corporations judged communist-infiltrated, including the Globo conglomerate—an ironic development, given Globo's well-known support for the regime.[65] National security reports took issue generally with Globo's reporting on male homosexuality, for the reasons noted above; but they also saw communism, for example, in the network's development of the "subversive" play *O berço do herói* and the telenovela it inspired (*Roque Santeiro*, censored before it could air). The reasons for censoring the novela included "love affairs; guys visiting young women after 11P.M.; tendencies toward Free Love; sabotage; civic disturbances; agitators convoking the people to participate [in protest]" and "references to terrorism."[66] In a letter, federal police chief Moacyr Coelho clarified that *Roque* and the novela *Gabriela* must be censored for reasons that blurred cultural and political security, because the novelas would "assault ... household [moral] standards" and thus "harm ... national dignity or interest."[67] Freely mingling cultural countersubversion with awareness of actual political opposition, SNI officials censored anti-regime periodicals *Opinião* and *Movimento* as "pornographic journals," representative of the plot of the "leftist press" to use pornography and tabloid for "the diffusion of their ideas."[68] In fact, SNI agents were wont to interpret any public, cultural, or moral aberration as global conspiracy; they even classified the brutal, sensational 1973 rape and murder of seven-year-old Ana Lídia Braga as part of such a plot. Wrought, as an SNI reckoning of "psychosocial" security would have it, by "drug-addicted sexual maniacs," the crime presented further "evidence" of a "global movement ... to corrupt the youth, with the goal of weakening national morality, according to the dictates of *guerra revolucionária*." Only a nationwide "campaign of moralization," the SNI report indicated, could restore national security.[69]

There was, then, sexually countersubversive outrage among those steering the country's various intelligence and police services in the 1970s—but police on the ground also took the theory of sex-as-subversion to heart. That is, observations of moral and sexual deviance figured in specific episodes of surveillance, condemnation, and/or arrest. Such observations were routine, and presumptive, and grew more shrill as moralists' power waned at higher levels. Take, for example, the 1981 case of a theater director, matter-of-factly accused by intelligence agents of "continuing her subversive activities" via "the processes employed by certain leftist organizations who are active in Brazil, principally among students, *that is, via promiscuity and sexual libertinism*." The investigating officers in this case were convinced that this director had tried to hatch an anarchic subversive plot—beginning with "hugging," "kissing," and an actress's "promiscuous" use of a toilet while in the company of other members of the theater troupe.[70]

In fact, wayward "girls" (for so security officials often called them) formed a particular node of concern for those who did the everyday work of surveillance and repression—concern that increased in 1968 and thereafter. This anxiety about the out-of-control sexual and gender behavior of middle- and upper-class women echoed the perceived "crisis of decency" of decades before.[71] Its latter-day pervasiveness brought something akin to the tales of young, female perdition via communist seduction—which we encountered above in incarnations from Muricy and *A Defesa Nacional*—to police reports and interagency correspondence. Among the most illustrative examples, the 1968 case of a university student (whom we shall call "Paula") demonstrates the ways in which police could link student activism to communism, seduction, and sexual ruination. The facts of the case, as compiled in a DOPS report of 27 November 1968, were sensational. A twenty-five-year-old social sciences student at Rio's Catholic University, Paula "was not possessed of great physical attractions" but did enjoy the privileges of wealth—her family lived on the exclusive Avenida Atlântica in Rio's southern littoral zone and "were people . . . of financial means." Paula's family had last heard from her when she telephoned from the airport on Monday, 7 October, to say that she and a male fellow student planned to travel to the soon-to-be-infamous National Student Union (UNE) Congress at Ibiuna, in southern São Paulo state. (On 12 October, police burst in, arrested hundreds of students, and broke up the congress, held in clandestinity because such gatherings, like UNE itself, were illegal at the time.) When she next appeared, at seven in the morning on Sunday, 13 October, Paula was getting out of a taxi, "with her nervous system in a desperate state, and completely covered with injection-marks." Committed to the Painel Psychiatric Hospital by an anonymous companion ("who rang the bell—and then fled"), Paula could never be induced to elucidate her fate, beyond repeating the phrase "he told me not to tell." Paula's family, likewise, did not wish to furnish details, fearing further damage to the girl's reputation and—according to DOPS agents—"reprisals from the students."

This apparent lack of any substantive information, however, did not discourage security agents from DOPS and CISA from drawing conclusions about Paula's fate. Observing, with a note of knowing triumph, that another young woman who had attended the Ibiuna congress had suffered a "nervous collapse" when the hundreds of students in attendance were arrested by security forces, the report affirmed that Paula must "have been lured to the UNE Congress and suffered a sexual assault" at the hands of student malefactors. This explanation seemed all the more likely when investigators affirmed that "the young woman had a history of psychiatric problems and was a communist."[72]

Branded victims of sexual subversion, its aggressive, gender-troubled agents, or both, women suspects suffered various modes of stigma. Even in cases less detailed and sensational than that of Paula, police reports often recreated something akin to the "lost girl" parables explored above in the context of *A Defesa Nacional*. Indeed, the Labor Ministry's intelligence force reported to the DOPS in October of 1970 that young women continued to become *subversivas* via a process hinging on sexual defilement. Describing a case in which a suspect allegedly lured young women into prostitution and subversion, the report concluded that such activity constituted the alarming "seduction or conduction of girls, very young girls, into subversive activities."[73] Yet more tellingly, DOPS reports nearly always ascribed sexualized subversion to female suspects and captives—young women whom DOPS agents inevitably described in terms of gender and sexual deviance, implying coterminous violations of moral, political, and legal codes of conduct. For example, a DOPS intelligence squad provided the following 1970 profile of an FNFi activist, whom we shall call "Laura": "She figures among those involved in the process of subversion of students in the State of Guanabara.... Among the women students she is the most dangerous, even persecuting and threatening her colleagues. She is violent and uses, when excited, the most lowbrow language. She is brazen, petulant, and highly revolutionary. She has cohabited with various male accomplices, but she married, after entering the Communist Party, another communist named João Magalhães."[74]

The "danger" that Laura posed, then, comprised "violence" and overt, aggressive subversion, as well as gender deviance (the unladylike language and the "brazen" attitude) and sexual promiscuity evidenced by her living habits—the mention of which might have seemed gratuitous had it not occurred in a context saturated with ideas about sexualized subversion. Indeed, some subversives were accused of even more scandalous sexual crimes. As early as 1966, political police in São Paulo warned that their rightist allies were at the mercy of a leftist operative who used her wiles to "seduce operatives of the Right in order to gain information" for her revolutionary superiors. DOPS agents vilified a female FNFi professor, labeling her a "known agitator" based on her subjection to a previous "inquest for practicing sexual acts with students inside the University." The duplicity of standards when it came to such gender and sexual deviance surfaced prominently in this report: though the report named four male accomplices, none suffered allusions to their sexualities, conventional or otherwise.[75]

The apparent gender imbalance in the prosecution of sexualized subversion did not, however, mean that male suspects were immune to similar conflations. If *A Defesa Nacional* warned against the sexual subversion of young men, police seemed keen to make connections between male suspects' subversive morality and politics. Indeed, despite an insistent, patriarchal focus on female suspects as sexual transgressors, records also show police willingness to conceive of male sexual or moral deviance— even outside the "gay movement"—as a symptom or component of actionable revolutionism. Police investigating suspects in a 1969 bank robbery attributed to armed militants from the group National Liberating Action (ALN) raided the upper-class home of a man whom they described as divorced and the lover of a single mother. A search of the suspect's house seemed to confirm his "subversive activities," as agents discovered that "in his luxurious home were to be found various obscene and pornographic images." This information was deemed important enough that army intelligence officials distributed it to various other agencies, including CISA, where the passage about pornography— bracketed and underlined—drew particular attention.[76]

Men were also the focus of moral countersubversion when security forces turned their gaze on the progressive clergy—generally portrayed, unlike female subversives, as aggressors rather than victims of sexual subversion. Kenneth Serbin has pointed out the ways in which priestly celibacy became the subject of politicized debate in the 1960s and 1970s— but intelligence officials investigating the progressive clergy had much more on their minds. Priests who leaned or appeared to lean left drew the ire and suspicion of the state's security foot soldiers not so much for engaging in anti-celibacy activism as for sexually subverting young people. After extensive investigation of priests in the Diocese of Barra do Piraí, for example, army intelligence agents informed their superiors of a litany of clerical offenses against the desired moral-political order. The lead investigative officer explained that "there are, in this area, various facts, linked to morality, that touch fundamentally on the bishop and the priests of the Diocese. They [the facts] are presented here, since one of the forms of subverting is, precisely, that of promoting and permitting moral degradation." Military intelligence officials reported, among other pertinent "facts," that one priest had distributed a sex education book entitled *Sex and Adolescence*, advocating communism alongside male and female masturbation; another priest had apparently been seen in a swimsuit in close proximity to young women. These and other "moral irregularities" were clear evidence, to the investigating agents, of communist subversion.[77]

Such surveillance thus incorporated sexuality as a reliable strand in a web of suspicion and incrimination. Police work emanating from this web had direct, repressive consequences, leading to censorship, loss of employment, and detainment in the fearsome machinery of the state; notably, the sexualized examples above cluster around the period of heightened repression after 1968. The São Paulo socialite whose luxuries included "pornography" may have had concrete ties to the ALN—ties that would certainly explain his ultimate arrest, torture, and exile. Even so, intelligence agents evaluating the case granted special attention to his "obscene and pornographic images." CISA and DOPS accused the above-mentioned university professor of using "homosexual and heterosexual acts" to "spiritually and sexually corrupt" students, leading them to "adopt a truly abject type of life, including declaring [themselves] openly communist." Removed from her position in 1968, she was arrested and subsequently went into exile. No doubt her personal links with leftists and her history of student activism were key factors in her fate—and yet her alleged sexual transgressions were the only infractions to appear in her 1970 police file.[78] The putatively dissolute priests in Barra do Piraí were relieved of their duties, too, as security officials and conservative clerics advocated their dismissal from the diocese. It is impossible to determine precisely how much weight security workers lent to imputations of moral and sexual deviance in such cases. Remarkably, however, accusations and/or observations of deviance appear to have seamlessly confirmed, awakened, or deepened police suspicions of individuals' "subversive activity," based on an ideological framework that presumed linkages between pornography, homosex, "sexual corruption," and the workings of a nefarious, global communist conspiracy.

If these ideas had the power to affect such repressive processes, how did they gain ground in this milieu and circulate among the guardians of the regime's dungeons? The driving concern with sex as subversion filtered into the various security forces not only via their leadership—that is, via the advocacy of national officials from the intelligence services—but also by way of on-the-ground agents' exposure to and affinity for the exponents of moral countersubversion whom we have encountered above. By the early 1970s, Corção, Pacheco e Silva, Muricy, TFP, Moral Re-Armament, and other advocates of moralism enjoyed esteem and even celebration within the ranks of the regime's spies and enforcers. Corção, for example, appeared across the gamut of security records as both inspiration and sage; admirers in the intelligence services referred to him as an expert on subversive tactics and even rallied behind him as an embattled leader, victimized by "a Global Plan from the Subversive Movement in the realm of Revolutionary Warfare, to neutralize the influence of writers and intellectuals who publicly contest . . . the psychological campaigns of that Movement."[79] Indeed, several security agencies recommended and even distributed the writings of Corção and other conservative Catholic activists. In April of 1971, officials from CISA asserted that articles by Plínio Correia de Oliveira and Gustavo Corção "represent part of the psychological action developed by this agency" against communism, and SNI agents in São Paulo were so taken with the moralistic anticommunism of Corção and Lenildo Tabosa Pessoa that they claimed these journalists as key "allies" in the war on subversion, especially when it came to articles on such illustrative themes as pornography, morality, communism, and authoritarianism. The conservative magazines *Hora Presente* and *Permanência*, noted a secret security memo in São Paulo, "support the interests of the Revolution of March of 1964, coinciding in . . . ideological, philosophical, and spiritual objectives. For examples, we suggest the reading of the following articles: 'Subversive Warfare and Revolutionary Warfare'; 'From Pornography to Desacralization,' 'Cinema and [Communist] Revolution'; and 'Military Force and Christian Love.'"[80]

Likewise, Muricy made his way into political policing, directly affecting the tenor and tactics of countersubversive operations. When he announced the results of his psychological profiling of subversives, federal police in São Paulo tried to operationalize those findings. A 1971 directive circulated among agents from several security forces in São Paulo state (including the fearsome CODI, or Center for Internal Defense Operations) affirmed that "terrorists . . . of both sexes" could be identified by family "traumas" and "problems in the realm of sexuality."[81] More than a decade later, after the end of dictatorship, one of the first major pro-regime memoirs defended extrajudicial measures in terms of Muricy's "studies," specifically the linking of youthful subversion to "psychological maladjustment," "broken homes," "drugs, prostitution (homosexuality, lesbianism) [sic], pornography."[82] So strong was this connection that it colored hard-liners' contemporary interpretations of even the most spectacular acts of resistance and terrorism: the 1969 kidnapping by armed leftist guerrillas of the U.S. ambassador to Brazil, Charles Burke

Elbrick. In a compendious report intended to explain the kidnapping, chief investigator General Tasso Villar de Aquino traced the "transformation of a young student into a terrorist at the service of communism"—a path that led, according to his and other reports, directly through the sexual corruption of adolescents by "agents of communism."[83]

Adolpho João de Paula Couto, among the most extreme of moralistic exponents, demonstrates the importance of such ideas to security practitioners. His work appeared in intelligence reports to underscore what he called "subversives' combination of themes of moral order with those of social and political order." More importantly, his essays and reports and books were forwarded and exchanged between police and intelligence agents, in a testament to his impact. When he fired off letters and reports denouncing homosexuality, women's liberation, black power, "the dissolution of the family, free love, the degradation of women, and . . . the moral dissolution of society," Paula Couto did not go unheeded. His letters reached officials at the Division of Censorship of Public Diversions, the Ministry of Justice Intelligence Service, CISA, and the Ministry of Education—and were circulated by these officials to agents and bureaucrats at other levels and in other branches of enforcement.[84]

Indeed, the stimulation of a morally counterrevolutionary crusade reached new, rather more formal heights with the distribution of materials specifically intended to instruct intelligence agents in the work of identifying and repressing moral subversion. In 1969, for example, cadets at several training institutions received excerpts from *Brazilian Catholic Radicalism*, by Alessio Ulisses Floridi, one of a series of alarmist, anti-Soviet analyses written by this Jesuit priest. The distribution of excerpts ostensibly intended to alert the anticommunist "Revolutionaries of 1964" to the dangers posed by moral subversion in the church. Like other sources linking progressivism to dissipation, the excerpt eschewed the celibacy debate, in favor of informing trainees about the moral and political perils represented by abortion and homosexuality. The danger, especially in the latter case, was that proponents would succeed in "normalizing" these "vices," precipitating a fateful social dissolution.[85]

The circular *São Paulo por Dentro*, meanwhile, was privately published and might at first glance have seemed the ravings of a fanatical civilian. Sent regularly to the DOPS intelligence chief by a pro-repression informant, *São Paulo por Dentro* sought to "present a panoramic, political-social view of São Paulo, focusing especially on the communist-subversive-terrorist aspect." The informant (whom I pseudonymously call "Fábio") reacted to the chaos he saw gestating in São Paulo in 1970; he sketched a metropolis beset by subversives bent on concomitant terrorism and moral profligacy. "Terrorists," the pamphlet read, engaged in "scenes of bacchanalia and libidinousness," celebrating the "victories of terrorism" by treating themselves to lavish sensual pleasures and cavorting "half-naked, caressing women and drinking poolside." Rote blasphemy rounded out the subversive program, whose adherents allegedly owned a poster that showed Saint Joseph kissing the Virgin Mary, followed by the question "Is she really a virgin?" The link between sexual blasphemy and revolutionary subversion seemed patent: "*As you can see*," wrote Fábio, "this [poster] is plainly subversion on the march!" This sensationalism did not prevent *São Paulo por Dentro* from having an impact on political police; police archives include dozens of issues of the pamphlet, and DOPS, SNI, and CODI units circulated its information between themselves.[86]

More ambitious even than *São Paulo por Dentro*, a full "theoretical and practical dictionary" of "National Security and subversion," 350 pages in length, emerged in 1977, authored by police delegate Zonildo Castello Branco and published by Rio de Janeiro's secretariat of public safety. It is impossible to know the extent to which the dictionary impressed Castello Branco's colleagues—but it nevertheless reveals the vision of subversion espoused (and disseminated) by a police official responsible for street-level enforcement. Castello Branco—and his dictionary—brought into the realm of practice the moralistic and sexualized vision of (counter)subversion that had gained such purchase at higher levels of government. The author's introductory note warned readers that the "tactics, methods, and diversified achievement of subversive actions" made his dictionary an absolute necessity for "each police officer"—a sort of everyday policeman's guide to the world of subversion. This guide defined the Cold War as psychological and moral, waged across battlefields of gender, sexuality, and the mores of young people. "Marxist propaganda," the dictionary averred, "seeks to destroy the family," and only widespread civilian "defense of morality and of good customs" might stave off this effect. In the dictionary entry for "Communism," Castello Branco described an international conspiracy with which we are now familiar—one that sought an utter debasement of morality, especially that of youth: "The objectives of the MCI [are to be achieved] by dismantling traditional values, by physical and psychological wearing-down, . . . by the implantation of communist values [which include] (1) the creation of social instability, by means of an excessive valorization of youth, . . . a 'youth power'; (2) the destruction of moral and spiritual values . . . through the promotion of free love, the exploitation of sex, disrespect for parents, . . . and belittlement of religious sentiment, etc."[87]

True to form, Castello Branco's *Dictionary* exhibited allegiance to fellow rightists in Brazil and abroad. Referring to a group of allies who shared his "patriotic" perspective, Castello Branco listed the LDN, the Anti-Communist Movement (MAC), and TFP; he expressed sympathy for the Command for Hunting Communists (CCC) and the ADESG, whose primary objective, he wrote, was to "preserve and project moral values." Indeed, the influence of the ESG itself surfaced in the dictionary's repeated citations not only of early-1970s ESG intellectual production but of the institution itself as a source of "constant perfection" of the Doctrine of National Security. When it came to the transnational coterie of anticommunist alarmism, Castello Branco showed himself well versed, borrowing widely from the likes of Suzanne Labin and J. Bernard Hutton.[88]

Conclusion

Zonildo Castello Branco's chilling solidarity with the violent CCC mirrored other moralistic conservatives' penchants for harsh repression. Security forces, of course, engaged in the quotidian work of capturing, torturing, and eliminating the enemies of the military state. This work often focused on the nitty-gritty, rather than the ideology, of countersubversion—on eliciting names, locations, and the structure of clandestine organizations. Then, too, in many cases the state's most committed enemies equally eschewed moral and sexual unconventionality. Yet the narrative of repression as a response to deviance persisted in police discourses, both classified and published. *São Paulo por Dentro*, outraged at police officials' failure to repress subversion, spoke with unstinting praise of the newly created Operation Bandeirantes (OBAN), whose infamous investigators and torturers ushered in a new era of corrupt, extralegal, and terror-laden policing in Brazil.[89] In *A Defesa Nacional*, the serial "Getting to Know the Internal Enemy" suggested new, preventive measures to protect youth from communist machinations. Still, the series insisted that direct repression remained necessary to "eliminate old militants and those who are already contaminated," objects of potential state violence whom the author identified as "errant and extravagant."[90] Just as Corção had sanctioned "good violence" against those who "ought to be punished, ought to be mercifully castigated," and just as Cardinal Jaime de Barros Câmara had warned against any "mercy" for those who "must pay," countersubversives in the military and police milieus we have explored in this chapter saw moral catastrophe not only as a ramification of subversion but also as a constituent justification for violent repression in the name of state security.

The saga of Colonel Carlos Alberto Brilhante Ustra, whose recollections opened this chapter, exemplifies the ways in which this vision of subversion continues to influence certain memories constructed around the turbulent events of the 1960s and 1970s. As of this writing, Ustra has just died, taking to the grave his controversial insistence that he and his companions "fought to preserve democracy . . . against terrorism." Until the last, Ustra joined ex-colleagues and partisans in contesting the nature and details of the violence they perpetrated; the colonel denied that state-sponsored torture ever happened, famously observing that "excesses occur in every war."[91] Yet Ustra, like others, did not hesitate to recall this "war" against subversion as an exercise in moral recuperation—read, in his case, onto the style, moral choices, bodies, and sexualities of young men and women. In his 2006 *The Suffocated Truth*, Ustra hearkened back to his testimony before a military tribunal thirty-five years earlier, around the time that repression peaked. Surely Ustra's legal jeopardy and legacy (not to mention the intervening decades) affected his latter-day account. Remarkably, however, the colonel's 1971 testimony, like his 2006 book, celebrated moral recuperation as a sign of victory over subversion. Referring to ex-political prisoners, Ustra testified that "they have demonstrated true repentance. . . . Some, for example, beyond having returned to their old boyfriends or old girlfriends (who did not share their [leftist] ideas), are now ready to get engaged."[92] Conventional sexuality, cemented by the marriage pact, would serve as proof positive that these youths had left subversion behind.

As we saw in the previous chapter, such attitudes emerged quite strongly at the ESG, where nationally respected intellectuals praised repression as a warranted response to moral crisis. The kind of thinking that led to such assessments of the national security situation extended, as this chapter has demonstrated, well beyond the ESG, to other forums of defense theory and even enforcement. Security workers, from the exalted corridors of military and governmental hierarchy to the police delegates in charge of everyday operations, shared and deployed a vision of subversion and countersubversion that fused these categories with morality, sexuality, and gender. In the chapter that follows, we shall investigate a public, legislative arena in which moralistic right-wingers promoted their vision for Brazil's moral-cultural path: Moral and Civic Education, the pet project of those who sought to morally "immunize" Brazil's youth against the dangers of subversion.

6

Brazil Counts on Its Sons for Redemption

Moral, Civic, and Countersubversive Education

Another mania of that period was *Moral and Civic Education*. Many of
the generals thought that all the national problems resulted from the
fact that children no longer received this material in school, as they
had in the old days.

—General José Maria de Toledo Camargo, former military
  government spokesman

Moral and Civic Education is the psychological labor that the
Government is doing together with Brazilian youth, with the aim
of arming youth ideologically, cultivating its spirit of Brazilianness,
enabling national democratic indoctrination, strengthening our
regime, preserving our history, and responding in that form to the
Marxist and Communist-Socialist indoctrination. That is why
communists react so strongly against Moral and Civic Education.

—Secret report from the Ministry of Justice Intelligence
  Division, 1971

In October 1971, General Moacir de Araújo Lopes, whom we witnessed
in chapter 5 denouncing subversive "exhibitionism," "fellatio," and
"anal eroticism," wrote a brief for the National Commission on Morality and Civics (CNMC), of which he was a highly influential, founding
member.[1] Lopes opened with a parable, meant as a call to arms: a teacher
at a certain Brazilian public school had assigned a book entirely unsuit-
able, to Lopes's mind, for her eighteen-year-old students. As the brief
explained, the book "reveals the extreme gravity of the state to which
Western Civilization has descended in terms of morality," a state which
bore comparison to "Babylon, the great prostitute of the Apocalypse."
Stressing the dimensions of moral and sexual outrage, Lopes mused that
Satan "is loosed among us, with his entourage of lubricity, filth, and
degradation." As for the book itself, Lopes provided few specifics, beyond pronouncing it debauched and concomitantly subversive. The
book "represented the most vile, ignoble, filthy, low, nauseating, and

unclassifiable material of which the human mind is capable"; promoted a "bordello-like mental atmosphere" among the young women who read it; and constituted "the gravest of moral crimes," primarily because its author was the "equivalent of . . . the disciples of the perverse and irresponsible Herbert Marcuse, the philosopher of the Hippies." As if to drive home the conflation of "lubricity," counterculture, and political disloyalty, Lopes quoted recent Brazilian laws affirming obscenity's threat to national security and insisted that the book was "all the more subversive because it ridicules the Family [and] the Armed Forces."[2]

This brief introduced yet another element in the history of sexualized subversion: a solution beyond those we have thus far noted (censorship, calls for retaliatory violence, and police monitoring of morality and sexuality). Lopes called for "the most severe repression" in such cases, but he used this parable chiefly to promote a new program that he designed and administered: Moral and Civic Education (EMC). Mandated at all levels of Brazilian education by Decree-Law 869 of September 1969, this new discipline showed the federal policy-making influence of countersubversive moralism. To oversee the program, the law also created the CNMC, a nine-member body appointed by the president. This quickly became a bastion of archconservatism. EMC, in other words, enshrined the perspectives and preoccupations of anticommunist moral panic in a program created and managed by such panic's adherents. As Lopes put it, EMC intended to combat subversive, Marcusian "lubricity," the "waves of moral depravity" that threatened "a free fall into the utter foundering of morality."[3]

Extant scholarship has begun the work of unpacking and contextualizing EMC, noting its breadth, conservative fundaments, and importance, and even hinting at the program's connections to Brazil's legacy of authoritarianism.[4] Yet EMC, I contend, represented more than the developmentalism, the general, statist patriotism, or the vague, Catholic fundamentalism that others have rightly observed. Conceived quite explicitly as a weapon to be deployed against the ever-vilified communist guerra revolucionária, EMC emanated from the most conservative, moralistic sectors of the Brazilian security establishment. Moral anticommunists, among them those we have already encountered, supported the program as a solution to "the youth problem," the destruction of the family, corrupt media, and other putatively communist-inspired means of moral subversion.

As a survey of debates about EMC reveals, the program's architects and champions viewed it as a direct response to the perceived sexual and moral subversion we have thus far discussed. EMC hearkened back to previous exponents of authoritarian reform—older Catholic, right-wing, and even fascist ideologues. This tradition in EMC codified a legacy of moralistic, biosocial conservatism championed by hygienicist and patriotic reformers of the early twentieth century as well as by those latter-day countersubversives whom we have seen pathologize notions of subversion. In many ways, the program's institutionalization fulfilled the hopes of generations of such conservative reformers, whose attempts to legally mandate conservative Catholic morality, biopolitical control, and anticommunism had hitherto met with only limited success. As we saw in chapter 1, the far-right, often deeply religious morality of certain actors in this earlier period did not achieve the installation of moral and civic instruction as a discipline; but the latter-day military regime brought the agendas of such actors to life in EMC, a Cold War program designed for the mass manufacture of a Brazilian subject idealized by a long tradition of elitists, reactionaries, and authoritarianists.

Patriotic, morally and sexually traditionalist, conventionally gendered (overwhelmingly masculine or—when female—devoted to cultivating patriotic masculinity), physically and mentally vigorous, and enthusiastic about civil and military service, this subject would not only fulfill the expectations of reformers dating back to the 1910s, but would (as a result of these qualities) staunchly resist communist subversion—or so the program's designers hoped. Much like these earlier expectations, EMC incorporated signal anxieties about girls and women—but did so in a way that marginalized them as instruments for the production of masculinity; gender trouble among women, in other words, was a major problem, but principally insofar as it affected men. EMC did not, of course, actually foment the universal remoralization that its proponents sought—it did not, for example, remove sexuality from public culture. By the late 1970s, moralists' triumph at instituting EMC gave way to insecurities about its effectiveness. Certain hard-liners blamed bad teaching and suggested further retrenchment. Nevertheless, the program does represent a remarkably far-reaching attempt to actualize visions of moral countersubversion and of its ideal soldier-citizens. In the latter section of this chapter, I rely on EMC textbooks to assess the extent to which this idealized subject made his (rarely, as we shall see, her) way into curricula and classroom materials. Pre- and proscriptions designed to create a masculinized, moral, hygienic, subversion-proof *brasileiro* surfaced in the schoolbooks of Brazilian children.

Constructing a "Protective Shield"

In twentieth-century Brazil, the fate of moral and civic education reflected the controversy and political passion that consistently surrounded it. Officially instituted in 1925 as Moral and Civic Instruction, the discipline underwent successive cycles of modification, abandonment, and revivification before its return to the mandatory curriculum in 1969. Significantly, this renaissance of morality and civics in the national educational agenda stemmed from the efforts of hard-line institutions and individuals with whom we are already familiar. From its embryonic stages, the 1960s movement to reestablish EMC made anticommunist moral panic its motivation and primary idiom. As early as 1965, future president and hard-liner Arthur da Costa e Silva began agitating for the return of moral and civic instruction—on the grounds that modernity, gender trouble (working women), and communism had debilitated the natural source of such instruction (the family) and thus imperiled national security. "The modern family," Costa e Silva wrote, "facilitates . . . the implantation and evolution of Guerra Revolucionária, such that, disturbed by economic and social changes, [the family] can no longer complete . . . its educational function. Frequently dissociated, particularly by dint of the work of women outside the home, its members are forced to operate outside of a traditional family structure." A moral and civic education program, he continued, would minimize the moral and political risks of the situation, instilling discipline, family values, and work ethic.[5]

These concerns, thus present at the outset of the regime, gained intensity and traction as the 1960s progressed. In late 1967, then-president Costa e Silva and Education Minister Tarso Dutra created a special commission explicitly to address the problems of "agitation" among Brazilian students and suggest measures for its elimination. General Jorge Boaventura, whose outrage at an "aggressive sea of pornography and licentiousness" appeared in *A Defesa Nacional*, formed part of the commission; and über-moralist General Carlos de Meira Mattos headed the group, lending it his name. Accordingly, the group's report (released just as protests intensified in 1968) adhered to moralistic, anticommunist standards, focusing on moral concerns and linking them implicitly to "democracy." Indeed—and here lay the rub, from Meira Mattos's point of view—there was "no way to regulate the in-class promotion of ideas [that are] *antidemocratic and contrary to morality*."[6] Advocating the educational reform that would eventually lead to EMC, Costa e Silva and the commission seemed bent on bringing hard-line morality into the classroom to address the concomitant problems of the immoral and the "antidemocratic," categories made tantamount by moral panic.

Costa e Silva and the Meira Mattos Commission, responding to moral and social change as well as to the acute crises of 1967–69, gave rise to the immediate impetus for reinstituting EMC: an ADESG-based working group that developed the legislative framework for Decree-Law 869.[7] Eloywaldo Chagas de Oliveira and Humberto Grande—both, as we shall see, eminent moralists and administrators of EMC—joined the above-quoted General Lopes at the helm of this working group, its perspective epitomized by its founder, adesguiano Wilson Regalado Costa.[8] Proudly remembering his role in reinvigorating EMC, Costa affirmed that the discipline was to serve as a bulwark against moral/Marxist subversion. Indeed, Costa held that anyone who did not support the reinstitution of EMC must be "pro-communist," a "sympathizer," or in fact "Marxist." The pre-1969 lack of a formal, curricular discipline for EMC, he continued, was "exactly what inspired and oriented the materialist avalanche" that had so disturbed him and his compatriots in the late 1960s. Reiterating the connection between subversion and moral and spiritual failure, Costa claimed that EMC's neglect had been the work of communists, "part . . . of an 'insidious technique' that many unwittingly accepted, playing right into the hands of the enemies of the Fatherland, of the Family, and of Religion."[9]

The discipline's founding and governing intellectuals published volumes of work confirming their vision of EMC as a moral weapon in guerra revolucionária. EMC, these thinkers confirmed, meant to redress moral crisis and to fight precisely the categorical problems (wayward youth, deviant sexuality, gender nonconformism, "pornographic" media) we have seen spark anticommunist moral panic in the late 1960s and early 1970s. Moral education activist and fellow CNMC founder Arthur Machado Paupério, for example, luridly elaborated the moral crisis in an essay on the "purposes" of EMC: "We are living in a time of an incredible crisis of moral principles. . . . The decadence of customs accompanies the uncertainty of principles that have guided human life since time immemorial.... Young people are undergoing an exceedingly grave crisis of moral dimensions. The incidence of criminality, of uninhibited sex, of drug abuse, and of materialism . . . among young people . . . has created an avalanche . . . that saps the remaining healthy energies."[10] Beyond these evocations of abandoned tradition and moral-sexual deviation, Paupério recurred to the time-honored (indeed, anachronistic) bugbear of the "third sex"—mingling, like other exponents of moral crisis, deviant sexuality, unconventional gender, and eugenics-style decadence (the vague, sapped "energies") in a vision of moral decline and chaos.[11]

Other CNMC members clarified that it was precisely because young people were so taken with sex and materialism that EMC must succeed—to concomitantly reinstate traditional morality and save Brazil from communist subversion. Geraldo Bezerra de Menezes (erstwhile president of the CNMC) affirmed that "we are living today in open guerra revolucionária" that could only be combated with "morality and civics" as a mandatory subject-course. EMC, then, meant to counteract the moral crisis, itself a direct result of communist revolutionary infiltration; moreover, it was to do so by addressing the quotidian behavior of citizens-in-training. Menezes delineated the "psychosocial agenda of the CNMC": to create, in EMC, an "instrument for the perfection of customs." This "instrument" would counteract the "moral permissiveness" wrought by communists' "ideological warfare." Such permissiveness featured "drug abuse, eroticism, violence, . . . the degradation of the family, . . . corruption, perversion, and subversion"—evils, which, he made clear, held "our civilization . . . suspended at present between salvation and the abyss." The choice, then, was clear: EMC and moral salvation—or perversion and the collapse of civilization via "ideological warfare."[12]

In the tense period surrounding its 1969 mandate and subsequent implementation, EMC's architects (like contemporaneous national security forums) saw such "ideological warfare" not only in youthful sex and drug abuse, pornography, and cataclysmic permissiveness, but in the emergence of an appalling "modern woman." Like many ideologues troubled about gender, these thinkers worried less about women themselves than about abandonment of women's role as stewards of their (presumably male) progeny. Communism, affirmed EMC's planners, sought to destroy marriage via the "emancipation of Woman: it separates her from domestic life, [and] makes her neglect her children."[13]

Humberto Grande, founding member of the CNMC, blamed subversive revolutionism for a Western plague of "gender inversion." His prescriptive guide *Moral and Civic Education of Women*, reiterating fears about degeneracy via the "third sex," denounced "pathological cases of man-woman and woman-man, the result of confusion and sexual indifferentiation... a phenomenon of decadence, and of the inexorable death of a people." EMC was to combat such revolutionist decadence via retrocession to a premodern moral past, precluding the development of "woman-man" and "emancipated woman." Grande longed for "the respect that was had for Woman in the Middle Ages," which "made that period... one of the most healthful in the history of human development."[14] Because guerra revolucionária had taken women away from their proper place at the homebound helm of moral and civic instruction, official, state-mandated EMC would have to step in as what Lopes called "a protective shield against the attacks of international communism."[15] These ruminations, all of them appearing between 1967 and 1974, clarify a key point in EMC, consonant with other arenas of moral panic. Though women were, as we have seen, a major node of anxiety, that anxiety did not displace the masculinity of the ideal *brasileiro*. The trouble with "modern woman," here as elsewhere, in the 1970s as in the 1930s, was her "neglect" of child-rearing, with its implications for "healthful human development" and the potential "death of a people."

Rounding out the established litany of rightist moral plaints, EMC's proponents and administrators affirmed that mass media and guerra revolucionária would form central nodes of cultural countersubversion.[16] In 1970, shortly after its inception, CNMC developed an "emergency" plan to redress the "state of affairs observed in the Western world today, the results of the exacerbation of sex and violence" wrought by "social-radical context" and "foreign ideologies." EMC sought to combat the influence on youth of "mass communication—TV, radio, cinema, theater, magazines, journals—[which] profoundly perturb the educational efforts in the moral and civic arena." The CNMC mandated lessons on communist warfare, making the link between immorality, mass media, and subversive, "foreign ideologies" clear even in the prescribed curriculum. EMC courses were to cover "the importance of the psychosocial field in *Guerra Revolucionária*. Propaganda and counter-propaganda. National Security. Internal Security. The International

Communist Movement. The international communist fronts. Operations against subversion."[17]

EMC as Countersubversive Rallying Point

This vision of (and plan for) EMC as a savvy, wide-ranging armament against moral subversives suffused the top minds not only of EMC administration itself but also of moralistic countersubversion in milieus across Brazil's national security apparatus. The crisis-mongers of the security forums and forces discussed above promoted EMC as a quintessential solution for that familiar litany of concerns—youth, sexuality, "modern" women, public morality, and pathology. They saw EMC as the spearhead of a moralizing campaign that (like their shared moral-hygienic anxieties) linked the moralistic anticommunists who supported EMC with rightist reformers of decades past. General Antônio Carlos da Silva Muricy himself, whose nationally published "psychological profiles of subversives" pathologized youthful rebellion, demonstrated the readiness of fervent moral countersubversives to champion EMC as an ideal solution. Muricy recommended EMC—alongside psychotherapy in the most acute cases of sexualized subversion—as the solution to the problem of massive adolescent subvertibility. "The base of our [countersubversive] work," Muricy reported, "should be giving youth a solid moral structure" via EMC, "a vigorous element for the defense [of youth]." Muricy's report affirmed, via "scientific" study, that "solid moral structure" and the values enshrined in the traditional family home made for the most effective shield against subversion. He and others pointed to EMC as the means of providing such a shield. In the words of one esguiano, the 1969 EMC legislation would save Brazil's "children [from] *ideological and moral* subversion."[18]

Esguianos' general fidelity to the hard-line precepts of Costa e Silva and of EMC's administrative intellectuals makes sense, given the institutional and personal closeness between the ESG and the EMC establishment. Multiple members of the CNMC and the Federal Education Council (CFE, a government body that shared authority over EMC) studied or even taught at the school, including, of course, some whom we have already encountered.[19] Indeed, CNMC co-commissioners Moacir de Araújo Lopes and Adolpho João de Paula Couto used their time *at* the ESG to develop Moral and Civic Education.[20] Paula Couto, praising Lopes himself as the "driving force" of the CNMC, wrote a term paper in which he linked the commission's curricular program to the campaign to "combat the patent effects of the agents of Guerra Revolucionária within the schools." Demonstrating the ways in which EMC proponents conceived of their project in transnational context, Paula Couto quoted Fred Schwarz, J. Edgar Hoover, and well-known French tactical theorists on the ways that religious faith and "Western values" must form the primary defense against communist subversion.[21] The singularity of institutional vision between the ESG and EMC administrators only increased as official collaborations "offered the opportunity for further integration between the CNMC and the ESG." The CNMC established exchange programs with the ESG, where the commission's assessors participated in ESG courses, while CNMC members were invited to publish theses and give lectures at the ESG and ADESG.[22]

Right-wing moralists of all stripes joined in enthusiasm for EMC. Civilian right-wing organizations, including Moral Re-Armament and the National Defense League, also offered their public support, the former going so far as to send representatives to "place the Moral Re-Armament Movement at the disposition of the CNMC." Marília Mariani, who had contributed to *A Defesa Nacional*'s series on youth in crisis, delighted in the prospect of moral and civic education, which she saw as a means of preparing boys for the military and girls for homemaking. She lauded EMC in a speech at the First South American Congress of Women in Defense of Democracy—organized by CAMDE, the group of women who in 1964 had led pro-coup marches of the "Family, with God, for Liberty."[23]

CAMDE itself had always championed "remoralization" as a means of fighting communism. As noted above, its mid-1960s, anticommunist youth clubs in Rio de Janeiro and São Paulo sought goals including "religious and familiar education" alongside the "moralization" of media.[24] Mariani and CAMDE underscored the prevailing notion that EMC should resolve gender trouble among women largely for the sake of relegating them to the role of homebound cultivators. Most EMC texts specifically prescribed military service for young men, yet only a handful contained equal or correspondent measures for young women, and then only in the service of patriotic motherhood. Mariani, for example, vaguely suggested that female students should visit "orphanages" as training to become productive "citizens and homemakers."[25] *A Defesa Nacional*, meanwhile, brimmed with contributions and editorials celebrating EMC as the solution to the moral "involution" putatively instigated by communists. The magazine's guide to "Getting to Know the Internal Enemy," having listed literal seduction as one of the principal "reasons that impel youth toward subversion," suggested EMC as an immediately necessary solution.[26]

Key state functionaries also got into the act, championing and monitoring EMC at the various levels of overt and covert governance. Public relations chief Hernani d'Aguiar lauded EMC as a way of counteracting "the explosion of instincts that we are experiencing," and Minister of Education Jarbas Passarinho backed the program as a redress for the moral crisis in which "the entire world is subjugated to a propaganda centered around eroticism [and] the appeal to sex."[27] As indicated by this chapter's epigraph, such ideas were widespread at the top levels of the military regime. Yet lower-level security forces, including spies and police, also displayed marked concern with EMC. Intelligence agents classified EMC as a defensive measure to keep "young people from being criminally induced to engage themselves in the subversive-communist process." A 1970 brief urged cooperative action, as the situation "demands that we in the Brazilian Air Force take care to develop a true program of Moral and Civic Education, which can be obtained from and oriented by the National Commission on Morality and Civics, which utilizes sectors specialized in the Implantation and Maintenance of Doctrine."[28] The watchers assigned to surveil and curtail any student activism at the University of Brasília, meanwhile, were yet more explicit about these connections. By 1976, spies at the university were convinced that the MCI (the abbreviation referring to an imagined, well-articulated "International Communist Movement") had "flagella that especially attack the youth of developing countries: drugs; moral licentiousness; unconditional failure to appreciate the traditional values and History.... In a thousand and one ways, the MCI strives toward these points, because it knows that they subjugate and condition [our] youth." The solution, they proposed, was EMC, part of a "total" strategy: "It follows that, to combat subversive infiltration in the schools, we are compelled to apply a total treatment ... as the strategy of the enemy is also global."[29]

The foot soldiers of the "war" on subversion thus had high hopes for Moral and Civic Education, and consequently surveilled the discipline's teachers. Interestingly, by the late 1970s, these foot soldiers seemed increasingly dissatisfied, not with the idea of EMC, but with its execution.

A 1978 SNI memorandum, for example, complained that the discipline was losing the battle against "subversive proselytism among students"; the solution, according to the SNI, lay in hiring better teachers. These, the memo continued, should be drawn directly from the source: "civilian and military reserve graduates of the Escola Superior de Guerra."[30]

The Barracks as Schoolhouse: Military Service and EMC

EMC's rightist champions, in keeping with their masculinist orientation, envisioned the discipline working in tandem with military service and physical fitness. Here moral, civic, physical, and patriotic inculcation emerged as part of a schematic connecting post-1969 EMC with the moral-hygienicist, even eugenicist, reformers of bygone decades. The sanitizing elites of the early twentieth century had dreamt of "cleansing" public health, fitness, and behavior, and had connected such cleansing to national viability.[31] Moral countersubversives in the 1960s and 1970s likewise saw EMC as a means of constructing the citizens of an idealized—and heavily masculinized—public, a public whose all-around vitality would mean victory against guerra revolucionária. "Integral" pedagogy, reminiscent of bygone reformers, concatenated hygiene, physical prowess, moral rectitude, social or political fitness, and—invariably—military service, and was the focus of moral anticommunists in the post-1964 period. Here the EMC vision of the ideal *brasileiro* as male—a vision consistent with decades of right-wing moralists' relegation of women to reproductive and puericultural functions—appeared with greatest clarity. Only very occasionally (as in the case of Mariani, noted above) did moralists make specific provision for a gender-appropriate analogue to military service for women, and then only to underscore the need to cultivate nurturing, patriotic mothers.[32]

Proponents linked morality to physical health in terms that likewise approximated the earlier dreams of biocontrol, with specific emphasis on the ways that military service and physical fitness might directly address the subversive "youth problem." Reformers in the 1960s and 1970s followed the tradition of Olavo Bilac, who in the 1910s had proposed universal conscription as the engine of a hale, hearty, and politically sound citizenry. Where some Cold War moralists worried at the physical unsuitability for military service of fifty percent of Brazil's young men—by reason of their "bestialization" and "sexual exaggerations"— security theorists made clear that only obligatory military service could effect the necessary moral, civic, and physical honing of vulnerable youth into ideal, countersubversive, masculine citizenry.[33] (This ideal citizenry would be circumscribed not only by masculinization but by maleness, since women did not serve in Brazil's armed forces until the 1980s and have never been subject to obligatory service.) Colonel Germano Seidl Vidal epitomized this tendency, extolling military service as a training ground for moral, physical, and political fitness. Fondly recalling his own days as a cadet, Vidal stressed the importance of EMC via military service, for the "containment of Guerra Revolucionária." Vidal listed the topics that such service-based moral and civic education should cover, demonstrating the focus on morality, fitness, and anticommunism: "Notions of Nutrition," "Sexual Education," "Venereal Prevention," "Hygiene and First Aid," "the Spirit of Family," "Moral and Spiritual Values of Man," "Notions of the History of the Pátria," "Civil Rights and Obligations," and "the Sense of Democracy."[34] Military training, according to Vidal's prescription, would create disease-free, well-nourished, hygienic, morally rigorous, civic-minded, and democratically countersubversive citizens.

Total war made these citizens indispensable and thus necessitated obligatory service. "Modern warfare," General Almério de Castro Neves explained, because it "is not fought with Armed Forces realizing [traditional] military operations," required not only technical training but the mobilization—and militarization—of an entire citizenry for engagement in moral and psychological combat. According to Neves, "Preparation for war must include the entire population, technically and spiritually, seeking not only the people's cooperation in defensive measures, but also their capacity to withstand the effects of war, principally psychological war." If, since the time of Olavo Bilac, military service intended to furnish not only military strength but a vital citizenry, Cold War exigencies reinforced the need for universal service. Neves lamented that contemporary youth made "easy prey for . . . extremist agitators, who will exploit this virgin territory at grave risk to national security." He lobbied for obligatory service to "administer moral and civic education to our youth, . . . so as to neutralize subversive propaganda [of the] communists" and prepare "all Brazilians" (that is, all male Brazilians) for "participation . . . in national security."[35] The CNMC's own public intellectuals warmly endorsed military service and stressed the dangers of codependent moral and physical degeneration via communist subversion. "The final objective" of subversion, wrote Moacir de

Araújo Lopes, "is the *physical, moral, and spiritual enervation* of our people, especially our youth." With a certain redolence of eugenics, Lopes demanded that EMC address the "degradation of Woman," but he emphasized patriarchalist concern with puericulture—because women's moral decadence meant, in Lopes's view, a concomitant somatic weakening of women as child-bearers or—in Lopes's own words—the physical "prop of the race."[36]

Race (*raça*) here referred less to skin color or ethnicity than to a time-honored notion of national "stock," or common physical, reproductive, and genetic makeup—a notion that had preoccupied eugenicist reformers of earlier decades.[37] This echo of eugenics reverberated through EMC's construction, as proponents worried about concomitant moral and physical debilitation. Lamenting the brevity of military service, one expert argued that EMC must use "sporting and cultural activities" to counteract moral-hygienic neglect, which would otherwise "compromise our very future generations by *genetically weakening* man and channeling the biological energies of young people into antisocial activities" like pornography, unconventional music, and pleasure seeking.[38]

Eugenics haunted latter-day EMC, often via venerable educational authorities. CFE Secretary-General Celso Kelly's own career stretched back into the 1930s, and his 1970 *Introduction to Moral and Civic Education* linked the former era to the latter. Kelly explained that EMC sought "the betterment of the race, not in a discriminatory sense . . . but in terms of the improvement of the people's fitness," endangered by contaminants like "drink" and "excessive pleasures."[39] Like Kelly, Pedro Calmon had been a recognized public health authority since the 1930s, when he had championed Brazilian youth's "spiritual militarization" and "anthropo-psychic regeneration" via military service.[40] Calmon, too, conveyed such moral-hygienic ideas into the late 1970s, furnishing EMC administrators with counsel that hearkened back to interwar Brazilian variants of José Vasconcelos's "cosmic race." In a 1982 essay on civic education, Calmon begged, in the name of Brazilian "sovereignty," that authorities "maintain the rigidity of our race, forged . . . in the formidable *mestiçagem* [racial mixture] of our people."[41] National security, in other words, depended on what earlier reformers had envisioned as a "eugenics" of controlled (often Eurocentric) racial mixture, designed to foment heritable moral, physical, and masculinist superiority.[42]

The army's own pedagogic manuals operationalized the articulation between EMC, physical vigor, and military service. In a 1971 basic training manual, for instance, a segment on "preparation for guerra revolucionária" stressed the special characteristics of this type of warfare—then informed trainers and trainees that "moral and civic instruction" constituted the first item of said preparation. Such moral and civic education linked moral and corporeal strength and fitness, seeking to cultivate "aggression, audacity, and initiative [to] fight in isolation, subjected to burdensome physical exertions, in arduous terrain" as well as the "spiritual makeup" necessary to maintain the "absolute and sacred character of the mission."[43] Internal defense—also known as countersubversive or counterinsurgent warfare—thus depended on this all-encompassing combination of preparatory fields. Indeed, basic training manuals granted EMC its own, exclusive section, drawing on Father Bastos de Ávila's *Little Encyclopedia of Morality and Civics* to insist that military training should scrutinize trainees' social, sexual, and leisure behavior. Troops must learn "good military manners," including "relations with women" and particularly "responsible conduct . . . in public places (bars, theaters, . . . sporting arenas, etc.)."

Finally, the basic training would explicitly seek to regulate soldiers' sexual lives, for reasons that combined morality with public and sexual health. Topics included "sexual hygiene, venereal diseases," "substance abuse and alcoholism," and "eugenics: notions about sexual education, family planning, and prenuptial and prenatal assistance."[44] The "eugenics" articulated here appears to have drawn on the notions of Latin American authorities who, in the 1920s and 1930s, tried to "eugenize public health" via a "positive eugenics" that saw "racial poisons" like nicotine, alcohol, and venereal diseases as national liabilities. Indeed, the leaders of the once-prominent São Paulo Eugenics Society had declared that "Sanitation-Eugenics is order and progress."[45] After 1960, Brazilian military intellectuals replaced the latter couplet with "security and development," the core precepts of Cold War countersubversion.

"Clean of Body and Soul": Boy Scouts and Beyond

To ensure "integral" (moral, civic, and physical) education, EMC-minded reformers reached beyond military service itself to extracurricular activities. Among the most oft-suggested programs—and the most telling in terms of conceptual continuities across the decades—Boy Scouts (*escotismo*) received near-constant mention by EMC supporters bent on using scouting as a font of discipline, regimentation, and indoctrination. CNMC founding member Álvaro Neiva, in his guide to the application of EMC outside of the classroom, called scouting the "perfect, central font ... of a disciplined conscience." Pathologizing student disturbances as "clinical cases ... of maladjustment" that needed "biological, psychological, and sociological" treatment, Neiva lionized Baden-Powell, affirming that scouting would immunize Brazilian youth against subversive "student actions." Rather than protesting, scouts would remain "loyal," "courteous," "obedient and disciplined," zealously dedicated to "honor," and—in classic moral-hygienic terms—"clean of body and soul," just as Baden-Powell himself had prescribed at the turn of the century. Scouting provided an "efficient tool" for the explicitly masculinist goal that Neiva set for EMC: that of creating "the New Man."[46] Reflecting the male-oriented reformism of scouting advocates past, the EMC-related documentation I was able to examine made little or no mention of Girl Guides (*Bandeirantes*).

Links between scouting and EMC went beyond ideological affinity. As we shall see, scouting appeared in EMC curricular materials, and CNMC President Admiral Benjamin Sodré was the veritable face of Brazilian scouting. Known as the "Old Wolf"—a reference to "Little Wolves," the Brazilian analogue of U.S. Cub Scouts—Sodré championed and oversaw the unification of Brazil's various scouting associations, and received the national scouts' highest decoration. Moacir de Araújo Lopes himself, as EMC's own "old wolf," advocated scouting as the perfect combination of religious morality with discipline and civic consciousness. He, too, venerated Baden-Powell, who appeared in Lopes's advisory list of texts for teaching the discipline.[47] Having established that "explicit linkage to MORALITY" would make or break EMC, Lopes praised *escotismo*'s emphasis on the "importance of well-formed *character*, guided by morality, founded in ethics, and taking God for its source." He implied that even Marxist subversives recognized the centrality of such scout-borne morality to *guerra revolucionária*: "The importance of Scouting's theist philosophical foundation ... is cast into relief by the attempts by materialist, radical socialist, or ... Marxist elements to destroy it."[48] So important, in fact, did scouts prove to moralistic national security that a 1971 presidential decree amended Decree-Law 869 to include scouting units as official "civic centers" of EMC.[49]

For older youths beyond the reach of scouting, supporters of morality and civics as countersubversion recurred to other extracurricular
programs designed to combine religious, moral, and physical resilience.
Here the favorites (especially among esguiano advocates) included the
government-sponsored service programs Project Rondon and Operation Mauá. Instituted in 1967 and 1969, these Peace Corps–like initiatives aimed to remove students from the milieu of urban protest and
channel their energies into government-approved development projects. Sending hundreds of thousands of Brazilian university students to
remote areas of the country to participate in the state's developmentalist
initiatives, the programs intended "not to provide assistance to Brazilians living in the wilderness but rather to change the perceptions and
opinions of student participants."[50] Moreover, these were explicitly
masculinist overtures, designed to reconstruct youthful "vigor" in a
time when traditional gender seemed under countercultural attack.[51]

As such, EMC supporters and administrators were quick to link Project Rondon and Operation Mauá to the holistic goals of moral, civic, and
physical perfection. One esguiano proponent, for instance, praising the
"heroic remedy" of "Moral and Civic Education, . . . destined . . . to forge
the new Brazilian man," included Rondon in that grand destiny: "The
philosophy and purposes that inspired the creation of Project Rondon
are the same ones that guided the institutionalization of Moral and
Civic Education."[52] A report on incorporating youth into "National Objectives," meanwhile, saw Rondon and Mauá as a reaction that, together
with sport, would counteract the "International Communist Movement"
and its "constant appeal to sex and violence." The government's programs, in this account, would promote the "fundamental role of Sport
[as] an escape valve for . . . youth" and "occupy young people [so that]
there won't be time for marijuana, for violence, or for terrorism." Mauá
and Rondon, then, would complement EMC, counteracting subversion
by promoting constructive physical activity for young people.[53] An ESG
essay reinforced the holistic approach, advocating resolution to the
problem of students who "protest just to protest" via "Moral and Civic
Education . . . Military Service, and programs like those that are being
developed with such success by Operation Mauá and Project Rondon."[54]
Work, it seemed, would set troubled youth free from the fetters of
moral subversion.

Mauá and Rondon were explicitly linked to national security, the
maxim "integrate, don't abdicate" (*integrar para não entregar*) evoking

long-standing fears of the "loss" of Brazilian sovereignty to shadowy, foreign threats. Supporters of the projects seamlessly imbricated this territorial idea of security with the ideological and moral-physical security mandated by ideas of total war and, they hoped, provided by moral and civic training in and out of the classroom. An *A Defesa Nacional* paean to the ideal Brazilian youth, for example, affirmed his conventional style ("he can't be called a 'Hippie'" or have long hair) and gender (he had a girlfriend and played sports). Instead of engaging in "strikes" or "movements of revolt," he fulfilled the promise of Project Rondon, "turning toward the gigantic interior of Brazil" with "ideological maturity." Regime propaganda czar Octávio Costa, meanwhile, brought several of EMC's linked threads together, advocating EMC as a countersubversive measure to stem student protest—a measure that would count on Project Rondon as an escape valve and on "the barracks" (military service) as a formal "fourth realm" of EMC. Some supporters even suggested that students who served in Rondon should receive EMC credits—but, tellingly, this proposal was quashed by the archconservative CNMC, its members bent on maintaining the long-term rightist objective of Moral and Civic Education as a stand-alone discipline.[55]

From Commission to Curriculum: EMC in the Classroom

We have thus far concerned ourselves with the ways in which moral panic among members of Brazil's military-bureaucratic establishment inspired EMC as a counterrevolutionary weapon, designed to vanquish problems ranging from eroticism to protest to moral-physical degeneration. These conceptual forays into countersubversive and antimodern pedagogy are significant insofar as they reflect the ways that moral panickers translated their anxieties into legislation (Decree-Law 869) and policy (the creation of the CNMC, followed by the various guidelines set forth by its commissioners and those of the CFE). Yet EMC went beyond legislative and policy debate—it made its way into classrooms across Brazil, where millions of students confronted it in lectures, assignments, and textbooks. I turn now to these textbooks as a means of assessing moral anticommunism's diffusion into the on-the-ground curricula to which young Brazilians were exposed during EMC's tenure.

Such textbooks varied widely, produced as they were by disparate authors and publishing outfits; indeed, regulation of texts to be used in EMC classes proved haphazard enough to frustrate moralists and administrators who would have preferred much tighter control of what students read. In 1980, for instance, CNMC President Geraldo Bezerra de Menezes would lament the fact that some EMC courses relied on textbooks not approved by his commission; and there was competition between the CNMC and the CFE over the right to regulate textbooks. This is not to say that oversight failed utterly; the more rigid CNMC, it seems, tended to carry the day when it came to jurisdiction. Textbooks submitted for inspection underwent a review process that sometimes mandated the removal of "negative aspects"—such as, in one case, a failure to adequately emphasize "moral conscience."[56] I have tried to rely on books with at least some indications of vetting and of classroom use, but the issue of regulation and implementation dogged EMC curricular materials throughout the discipline's tenure.[57] Moreover, students and teachers may of course have had latitude of interpretation, and it is difficult to get a reliable idea of how students reacted to these materials. Though many students seem to have taken EMC in stride or simply ignored it, there was some resistance to EMC, at least from university-level students who militated against the government. At the Federal University in Minas Gerais, for example, a militant student denounced "the fascist behavior and mentality, like alienation, authoritarianism, and the imposition of an official ideology" represented by EMC. (Security forces at the university, notably, interpreted this as communist subversion and sought the expulsion and arrest of the student in question.)[58] One former primary teacher, meanwhile, recalled adhering to the letter of EMC mandates: "We just passed along the content. It was like this:... 'Open your books to such and such page,' and you'd talk about that content."[59] My survey of textbooks from across the levels of study provides, then, a basic sense of how closely classroom curricula (if variably deployed and received) adhered to the prescriptions of pro-EMC moralists—particularly as the CFE and (more often) the CNMC and Moacir de Araújo Lopes authorized some texts and not others.

Moralism made its way quite emphatically into these materials, which—to a rather surprising degree—featured the hallmarks of moral panic and of the counterrevolutionary remoralization we have seen in EMC's formative and administrative debates. Textbooks referred directly to moral crisis, and to EMC's intent to counteract it; tended to define morality in terms of young people's day-to-day behavior, making specific mention of sexuality and communist subversion; expressed concern about gender deviance—especially women's liberation, though specific prescriptions for feminine behavior remained vague and exclusively reproductive/puericultural; inscribed sin and subversion into an age-old continuum between civilization and barbarism; and, accordingly, drew the same, synthetic connections that EMC authorities did between physical vitality, moral health, and national viability.

A Textbook Moral Crisis

Reinforcing planners' vision of EMC as a response to moral crisis, textbooks introduced in the 1970s rang with moral panic quite equal to that we have already encountered, in terms both of scope and fervency. Students read unmistakable messages that they were living through an epoch of moral catastrophe. "Man . . . has lately allowed vice to enslave him," cautioned one CNMC-approved textbook; "liberty," mourned another, "has become libertinism," in a modern world that "makes morality an inconvenience"; a third warned students of "the derailment of a large section of our young people," a critical phenomenon stemming from the replacement of "true, legitimate," marital love with "transitory erotic attraction."[60] The comprehensive *National Encyclopedia of Moral and Civic Education*—still locatable, as of this writing, in school library collections—described a multifaceted "crisis of adolescence" buffeting contemporary youth: "crisis of sexuality, of love, of religion, and . . . crisis of liberty. This is what makes this period so tragic because, given a badly oriented education, the man of tomorrow will not overcome any of these crises and will live a completely incoherent adult life. . . . The crisis of sexuality, having completed its physiological phase in the first few years, will become a blossoming conflict of liberty [itself]."[61]

Most such cries of "Crisis!" clarified that the moral decadence in question centered on youth behavior. The textbooks focused unambiguously on the day-to-day activities and attitudes of their readers. Morality, many a textbook affirmed, was the "science of customs," of "good habits," and comprised "the comportment that you display before God and other people."[62] Moreover, morality was "immutable" and only varied for execrable "materialists."[63] Textbooks explicitly aimed to guide students to "good habits" in their daily lives—or, as Marília Mariani's 1970 *Guide to Civics* put it, to promote "the self-discipline that will regulate your moral life, your social, emotional, and sexual behavior."[64]

Indeed, sexual behavior lay at the center of such textbooks' pre- and proscriptions, so much so that informing students about moral crisis nearly always involved linking that crisis to sexuality. One primer warned students that human beings had come to resemble irrational, instinct-driven beasts. This "regression to the level of animals," continued the author, "is the principal cause of the wave of sexual unruliness and perversion that inundates our planet.... Today, the most complete and absolute libertinism is encouraged."[65] Amid warnings of "sexomania," or "exacerbation of sex all over the place," *Course in Moral and Civic Education* rhetorically asked students if "the taboo status of virginity is dying." The answer seemed to be a hand-wringing affirmative, as, according to the book, "we are seeing the creation of a new sexual morality, abetted by the wave of eroticism, by festivals of pornography, by *hippies*, by transparent dresses, by nudist magazines, by the cinema, by the progressive disrobement of women, by topless swimsuits, in waves that disaggregate the family and marriage. This new sexual morality must be combated; it must be opposed and defeated."[66]

Here, as among the moralists of the ESG and other security forums, "social communications" bore the blame for the explosion of illicit sexuality. "Cinema, magazines, theater, journals, and television," one book informed students, joined "immoral and pornographic publications, which terrifyingly invade newsstands, schools, and homes."[67] A chorus of textbooks concurred, blaming the "wave of eroticism" on "mass communication," "means of social communication," the globalization of "hippies" and/or counterculture, and even novels and Hollywood, which together had generated the very amalgam that these textbooks warned students to avoid: "the drug addict, political dissident, and sex maniac."[68]

Beyond identifying this moral and sexual crisis, EMC textbooks concerned themselves with prescriptions for appropriate comportment in these areas. Authors stressed the sanctity of marriage, stigmatized premarital sex, and commonly included lists of "duties" (like the "duty not to abuse sex").[69] The textbooks commonly included entire sections meant to serve as youth sexuality guides, like Gleus Damasceno Duarte's chapter "Sex and You," whose complaint about the "wave of sexual unruliness and perversion" we noted above. The reader *Building Brazil*, which equated eroticism with "guerrilla warfare," included just such a guide to adolescent romance, titled "Orientation for Courtship and Engagement." Here the authors warned teenage readers against "manifestations of affection by means of touch," as, "obviously, sexual intimacy is immoral and inappropriate at [your] age." Courtship, this section stressed, "is not an initiation to sex, but a training period for love." The text sought to reinforce traditional gender roles in this arena, charging girls with safeguarding virtue against adolescent sexual fumblings: "It falls to the young lady to repel egregious liberties during the courtship, since these might cause her irreparable harm."[70] This was one realm in which the neglect of girls and women in cultural counterrevolution did not attain so overtly as in other areas (like military service) of focus on male youth; textbooks for EMC *did* address girls and young women directly, albeit in a vague form consistent with the breadth of moralistic fears.

Textbooks for Modern Womanhood

EMC curricular materials brimmed, that is, with concern and prescription not only about sexuality but also about gender, mirroring the preoccupation with traditional womanhood and family life in other arenas of moral panic. As we have seen, the very founding principles of EMC, elaborated by future President Costa e Silva himself, focused on the imperiled, "educational" function of the family—the problem with modernity and working women consisting almost solely in the effects of these on puericulture. Accordingly, young women reading EMC textbooks would have found implicit and explicit messages denouncing the "new woman" and anything approaching "women's liberation"— categories that the textbooks, true to the discipline's guiding philosophy, identified as the doom of prized, republican motherhood. The CNMC's Humberto Grande had declared that "the emancipated woman" with "her own apartment, her own automobile, [and her] various lovers, for so long as [her] physical charms last," was "culpable for modern social disorganization"—and EMC textbooks accordingly sought to preclude the development of this specter.[71] Some restricted themselves to rather bland denunciations of "the new image of woman" or instructions that "the woman should seek to be a good housewife."[72] One EMC primer explained this in terms characteristic of a cult of patriotic domesticity, where women's role as child-rearers trumped all other considerations: "Of the utmost, especial importance, is the mission of the Mother—first educator, great molder of man's mentality and sentiment. It is from the Mother, in the home, that the human being receives his first and usually most decisive influence.... That is why the responsibility of the Mother is so great."[73]

Yet EMC authors also waxed more aggressive, directly denouncing modern and/or liberated women. Though these textbooks did address women and girls directly, they replicated the message of other moralists vis-à-vis *brasileiras*: that they mattered (and their morality mattered) only insofar as they affected the creation and cultivation of male offspring. "Woman," the *Guide to Civics* insisted, "has always been the guardian of morality in the home [and] the primary party responsible for the rearing of patriotic men"—wherefore the *Guide*, echoing like-minded moralists at the ESG and higher up the EMC administrative chain, blamed unconventional women for the perceived moral and social crisis. "When families fall apart," it advised, "when homes are abandoned, when many people leave off their responsibilities—in short, when a nation lacks *men* (in the highest sense of the word), it is because it lacked women before—mothers and teachers, who might have raised [men]."[74] Edília Coelho Garcia, herself a CFE member, authored a textbook that ridiculed the "so-called 'equality of the sexes.'" Willing to acknowledge that women should not be relegated to their nineteenth-century "slave" status, Garcia nevertheless asserted that "modern woman" had "brought serious problems." Since "an employed woman is away from home for the greater part of the day," Garcia informed students, "her children are left with little care"; indeed, "woman's liberation . . . separates her from her domestic life [and] makes her neglect her children."[75] As these examples make clear, EMC's prescriptions for girls and young women, though perhaps more focal than other moralizing programs (scouting, for example), remained vague, with little to direct female readers beyond general, patriarchal traditionalism.

Pathologizing Student Subversion

Joining long-standing ideas about patriotic motherhood with the gendered security theories we have previously encountered—ESG worries, for example, about the "biological" and "psychic" effects of working women on national viability—EMC textbooks' guides to sexuality and gender tended to engage in certain pathologizations. Steeped in a pseudotheory of progress, these pathologizations linked morality, physical and sexual pathology, national viability, and an age-old struggle between civilization/refinement and barbarism/instinct. EMC primers railed constantly against "instinct" as a sign of "animalization," or "regression to the level of animals" and to barbarism.[76] They further tied such fearful reversal in the march of civilization to the moral-cum-physical consequences of instinct-driven life. Afonso Rodrigues's *Ethics and Civics* opened with an exemplary passage, warning students that capitulation to animal "instinct" led not only to degradation but to degenerative "mental disease." Among examples of the latter, Rodrigues included "the drunk" and (in a burst of anachronism) "the hysteric." Rodrigues explained that "Man can degrade himself and act like a brutish animal, dragged along by inferior tendencies. . . . This errant type is one characterized by bad habits . . . the drunk, the hysteric, the paranoiac. Mental diseases accompany moral vices."[77] Another textbook told students they must avoid "anomalies and vices, from disorderly practices to deviances against nature" because these were likely to cause maladies of the body as well as of the soul. Exercising "discipline in sexual life," warned author João de Oliveira Torres, "and conditioning [sex] to the elevated interests of the spirit constitute a factor of *physical and spiritual health* and a necessity for a regular social life."[78]

Perhaps the most illustrative example of such pedagogical pathologization, however, emerged in the books of José Hermógenes de Andrade, something of a self-help celebrity whose books can still be purchased or obtained at public and school libraries.[79] Andrade's convoluted logics indicated a causal relationship between sexual, physical, and psychological ill health. Andrade, whom Moacir de Araújo Lopes sanctioned as an EMC pedagogue, warned young readers against "problems like masturbation, menstruation [*sic*], impotence, venereal disease, and sexual anomalies," which, without treatment, would surely lead to "psychological or organic diseases that manifest themselves through aberrations or deviations from what is normal, healthy, and pure." Such "aberrations," according to Andrade, included "homosexuality," which also "must be treated."[80] Andrade's 1975 *True Youth* further inscribed sexual behavior and pathology into a continuum in which health, civilization, and morality diametrically opposed degeneracy, regression, and dissipation. The book bemoaned the contemporary emergence of a "pseudoyouth," whom Andrade's illustration showed barefoot, long haired, bearded, surrounded by unhygienic-looking flies, reclining on a sidewalk, accompanied by an empty liquor bottle, and extravagantly clothed in jewelry, jeans, a large belt buckle, decorative patches, and sunglasses (see fig. 7). As if the picture did not fully express the pathologically regressive, moral and physical waywardness of this youth, Andrade described his "quasi-scientifically produced degradation," his

Para outros segundo a "onda" do momento, jovem é o rebelde agressivo, supostamente liberto ("avançado"), "inserido no con-

PSEUDO JOVEM

Figure 7 José Hermógenes de Andrade's "pseudoyouth," surrounded by the trappings of degeneracy. In Andrade, *Juventude verdade*, 78. Photo by author.

"laziness, libertinism, and . . . return to animal behavior, which humanity had left behind."[81]

Progress-halting pathology also carried thinly veiled racial implications. In a section titled "Morality and Love," Andrade included a pair of images designed to differentiate the sexually dissipate from the "normal, healthy, and pure." Representing the former, a racial- and bestialized man and woman, whose physical features suggested mixed racial heritage, whose unshaven face and dark lipstick suggested slovenliness and poor taste, and whose gaping, nearly drooling mouths suggested developmental incapacity, appeared beside the words SEX = LOVE; immediately below this, an obviously white, blond couple, clean cut and shaven, looked on a cloud labeled LOVE, in which SEX made only a minor appearance. The caption sought to drive home the point that backwardness, ugliness, unhealthfulness, and even racial degeneration accompanied sexual immorality and the confusion of sex with love. "The primitive confuses sex and love," it read. "For the evolved man, sex is just a component and an aspect of love" (see fig. 8).[82]

Given this tendency toward pathologization, EMC textbooks required very few pedagogical or conceptual leaps to coordinate with

Figure 8 Illustrating the proper relationship between sex and love. The "primitive" couple, above, confuses sex with love, while "Evolved Man," below, knows sex to be just a small component of love. In Andrade, *Juventude verdade*, 87. Photo by author.

physical education and physical health. Indeed, the textbooks combined warnings against vice with prescriptions for exercise and advice about the body's interactions with the physical world. Ebenézer Soares Ferreira included a section (common to many an EMC primer) on "Duties with Regard to the Body," in which he affirmed that "disrespect for the body is common when Man abandons himself to sexual practices that are contrary to nature, when he allows himself to tread the path of fornication and adultery, when he engages in sloth."[83] Textbooks once again made clear the linkage of such ideas with a history of bygone reformers: citing Baden-Powell and Monteiro Lobato (creator of the famously pathologized *caboclo* Jeca Tatú), *Principles of Moral and Civic Education* described the inextricability of physical health and moral character. "Health is an important factor in the formation of character," it read, relating the sins of "sloth" and "indolence" to "lack of healthfulness."[84]

Beyond such warnings, the texts offered recipes for moral-physical vitality, generally promoting exercise and physical education.[85] The books often offered counsel reminiscent of eugenicist theories about "racial poisons," arguing that "physical environment ... acts decisively in the formation of people's character and behavior." One *Course in Moral and Civic Education* counseled that "excessive, continuous heat enervates the muscles [and] weakens the will"; but that "cold, on the other hand, pleases the senses, relaxes all the impulses of life, and is therefore a conservator, a preservative of strength."[86] The books often returned to these themes, from bullet-point insistence on "observation of the precepts of hygiene and temperance" to entire chapters on habits of cleanliness and fitness.[87]

Logically, given the disposition of EMC authorities toward scouting, Baden-Powell and his generations of followers made many textbook appearances. Where Maria Caiafa's mnemonic primer praised scouting as "a worldwide organization ... whose objective is moral, physical, practical, and civic training of children and youths," *Building Brazil* indicated *escotismo* as a solution to the challenge of combining "training" and "leisure"—one that "fulfills both of these goals very well." Some EMC textbooks went further, dedicating extensive space and praise to scouting's "clean[liness] of body and soul." Lurdes de Bortoli's 1978 primer, for example, pictured scouts on its front cover and used scouting as an organizational motif for the book's lessons, which ran the gamut of EMC tenets, from the denunciation of "instinct" to the juxtaposition of "virtues" and "vices," to the differentiation of "indigenous society" from "civilized society."[88]

Guerra Revolucionária: Frontal Attacks

EMC textbooks kept pace with other forums of anticommunist moral panic in one further regard. We have seen that moralists envisioned EMC as a weapon against Marxist guerra revolucionária—and the books, despite the youth of their readers, peppered the moral, hygienic, sexual, and gendered counsel we have just explored with explicit denunciations of communism as the source of moral, political, psychic, and even bodily ruin. In this sense, these textbooks served overtly as primers for the study of countersubversion. The books commonly included a section or chapter entitled "Godless Communism," which invariably denounced communist materialism and immorality.[89] These chapters

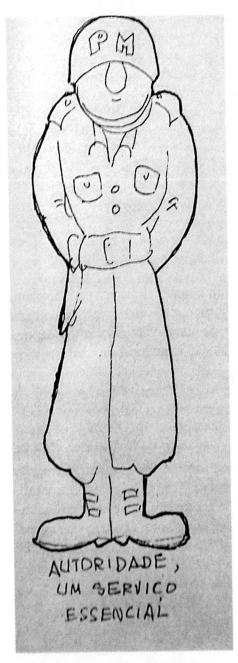

AUTORIDADE,
UM SERVICO
ESSENCIAL

Figure 9 "Authority: An Essential Service." The textbook *Juventude verdade* sanctioned military authoritarianism as not only warranted but beneficial. Next to an illustration of a blithely smiling, armed military policeman, author José Hermógenes de Andrade implicitly responded to critics of the regime's tactics, contending that "authority . . . is a public service. . . . It is not only a source of 'repression,' as has sometimes been said." In *Juventude verdade*, 17. Photo by author.

often read like an adolescent's introduction to National Security Doctrine. One such entry, referring students to the "precious book *Do You Know Communism? Do You* Really *Know It?*," warned that "Lenin affirm[ed] that . . . morality" was subordinate to the revolutionary struggle for "communist dictatorship." The author even listed the techniques that communists would putatively use in their takeover, including "agitation," "infiltration," "kidnappings," and attempts to undermine "the student population [by] recruiting everyone into subversion."[90] A curricular variant of the moral panic–borne theory we have already encountered, this type of direct, anticommunist admonishment sought to enlighten young readers on their own vulnerabilities to communism. Indeed, the *National Encyclopedia of Moral and Civic Education* strove to alert students to the fact that "part of the student population has fallen victim to the ardent Marxists who so ably exploit" it, leading to a plague of "waywardness, often delinquency, in modern youth."[91] *Principles of Moral and Civic Education* assured students that this waywardness and the concomitant moral-physical degradation constituted communist tactics: "Take note that the experts in [communist] doctrines use the weakening and corruption of youth as a weapon [in order to] destroy the physical and spiritual strength of their pitiable victims."[92]

Fonts of Moral Anticommunism

However striking the directness of EMC texts in denouncing international communism to a young audience, the texts' general adherence to the precepts of administrators and bygone moral-hygienic reformers follows logically from the bibliographic influence of these administrators and reformers, as well as of moral technocrats, on the textbooks. It is difficult to gauge the degree to which these materials were embedded in the network of countersubversive moralism we have explored, as textbooks traditionally do not follow citation guidelines. Nevertheless, those textbooks that had bibliographies cited a familiar cohort of moralists—and those that did not have formal bibliographies included such moralists in their acknowledgments or in textual citations. Andrade's *Juventude verdade*, for instance, featured a source list that included "reports and conferences from the Escola Superior de Guerra," as well as more specific referents: Suzanne Labin, the ESG-influential author of *Hippies, Drugs, and Promiscuity*, and José Leme Lopes, the psychiatrist-turned-moraltechnocrat whom we met in chapter 4. Reproducing this penchant, other textbooks cited Father Bastos de Ávila (whose worries about "perverted" education we explored in chapter 4), Nilda Bethlem Bastos (an *A Defesa Nacional* expert on the "youth problem"), CNMC member Arthur Machado Paupério, Djacir Menezes (ESG lecturer and LDN collaborator, whose antipornographic outrage we witnessed in chapter 3), and Gustavo Corção himself.

Reaching further back, EMC authors demonstrated a proclivity for reformers of a bygone era. Textbooks cited 1930s Integralist leader Gustavo Barroso; Everardo Backeuser, whose vehement, interwar denunciations of Soviet "free love" and "moral putrefaction" we reviewed in chapter 1; Oliveira Viana and Nina Rodrigues, both eminent, racist theorists in fin de siècle Brazil; Pedro Calmon (who, as we saw in this chapter, continued to contribute to EMC after 1969); ESG "characterology" favorites Eduard Spranger and Nicola Pende; and the patriarch of Brazilian patriotic education, Henrique Coelho Neto.[93] The eugenicist moral panic of Coelho Neto's 1921 *Civic Primer* echoed down through the decades in EMC textbooks, which tended to include his "commandments" and venerate him as the founder of Brazilian civics. Ferreira, for instance, quoted Coelho Neto to demonstrate that "civics" comprised "morality," "honest comportment," and "the habits that [have been] transmitted" from parents and teachers; and that the "base" of this moral-civic-behavioral conglomerate was, of course, "the hearth."

Conclusion

Brasil conta com seus filhos para a sua redenção—the boldface epigraph of the *National Encyclopedia of Moral and Civic Education*—suffers from certain ambiguities of meaning. *Filhos*—"sons" or "children"—might indicate only male offspring or include both sexes. The possessive pronoun *sua*, meanwhile, could mean Brazil's own "redemption" (*redenção*)...or that of the *filhos* themselves. As we have seen, women and girls were the focus of much anxiety but comparatively little in the way of specific prescription for redressing supposed moral ills. In large part, this stemmed from moralist reformers' *longue durée* relegation of women to the status of child-makers and child-rearers. Did Brazil, then, count on its sons, or on all of its children, for redemption? For their own redemption, or that of the country as a whole? For both? Whatever its translational vagaries, the phrase contained little ambiguity in one respect. Redemption here meant salvation from moral-subversive crisis, in whose stormy throes Brazil and Brazilians faced communists' concomitantly sexual, moral, physical, and psychological warfare—an assault that only effective EMC could counteract. As we have seen, the *Encyclopedia* contained further admonishments for student readers, whom it warned against the "crisis of adolescence" and the sad fate of young compatriots who had "fallen victim" to Marxists' able plotting.[94] This book enjoyed at least some distribution to students; it can still be found in public and school libraries.

Significantly, for our purposes, the *Encyclopedia*'s editors dedicated the book's predominant section (nearly sixty pages, or half of the volume) to discussion of love, sex, and marriage. Students read about "the nature of love," the "psychology of the sexes," "personality maladjustments that cause marital difficulties," and "vices," including "excessive preoccupation with pleasures," "gambling," "drinking," and "extraconjugal adventures."[95] Here, as in other EMC textbooks and foundational treatises, sexuality, sin, and subversion formed the core of the discipline's raison d'être. From its embryonic phase, as the brainchild of Costa e Silva and certain adesguianos, through its development into law, EMC enjoyed the support of hard-line moralists who saw moral and civic instruction as—to quote EMC honcho Moacir de Araújo Lopes—a "protective shield" against the moral-subversive apocalypse they perceived on the horizon.

The reactionaries who designed and administered EMC, beyond philosophizing about its remoralizing-cum-countersubversive effects, seem to have had some success at affecting the curricula that students might encounter in their everyday studies. Indeed, students' daily lives were precisely what EMC sought to regulate; as textbooks from the discipline's critical period demonstrate, classroom materials adhered to EMC administrators' morally panicked prescriptions. In the books surveyed for this chapter, students could read about the moral crisis putatively enveloping them; its unambiguous, sexual and gendered nature; the ways in which moral failures might pathologically affect physical health (true to form, the *Encyclopedia* also warned that "excessive preoccupation with pleasures" would "annul one's capacity for exertion"); and the nefarious activity of communist subversives at the base of the moral-sexual crisis.[96] In terms of its state-sanctioned intrusion into the daily lives of students, and its focus on holistic education that sought the inextricable moral, physical, spiritual, intellectual, "aesthetic," and political perfection of the public, EMC followed the prescriptions of bygone generations of reformers, whose visions of a "eugenically" cleansed, orderly citizenry lived on in the morally countersubversive eugenics of military manuals, EMC textbooks, and prescriptions for physical, moral, and military instruction.

7

From Pornography to the Pill

Bagunça *and the Limitations of Moralist Efficacy*

The nude is not considered erotic, solely by virtue of its exhibition.

—Wilson Aguiar, chief censor, approving the staging of *Hair* in 1970

The Abandonment of Youth: Our youth was abandoned ... Once the opponents of the [military regime]—communists, men of the left, and friends of exiled politicians—perceived the [government's] timidity in the propaganda sector, they lost no time launching themselves into counterpropaganda. ... [Communist] propaganda has acted and acts freely. And subversive impregnation has found fertile ground in our unsheltered and abandoned youth, inducing them to hedonism as the only objective of life.

—General Sylvio Frota, a hard-line opponent of democratization, on
  the failures of the waning military regime

In the regime's principal intellectual institutions, among security forces, and in educational legislation and practice, then, perspectives took hold that operationalized the ideological intervention we have now witnessed at several levels—an intervention that firmly associated moral and sexual deviance with communist subversion.[1] As we have seen, police fretted over and surveilled the sexual and gender activity of suspected *subversivas*; intelligence services shared information about supposed orgies among left-leaning faculty; top military minds envisioned the "loss" of young people (particularly young women) to subversion in explicitly sexual terms; the "dictionary" disseminated to the front lines of the war on "terrorism" defined communist subversion in terms of "free love" and "the exploitation of sex"; and students across Brazil were slated to learn how to be masculinized anticommunists or to think of themselves as patriotic mothers, all in the service of combating moral guerra revolucionária.

Nevertheless, Wilson Aguiar, head of the state Service for Censorship of Public Entertainment (SCDP), approved the staging of *Hair*, reasoning, as noted in the epigraph above, that "the nude" did not have to be "erotic." Aguiar's green light for the musical and his remark on theatrical nudity indicate the possibility for controversial media productions (*Hair* had garnered fame and infamy internationally) to pass muster even with notoriously strict censors like Aguiar, who himself stated that his office existed to enforce the "exigencies" of "morality" in the name of national security. With hard-liners preoccupied with "pornography," libidinousness, and public displays of almost any suggestiveness, Aguiar's response to *Hair* seems remarkably nuanced, and somewhat out of place.

In fact, this type of contradiction often affected the implementation of regime policy on morality and sexuality across the decades of dictatorship. This proved especially true as hard-line and moralistic influence began to wane in the regime's later years; after 1974, more moderate voices came to power within the regime, and a gradual (not to mention halting and sometimes violent) process of democratization began. By the latter half of the decade, this process had attenuated the hard-line moralistic primacy (the victories of ESG legislation; the public sway of the likes of Gustavo Corção, Antônio Carlos Muricy, and Moacir de Araújo Lopes) of the preceding years of lead. When it comes to sex, dictatorial policies have rarely been treated, and even then as a monolith, as "*the* authoritarian state."[2] Journalist Elio Gaspari's characterization of the dictatorship as a *bagunça*—a "mess"—comes closer to the truth: that competing factions and cross-purposes governed authoritarian Brazil. This messiness certainly extended into the realms of morality and sexuality, such that attempts to police sexual and moral practice for national security reasons varied in terms of success, both temporally and between the agencies and subsectors of the military government. Despite the presence of a clear, moralistic agenda, which rightists promulgated in the peak years of state violence (1969–73), implementation remained problematic.

As the foregoing chapters demonstrate, method did rule this madness in key ways—from the top echelons of military rule to the foot soldiers of intelligence and police forces, sexual subversion constituted a significant and sometimes obsessive concern. However, as the dictatorship entered its final years—once the period of most intense state repression had ended—other forces and factions came into play, competing with moralism for control of the regime's mission and message. Though sexual and moral panic and paranoia continued to rankle among the most violent governmental and paragovernmental authoritarianists, the murky waters of the bagunça grew even more obscure. The state, somewhat unwittingly, financed soft pornography; censors seemed continually unclear as to jurisdiction (between competing censorial agencies) and the precise measures needed to combat moral and sexual subversion; and by the end of the 1970s, government planners had seriously considered the idea of state-sponsored birth control. In one sense, this reflected the waning of hard-line influence within the regime and the effect of *abertura*, or democratic opening—something clearly felt by the enraged partisans of the AAB, whose above-noted outrage dovetailed with a general desperation among moralists as the 1980s dawned. On the other hand, confusion in sexual and moral policy showed the ongoing disorder and disjunction that characterized much of the period of military rule.[3]

"The Police Don't Know How to Censor":
Bagunça and the Mysteries of Moral Censorship

Chaos and contradiction dogged moral censorship even in the early years of the dictatorial period. The nuts and bolts of *what* was to be censored, by whom, and when quickly became one of the sites where centralized authoritarianism most visibly frayed and deteriorated. Censors themselves have attested to the presence of some organizational scheme—chains of command, occasional communication across agencies—but even here it would be more accurate to refer to organizational "schemes," in the plural. Cuts to or prohibition of news media, literature, art, music, theater, and cinema could come from several state agencies—the fifteen-member Superior Council of Censors (CSC), for example; the Division of Censorship of Public Entertainment (DCDP), nominally if not always functionally governed by the federal police; the presidential press secretary; the heads of military departments; or individual government ministries. Then, too, the press and artists also engaged in wary gambits of self-censorship, for reasons ranging from direct censorial guidelines to efforts to maintain revenue sources. Certain media outlets (notably the motley, often oppositional, "alternative" press) were subject to harsher strictures than others, and prior censorship reigned during the harshest years of dictatorship. Some censors received detailed training, while others did not, and failures in communication were common, as was uncertainty even as to what resources would be necessary to properly censor morally questionable materials. One former censor recalled personal access to federal police chief Moacyr Coelho on questions of censorship—but also the vagueness of communication between Coelho and the Ministry of Justice (also responsible for censorship). Coelho himself, moreover, admitted that his organization did not have, for example, the translational resources necessary to censor foreign (and potentially subversive/pornographic) films.[4]

In a signal example of the byzantine, often paranoid, and seemingly haphazard application of moral censorship, Ministry of Education officials censored the pro-morality masterpiece of Fernando Bastos de Ávila, whom we have already encountered as one of the ESG's leading lights in the struggle against "perversion" as a "psychosocial" and subversive problem. Ávila's 1967 *Little Encyclopedia of Morality and Civics*, designed to inoculate young students against sexual and moral subversion, itself came under fire from a shadowy and ultimately equivocating network of censors. Showing that the terms (quite literally) of moral subversion could be contested, even among allies in the "good fight" against such subversion, a commission cut several entries from the *Encyclopedia*: "communism," "Marxism," "consciousness raising," "politicization," "abortion," "religion," "cassation," "dictatorship," "coup d'état," and "democracy."[5] The obscure rationale behind the cuts—which left entries like "chastity" and "courtship" intact—could potentially have objected to the mere inclusion of concepts like "Marxism" and "consciousness raising"; to the failure to specify Christianity in the explanation of "religion"; and to the sensitive nature of an entry like "dictatorship" (though Ávila did not mention Brazil and was in fact a supporter of the government). Explanatory conjecture falters, however, in the face of censorship of the encyclopedia's entry on abortion, which adhered to a very conservative politics of reproduction and gender: "Abortion is criminal and is, in the final analysis, the murder of a defenseless being; it merits the execration of all men. There is no reasoning that can justify it; any attempt to consider it a last resort for the good name of a young woman ... is nothing more than an unworthy sham, of the lowest selfishness. ... The honor of a young woman depends, fundamentally, on her attitudes and behaviors with relation to young men. (See *sexual education, courtship*.)"[6] The flap over the *Encyclopedia* grew still more confused when outcry against its censorship forced Minister Tarso Dutra to revoke the censorial commission's authority to tamper with the original work. Instead, a new commission was convened to "decide about the encyclopedia, in its totality, offering suggestions to the Minister."[7] Notwithstanding its rocky start, the *Encyclopedia* went on to have several further editions.

Disagreement between different forces within the government and ambiguity about where the censorship buck stopped recurred frequently across the years of military rule. For example, though officials from the Army Intelligence Service (CIE) execrated *Hair* as a touchstone of "authentic moral degradation" and part of a plot of "moral subversion," the SCDP under Wilson Aguiar made the musical's production legal in early 1970. Expanding on the comment with which this chapter opened, Aguiar showed that censorship could be relatively nuanced (recognizing distinctions between nudity and eroticism)—but also incoherent, as the ideas expressed here by Aguiar were not shared by security theorists or applied across time and agencies. While he held that nudity did not necessarily entail eroticism, Aguiar went on to insist that "what government censors will not permit is that erotic gestures be made or that the nude is used to awaken eroticism." General José Maria de Toledo Camargo, sometime head of the government's public relations machine, remembered the *Hair* episode in terms of its implications for divisions in the regime and for the rampant moralistic fears of right-wing hard-liners. In a memoir written decades later—when he somewhat problematically identified wholly with the "soft-line" elements of the regime—Camargo referred to anticommunist "paranoia" vis-à-vis "global communist action . . . via the theater, *to do away with the structure of the family*. This included *Hair*, because it had a scene of frontal nudity and preached peace."[8] Camargo's dismissiveness itself demonstrates the vicissitudes of moralism within the regime, as his attitude diverged from that of the previous public relations czar, who argued in a public 1968 treatise on revolutionary warfare that communists used "sexual revolution . . . to dismantle love [by] completely sexualizing it, with the consequential dissolution of the family and of juridical and moral order."[9]

Reflecting such conceptual disagreements, the machinery itself of government censors could be unworkable—if what to censor was ever contentious, questions continually arose about *who* had the authority to censor. In an exposé entitled "The Rio State Police Don't Know How to Censor," the *Jornal do Brasil* reported on confusion among the Federal Police in Rio about how to proceed with the censorship and liberation of a book that had been duly submitted for approval. Censorial law stipulated that material must be submitted at local subdelegations of the

Federal Police, but suggested that actual censorship should happen at regional facilities. Inspector Eudo de Luna, frustrated with the lack of clarity, asked the regional delegation for clarification on "the jurisdiction and the form for permitting...publication."[10] Significantly, political police demonstrated their certainty that erotic literature conveyed a subversive threat, as well as their simultaneous *un*certainty about how, exactly, to measure and confront that threat. The Guanabara state DOPS compiled detailed information on authors, publishers, and vendors of works considered "offensive to public morality and to the good customs of the Brazilian family." Even as they seized some books and threatened authors and translators, however, agents lamented that "this DOPS still does not have operatives better qualified in the speciality [of censorship], nor do we know the criteria...of the Minister of Justice. As a result, a deeper analysis of the [potentially subversive] material is necessary."[11]

Such confusion reflected a crisis in the operationality of censorship, encompassing both incompetence and much higher-level battles over the right and responsibility to censor in the name of morality and anti-communism. As early as 1968, the newspaper *O Globo* referred to an "'internal war' among the policing powers" about the nature, extent, and jurisdictional details of censorship.[12] That "war" reflected increasing division within the regime and, as the 1970s wore on, a sense of embattlement and disempowerment on the part of hard-liners. Indeed, as former regime nabob Camargo retold it in his 1995 memoir, this division was experienced as a gendered fractiousness, where hard-liners adhered to moralistic countersubversion and dismissed those who did not as failed soldiers and patriots. Identifying (albeit retrospectively) with the opponents of the hard line, Camargo claimed that he and others who did not share moralistic paranoias were figuratively, by the mid-1970s, emasculated by more hard-line colleagues: "[We were] seen as a band of loafers, preoccupied with gossip and idle chatter, and who didn't realize that the country was at war."[13]

As the *Globo* reference to "internal war" indicates, such division reached a remarkable pitch in disagreements between censorial bodies, particularly in the late 1970s, as democratization attenuated hard-liners' power within the regime. In 1983, for example, officials from the federal police joined the director of the Division of Censorship of Public Entertainment (DCDP, which saw itself as the paramount censorial authority) in complaining about the interference in their censorial work of another government body, the Superior Council of Censors (CSC). DCDP Director Solange Maria Teixeira Hernandes, who had been appointed precisely for her moralistic severity, railed against the relative liberalism of the CSC, which by this point comprised not only members from the Ministries of Justice, Communications, and Foreign Relations, but also representatives from state arts agencies and nongovernmental organizations. Lamenting the lack of clarity about censorial hierarchy, Hernandes struggled to keep the DCDP on track as a seawall against the tide of "leftist" moral subversion in the media; she saw the CSC as a principal collaborator with the enemy. Contending that her organization should have ultimate authority, she alleged that the CSC representative from the Brazilian Press Association, Roberto Pompeu de Sousa Brasil, "has the habit of liberating every pornographic film that comes across his desk." She and her allies in the federal police grew particularly exercised over the film *Eva, the Principle of Sex*, in which they decried "normal, abnormal, and homosexual sex scenes, male and female nudes, . . . fellatio and cunnilingus . . . with much intensity." The DCDP, in fact, had barred the movie, a decision upheld by the police—but the ongoing power struggle between the DCDP and the CSC resulted in the film's release to audiences over the age of 18.[14]

Even in cases of clear jurisdiction, hard-liners felt themselves pressed to maintain the stringency they desired. Moralists in government, though they held positions of power, sometimes had to police censors themselves in order to realize moral and sexual countersubversion. Thus in 1973, with conservatives still leading the war on "subversion," federal police chief General Antonio Bandeira ordered the certificates of exhibition of ten films revoked in one fell swoop. The films had already reached the public, but the notoriously conservative General Bandeira disagreed with the rather more liberal decisions of his underlings. According to the federal police, "licentiousness, violence, and subversion . . . are intimately related between themselves and in the final analysis simply contribute to 'undermining the roots of Brazilian society so as to destroy it.'" Hence censorship sought to "impede that process [in order to] preserve national security itself." Bandeira not only ordered the films taken out of theaters but "called a meeting of various censors demanding more rigor in their work." Even in this case of direct and unilateral intervention, however, bagunça remained in play:

the films continued to be shown throughout the weekend and were only prohibited—"rigorously"—starting the Monday following Bandeira's announcement.[15]

The "mess" of dictatorship, then, certainly encompassed censorship, with erratic methods and regulation even within organizations headed by hard-liners. The disconnect between message and policy at the top and actual practice at the bottom grew so marked that officials even more exalted than General Bandeira found themselves in sticky situations. Education Minister Jarbas Passarinho, for example, tried to temper the government's increasingly unpopular message on censorship in 1973, claiming that he was against the "total censorship of theater performances," though not "against censorship itself." Passarinho insisted that the government had not "augmented the rigor of censorship but simply tried to defend itself and the public against explicit and implicit subversion in certain plays and, particularly, against aggression and pornography." Unfortunately for Passarinho, much of his message was lost in an embarrassing lapse in which it became clear that he himself had faulty information on what was being censored. As an "example of Government liberality," the minister cited the release of *Navalha na carne* (*Razor in the Flesh*)—which in fact suffered total censorship and would not be legally shown in Brazil for thirteen years. "This," observed *O Estado de S. Paulo*, "the minister did not know."[16]

As *O Estado*'s observation makes clear, even those outside of government could not help but note the contradictions and fitful vagaries of censorship. In a trenchant critique that itself came to the attention of intelligence agents on the hunt for "subversive" material, a student newsletter at Fluminense Federal University pointed out the ways in which the government seemed at odds with itself when it came to cultural policy. "Cultural life," the students complained, "is submitted to violent and absurd censorship. Organized almost as an autonomous sector, [censorship] enters into conflict even with other governmental organizations, as in the case of the prohibition of the play *Rasga coração* [which was the] winner of the National Theater Service Prize."[17] Likewise, critic Flávio Galvão wrote that in its obsessive attempt to combat "sexual revolution" via censorship, the government had become "ridiculous" and "laughable." As Galvão went on to point out, the focus on censorship made little sense from a legal standpoint—government disorganization on this front had reached such heights that the regime seemed to ill understand extant legislation: the government (or at least elements within it) "was beating a dead horse because publications . . . harmful to morality and to good customs were already crimes . . . and, as such, their repression was already legally provided for," with or without hard-liners' focus on national, moral security.[18]

"Amorous Relations with Watermelons": *Pornochanchadas,* Embrafilme, and Dictatorial Pornography

Perhaps the most striking example of the bagunça in sexual and cultural policy, and of censorship's contradictory implementation, lies in the story of the government film corporation, Embrafilme, and the most popular subset of movies that it produced: *pornochanchadas.* Created in 1969, Embrafilme (formally Empresa Brasileira de Filmes, or Brazilian Film Enterprise) eventually supplanted the controversial and somewhat ineffectual National Cinema Institute. In its first several years, Embrafilme functioned principally as a distributor, but between 1974 and 1979 the organization's budget increased thirteenfold, as it took on the distribution of 30 percent and the production of 25–50 percent of national film production. In many ways, Embrafilme achieved its mission— teaming up with Brazilian filmmakers, the state agency managed to vastly increase output and Brazilian viewership of nationally produced cinema, undergirding resistance to the implacable onslaught of imported films.[19] In the same interview in which he erred in citing *Navalha na carne,* Passarinho referred to the state's project of fomenting national film production and taking a stronger hand in the politics of national culture. Government, Passarinho averred, would not engage in "dema-gogic and antidemocratic" propaganda; he also insisted that state spon-sorship would not "fall into the ingenuity of financing subversion or pornography."[20]

Even as Passarinho spoke, however, Embrafilme was moving toward one of its key legacies: the financing of its most popular and successful genre, the pornochanchada. These films combined soft-core pornogra-phy with an older style of light comedy (*chanchada*) based on traditional tropes of mistaken identity, idiosyncratic and/or obsessive characters, and rusticity contrasted with the modern and the urbane. Dismissed by some, pornochanchadas have also been historiographically validated as important contributions to Brazilian popular culture, especially insofar as they developed out of innovative, antiestablishment filmmaking in 1970s São Paulo.[21] Pornochanchadas preceded hard-core pornography, and most of their eroticism lay in the power of titillating suggestion. Illustrative titles include *As secretárias . . . que fazem de tudo* (*The Secretaries . . . Who Do Everything*); *Eu dou o que ela gosta* (*I Give Her What She Likes*); *A noite das taras* (*The Night of the Fetishes*); *Ninfetas do sexo* (*Sex Nymphets*); and *As cangaceiras do sexo* (*Sex Bandits*). Scenes of explicit intercourse were rare, and nudity often partial. To quote one critic, "the major failing of the pornochanchada is not that it is porn, but that it is so little porn."[22] Indeed, some have argued that pornochanchadas ultimately reinforced moral conservatism, via plots that punished sexual deviance while relying on "fantastical happy endings" of conventional marriage to reward heterosex, fidelity, and monogamy.[23] Nevertheless, the films (which numbered in the hundreds) featured bodies and sexualities in ways that transgressed previous standards of permissibility.[24]

The popularity of pornochanchadas made them the only viable means of fulfilling the quotas established for exhibition of nationally produced films. Hence, though Embrafilme did not finance all pornochanchadas, a great majority of them (especially after 1980, when both moralism and dictatorship were unquestionably in decline) received government support. By 1980, in fact, the linkage between the state film corporation and sponsorship of pornography had received enough public attention that Minister of Justice Abi-Ackel openly favored shutting down Embrafilme rather than continuing to fund "that kind of production."[25] The DCDP, meanwhile, directly blamed Embrafilme for the production of films harmful to "morality" and "decorum"—yet continued to allow the production of the offending pornochanchadas. Indeed, as William Martins has argued, there was a "tacit agreement" between Embrafilme, government censors, and many (though not all) film critics that "pornochanchadas were terrible, but they guaranteed the survival of national cinema."[26] In a compounded irony, national production entered a period of decline once pornochanchadas began to suffer competition from foreign, hard-core pornographic films—a development that followed the end of censorship and the consequent permissibility of those imports.[27]

Thus, despite the best efforts of powerful moralists, and the conflation at various government and administrative levels of sexual and moral deviance with communist subversion, the state found itself financing transgressively erotic movies. This irony was starkly illustrated every time the lights went down in theaters showing the movies, as cinema operators had to play stilted government propaganda shorts before any feature film, including the chanchadas.[28] The incongruity can be attributed, in part, to bagunça itself, to the several government agencies and individuals whose divergent agendas converged at this site. Censors, bound to stamp out eroticism, were equally or perhaps more bound to support the national film industry. Indeed, the confusion became so apparent that even the government's critics noted the irony of state finance for pornochanchadas. Oppositional student groups complained that "Brazilian art finds itself in a state of crisis" based on the government's nonsensical support for "all the pornochanchadas, which . . . use mediocre humor and cheap sex to stimulate moralistic and reactionary concepts about sex."[29] Condemning censorship more broadly, one student bulletin pointed out the deep ironies of the government's selective moralism, including the 1976 censorship of a transmission of the Bolshoi performing *Romeo and Juliet*. The students pointed out that "Films held by the censors to be harmful to the Brazilian public are prohibited or mutilated (*Iracema*, by Orlando Senna, *Z*, by Costa Gavras, etc.), while torrents of subproducts like *kung fus* and pornochanchadas are launched into the marketplace; books by famous and respectable authors disappear from the bookstores, and the press lives with prior censorship always at its back . . . not to mention the possibility that journals and magazines might be taken off the newsstands at any moment. The arbitrariness of censorship has reached the ridiculous point of prohibiting the presentation of the Bolshoi Ballet, on TV."[30]

The issue of pornochanchadas dogged Embrafilme from its inception until its abolition by President Fernando Collor de Mello in 1990. Indeed, the delicate relationship between the state film company and the censors who should have been (and sometimes were) its greatest antagonists seemed to hinge on the cross-purposes that forced a tenuous and ironic cooperation. Embrafilme and the DCDP remained uncomfortably linked as long as both existed, because Embrafilme wished to avoid complete veto of its productions, while DCDP functionaries felt pressure "not to completely censor a nationally produced film, especially if it had received state funding."[31] In this sense, Embrafilme was representative, as the interrelated problems of censorial jurisdiction and reluctance to censor national production spread into other areas of the arts. In 1976, the SNI would complain that the state's National Theater Service (SNT) rivaled Embrafilme in this respect. Agents reported that "the SNT offers . . . plays that, though they have been submitted to censorship, present, in their texts, politico-ideological and erotico-pornographic connotations, which should disqualify them from receiving aid from an official agency." The sticking point, it seemed to SNI officials, lay once again in the issues of competing mandates and censorial bodies.[32]

Recent scholarship on Embrafilme has noted its relative autonomy from the Ministry of Education and Culture—the state parent agency to both Embrafilme and the SNT—and the ways in which this meant constant stylistic crises and conflicts. Embrafilme produced and coproduced a wide variety of films (242 in total between 1970 and 1981), with an according variation in the degree to which production dovetailed with the ideological and aesthetic guidelines favored by different elements of the state.[33] Among the most pointed examples of films that challenged and even mocked moralistic state prerogatives, Joaquim Pedro de Andrade's eighteen-minute *Vereda tropical* (*Tropical Way*, 1977) showcased erotic parody (indeed, biting political commentary) on Embrafilme's dime. Andrade made the short as part of a series called *Contos eróticos* (*Erotic Tales*), for which he had already produced another satirical film centering on sex (*Guerra conjugal*, *Conjugal Warfare*, 1975). *Vereda tropical* starred Cláudio Cavalcanti as a thirty-something with a sexual preference made absurd by the film: the character favored intercourse with watermelons (see fig. 10). Cavalcanti's character, like *Vereda tropical* itself, parodistically eviscerated the regime's cultural and moral policies—Cavalcanti portrayed an effete intellectual suffering from erectile problems and only capable of sex with fruit. His tender and sometimes disturbing (borderline sadomasochistic) attentions to a watermelon (culminating in its sexual penetration) ridiculed both the male chauvinism and the hypocrisy of the pornochanchada genre.[34] When the film was censored in 1977, Andrade gave an incisive interview to the *Jornal do Brasil*: "*Vereda tropical* is a film that is already self-censored within the obvious limits of censorship, insofar as I know where I live and I make films to get by [censors] and not incur prohibition. When [censorship] happens, it is as though the film had ceased to exist. [*Vereda tropical*] does not have profanity, does not have naked women, and yet still cannot be shown."[35]

As filmmaker and critic Jean-Claude Bernardet pointed out, *Vereda tropical* threw censorship into precisely the kind of upheaval that Andrade's ironic critique had intended. While it was "easy to censor" a pornographic film, Bernardet wrote, Andrade "has created a universe of

As Três Virgens, de Roberto Palmari, conta a história de uma jovem confiada à tutela de tias solteironas pelos pais descontentes com seu comportamento

Em *Arroz e Feijão*, de Roberto Santo- (acima), Joana Fomm vive um romance com o sobrinho. *Vereda Tropical*, de Joaquim Pedro, foi vetado pela Censura por relatar as aventuras eróticas de Cláudio Cavalcanti com uma melancia

"Vereda Tropical," de Joaquim Pedro de Andrade CENSURADO AQUI. CONVIDADO PARA FESTIVAL EM NOVA IORQUE

Figure 10 News coverage of censorship of *Vereda tropical*. In Caderno B, *Jornal do Brasil*, 25 February 1979, 5.

pleasure without culpability." Hence censorship of *Vereda tropical* must be "exclusively ideological" and necessarily reveal the ridiculousness of that ideology.[36] Two years later, the Superior Council of Censors (CSC) reversed DCDP's decision, allowing the film to be shown without cuts and adding: "It seems absurd to us to cut the episode *Vereda tropical*, an almost criminal comedy, as we do not have, at any moment, the worry that it will induce in viewers the desire to have amorous relations with watermelons."[37]

As is well known, pornochanchadas were just one of the filmic ways in which Embrafilme challenged the state's more moralistic factions and agencies. Within the system of partial financing from Embrafilme, artists seem to have felt a certain amount of creative and even political freedom, extending beyond pornochanchadas into films that contravened the countersubversive hard line more thematically. As filmmaker Carlos Diegues (famously a critic of Embrafilme) pointed out, "It is a mistake to talk about a single economic project of Embrafilme. The great quality of Embrafilme is . . . pluralism."[38] That pluralism included several artistic avenues of deviation from the prerogatives of authoritarianists at the heart of the regime, including Diegues's own *Bye Bye*

Brazil, Ruy Guerra's *The Fall*, Roberto Farias's *Pra frente, Brasil*, and films from the oft-controversial Cinema Novo group. Even to Diegues, Embrafilme represented something of a "victory" for certain radical artists of the 1960s, who benefited from the state's underwriting of national cinema; Guerra argues that the self-censorship which many artists exercised under the dictatorship was attenuated by Embrafilme, which at the very least allowed them to avoid "the extremely violent economic censorship that results from a structure completely dominated by the foreign film, by large distributors, by exhibition networks."[39] Pornochanchadas, though sensational, were only the most obvious of films that subtly countered the regime's more authoritarian prerogatives.

Indeed, Embrafilme went beyond these subtle, film-based challenges noted by scholars of the period's movies and moviemakers. By the close of the 1970s, the organization had involved itself with more radical, direct denunciations of the regime. Embrafilme sponsored the First National Symposium on Brazilian Film, held in Rio in September 1978. The symposium "celebrated the union of two historically antagonistic classes in national cinema: producers and exhibitors"—and this union produced a certain degree of open revolt. Embrafilme published proceedings of the meeting, presented as the will of "representatives from all the sectors of our cinematographic community." These representatives, according to the proceedings, demanded not only an end to censorship but retroactive restoration of any films prohibited or "mutilated by censorship in their original version." Furthermore, and perhaps most impressively, the attendees called for cultural and economic redress or repayment for the harms of censorship: "reparation from the State for the damage caused by the action of Censorship to the cultural patrimony of society and to the patrimony of each of the individuals involved in the processes of [film] distribution." Though the military establishment did not meet these demands, they were a sign of liberalizations happening via Embrafilme, itself a state agency.[40]

Policing and Promoting the Pill

The relationship between censors, the moralistic prerogatives espoused in regime power centers, and government-sponsored film production thus reflected the temporal vagaries of clout within the regime, and the messiness of attempts to streamline sexual and cultural policy. This bagunça met its match, however, in a demonstration of governmental factions' cross-purposes in an altogether separate—and perhaps more surprising—arena: debates over birth control in the late 1970s. At this point, though repression continued, the most intense years of extralegal detainment and disappearance had ended. While the armed Left lay in tatters, the power of extreme-right elements within the dictatorship appeared in many ways to wane. Perhaps for that very reason, plans emerged that would have seemed unthinkable only a few years earlier. By 1977, a program appeared to be in place to distribute two million government-purchased birth control pills. The fate of the pills—and, presumably, of the nearly 100,000 women whom the program intended to serve—reveals the byzantine nature of government policy on morality and reproduction; the outrage and desperation of extreme-right moralists, who felt themselves losing ground; and the confusion, even at senior levels, about how to manage competing prerogatives of moralism and developmentalist population control.

As late as 1973, government and security forces displayed—publicly and confidentially—rigid opposition to birth control. At a meeting of the United Nations Economic and Social Council (ECOSOC), Brazilian representative Mauro Sérgio Costa Couto "reiterated that our government does not see any necessity to incentivize birth control." This announcement represented a frontal attack on BEMFAM, the family-planning services NGO founded in Brazil by the International Planned Parenthood Federation (IPPF) in 1965. IPPF, sponsored in large part by the United States government, worked to curb population growth and raise awareness of reproductive strategy. These activities roused suspicion and hostility from a variety of quarters, including moralists; such sentiments crested in 1967, when a congressional inquiry addressed sensational accusations of "massive sterilization" of rural Brazilian women by "foreigners" (among them North American missionaries).[41] As the Catholic magazine *O São Paulo* crowed following Couto's appearance at ECOSOC, "The non-Brazilian interest of the activities of BEMFAM and of some Brazilians has now been recognized, in their campaign . . . denounced as anti-patriotic, not to mention . . . amoral."[42] If *O São Paulo* reveled in this rejection of birth control, the SNI remained highly suspicious of BEMFAM itself, reflecting—at this apogee of rightist security forces' power in the regime—the active opposition to birth control within the machinery of repression. The SNI maintained vigilant surveillance of BEMFAM and anyone related to it. As a (clearly shocked) SNI functionary wrote in a classified memo, BEMFAM had been active in the state of Guanabara, treating "issues linked to sexual education, even recommending the use of contraceptives." The memo sought information from other intelligence services, especially "if BEMFAM creates propaganda, distributes, sells, or recommends the use of . . . contraceptives."[43]

Nevertheless, later in the 1970s, as the dictatorship tilted toward re-democratization, concern about population control did begin to creep into public discourse in Brazil. By the time of the 1974 UN Conference on Population in Bucharest, Brazil's representatives—though still insisting on natalism and population growth as the way forward for Brazil nationally—were willing to entertain the validity of North Atlantic anxieties about the "demographic explosion." Brazil joined a bloc of African and Latin American countries in denouncing IPPF at the conference, but did begin to consider the government's potential role in providing birth control to low-income families, should they demand it.[44] As the official statement by Brazil's delegation put it, opposing the proposed World Population Plan of Action, "Birth control is a decision for the family unit, which in this context should not be subject to government interference; being able to resort to birth control measures should not be a privilege reserved for families that are well-off, and therefore it is the responsibility of the state to provide the information and the means that may be required by families of limited income."[45]

By this point, then, some members of Brazil's military government had turned a corner in terms of attitudes toward fertility and reproductive rights. No sanction emerged regarding activities like those of BEMFAM, but ideas about family-centric limitation of progeny and concern with the reproductive health of poor women did creep into public and governmental discourse. Much of the new discussion revolved around population control and the concept of *gestantes de alto risco*—women likely to have "high-risk pregnancies." According to an *O Estado de S. Paulo* report in June 1977, the latter represented cause for public alarm: 29 percent of Brazilian women fell into this category, "running the risk of [uninduced] abortion, premature labor, or even the birth of children with congenital deformities."[46] That same month, the Ministry of Health confirmed that a new program would indeed take international population control efforts into account, in accordance with the statements set out by the Brazilian delegation. While no grand plan for limiting reproduction was to be entertained, the government must take responsibility for facilitating parents' (especially poor parents') own decisions to stop having children.[47]

The program in question, rolled out by the government in fits and starts between 1977 and 1979, reflected the high-stakes nature of the issue and a contradiction redolent of bagunça: ambivalence and hostility to birth control in some quarters of the regime even as other representatives of the state took steps to sponsor broad family-planning interventions. The initiative, developed by the Ministry of Health, was dubbed the Program for the Prevention of High-Risk Pregnancy (PPGAR)—the name itself reflecting a public relations campaign determined to limit the program's focus to the health of at-risk women. Preliminary plans remained vague and suggested a very limited scope. Although, in the initial phases of discussion, sources claimed that the government would spend 2.7 billion *cruzeiros* and distribute 2 million boxes of free birth control pills, these promises appear to have fallen by the wayside; and those numbers that did materialize more clearly made the program appear quite small-scale. At its outset, PPGAR sought to attend only 81,700 women over the course of four years. By November 1977, the state of Rio Grande do Norte was the sole beneficiary and a modest 13,200 "patients" had received care.[48]

Meanwhile, officials were scrupulously careful about distancing the program from birth control as such. The focus of implementation and of public representation remained strictly wedded to the titular high-risk pregnancies, making PPGAR, both in deed and in appearance, more a social welfare program than anything resembling a population control measure. In this regard, in fact, the program fell in line with the maternalism that characterized rightist prescriptions for the redress of "modern" womanhood; no matter what the concern about women, redress took the form of promoting "healthy" motherhood. According to the 1978 annual report from the National Division of Maternal and Infantile Health (DINSAMI), the responsible department within the Ministry of Health's National Secretariat of Special Health Programs, PPGAR's agenda limited itself to basic puericulture. DINSAMI reported its goals and achievements in the realms of "attending pregnant women," "attending births," and "attending children less than a year old," but made absolutely no mention of birth control, focusing instead on vaccinations and pre- and postnatal care.[49]

When government officials addressed the program publicly, they stressed its orientation as one that tended *away* from birth control, and took care not to offend moral sensibilities. The regime's public relations honcho, then-Colonel José Maria de Toledo Camargo took the proactive tack of deciding that PPGAR would get no radio or television publicity at all because it was an "issue of an intimate nature." (This, of course, begged the question of how potential beneficiaries were to discover the program.) In a statement, the colonel clarified that his decision conformed to the government's "politics of social communications" (the attempt to carefully manage public information, especially that of a sensitive, potentially subversive nature). He made a point of mentioning the Pill as precisely the live wire that AERP (the aforementioned government public relations bureau) wished to avoid: "The adoption of contraceptive pills, for example, . . . cannot be disseminated generally, as it hinges on medical criteria and involves prejudices and religions."[50] The government's chief spokesperson thus placed a kibosh on public discussion of PPGAR beyond its emphasis on the *promotion* of reproduction via gestational health.

Even the minister of health himself strove to publicize the less controversial aspects of the program, "such as supplementary alimentation, prevention of mental deficiencies in newborns, and assistance granted to pregnant women, breastfeeding mothers, and children." Representatives of the program repeatedly emphasized the Ogino-Knaus (rhythm) method as the principal focus of birth control within the program. Approved by the Catholic Church, this tactic (sometimes called natural family planning) was lauded by officials as "the most traditional method, which consists in the abstinence of sexual relations during the woman's fertile period."[51] Stressing this point, Cyro Coimbra, director of DINSAMI, told reporters that the program's goal was to "save lives"; therefore, the PPGAR held the position that "the only totally innocuous method is the Ogino-Knaus chart."[52]

Government ambivalence vis-à-vis public messages about the program grew so pronounced that critics decried its limited scope and its half starts. Elsimar Metzker Coutinho, a Brazilian-born global authority on endocrinology, family planning, and contraceptive pills, noted that the PPGAR represented a "sign of evolution in government politics with relation to family planning . . . a position that is long overdue." Nevertheless, he complained of the program's crippling shortcomings and contradictions. The much-touted focus on women with high-risk pregnancies, he wrote, would leave "unprotected those healthy women to whom methods of avoiding pregnancy will be denied. By means of this blatant discrimination, the Program will exclude the great majority of women of fertile age." The PPGAR, he argued, should seek to attend far more women, irrespective of their gestational health, and should stop equivocating when it came to more politicized means of birth control. The rhythm method, Coutinho pointed out, was "completely ineffective" in most cases, and should be replaced not only by the Pill but by IUDs, whose principal obstacle in Brazil was "an unjustified campaign of defamation inspired and fed by the enemies of family planning."[53]

If the regime's public pronouncements about PPGAR displayed ambivalence and lack of coherence around goals, methods, and message, the program's deployment made this confusion even more apparent. When authorities began discussing the possibility of actually distributing contraceptive pills, PPGAR's leadership made it clear that such distribution would be strictly limited. Many women—especially those at "high risk," on whom the program intended to focus—would "be counseled to use other methods of contraception," and it was here that Coimbra reemphasized the program's intent to "save lives."[54] In fact, the fate of the two million planned boxes of free pills remains unclear, at least insofar as I have been able to determine. While several thousand boxes of pills were sold to paying customers (in private pharmacies) between 1976 and 1978, funding for the government-subsidized pills still had not materialized two years later. In 1979, some 594,000 women, instead of receiving birth control, were slated for "preconception orientation."[55] Later that year, in September, the third National Development Plan (PND) officially canceled the Pill as part of government programs. Reiterating the puericultural importance of "maternal and infant health" and even of "the prevention of venereal diseases," the plan discouraged contraception more generally, instead opting for "family planning" that was, by default, "natural" and likely to be limited to the Ogino-Knaus method. The PND "discouraged . . . the adoption of mass programs of birth control . . . recommending governmental action in the realm of family planning."[56]

The lack of unity in message and implementation continued into 1980, when those who had tried to introduce birth control appeared to realize that the Pill had placed the program as a whole in serious jeopardy. Observers noted that PPGAR's continuing supporters were "timidly" preparing a draft bill in which the only contraceptive methods proposed were "natural"—so-called "radical" birth control was entirely eliminated from the program. Even the eviscerated version of the program, however "timidly" presented, had been placed on the back burner, with no date set for its approval by the president, much less for its deployment. Minister of Health Waldyr Mendes Arcoverde summed up this effective retreat from anything resembling the birth control initiatives imagined a few years earlier: though the ministry "cannot ignore the existence of chemical and radical contraceptive methods," his administration would exclude such methods entirely. Instead, the revamped PPGAR would emphasize the "educational facet," in which "gynecological clinics will give women knowledge about the physiology of human reproduction." As Minister Arcoverde put it, the idea was "to immediately make natural family-planning methods catch the eye."[57]

Contemporary consensus, dovetailing with Elsimar Coutinho's assessment, concluded that this privileging of Ogino-Knaus and coitus interruptus (the "pull-out" method), both approved by the church, emerged in large part to evade "criticism from radical sectors, who hate any type of birth control."[58] Among those radical sectors, as we shall see, church leaders and radical rightists found themselves in a somewhat unlikely alliance, but a principal font of the anti-Pill groundswell emanated from the ESG, which still—true to form—loomed large at this nexus of moral and social planning issues. Developmentalists at the ESG opposed birth control for at least two reasons: (1) the idea that as economic conditions improved, families would "naturally come to limit the number of children," and (2) the dearly held notion that Brazil had a huge "territory to be populated" and thus sterilization and the Pill (the two methods of contraception referred to under the rubric of "radical") were, in some sense, unpatriotic. Indeed, Arcoverde affirmed that the ministry's line on birth control would follow "the doctrine proposed by the Escola Superior de Guerra." Accordingly, it would avoid undue "impact" and would "not defend radical and irreversible contraception . . . nor will it use contraceptive pills as a mass method."[59]

The prospects for sponsored birth control seemed particularly dire at this point, given the personal opposition of the president himself. General Figueiredo, whose crusade against the "pornographic surge" included an alliance with archconservative evangelical pastor Nilson Fanini, was no friend of contraception in general. When asked by two schoolgirls (aged fourteen and sixteen) about birth control, Figueiredo responded enigmatically, "The surest contraceptive is not to have love for the person, not to like the person. Otherwise, as I see it, there is no human force that can impede conception." Figueiredo added that, in his capacity as director of the SNI, he had identified the antifamily attitudes of subversive captives as their distinguishing characteristic. "They didn't know what they wanted. They were lost," he concluded.[60] Reinforcing this sense of moralistic, family-centric countersubversion at the top, Federal Deputy João Alves de Almeida went on record in 1981 to proclaim his own and Figueiredo's opposition to "family planning" in general. Citing "free sex" and "dechristianization of the world," Almeida wrote a letter to the air force director of civil aviation expressing displeasure with national consideration of "'family planning,' a euphemism for birth control, a process by which in a short time we will arrive at the justification and legalization of abortion." The letter came to rest with agents from the air force's secret intelligence service, who archived it and underlined its key provisions (about "nations in social decomposition" and the idea that "family planning serves to cover up more serious crimes"). In this letter, as well as in a speech in the Chamber of Deputies, Almeida assured listeners that Figueiredo, his personal friend, "abominates family planning."[61]

"Imminent Risk of Harm": Moral Panic and the Desperate Right

Despite the friendly overtures of President Figueiredo, by the 1980s, the messiness of government policies on morality, from censorship to birth control, appears to have thrown moralistic right-wingers into a state of desperation and outrage. More broadly, extreme-right, hard-line elements of the regime felt a sense of marginalization following on the heels of democratization; *abertura*, even in the more recent memoirs of former Cold Warriors, represents disempowerment and, to some, defeat.[62] Moralists, bound ideologically and personally to the hard line, linked this disempowerment with an impending triumph of cultural and sexual subversion. Deputy Almeida's abovementioned speech rang with a moral panic that reflected moralists' sense of losing the "good fight"—he referred to an inexorable march toward abortion, marked by "entirely uninhibited sex, exacerbated eroticism, vices, drugs, and criminality." In Brazil, as elsewhere, this manifested in "the ever-growing intervention of the State in family life, with methods that ... deteriorate the genetic patrimony and weaken the biologic quality—so ruined already—of our population." Such methods would leave Brazil in "a biological, social, and moral state worse than that of any other nation on earth," said Almeida.[63]

This sense of the inexorable, of a turning point that had left the heady days of moralistic power behind, cropped up in other right-wing quarters. Corção himself viewed birth control cynically, as a legislative descendant of the 1977 legalization of divorce. For that reason, Corção and other conservatives "did not react with much surprise to the decision of the government" to consider sponsored contraception programs. In a statement, Corção bemoaned the situation, but took the view that this moral dissipation was inevitable and that his *bom combate* (good fight) had at long last proven unwinnable. "This goes beyond the pale, unfortunately . . . but ultimately it is just one more sad event against which I have fought for my whole life and, it would seem, fought in vain."[64]

Intelligence and security forces, meanwhile, felt themselves beset by a moral-sexual conspiracy mounted by enemies on the Left. This sense of embattlement increased to the point of routine in the later 1970s and early 1980s. One report from the Justice Ministry's intelligence division generated a laundry list of such enemies, including the usual suspects: artists, the oppositional Brazilian Press Association (ABI) and Brazilian Bar Association (OAB), feminists, and several gay and lesbian rights groups, including the pioneering Somos, Lesbian Feminist Action Group (GALF), and "some other thing about sexual action" (an apparent reference to the São Paulo group Outra Coisa/Ação Homossexualista). Imputing subversion to the activists in question, the report declared vaguely that they had "shown almost extremist behavior." The report's conclusion made clear that the moral issues at stake in censorship were inseparable from the political ones. Activists' "systematic" and "declared campaign" against cultural repression imperiled the "moralizing and relevant action lent by censorship on behalf of Brazilian society"—that is, censors' struggle against communist "attempts to manipulate the outlets of social communication."[65] An SNI report, similar in focus, waxed bitterer, reflecting the increasing desperation of moralist hard-liners. "The broaching of themes that attack morality and good customs, in flagrant disrespect . . . of Article 153 of the Constitution, on the part of the most varied publications, grows ever more abundant." The report, secure in its righteousness if not in its effectiveness, also expressed incredulity at the proliferation of eroticism in public culture when both the minister of justice and the president had spoken out against the "excess of licentiousness that has been occurring in that area."[66]

Higher-ups did, indeed, engage in the moralistic hand-wringing of this moment. Justice Minister and former Integralist Ibrahim Abi-Ackel, who at one point endorsed mob attacks on bikini wearers at Ipanema beach, complained bitterly and consistently of the growing "excesses" of licentiousness provoked, to his mind, by political democratization.[67] In September of 1980, he wrote letters to the governors of Brazil's states, soliciting their help in "preserving public morality and good customs." Separate letters to the presidents of the state appellate courts ratcheted up the urgency of this solicitation, citing "imminent risk of harm" from attacks on morality.[68] In the Chamber of Deputies, right-wing moralists hammered home the message about morality as a safeguard against subversion. In a 1983 address entitled "The Current Situation of Subversion in Brazil," Federal Deputy Sebastião Curió Rodrigues de Moura—the (in)famous "Major Curió" of the military's 1970 counterguerrilla offensive—sought to inform his fellow legislators about the dangers of *abertura* and amnesty. Exercised about "clandestine organizations, who were said to have been extinct, or at the very least 'converted' to democratic ways," Moura held forth about Marxism as an ongoing problem in Brazil, "subversion that proceeds via the progressive infiltration of communists in all the sectors of human activity." Armed with a list of "communist organizations . . . that are active today in Brazil," Moura began with accusations of moral subversion. The principal "communist organization" (or series of organizations) to which he pointed was "anarchist groups who preach the liberalization of marijuana, of abortion, of homosexuality, in short of everything that can disaggregate the family and weaken society."[69]

New rightist organizations also emerged to bring this message to national attention. Perhaps the most visible of these, the Senhoras de Santana (Ladies of Santana) coalesced in a wealthy neighborhood of São Paulo's northern metropolitan region. The Senhoras presented themselves—in an ironic mirroring of the Mothers of the Plaza de Mayo and similar *anti*authoritarian groups—as worried *donas de casa* (housewives and mothers) who sought to protect their families from a "crisis" of immorality and eroticism. In 1981, led by Marlene Schmidt Rodrigues, Maria da Luz Duarte Mendes, Maria Helena Maluf, and several other women, they presented a statement—titled "We Are Just Concerned

Mothers"—to the national congress. The statement read like notes from an ESG workshop or a passage from one of the school's manuals. "It is in the realm of the moral," held the Senhoras, "that we encounter the most profound crises of our time. We are being victimized by a continuous psychological action designed especially to prejudice young minds." They identified the moral crisis as principally sexual and media-borne: "What we are seeing on our televisions, cinemas, and magazines is the most profound inversion of values. Conjugal infidelity . . . lack of familial love . . . rapes, masturbation, spouse swapping . . . are valorized." The women lionized Figueiredo as a president committed to the kind of moral change they wanted to see. His declared war on pornography, like his support for other moralistic initiatives, thrilled the paulista women's group. "We here in São Paulo," the statement enthused, "are elated with this decision of our government, in its attempt to weaken the effects of this pornography." They closed by associating sexual liberalization with *abertura*. While they did not directly oppose democratization, they—like Ruy Côdo, the deputy who introduced them—held it responsible for "licentiousness" and for "pornography that wounds and sickens the Brazilian family."[70] They were not alone: two years earlier, the Feminine Civic Union (UCF), a similar group in Santos, accused "men who are trying to teach perverse things" via "pornography" of "threatening National Security."[71] Like other moralistic anticommunists, the Senhoras and the UCF experienced the late 1970s and early 1980s, the era of redemocratization, as a waning of the power of rightist moralism and a dangerous backsliding into the territory of subversion.

Reflections on Bagunça: Strange Bedfellows

Even as the Senhoras made their advance on the legislative floor, however, there were those willing to oppose them—legislators who, as redemocratization gained momentum, identified the Senhoras and their ilk with "false moralism" and "the return of indiscriminate censorship" and authoritarianism.[72] Likewise, there were those, including several opposition legislators and the secretary of health in nearly every state, who supported government-sponsored birth control.[73] In fact, by this point (1981), moralists felt their star waning. President Figueiredo himself was a staunch ally in the *bom combate*—but the triumphs of broad censorship, of Moral and Civic Education, and of the successful intimidation of lesbians, gays, feminists, and other gender-sexual heterodoxy seemed bygone. This was so much the case that, despite the ongoing friendship of Figueiredo and Abi-Ackel, and despite the continuing conviction of extreme moralists inside and outside the security apparatus that moral dissolution represented active subversion, the lines between Left and Right, "subversive" and sexual, grew increasingly blurry. In the late seventies, progressive sectors (including, at times, feminists) openly voiced *their* opposition to birth control and media-borne immorality, making for an unlikely and sometimes uncomfortable fellowship with their longtime right-wing detractors.

The progressive clergy, ever the targets of Gustavo Corção's alarmist derision, found themselves siding with him, as Catholics, in opposition to birth control. Thus when Corção denounced the advent of the Pill as "a descending arc of morality," whose starting point was the 1977 legalization of divorce, Dom Ivo Lorscheiter joined him. Lorscheiter, a leading antagonist of the regime in the human rights debate, announced that "distributing pills is like handing out poison . . . it will be a disaster for the people and for the Country, which, continuing this way, will become an authentic cemetery." Dom Ivo's cousin and fellow progressive, Dom Aloísio Lorscheider, laced his comments with unequivocal moral panic. Nearly echoing Corção, he pointed to a wave of libidinousness in Brazil that "began with divorce, now includes the Pill, tomorrow will be abortion, and after that, homosexuality. Then it will be the end."[74] Dom Avelar Brandão, a relative moderate whom the regime and conservatives nevertheless branded a "dangerous element" (on the basis of his association with human rights and social justice), likewise spoke out strongly against contraception.[75]

Other progressives took the regime and its allies to task on the significance of government-sponsored pornochanchadas and birth control. These issues thus created a contradictory triangulation within which regime hard-liners, moralist right-wing civilians, and left-wing opposition groups found themselves in agreement about morality—if about nothing else. This, as anthropologist Paula Montero summarizes, was less an alliance than a "confluence of divergent interests" that supported "more ethico-moral control of television shows."[76] As noted above, the reformist Catholic newspaper *O São Paulo* and its publisher (the archdiocese) decried a "wave of eroticism" and celebrated impediments to the liberalization of birth control. Yet *O São Paulo* saw "permissiveness" and the relaxation of sexual and reproductive culture and practice as outgrowths of *capitalism*, the "society of consumption" promoted by the regime and against which the regime's "censorship in and of itself will be ineffective."[77] Concurring with the anti-pornochanchada student groups mentioned above, the newsletter *Campus* (published by students at the Federal University at Minas Gerais, UFMG) ridiculed the government's self-ascription of the word "revolutionary" and blamed "the famous pornochanchadas" on government support and the capitalist opportunity that they represented for "producers who see in them a prime investment."[78]

These voices on the Left echoed those of other progressives who more broadly denounced birth control as an imperialist, capitalist-led war on the world's poor. Such voices included some Brazilian feminists, whose birth control politics did not necessarily mirror those of their North Atlantic counterparts. Indeed, given the configurations of dictatorship and opposition in 1970s Brazil, many feminists focused more on broad-based alliances with other anti-imperialist, pro-democracy, and pro–human rights constituencies, notably the Catholic Church. The complexity of this position led, for example, to contradictory articles in the feminist magazine *Brasil Mulher*, which alternated between advocating abortion rights and advising readers to "throw out [their] birth control pills."[79] Catholic progressives had long cast their opposition to birth control as anti-imperial pro-natalism; as early as 1967, Dom Jorge Marcos de Oliveira deplored birth control programs as a North Atlantic plot, coinciding with right-wing moralists in his opposition to the Pill and in his pro-natalist stance (which, in and of itself, would have found welcome at the ESG). At a labor day rally, Oliveira exhorted the crowd to consider "this story of the Pills, they've got Pills in North America, but today what we need in Brazil is many Brazilians who nurture in their hearts the seed of idealism and of struggle." His charge that family planning emanated from "North American missions, invading . . . to decimate our families, to sterilize our women, to destroy the vigor of our men, to destroy the possibilities of a great nation" met with applause and a chorus of "Americans, get out!"[80] Catholic literary critic and regime detractor Otto Maria Carpeaux likewise read the promotion of birth control as a cynical capitalist ploy. "They [foreign imperialists] are no longer interested in the presence of millions of individuals who, for total lack of resources, are not even potential consumers of American merchandise. Instead, they wish to diminish the demographic pressure that might be capable of generating revolutions in underdeveloped countries."[81]

Conclusion: Rethinking the Politics of Opposition and Morality

In a tour de force on the contradictory relationships between authoritarian government, right-wing reaction, and policy on morality, sexuality, and gender in southern South America, political scientist Mala Htun has argued that the Brazilian government legalized divorce in 1977 as a counterattack against the left-leaning currents in the Catholic hierarchy who had made trouble for the regime. There is much to be said for Htun's interpretation—but what we have seen in this chapter problematizes her explanation. Why would the government use divorce to assail the church in 1977, only to retreat from state-sponsored birth control—in accord with conservative and progressive clerical opposition—in 1980? Why, in a later interview, would former minister of justice (and longtime moralist) Armando Falcão claim he had capitulated to divorce legislation as a "necessary evil"—despite his own views and at the regrettable expense of alienating his personal friend (and human rights spokesperson) Dom Eugênio Sales?[82]

The legalization of divorce, near the end of a tumultuous decade in Brazil's politics—both generally and in specific terms of culture, morality, and sexuality—is significant less for its potential as a weapon against the progressive church than for what it tells us about the complexity and trajectory of the regime and its subfactions, including moralists. Where Falcão himself idealized marital unions that "transform[ed] the life of two people into a paradise" and obviated divorce, President Geisel, author of *abertura*, declared that he had always, as a Lutheran, been a proponent of divorce.[83] By this point in the dictatorship, divisions within the regime were more than evident: fractious debates over succession had even brought the country to the brink of a coup from within the government, and the fortunes of hard-liners and conservatives were on the wane. When it came to moral and sexual policy, these divisions exacerbated what was already a bagunça: the morass of state and civil actors competing for control of message, policy, and implementation on these issues. Right-wing moralists held important bastions of power within the regime and especially within the ideological fonts of Brazilian authoritarianism, and they even had a friend in President Figueiredo and his morality campaign, but the combined processes of redemocratization and increasing dissolution of the military state made moralism harder to prioritize and enforce. For this reason, other individual and state prerogatives competed with moralism and sometimes triumphed—as in the case of Embrafilme's production of pornochanchadas or the serious (if ultimately fruitless) consideration of state-sponsored birth control. Moralists, in turn, consciously experienced redemocratization as a setback in their millennial struggle to reinforce traditional political, gender, sexual, and cultural hierarchies.

Conclusion

In September of 1980, a late hour in the "war on terror" in Brazil's cities, the intelligence branch of the federal police in São Paulo circulated a report to several military, political police, and intelligence units, both local and national. Entitled "Subversion: Clandestine Organizations," the report represented the latest effort to surveil, and curtail, the activities of communists in Brazil—an effort that, to security forces, seemed increasingly embattled. The secretive agents of subversion, the report noted, had grown ever bolder, to the point of showing themselves openly on the streets of the city:

> [Clandestine communist organizations] have been forming their base cells in the homosexual milieus and among prostitutes, orienting [homosexuals and sex workers] to organize themselves in associations designed as tools of pressure and propaganda. Several of these associations, already constituted, have participated in meetings and marched in parades organized by the Trotskyists. . . . Although they are an insignificant minority [in numbers], they represent, without doubt, fronts of reinforcement for the activities of subversion.[1]

The report listed specific gay rights organizations and included organograms—a favorite device of intelligence and security practitioners in Cold War Brazil—designed to clarify the structure of the putatively subversive movement. The graphics lent a familiar, technocratic air of certainty to the assertion that homosexuals and sex workers were, in fact, representatives of the enemy. The "Fourth Trotskyist International," according to the federal police, headed a pyramidal organization at whose pedestal lay local "base cells," made up of sexual deviants.

The São Paulo police may have been responding, at least in part, to leftist organizations' embryonic, and glacial, movement toward the inclusion of sexual minorities. As noted above, some leftist groups did begin to advocate sexual liberalization, late in the period of dictatorship. The Workers' Party (PT), a key coalition of the regime's opponents and powerful player in post-authoritarian national politics, contemplated the inclusion of gay and lesbian activist groups in the 1980s. (A lasting gay rights group did not emerge in São Paulo's PT until 1992, and the party did not formalize recognition of a gay and lesbian "sector" until 2001.)[2] Then, too, it is possible that in 1980, with the armed Left long since dismantled, with democratization gaining strength, and with their own influence and future role inscrutable, hard-line security forces' increasing frustration made them shrill. Nevertheless, federal police at this time did not interpret gay rights demonstrations as a departure—rather, the police saw activists within a conspiratorial continuum, as further evidence of a relationship rightists had long presumed between sexual deviance and so-called subversion. According to this logic, if movements for sexual minority rights were emerging and gaining strength, communists must have incited them to organize and make a play for public attention. The marchers in São Paulo, like the sexually liberal pronouncements of certain leftist organizations, seemed precisely what countersubversives expected to see—subversive "reinforcements," thinly disguised, plotting to exert influence on the future of Brazilian democracy via noxious "pressure and propaganda."

By this point, moral panic among security forces had become de rigueur, and presumptive—a broadly conceived reaction against any deviation from moral, gender, or sexual traditionalism. Feeling themselves deluged by an onslaught of youthful sexual deviance, women's liberation, gay rights, and sexually explicit media, officials sought to surveil and monitor—when they could not directly repress—all of these manifestations of enemy plotting. Agents infiltrated women's meetings; condemned unionization and pornography in the same breath; fretted that Carnival celebrations in Rio "emphasized scenes of libertinism, where eroticism and sex are exploited, giving the impression of an atmosphere of open orgy and libertinism [sic]." These developments, complained an army intelligence memorandum, were the troublesome fruit of "the waves of 'modernity'" and, ominously, increased "discontent among the military."[3]

These ideas, as we have seen in the course of this book, had a long history of waxing and waning impact. Countersubversives, from activist individuals and organizations to high-ranking government officials, and from technocratic security theorists to police on the ground, had made moral panic a common rallying cry and a constitutive element in authoritarian repression. These Cold Warriors blamed communist subversion for alarming and much-ballyhooed developments in the areas of youth, sexuality, media, and women's public roles. The conflation of sexuality and subversion helped lend a coherent, doctrinal narrative to right-wing efforts to name, identify, and punish the internal enemy. Priests, students, university professors, artists, and other civilians refashioned into foes of state and society were thought to use morally dissolute practice and propaganda to turn Brazil into "another Cuba."

Just as such ideas stretch back in time, so they have shown remarkable durability in the decades since the end of the Cold War. Prominent ex-partisans of dictatorship have come forward to denounce and even ridicule democratization as a mistake, borne of the victories of moral subversion. Armando Falcão, who succeeded Alfredo Buzaid as minister of justice, later remembered Brazil's return to democracy with decided bitterness. In an interview granted years after the military's retreat from power, Falcão regretted the end of dictatorial strictures. As a result of the "total extinction of censorship," Falcão contended, "today excess has no limits. Look at the way television is, the way the radio is: everything at the service of debauchery, of immorality, of indecency. It's a shame what's happening in that sector." Falcão's critique encompassed antiauthoritarian "propaganda," which he lumped together with mass-media "debauchery." The former minister lamented the way in which "people say all that stuff against Pinochet" and against the autocratic measures of Falcão's own government. "That," he declared, "is propaganda of the extreme Left or of useful innocents." General Everaldo de Oliveira Reis, an ESG graduate and former instructor at the Officers' Finishing School (EsAO) who helped shape the doctrinal tenets of guerra revolucionária, likewise implied that authoritarianism's merit lay in its control of public morality. "What we have today," he told an interviewer, "disgusts even the [current] Minister of Justice, who was one of those who complained about the lack of freedom . . . back then [during the dictatorship]. . . . I'm horrified by what my grandchildren see on television. And don't tell me that is freedom of expression. In my day, we had another word for that sort of thing."[4]

Some rightists, in Brazil and the North Atlantic, have strayed even less from the moral countersubversion of the Cold War. There are those who do not acknowledge the end of the Cold War itself—a perspective intimated in Falcão's use of the vintage term "useful innocents"—and continue to react against cultural change, envisioning a global Marxism that weaponizes gender, sexuality, and morality. Ten years after the end of dictatorship, Jorge Boaventura (whom we encountered in chapter 4) published *The Suffering and Chaos of This Fin de Siècle (Its True Causes and the Potential Restoration of Justice and Peace)*. Boaventura's jeremiad denounced secularization, democratization (which he called "paganization"), and counterculture as Marxist subversion. True to form, Boaventura cited Brazilian and transatlantic stalwarts of Cold War thought, including Frank Buchman, Peter Howard, Luciano Cabral Duarte, and Arnold Toynbee.[5] (At the time, Boaventura was a candidate for the Rio de Janeiro State Senate, nominated by an important player in Brazil's *new* Right: the fundamentalist Universal Church of the Kingdom of God, or IURD.) As of this writing, conservative blogs in Brazil continued to decry a left-wing "culture war" perpetrated by what rightists call *gayzismo*—a putatively Marxist-inspired fusion of homosexual (*gay*) rights with fascist totalitarianism (*nazismo*).[6]

Hemispherically, meanwhile, the legacy of moralistic anticommunism lives on with equal virulence. "Cultural Marxism" has become the rallying cry of extreme rightists in Europe and the United States intent on conjuring a Cold War Left whose dissipate moral-cultural agenda, to quote William S. Lind, is "Dead but Not Gone."[7] According to Lind, Pat Buchanan, Paul Weyrich, and a host of other paleoconservative spokespersons, political correctness and multiculturalism represent thin veneers for the moral dissolution with which Marxists persist in undermining Western civilization.[8] The Christian Anti-Communist Crusade (founded by Fred Schwarz, with whom we are now familiar) continues to publish *The Schwarz Report*. Beneath the perennial, headline-level photograph of Schwarz himself, recent issues have included the claim that "communism . . . is nearing complete implementation in America"; Phyllis Schlafly's accusation that U.S. President Barack Obama is a "socialist . . . captivated by the un-American notion of running the country through Russian-style czars"; and Jeffrey T. Kuhner's contention that present-day "fascism and Marxism" are "evil twins," actively at work in destroying "capitalism, the sovereignty of the family, and Judeo-Christian civilization."[9] In 2011, the Crusade republished *You Can Trust the Communists to Be Communists*—retitled *You Can Still Trust the Communists to Be Communists (Socialists and Progressives, Too)*—which received praise from leading lights of the Right, including best-selling author and evangelical activist Tim LaHaye. According to LaHaye, the "poisonous waters of Marx," with their "swarming collectivist agents" still maintain a "relentless attempt to dethrone God and destroy Capitalism."[10]

LaHaye notwithstanding, the history of these ideas, part of which we have explored in these pages, should make us hesitate to dismiss them as powerless and marginal. Schlafly, as is well known, has had so significant an influence on American politics and culture as to splash the pages of standard textbooks. And Schwarz, as we have seen here, made such ideas meaningful and important during a transnational career that merits further attention than I have been able to give him. Right-wing reaction, moral panic, and countersubversion have a latent potency that may—as in the case of Brazil in the 1960s and 1970s—spring into effect. As the stories of the late twentieth century make clear, "progressive" notions of linear historical movement toward rights and inclusion, whatever their identitarian limitations, have also been belied by the resurgence of conservative moral and cultural politics.[11] The salience of this point cannot be ignored in Brazil and the United States, where cultural conservatives have determined the agendas of burgeoning evangelical Christian constituencies, placing moral fundamentalism at the center of national political debates. Indeed, by the late 2000s, conservative Pentecostals in Brazil, the United States, and Canada consistently drew on each other's struggles for example, inspiration, and strategy in the "war" for Christian values.[12]

The extremist individuals and organizations that we have encountered in this account demonstrate one, historical form of such resurgence. They did not, as we saw in chapter 1, always manage to make their moral agendas a state priority. Indeed, commitment to moral countersubversion *per se* appears to have been relatively weak among Vargas-era authorities. Rightist individuals and organizations who agitated for remoralization and even a return to the Middle Ages found their agendas neglected by a state more concerned with the industrialized, productive future. Rightists of eugenicist and fascist bent met with frustration when policies on the family, education, and youth failed to meet their expectations. Some of these rightists—notably those of the LDN and the TFP—would return with a vengeance in the 1960s, but for the duration of the interwar period they had little recourse but to seek compromise with Vargas or complain of the regime's misplaced (that is, not sufficiently moralistic) authoritarianism.

During the Cold War, however, moral, sexual, and gender conservatism pervaded state forums on national security, enmity, and authoritarian repression. Amid growing tension and concern about cultural change in the 1960s, the distinction that developed between counter-subversive warriors and their "internal enemy" informed the emergence in Brazil of an empowered, right-wing, conflationary vision of subversion. As we saw in chapter 2, this vision had several alternatives in the late 1960s, when commentators and experts weighed in with a variety of perspectives on the relationships (or lack thereof) between youth, style, sex, morality, radical politics, protest, and subversion. Rightists' rejection of cultural and moral change emerged at a time when such change had attracted the attention, positive and negative, of a spectrum of observers and activists. Yet if questions about the nature of an emergent category of youth, about gender and sexual behavior, and about countercultural style generated significant discussion in this period, the Right's and the military's most ardent opponents on the political Left did not share in the sexual radicalism of which they were accused.

Despite this contradiction, and despite the seeming extremism or even marginality of their ideas, a network of rightist individuals and organizations made moralism a touchstone of national debates about security. Horrified—and emboldened—by contemporary developments in mass media, gender roles, and youth consumption and behavior, these rightists decried a "crisis of modernity," linked, as they saw it, to communist strategizing. This perspective, borne into the halls of power by right-wing individuals and organizations like IPES, IBAD, the LDN, and TFP, gained traction in articulation with transnational currents of moralistic, anticommunist thought. Via firebrands of this persuasion, from Brazil and elsewhere in the Atlantic, sexual and gender unconventionality became presumptive aspects of the "internal enemy." This presumption took on particular salience in the so-called years of lead (1968–74) of Brazil's dictatorship—security forces and cultural conservatives, embroiled in witnessing and remembering student activism and cultural change in the late 1960s, implicated protests alongside pornography, social justice alongside sex, in the fight against guerra revolucionária, then at its most violent.

Such anticommunist moral panic made its way into the military state's institutional security thought and planning. This incursion happened via a "moral technocracy," whose expertise became doctrine—a doctrine of national security both bolstered and circumscribed by the transnational literatures (often anachronistic or exclusively and extremely conservative) that informed it. Echoing, in several ways, the conservatisms of decades past, this moral technocracy equated subversion with earlier notions of degeneracy and wrote the struggle for Cold War national viability across the bodies, sexualities, and consumption patterns of middle-class young people. At the ESG, as at other institutions of military training and security planning, modernization's effects on youth, media, and gender seemed acute and cataclysmic, and were interpreted as the work of repressible subversive enemies. This interpretation gained a lexicon all its own, via stock categories: "the youth problem," "social communications," and "women's liberation," all thought to be arenas of communist revolutionary warfare. "Communists," wrote one esguiano, attempted to discredit "middle-class morality" and "moral indignation" vis-à-vis liberalization—and it fell to the "armed forces, [which are] the middle class in arms" to restore moral and political order, via authoritarian repression.[13]

Finally, this moralistic approach to anticommunism, with its component demonizations of modernity, made inroads into policy and practice. State security forces embraced moralistic countersubversion. During the years of harshest repression (1968–74) and then after the armed Left had been decimated, associations between moral and political deviance were part of the armature of repression. Hierarchs of the intelligence and enforcement agencies, from the National Intelligence Service to the departments of justice and political policing, assured each other and their subordinates that pornography, orgiastic parties, homosexuality, hippies, and other sexual unconventionalities (especially where these involved young people) were signs and symptoms of communist "total war." Surveillance or suspicion of deviant sex and gender behavior appeared in individual cases of "subversive activity"—and such behavior, to the police who worked these cases, seemed seamlessly or implicitly imbricated with the processes of clandestine warfare. Those who kept the day-to-day machinery of repression running, in other words, deployed moralism as an integral part of the framework for policing the internal enemy.

Cultural and moral countersubversion also achieved certain public, legislative success. Moral and Civic Education, the large-scale cultural offensive launched by the rightists we have met here, became a platform from which to wage a defensive, desperate war against what EMC proponents called "the incredible crisis of moral principles." From planning to execution—in textbooks designed to reach EMC classrooms across Brazil—Moral and Civic Education operationalized the antimodern concerns of countersubversives, denouncing "modern woman," "mass communication," "materialism," and general "hedonism" as weapons in an ideological and cultural war for the very survival of Western civilization. These concerns reflected the precise anxieties that rightists had traditionally decried, and whose growth, in their eyes, became explosive in the 1960s and 1970s. At least some of the texts analyzed here reached classrooms and school libraries across Brazil. Teachers and students, of course, can have interpreted these messages from on high in myriad ways—but here were moral conservatives doing their utmost, wielding the power of the state to bring the messages of moral panic and anticommunism into the everyday lives of Brazilians.

Several factors, however, complicated the ascendancy of moralistic countersubversion, at the broadest, sustained levels. Timing, the process of democratization, and the general disorder that reigned within Brazil's unwieldy military government made the Right's morally anticommunist perspective difficult to enforce universally. Moralism informed the ideology of top officials and provided an impetus to repression, but it also reached the limits of effectiveness that stymied many of the military period's initiatives. This happened as competing interests within the regime—notably the desire to promote a national film industry and the willingness of some to consider birth control a developmentalist prerogative—alongside the gradual waning of hard-line supremacy led to an attenuation of moralistic power in certain realms of government. The reactionary state thus unwittingly sponsored soft-core pornography, despite the denunciation of this practice by moralistically countersubversive ministers and censors, and high-level authorities laid plans to override rightist objections and implement government-sponsored birth control programs. That the latter did not succeed had to do, at least in part, with the united opposition of conservatives *and* progressives.

Nevertheless, the confluence in the 1960s and 1970s of these phenomena—an empowered Right, integrated at the top levels of government; a security establishment suffused with rightist moralism; programmatic plans to eradicate the sexualized threat to the country's youth; and the ongoing hand-wringing of cultural conservatives—created strongholds of anticommunist moralism that spanned government agencies, informed repression, and generated attempts to control and even change quotidian behavior. The EMC textbook *Guide to Civics*, quoted in the introduction to this book, told students it would instill "the self-discipline that will regulate your moral life, your social, emotional, and sexual behavior."[14] That mission had special importance for rightists like Dom

Luciano José Cabral Duarte, a conservative, government insider, and proponent of remoralization as anticommunist prophylaxis. A supporter of the government's authoritarianism, Dom Luciano was an SNI informant; he represented reactionary opposition to the progressive clergy and to "radical" leftists within and outside of the church. He helped found the CNMC and authored its guidelines for moral and religious education. In 1985, with dictatorship ever more on the wane, Duarte expressed conservatives' ongoing anxieties about moral crisis and its portent for Brazil's national security. At a conference on the future of EMC, Duarte joined colleagues in a denunciation of the alarming ways that new technology would further degrade young people, women, and morality in general, leaving the country open to attack by a subversive "minority." For Duarte and like-minded fellows in the security and intelligence community, EMC represented the last, best, desperate hope of a core of patriots determined to rescue Brazilians via education. Where military officials and intelligence officers had fretted over the vetting of EMC teachers, Duarte praised them as heroes, straining to withstand an onslaught of destructive moral pollution. "I can only imagine," he told his audience, "the struggle waged by the Professors of Moral and Civic Education in today's Brazil. How to motivate, at this height of necessity, . . . adolescents so drunk with rock, with sex, with futility, and with drugs?" This question, like those about the role of new media, women, and sex in the public sphere, motivated conservatives like Duarte and intelligence and government officials with whom he collaborated. For them, drugs, sex, and rock music were the work of the nation's subversive enemies, and the challenge of its defenders.

IN MAY OF 2012, Brazil opened a new chapter in the story of its own authoritarian past and in the broader history of Cold War atrocities and post-democratization attempts to negotiate justice for the victims of state and paramilitary violence. Brazil's National Truth Commission (CNV) became the latest of a series of bodies, spanning at least two decades, that have sought to record or redress the human rights violations of post–World War II dictatorships in the Americas. In August, the CNV moved to subpoena Carlos Alberto Brilhante Ustra, who in 2008 had become the first Brazilian military official to be formally recognized as a torturer.[15] After several unsuccessful appeal attempts, Ustra appeared before the CNV in May 2013. While he continued to deny wrongdoing, former victims denounced him in dramatic and sometimes emotional testimony.

Many—if not most—Brazilians look back on the dictatorship as a dark chapter in Brazilian history, marked most notably by repression and abuse. Indeed, this is so much the case that in some ways the historical memory of dictatorship giving way to democratization has eclipsed awareness of police and state violence *since* 1985.[16] Nevertheless, Ustra is not without his supporters, even—or perhaps especially—now that he has died. Amid continual consternation about the linked evils of democratization, dissipation, and subversion, rightists of several stripes have rallied to his cause, decrying the truth commission and post-authoritarian justice more generally as *revanchismo*—vengefulness. Defending Ustra is just a small part of these critics' broader agenda. According to such revisionists, the "war on terror" was justified, hard fought, and only temporarily successful. The Cold War, they claim, continues; clandestine communists have now gained power in Brazil and across the West, and Ustra was only the latest victim of a long-running leftist conspiracy. That conspiracy, they argue, continues the work of linking sexual and moral degeneracy, communist ascendancy, and the discrediting of Brazil's military rulers. The largely ex-military pressure group Terrorism Never Again (Ternuma), intimately linked with Ustra's public defense of his record, complains of communists' predominance in "the 'democracy' which is being imposed on us not by law, but by . . . licentiousness and impunity."

Ternuma distributes *Orvil: Attempted Takeovers*, a book-length study compiled by ex-officials of the Army Intelligence Service and designed to further rebut the history of state violence and human rights abuse. *Orvil*, like other reactions to so-called vengefulness, seeks to set the record straight—by contextualizing Cold War countersubversive excesses as part of an honorable struggle against the morally bankrupt designs of international communism. Just as Ustra's ongoing self-defense affirmed the moral, sexual, and gendered aspects of his errand into countersubversion, so *Orvil* seeks to make the argument about subversion that rightists have been making for nearly a century—that communists sought to sexually corrupt Brazilians, especially young Brazilians, and that repression was a merited and necessary response. "Sex," the report claims, "was used in terrorist circles as a tool for the attraction and entrapment of inexperienced youths."[17] Ternuma's initiates make the case that this process continues to this day, as moral crisis has once again aligned the forces of communism, immorality, and conspiracy against the military defenders of Brazilian sovereignty. "We are living," writes one Ternuma officer, "in a time of iniquity, in which the national program of human rights . . . promotes homosexuality. It inveighs against religious tradition. It renews persecutions that were buried with amnesty."[18] Complaining of a new "dictatorship" of "communist governors," Ternuma partisans attempt to breathe life into the not-so-restful ghosts of authoritarian moralism. "What kind of dictatorship," asks one rhetorical post, disgusted with current morality, "was that [of 1964]? Ah, yes. That dictatorship prohibited marriage of one man with another, prohibited explicit sex reaching children via television, prohibited the lack of shame."[19]

Notes

Introduction

1. Cristovam Breiner, "Causas da decadência," *Boletim do Diretório da Liga de Defesa Nacional* 96 (1974): 4 (emphasis added). Unless otherwise noted, all translations from the Portuguese are my own.

2. General Breno Borges Fortes, speech, Conference of American Armies, Caracas, 3 September 1973, quoted in "Brasil contra novos conceitos de segurança," *O Estado de S. Paulo*, 9 September 1973, 17.

3. Corção, "Terrorismo cultural?" *O Globo*, 12 May 1964, 5; Corção, "Perversos e tolos," *O Globo*, 9 December 1971, 2.

4. Camargo, *A espada virgem*, 131.

5. Archdiocese of São Paulo, *Brasil: Nunca mais*; Comissão Nacional da Verdade, *Relatório*.

6. Brands, *Latin America's Cold War*; Harmer, *Allende's Chile*. A notable, cultural-history exception is Joseph and Spenser, *In from the Cold*.

7. See, for example, Bertonha, "A Direita Radical."

8. Gaspari, *A ditadura escancarada*, 24.

9. Perelli, "Military's Perception," 96. Carlos Fico suggests that after the regime's early-1970s victory over armed groups, countersubversives turned to "ethico-moral" definitions of subversion. Rightists, as I demonstrate, had long before made such definitions a part of the rationale for military government and repression. *Como eles agiam,* 133, 218.

10. Margaret Power and Sandra McGee Deutsch have suggested that academics avoid studying the Right so as not to "examine a viewpoint they find repugnant or depressing." Deutsch, *Las Derechas*, 1. Recent scholarship has begun to redress certain aspects of rightist mobilizations and legacies, especially in Argentina and

Mexico. See Pensado, *Rebel Mexico*; Pani, *Conservadurismo*; Walker, *Waking from the Dream*; and Finchelstein, *Transatlantic Fascism* and *Dirty War*.

11. Examples include Johnson, *Lavender Scare*; May, *Homeward Bound*; and Dean, *Imperial Brotherhood*.

12. Johnson, *Lavender Scare*, 2.

13. Visions of the Cold War as a moral and cultural struggle transcended even the period's greatest geopolitical divides, as Soviets and Cubans, too, linked sexual and moral deviance with threats to state and society. See Peña, *¡Oye Loca!*, esp. chap. 2; Tsipursky, "Citizenship, Deviance, and Identity."

14. Eidelman, "Pornografia y censura estatal," 7; Kuri, "El lado oscuro," 529. See also Manzano, *Age of Youth*; Pensado, *Rebel Mexico*; and Carey, *Plaza of Sacrifices*.

15. Johnson, *Lavender Scare*; Kinsman, "'Character Weaknesses.'"

16. Examples include McGirr, *Suburban Warriors*; Self, *All in the Family*; Perlstein, *Before the Storm*; Brennan, *Wives, Mothers*.

17. Margaret Power has examined Brazilian, Chilean, and U.S. women's transnational activism, noting that right-wing nationalisms have not historically precluded transnational collaborations. Power, "Transnational Connections," 21–33.

18. Pacheco e Silva, *Hippies, drogas, sexo, poluição*, 8–9, 44–45.

19. May, *Homeward Bound*, 82; D'Emilio, *Sexual Politics, Sexual Communities*, 41–48.

20. René Dreifuss's landmark study on the coup was the first to characterize the dictatorship as an exercise in "conservative modernization"—economic growth and modernization without redistribution of wealth or change in class structure. Dreifuss and others have applied the term to analogies between the regime slogan "Security and Development" and longstanding elite dreams of "Order and Progress." Dreifuss, *1964*, 80.

21. On this tendency, see Wolfe, *Autos and Progress*.

22. Alvarez, *Engendering Democracy*, 9, 43–53; Ribeiro and Ribeiro, *Família e desafios*, 173; Sodre, *O monopólio da fala*, 90–95; and Barbosa, "Mulher e contracepção."

23. Cohen, *Folk Devils*; Goode and Ben-Yehuda, *Moral Panics*.

24. Generally, Latin American students have received considerable scholarly treatment, with relative inattention to youth as such, to sexual revolution (or lack thereof), to generational conflict, and to the various constructions of and responses to this category. The most notable exception is Valeria Manzano's *The Age of Youth in Argentina*. Christopher Dunn's research on Tropicália, though it does not explicitly take up conceptualizations of youth, does begin to note the ways in which young people's (counter)cultural activities loomed large in the national imaginary. In Mexico, Eric Zolov argues, a cultural fascination with *rebeldismo* (rebelliousness) among youth led to anxiety about *"buenas costumbres"* ("good behavior"); I contend that in Brazil the same phrase (*bons costumes* in Portuguese) emerged to articulate anxieties that were more structural in their origins but were expressed culturally. Dunn, *Brutality Garden*; Zolov, *Refried Elvis*. See also Patrick Barr-Melej, "Siloísmo and the Self."

25. For a labor and cultural history of the church and its relations with the state, see Serbin, *Needs of the Heart and Secret Dialogues;* Vieira de Sousa, *Círculos operários*. Though this book is not a history of the Cold War church, I build on these works to consider church politics (both moral and economic) and midcentury upheaval as parts of a larger story—one less about Brazil's Catholic hierarchy than about the force of moralism inside and outside of the church.

26. See chap. 7; Della Cava and Montero, *E o verbo se faz*, 150.

27. See, for example, Durham and Power, *New Perspectives*, 1–2.

28. Blee and Deutsch, *Women of the Right*, 3.

29. Stepan, *Rethinking Military Politics*, 47.

30. Strub, *Perversion for Profit*, 7, 89.

31. The term "modernizing conservative" comes from Dreifuss's above-noted analysis. Dreifuss, *1964*, 71, 79.

32. Dreifuss, *1964*, 370; Motta, *Em guarda*, 67, 240, 281.

33. Mariani, *Guia de civismo*, 13.

34. Recent work that complicates dictatorship and resistance more generally includes Dávila, *Hotel Trópico*; Green, *We Cannot Remain Silent*; and Martins, "Produzindo no escuro."

35. Decreto-Lei No. 900, 29 September 1969, Diário Oficial da União, 30 September 1969 (Brazil), 8201; Conselho Nacional de Segurança, "Avaliação da conjuntura. Expressão psicossocial," AN/COREG, Fundo CSN, BR-AN-BSB-N8-001E-B; "Relatório do tema 25/Campo psicossocial/A família" (1975), ESG BGCF, TE.75.C.PSICOS.T.25, 13.

36. Polícia Militar do Estado de São Paulo, "Localização de livros subversivos" (14 September 1970), AN/COREG, Fundo CISA, BR-AN-BSB-VAZ-061-007.

Chapter 1

1. The original source of the epigraph is Vargas, "Saudação à juventude Paulista," *Cultura Política* 1, no. 10 (1941): 146.

2. On militarization, youth, and the "fascistization" of the body under Vargas, see Lenharo, *Sacralização da política*, discussed below. On the early Right's preference for antiliberalism, see Trindade, *Integralismo*, and Silva, *Onda vermelha*, 92, 106–7.

3. Bruneau, *Political Transformation*, 40–42; Mainwaring, *Catholic Church*, 27–38; Williams, "Church and State"; Isaia, *Catolicismo e autoritarismo*, 147–55; Schwartzman, Bomeny, and Costa, *Tempos de Capanema*; Aderaldo, *Educação e política*; Oliveira, Velloso, and Gomes, *Estado Novo*; Velloso, "A Ordem"; and Chauí, "Apontamentos." As noted below, Vargas did cooperate with and seek the support of major church leaders—like his personal friend Archbishop Sebastião Leme—and worked with Catholics on certain social projects, especially the labor code. This makes acrid disagreements over moral and religious priorities all the more striking.

4. Mainwaring, *Catholic Church*, 38.

5. Williams, "Church and State," 458; Isaia, *Catolicismo e autoritarismo*.

6. On the rural orientation of rightist agitation, which mirrored European fascism, see Isaia, *Catolicismo e autoritarismo*, 169.

7. In Brazil, historians have highlighted the need to investigate the roles played by the remnants of the prewar extreme Right in the coup of 1964 and its aftermath. Calil, *O integralismo*, 384; Deutsch, *Las Derechas*, 331–32.

8. Gilberto Vasconcellos suggests, in general and theoretical terms, that "moraliz[ing] pleasure" and "hatred of sexuality" have characterized authoritarianism everywhere, including Brazil. Vasconcellos, *Ideologia Curupira*, 38, 66.

9. Wolfe, *Working Women, Working Men*; Dennison and Shaw, *Popular Cinema in Brazil*, 38–48; Green, *Beyond Carnival*.

10. Deutsch, *Las Derechas*, 108; Calil, *O integralismo*; Silva, *Onda vermelha*, 87, 94, 110; Vasconcellos, *Ideologia Curupira*, 29; Trindade, *Integralismo*; Motta, *Em guarda*; Caulfield, *In Defense of Honor*; Beattie, "Honorable Masculine Social Space"; and Salem, "Do Centro Dom Vital." On links between prominent Catholic hierarchs, laypeople, and the Integralist far Right, see Williams, "Integralism"; Lustosa, "A igreja e o integralismo"; and Trindade, "O radicalismo militar," 124. Rodrigo Motta describes some of this moral outrage, omitting the centrality of morality, sexuality, the body, modernity, and youth to ultra-right anticommunism in this period. Motta, *Em guarda*, 63ff, 214.

11. Belisário Penna [*sic*], "A mulher, a família, o lar, a escola," in *Enciclopédia do Integralismo*, ed. Everardo Backeuser, vol. 9, *Integralismo e a educação* (Rio de Janeiro: Livraria Clássica Brasileira, 1959), 41–45, 49.

12. As Deutsch (*Las Derechas*, 255) and Vasconcellos (*Ideologia Curupira*, 27) point out, Salgado himself drew on rightist and racist thinkers of previous generations, including Oliveira Viana, Alberto Torres, and Olavo Bilac.

13. Plínio Salgado, "Educação," in Backeuser, *Integralismo e a educação*, 119–27; Plínio Salgado, "Panorama do mundo occidental," in Backeuser, *Integralismo e a educação*, 105.

14. Backeuser, *A sedução do comunismo*, 47.

15. Ibid., 55.

16. On "positive" eugenics in Latin America, see Stepan, *Hour of Eugenics*.

17. D'Elboux, *O Padre Leonel Franca*.

18. Franca, *A crise do mundo moderno*, 10, 278–79. On Franca's role in national debates, see Schwartzman, Bomeny, and Costa, *Tempos de Capanema*, 60ff.

19. "Pregando," *Estrela do Sul* (Porto Alegre), 28 September 1939; Isaia, *Catolicismo e autoritarismo*, 172.

20. Deutsch, *Las Derechas*, 276; Maio, "*Nem Rotschild nem Trotsky.*" Cytrinowicz, "Integralismo e anti-semitismo." Anti-Semitism cropped up commonly in Brazil's authoritarian rightist intellectual tradition. Silva, *Onda vermelha*, 162; Vasconcellos, *Ideologia Curupira*, 37.

21. Barroso, *Judaismo, maçonaria e comunismo*, 127.

22. Barroso, *Espírito do século XX*, 260.

23. Caulfield, *In Defense of Honor*, 82–83. Brazilian conservatives were, of course, not alone in their reaction against "modern" females who emerged with

industrialization and urbanization. See also Rubenstein, "The War on 'Las Pelonas'"; Weinbaum et al., *Modern Girl around the World*.

24. Penna, "A mulher, a família," 41.

25. Vasconcellos, *Ideologia Curupira*, 29. See also Silva, *Onda vermelha*, 94, 110.

26. For other intellectuals' and reformers' approaches to these themes, see Caulfield, *In Defense of Honor*, and Besse, *Restructuring Patriarchy*.

27. "A mulher para o lar," *O Diário de Minas Gerais* (Belo Horizonte), 29 August 1937. Such ideas, of course, were limited neither to Brazil nor exclusively to the Right. On Chilean, Argentine, and Mexican variants of such thinking, see Rosemblatt, *Gendered Compromises*; Ruggiero, *Modernity in the Flesh*; Guy, *Sex and Danger*; and Vaughan, *Cultural Politics in Revolution*.

28. Penna, "A mulher, a família," 41–44.

29. As Sandra McGee Deutsch points out, some Integralists—unlike other rightists—"extended domesticity to its limits" by theoretically allowing limited public roles for women "as long as they attended to their duties in the home." However, AIB men and women privileged highly traditional gender roles, affirming that "only the restoration of the 'patriarchal and Christian' family could ensure stability and happiness." Deutsch, *Las Derechas*, 283–89.

30. Mônica Pimenta Velloso and Maria Sadek have insightfully catalogued the ideas and roles of these two fonts of reaction, albeit without noting their central conflations of morality, sexuality, and subversion. Velloso, "A Ordem"; Sadek, *Machiavel, Machiavéis*.

31. See, for example, "A volta da mulher ao lar," *A Ordem*, May/June 1933, 460.

32. Justino Maria Pinheiro, "O congregado mariano—a sociedade e a Pátria," *A Ordem*, November 1937, 439, 444, 447–48; Alceu Amoroso Lima, "Discurso," *A Ordem*, October 1937, 373–76; and Lima, "O homem e a mulher (ensaio de caracterologia)," *A Ordem*, November 1937, 470–71. Lima would break with the far Right after 1964. He maintained his devout Catholicism but sided with progressives in the church as the schism between conservatives and social justice–minded Catholics widened in the 1950s and 1960s. In this, he was joined by at least two other noted rightists of the 1930s: Helder Câmara and Heráclito Sobral Pinto. Serbin, *Secret Dialogues*, 73; Da Costa, *Um itinerário no século*.

33. Pinheiro, "O congregado mariano," 444, 447–48.

34. Sadek, *Machiavel, Machiavéis*. Sadek locates Faria in the thick of a "spiritualist reaction" to revolution that encompassed Dom Vital, Farias Brito, Jackson de Figueiredo, Azevedo Amaral, and Leonel Franca.

35. Faria, *Machiavel e o Brasil*, 169.

36. Ibid., 105.

37. "O perigo do communismo," *Correio da Manhã*, 19 October 1934, 4. On widespread interest in (and confusion about) communism as a bloody experiment happening on Soviet soil, see Silva, *Onda vermelha*, 76, 210, 222; Dulles, *Sobral Pinto*, 9.

38. "O comunismo ateu: Carta pastoral e mandamento do episcopado brasileiro," *A Ordem*, October 1937, 286.

39. Nelson Hungria, "A mulher e o comunismo," *A Offensiva,* 17 September 1936, APERJ, setor Geral, pasta 49, dossiê 1 (emphasis added).

40. Backeuser, *Integralismo e a educação,* 17–26.

41. Auguste Viatte, "O catolicismo e a civilização nos Estados Unidos," *A Ordem,* December 1937, 501–10.

42. "A mulher para o lar," 3.

43. Ultimately loyal to Vargas, Góes Monteiro was a sometime Integralist sympathizer. Góes Monteiro to Benedito Olímpio da Silveira, 11 January 1935, AN, Fundo Góes Monteiro, SA 243, Film 047-97; Gustavo Capanema, "Sugestões para a unificação ideológica do país: Diretrizes de ação," CDPOC, Arquivo Gustavo Capanema, GC i 1935.12.00, reel 68, plate 57.

44. Caulfield, *In Defense of Honor,* 15. See also Caulfield, "The Birth of Mangue," 95; Wolfe, *Working Women, Working Men,* 72–73; Fischer, *Poverty of Rights,* 107–17, 125–41; and Besse, *Restructuring Patriarchy.*

45. Salem, "Do Centro Dom Vital," 116.

46. I depart here from Rodrigo Motta, who suggests that moralistic "demonization" of communism in the 1960s was merely a less pronounced shade of its 1930s predecessor. Motta, *Em guarda,* 49, 67.

47. Williams, "Church and State," 458; Schwartzman, Bomeny, and Costa, *Tempos de Capanema,* 44, 292.

48. Capanema, "Algumas informações sôbre a nossa atualidade católica," CPDOC, Arquivo Gustavo Capanema, GC i 1939.05.25, reel 71, plate 50–53.

49. Vargas, speech, Teatro Municipal, Rio de Janeiro, 2 December 1937, quoted in *Realizações 1: Panorama da educação nacional: Discursos do presidente Getúlio Vargas e do ministro Gustavo Capanema* (Rio de Janeiro: Ministério de Educação e Saúde, 1947), 9–10, 18.

50. Capanema, speech, Teatro Municipal, Rio de Janeiro, 2 December 1937, quoted in *Realizações 1,* 25, 30 (emphasis added).

51. Dávila, *Diploma of Whiteness,* 49–50.

52. Dulles, *Sobral Pinto,* 35; Schwartzman, Bomeny, and Costa, *Tempos de Capanema,* 60; and Bruneau, *Political Transformation,* 42.

53. Sueann Caulfield perceptively describes the Vargas government as traditionalist in its family and educational policy—a charge that rings true, for example, when it comes to the government's pro-natal policies. I seek to complicate the idea that these were outright victories for the Catholic, antifeminist Right, which failed in its efforts to push the government beyond the limits of statist morality and into a wholehearted embrace of moralism *per se.* As *Tempos de Capanema* points out, the Vargas government was much more interested in fecundity and procreation as the pillars of family policy—a distinction reflected in the sharp controversy over state recognition of children whose parents were unwed. Even the Estado Novo's moral censorship laws, designed to prohibit obscenity, defined the "obscene" as that which interfered with the family's "capacity for proliferation." Schwartzman, Bomeny, and Costa, *Tempos de Capanema,* 107–40. See also Hahner, *Emancipating the Female Sex,* 177–80; Levine, *Father of the Poor?,* 67–68, 120.

54. Capanema, "Das finalidades da educação física e do desenvolvimento dos programas," CPDOC, Arquivo Gustavo Capanema, GC 42.07.30, reel 56, plate 959/2 (emphasis added).

55. Lenharo, *Sacralização da política*, 83; Gomes, "A construção do homem novo," 151–66.

56. See "Brilhantes comemorações do Dia da Raça," *O Estado de S. Paulo*, 12 October 1937, 10.

57. See "Concurso de robustez da criança escolar do estado de São Paulo," *O Estado de S. Paulo*, 12 October 1937, 5. On state-centered puericulture as a challenge to the primacy of the church, see Maes, "Progeny of Progress," 159.

58. Oliveira, "Tradição e política," 41; Oliveira, "Autoridade e política," 56.

59. Velloso, "Cultura e poder político," 83, 90.

60. Mercedes Dantas, "Os regimes politicos e a realidade social do Brasil," *Cultura Política* 1, no. 5 (1941): 36–43.

61. Paulo Augusto de Figueiredo, "O Estado Novo e o Homem Novo," *Cultura Política* 1, no. 1 (1941): 133–37. See also Azevedo Amaral, "Realismo político e democracia," *Cultura Política* 1, no. 1 (1941): 157–76.

62. Peregrino Junior, "O desenvolvimento morfológico da criança brasileira," *Cultura Política* 1, no. 8 (1941): 51; Deodato de Morais, "Educação e o Estado Novo," *Cultura Política* 1, no. 9 (1941): 29–32; Batista de Melo, "A política nacional de família II," *Cultura Política* 1, no. 10 (1941): 129.

63. Lourenço Filho, "Secção de estudos gerais: Educação e segurança nacional" (speech, ECEME, 27 October 1939), *A Defesa Nacional*, no. 306–7 (November/December 1939): 1209, 1266 (emphasis added).

64. Imbiriba, *Breviário da instrução moral*, 14, 19–20, 80.

65. Góes Monteiro, speech, Colégio Militar do Rio de Janeiro, n.d., AN, Fundo Góes Monteiro, SA 627, microfilm 050-97, 40.

66. Salem, "Do Centro Dom Vital," 117.

67. Carlos de Oliveira Ramos, "A lei de proteção e amparo à família brasileira," *Cultura Política* 1, no. 9 (1941): 200–206; Batista de Melo, "A política nacional de família," *Cultura Política* 1, no. 10 (1941): 127–35; Caulfield, *In Defense of Honor*, 190–91. As Nancy Leys Stepan has pointed out, the church's opposition to "extreme" eugenics derived from Catholic hierarchs' unwillingness to cede authority over reproduction to secular powers, and from the curia's conviction that "spiritual values in marriage ranked higher than physical ones"—a conviction that Estado Novo intellectuals challenged via flirtations with "negative" eugenics. Stepan, *Hour of Eugenics*, 111–12.

68. Schwartzman, "A Igreja e o Estado Novo," 75.

69. Backeuser, *O communismo e a educação*, 2.

70. The 1942 law generally apportioned the cultivation of young minds and bodies to the state, reflecting a "preoccupation with reducing the influence of the family, of the church, or any other institution linked to the socialization of children and youths." Schwartzman, Bomeny, and Costa, *Tempos de Capanema*, 194.

71. On these global trends, see Mosse, *Image of Man*, 7, 15, 162.

72. Hugo Bethlem, "A segurança nacional e a juventude brasileira" (speech, Palácio Tiradentes, Rio de Janeiro, 8 April 1940) (Rio de Janeiro: Apollo, 1940), 16, 18.

73. Sternberg, *Escotismo*, 33.

74. Machado, "A 'Juventude Brasileira' e o escotismo," *Cultura Política* 1, no. 10 (1941): 59. Even Vargas weighed in to praise scouting as an engine of national honor, tradition, and defense. Sternberg, *Escotismo*, 63.

75. Schwartzman, Bomeny, and Costa, *Tempos de Capanema*, 123.

76. Leão Machado, himself a former scout, praised escotismo, but judged it "doctrinally . . . inappropriate to organize the *Juventude Brasileira* on the bases of scouting," since the latter was individualist and not expressly statist (61, 65).

77. Barroso to Vargas, 29 July 1939, CPDOC, Arquivo Gustavo Capanema, GC 1938.08.09, reel 52, plate 142–48.

78. Pinto, "Departamento de Educação da Mocidade" (n.d.), CPDOC, Arquivo Gustavo Capanema, GC 1938.08.09, reel 49, plate 901, 7.

79. Oldegar Vieira, "A organização da juventude brasileira," *Cultura Política* 1, no. 2 (1941), 155–66.

80. Gustavo Capanema, "Das finalidades da mocidade brasileira," CPDOC, Arquivo Gustavo Capanema, GC 1938.08.09, reel 52, plate 12.

81. Ibid.

82. Capanema to Vargas, 27 March 1939, CPDOC, Arquivo Gustavo Capanema, GC 1938.08.09, reel 52, plate 120.

83. Dutra, "Reservado: Organização Nacional da Juventude" (9 August 1938), CPDOC, Arquivo Gustavo Capanema, GC 1938.08.09, reel 51.

84. Müller's changing attitudes toward AIB remain somewhat inscrutable, but recent research demonstrates his ultimate disapproval of AIB-church alliances and his mercilessness in crushing the Integralists. Isaia, *Catolicismo e autoritarismo*, 154–56; Hilton, *Brazil and the Soviet Challenge*, 92, 132, 135–36; and Lemos, "Filinto Müller."

85. Aderaldo, *Educação e política*.

86. Sobral Pinto, "A reforma do ensino secundário," *A Ordem*, March/April 1931, 294–95. Sobral Pinto mounted his criticism despite Campos's own noted right-wing, corporatist, and even Integralist sympathies. Deutsch, *Las Derechas*, 321; Lenharo, *Sacralização da política*, 116; and Lesser, *Welcoming the Undesirables*, 96.

87. Dulles, *Sobral Pinto*, 30, 37, 192–94.

88. Sobral Pinto, who died in 1991, particularly deplored the entry of women into the public sphere. Dulles, *Resisting Brazil's Military Regime*, 191.

89. Sobral Pinto, "Chronica política (de 18 de março a 17 de abril)," *A Ordem*, May/June 1931, 286–89.

90. "Diretrizes para a educação nacional," *O Legionário*, 9 January 1938.

91. Franca, *A formação*, 35, 66.

92. Salem, "Do Centro Dom Vital," 119.

93. Manoel Marcondes Rezende, "Da nacionalização da escola," in *Algumas sugestões ao plano nacional de educação*, Centro Dom Vital de São Paulo (São Paulo: Revista dos Tribunaes, 1936), 16–32.

94. J. P. Galvão de Souza, "Como a união, os estados e os municípios prestarão assistência ao trabalhador intellectual?," in Centro Dom Vital, *Algumas sugestões*, 106–8.

95. L. Van Acker, "Que princípios de ordem geral devem orientar a educação no Brasil? Tais princípios devem ser formulados no Plano Nacional de Educação?" in Centro Dom Vital, *Algumas sugestões*, 35–39.

96. L. Van Acker, "O plano nacional de educação no Centro Dom Vital de S. Paulo," *A Ordem*, November/December 1936, 317.

97. Jaime de Barros Câmara, "Os programas de ensino de religião e o seu regime didático," CPDOC, Arquivo Gustavo Capanema, GC 42.07.30, reel 56, plate 962.

98. Lima to Gustavo Capanema, 16 July 1935, in Schwartzman, Bomeny, and Costa, *Tempos de Capanema*, 297.

99. Sobral Pinto to Capanema and Jaime de Barros Câmara, 27 March 1944, CPDOC, Arquivo Gustavo Capanema, reel 55, plate 683; Sobral Pinto to Pedro Góes Monteiro, [23?] October 1945, AN, Fundo Góes Monteiro, SA 432.3.

100. *Um homem, uma obra*, 53–54.

101. Calil, *O integralismo*, 148, 185, 224, 274–75.

102. "Coleta informal de dados: Luiz Feliciano Lotti," 25 November 1997, Centro de Documentação sobre a Ação Integralista Brasileira e o Partido de Representação Popular. Calil, *O integralismo*, 274n84.

103. Calil, *O integralismo*, 191.

104. Isaia, *Catolicismo e autoritarismo*, 14.

105. See chap. 3. Capanema, untitled essay (1963), CPDOC, Archivo Gustavo Capanema, GC pi S. ASS. 1963.00.00, reel 11, plate 103–33. This is not to say that Vargas, and much less Capanema, was an outright enemy of the church. The devout Capanema maintained personal and professional relationships with important Catholics on the Right, including Leonel Franca, whom Capanema encouraged to found the Catholic University at Rio de Janeiro (PUC) in 1941. See Gustavo Capanema to Leonel Franca, 16 February 1943, CPDOC, Arquivo Gustavo Capanema, GC g 40.00.00, reel 55, plate 433; Gustavo Capanema to Getúlio Vargas, 19 March 1943, CPDOC, Arquivo Gustavo Capanema, GC g 40.00.00, reel 55, plate 435.

Chapter 2

1. The source of the first epigraph is Costa et al., *Mémorias das mulheres*, 248; the source of the second is Murilo Melo Filho, "Quatro anos depois," *Manchete*, 6 April 1968, 13.

2. Memorial accounts of 1968 abound—for an example of the ways in which cultural and political deviance have blended and recombined in such accounts, see Matinas Suzuki, Jr., "Libelu era trotskismo com rock e fuminho," *Folha de S. Paulo*, 20 September 1997, 12.

3. Green, "Who Is the Macho," 447–53; Langland, *Speaking of Flowers*, 138.

4. Comissão Nacional da Verdade, *Relatório*.

5. Cowan, "Rules of Disengagement."

6. Cowan, "Sex and the Security State" (459–81) and "Moral-Sexual Panic."

7. Archdiocese of São Paulo, *Torture in Brazil*, 77. This report indicated that nearly 40 percent of torture victims were aged twenty-five or younger; significantly, 88 percent were male and more than half had university degrees, indicating their middle-class origins. In Argentina, too, truth report findings showed that young people suffered disproportionately—69 percent of Argentina's *desaparecidos*, for instance, were between the ages of sixteen and thirty. Comisión Nacional sobre la Desaparición de Personas, *Nunca más*.

8. Miller, *Latin American Women*, 66; Ribeiro and Ribeiro, *Família e desafios*, 173; Alvarez, *Engendering Democracy*, 9, 43–53. Carmen Dora Guimarães has even suggested that emergent consumerism among middle-class Brazilians involved a "progressive hedonization" that itself was generated by "the social and political restrictions after 1964." Guimarães, *O homossexual*, 105.

9. See Marwick, *Sixties*.

10. Ventura, *1968*, 34.

11. Green, "Who Is the Macho"; Langland, *Speaking of Flowers*, 138–39. Memoirs, oral histories, and journalistic accounts reaffirm the political Left's rejection of sexual and moral radicalism, and reflect the limited (and classed) extent of participation in such radicalism, especially in the 1960s. See Antonio Risério, "Duas ou três coisas sobre a contracultura no Brasil," in *Anos 70: Trajetórias* (São Paulo: Iluminuras, 2006); Dias, *Anos 70*; and Carmo, *Culturas da rebeldia*.

12. Bailey, *Sex in the Heartland*, 7–8, 11; Manzano, *Age of Youth*, 8; and Herzog, *Sex after Fascism*.

13. B. Peres, "Sexo e erotismo nas revistas brasileiras," *Paz e Terra* 5 (1967): 124; Fico, *Reinventando o otimismo*, 111–12.

14. Gaiarsa, *A juventude diante do sexo*, 298, 313, 593; "Você é contra ou a favor da educação sexual?" *Realidade*, July 1968, 48–50.

15. See, for instance, Euridice Freitas, "Aspectos e tendências da família em transição," *Arquivos Brasileiros de Psicotécnica Aplicada* 20, no. 1 (1968): 79–90; Freitas, "A família no processo de socialização," *Arquivos Brasileiros de Psicotécnica Aplicada* 20, no. 2 (1968): 44–52; Athayde Ribeiro da Silva, "Conflito de gerações," *Arquivos Brasileiros de Psicotécnica Aplicada* 20, no. 3 (1968): 55–60.

16. Freitas, "A família," 49–50; Edith Ramos, "The Male Dilemma," book review, *Arquivos Brasileiros de Psicotécnica Aplicada* 27, no. 4 (1975): 169–71.

17. Grünspun and Grünspun, *Assuntos de família*, 68–69, 121.

18. Ridenti, *Em busca do povo brasileiro*, 134. See also Pimentel, "*Paz e Terra*."

19. Lopes, "Somos o sexo que temos," *Paz e Terra* 5 (1967): 11–26.

20. *Manchete* (founded 1952) and *Realidade* (founded 1966) were Brazil's principal, modern glossies, known for rich imagery and investigative journalism; *Claudia* (founded 1961) was the most influential and widely read women's magazine of its day. Each had circulation in the hundreds of thousands. Peres, "Sexo," 124.

21. Silva, "Um garoto feliz: Só tem uma palmada para recordar," *Claudia*, May 1966, 30. See also Silva, "O conflito das gerações," *Realidade*, September 1967, 44–52.

22. Narciso Kalili, "Aqui está o adultério," *Realidade*, March 1968, 142. See also Duarte Pacheco and José Gaiarsa, "A juventude diante do sexo," *Realidade*, August 1966, 68–80.

23. Peres, "Sexo," 122.

24. Ronaldo Harari, letter to the editor, *Realidade*, March 1968, 5; Paulo Patarra, "Ninguém manda nestas crianças," *Realidade*, January 1968, 51–58. See also "Você é contra ou a favor da educação sexual?," *Realidade*, July 1968, 48–50.

25. Langland, "Speaking of Flowers," 105–23.

26. "Os hippies chegam com Hair," *Veja*, 4 June 1969, 58; "O asceticismo está retornando," *Veja*, 17 June 1970, 4–5.

27. Alberto Libânio, "O jovem universitário," *Realidade*, September 1967, 81.

28. Silva, "Eis o mundo deles," *Realidade*, September 1967, 31–38; José Carlos Marão, "Êles querem derrubar o govêrno," *Realidade*, July 1968, 35.

29. Silva, "Eis o mundo deles."

30. See, for example, David Ringel, "O enigma de Marighela," *Manchete*, 30 November 1968, 16–19. Advertisements and fashion spreads made subtle allusions to protest and rebellion. For example, the November 1968 issue included "Para não dizer que não falamos das cores"—"So they won't say that we didn't talk about colors"—a tongue-in-cheek reference to Geraldo Vandré's popular protest song "Para não dizer que não falei das flores" ("So they won't say that I didn't speak of flowers"). Langland, "Speaking of Flowers," 105–17.

31. "A rebelião universal dos jovens," *Manchete*, 13 April 1968, 16–23.

32. "Porque os estudantes se rebelam," *Manchete*, 20 April 1968, 144–47.

33. Narceu de Almeida, trans., "Marcuse: Todo poder aos estudantes," *Manchete*, 2 November 1968, 31–32.

34. Martins, *A rebelião romântica*, 54–55, 60–63, 68, 76.

35. Author interview with Fred Magalhães, 19 July 2006, Salvador de Bahia.

36. Ferreira, "Erotismo e subversão," *O Estado de S. Paulo*, 15 February 1970, 8; Galvão, "A liberdade de informação no Brasil—V," *O Estado de S. Paulo*, 13 December 1975, 69.

37. Author interview with Guilherme Santanna, 13 June 2012, Rio de Janeiro. I have used pseudonyms to identify all but one of my interview subjects.

38. Kon, *Sexual Revolution in Russia*; Lumsden, *Machos, Maricones, y Gays*, 64–65.

39. "E a nossa arte?," in *Unidade*, pamphlet in CISA, "Informação n° 105/CISA-RJ" (9 March 1977), AN/COREG, BR-AN-VAZ-064A-0027.

40. UNE, "Carta política da chapa da Une, gestão 68/69," and POLOP (Minas Gerais), "Normas de segurança" (n.d.), in SNI, Agência Central, "Documentos referents as atividades subversivas" (2 July 1969), AN/COREG, BN-DFANBSB-AAJ-IPM-0379, 1, 82, 84, 110, 141.

41. Dunn, "Desbunde and Its Discontents," 454–56; Green, "Who Is the Macho?"

42. Gabeira, *O crepúsculo do macho*.

43. Ventura, *1968*, 36. As James Green has demonstrated, homosexuality and gender deviance appear to have borne the brunt of a sexual and moral traditionalism

pervading the core of leftist factions. Green, "(Homo)sexuality, Human Rights" and "Who Is the Macho," 449.

44. Maria Helena Kühner, "Sexo, uma dimensão da liberdade humana," *Paz e Terra* 5 (September 1967): 82–83; Peres, "Sexo," 139.

45. SNI, "Serviço Nacional do Teatro" (21 October 1976), AN/COREG, Fundo SNIG, A1014171-1976.

46. Koutzii and Leite, *Che: 20 anos depois*; Goldenberg, *Toda mulher*, 37; Langland, *Speaking of Flowers*, 140. On the broader masculinism of Guevara-inspired militancy, see Lumsden, *Machos, Maricones, y Gays*; Saldaña-Portillo, *Revolutionary Imagination*; and Mallon, "Barbudos, Warriors, and Rotos."

47. On celibacy debates, see Serbin, *Needs of the Heart*.

48. "Para além da Micro," *O São Paulo*, 29 January 1972, 3.

49. Carlos Strabelli, "Problemas da família no Brasil," *O São Paulo*, 1 February 1980, 6.

50. "A serviço do erotismo," *O São Paulo*, 22 July 1972, 3.

51. Tristão de Athayde, "Demagogia ou realismo?" *Jornal do Brasil*, 12 January 1973, 6.

52. Ministério do Exército, "D. Waldyr Calheiros de Novães e outros," AN/COREG, Fundo CGI-PM, BR-DFANBSB-AAJ-IPM-0853, 12–14.

53. "Bispo auxiliar escreve ao Conselho de Presbíteros sôbre 'Missa Leiga,'" *O São Paulo*, 29 January 1972, 5.

54. CISA, "Organização Revolucionária Marxista-Democracia Socialista—atividades" (14 October 1983), AN/COREG, Fundo CISA, BR-AN-BSB-VAZ-101-0072.

55. CISA, "Manifesto do POR (Trotskista-Posadista)" (25 September 1978), AN/COREG, Fundo CISA, BR-AN-BSB-VAZ-077-0023.

56. For further discussion on this point, see James Green's mention of the emergence of a "left-wing sector" in the gay and lesbian rights movement in the late 1970s, where this link between traditional leftist politics and sexual rights had not existed before. Green, "Who Is the Macho," 466.

57. Nelson Rodrigues, As Confissões de Nelson Rodrigues, *O Globo*, 27 March 1968.

58. Nelson Rodrigues, As Confissões de Nelson Rodrigues, *O Globo*, 2 January 1968, 2.

59. Castro, *O anjo pornográfico*, 350, 342.

60. DOPS/Guanabara, Divisão de Informações, "Informação no. 834" (20 August 1969), AN/COREG, Fundo CGI-PM, BR-DFANBSB-AAJ-IPM-0527.

61. Freitas, "Aspectos e tendências" and "A família."

Chapter 3

1. CISA, "Organização Revolucionária" (see chap. 2, n. 54).

2. Fico, *Reinventando o otimismo*, 44.

3. Sigaud befriended conservative columnist Gustavo Corção; worked with TFP leader Plínio Corrêa de Oliveira on the Catholic journal *O Legionário*; met

with President Costa e Silva to promote TFP's agenda; and was cited in the most culturally conservative of ESG publications. See "Estudo conclusivo sôbre as repercussões da conferência tricontinental de Havana no movimento religioso no Brasil e sua possível evolução" (1970), ESG BGCF TG1-3-70/Eq. C.; *Um homem, uma obra*, 30; and "Presidente recebe d. Sigaud," *Correio da Manhã*, 14 September 1968, 3.

4. Sigaud, *Catecismo anticomunista*, 64.

5. "Lojistas colaboram com a CAMDE-Tijuca," *O Globo*, 20 August 1964, 19; Elisabetta Maria Martinelli to "Excelentíssimos Senhores Pais" (15 August 1965), AN/COREG, Fundo CAMDE, BR-AN-RIO-PE-0-078-D; "Minhas Prezadas Amigas desta longa e árdua luta" ([23?] October 1965), AN/COREG, Fundo CAMDE, BR-AN-RIO-PE-0-078-D, 86; Simões, *Deus, pátria e família*; and Cordeiro, *Direitas em movimento*, 132.

6. Dreifuss, *1964*, 162, 174, 230, 233, 244; Blume, "Pressure Groups," 218–19; Gaspari, *A ditadura envergonhada*, 153–58.

7. Rodrigo Motta's otherwise excellent study (arguing that sensationalistic moralism was less pronounced in 1960s anticommunism than in that of the 1930s) does not delve into the moralisms that characterized the latter period. Motta, *Em guarda*, 67.

8. "Agitação comunista no meio estudantil," *Noticiário*, August 1962, 5–6, AN, Fundo Paulo de Assis Ribeiro, caixa 52, pasta 3.

9. Ibid., 17.

10. Jean Manzon, *Criando homens livres* (1962), videocassette, AN, Seção de Documentos Sonoros e de Imagens em Movimento, Fundo IPES.

11. Penna Botto's extremism in the 1950s made him something of a Brazilian Joe McCarthy. Indeed, *penabotismo* became a "synonym for fanaticism, for exaggerated and irrational anticommunism." Motta, *Em guarda*, 144. See also "Que querem os estudantes brasileiros?" *Carta Mensal do IPÊS São Paulo*, June/July 1968, 4, AN, Fundo IPES, caixa 29, pacote 2; and Fernando Bastos de Ávila, "Objetivos e métodos da educação brasileira" (speech, IPES Forum de Educação, Rio de Janeiro, 14 October 1968), AN, Fundo Paulo de Assis Ribeiro, caixa 56.

12. Blume, "Pressure Groups," 215; Seganfreddo, *UNE: Instrumento de subversão*, 116.

13. Seganfreddo, *UNE: Instrumento de subversão*, 12–13, 18.

14. On these links, see Dreifuss, *1964*, 103, 163.

15. Dockhorn, *Quando a ordem*, 102.

16. "Você sabia que . . . ," *Ação Democrática*, March 1962, 16; *Ação Democrática*, February 1962, cover (see fig. 2), 14–15; and *Ação Democrática*, December 1961, 9.

17. "A família na Rússia," *Ação Democrática*, February 1963, 18; "Para onde querem levar a criança brasileira," *Ação Democrática*, September 1962, 20–21.

18. "Cuba exporta cocaína," *Ação Democrática*, May 1962, 11.

19. A. Fragoso Dias, letter to the editor, *Realidade,* March 1968, 5; Yara Alves, letter to the editor, *Realidade,* March 1968, 5.

20. Guarany to Muricy, 13 April 1969, CPDOC, Arquivo Antônio Carlos Muricy, ACM pm 1964.07.20, reel 1, plate 644.

21. Farias, "A conjuntura brasileira" (1980), CPDOC, Arquivo Cordeiro de Farias, CFa 1964.01.11.

22. See chap. 7.

23. Johnson, "Regarding the Philanthropic Ogre," 336.

24. Sadek, *Machiavel, Machiavéis*, 113. Other appointees included Hélio Viana, a former Integralist and editor of the right-wing periodicals *Hierarquia* and *A Offensiva*; Pedro Calmon, a Vargas-era supporter of "spiritual militarization" on behalf of the state; Manuel Diegues Junior, whose later work would denounce "playboys" as harmful to national institutions like the family; Gladstone Chaves de Mello; Father Fernando de Ávila; and Djacir Menezes, a fellow ESG moralist and friend to the CFC's most famous (and most famously reactionary) member, Gustavo Corção. Williams, "Integralism," 442; Lenharo, *Sacralização da política*, 80; and Manuel Diegues Junior, "Elementos básicos da nacionalidade— as instituições," *A Defesa Nacional*, July/August 1968, 13.

25. Farias, "A conjuntura brasileira."

26. See Corção, "Curriculum vitae," *O Globo*, 16 June 1969, 2.

27. See "Homenagem a Gustavo Corção," *O Globo*, 10 February 1973, 2.

28. In her excellent portrait of Corção's journalistic career, Christiane Jalles de Paula has argued that he lent legitimacy to the anti-Goulart campaign and helped celebrate the coup as a campaign to "recoup the soul" of Brazil. I argue that sexual moralism—briefly noted by Paula—dominated Corção's perspective and made him an effective spokesperson for Brazil's most right-wing, hard-line factions. Paula, "Combatendo o bom combate," 155, 188.

29. Paula, "Combatendo o bom combate," 165–66; Antoine, *O integrismo brasileiro*.

30. Corção, "Perversos e tolos" (see introd., n. 3).

31. Corção, "O cochilo da CNBB," *O Globo*, 13 November 1971, 2; Corção, *O século do nada*, 47; and Corção, "A educação sexual" (draft), BNGC 31, 1, 9, n. 019.

32. Corção, "Mais um catecismo," *O Globo*, 4 December 1971, 2.

33. Sales to Corção, 29 Decemer 1971, Eugênio Sales, BNGC, CE.

34. Corção to Padre Boaventura Cantarelli, 13 December 1971, and Corção to Sales, 30 June 1971 and 17 September 1971, Eugênio Sales, BNGC, CE.

35. Corção, "O apostolado da oração," *O Globo*, 9 October 1971, 2.

36. On debates over celibacy, see Serbin, *Needs of the Heart*, and Alves, *A Igreja e a política*, 95.

37. Corção's and TFP's brand of culturally conservative anticommunism both ante- and postdated the watershed events of 1968, but their activities intensified around 1970. Indeed, TFP grew notably more militant in 1970–71. Antoine, *O integrismo brasileiro*, 37–41.

38. "Grupos ocultos tramam subversão na Igreja," *Catolicismo*, April/May 1969, 2.

39. Plínio Corrêa de Oliveira, "A Igreja Católica infiltrada por adversarios velados," *Catolicismo*, April/May 1969, 4.

40. Antoine, *O integrismo brasileiro*, 43.

41. Corção to Scherer, 19 August 1966, Vicente Scherer, BNGC, CE. In a letter to Corção, his friend Gladstone Chaves de Mello used sexual metaphors to disparage Catholic "neo-modernists." Mello to Corção, 23 March 1973, BNGC, CR.

42. Molnar to Corção, 12 October 1966 and 16 March 1975, Thomas Molnar, BNGC, CR; Corção to Gerez del Arco, 31 July 1975, BNGC, CE.

43. Corção to Scherer, 19 August 1966.

44. Roberto Marinho to Corção, 30 January 1976, Rio de Janeiro, Roberto Marinho, BNGC, CR; SNI, "Apreciação sumária, campo interno no. 15/GAB/75" (1 December 1975), CPDOC Arquivo Ernesto Geisel, EG pr 1974.03.00, reel 1, plates 1059–67.

45. See Paul-Eugène Charbonneau, "A juventude da velhice," Ilustrada, *Folha de S. Paulo*, 21 December 1969, 2.

46. Capanema, "Catolicismo e capitalismo" (1963), CPDOC, Arquivo Gustavo Capanema, GC pi s. ass. 1963.00.00, 24, 54–55.

47. Among the signatories were Machado Paupério, Djacir Menezes, and the former minister of education and culture Raimundo Moniz de Aragão. "Homenagem a Gustavo Corção."

48. Corção to Sales, 30 June 1971.

49. Corção to Passarinho, 6 June 1972, BNGC, CE; Lacerda to Corção, 30 September 1965, BNGC, CR; Legislature of Minas Gerais to Corção, BNGC 31,3,1, n. 021; "Ofício no. 012 AERP/Bsb," Aguiar to Corção, 3 March 1969, BNGC, CR.

50. Mello obtained the appointment. Corção to Costa e Silva, 20 January 1968, A. Costa e Silva, BNGC, CE.

51. "Corção com Costa e Silva: Crise estudantil," *Correio Popular* (Campinas), 28 May 1968.

52. Corção, "Carta ao Presidente da República," *Diário de Notícias*, 23 December 1964, 2.

53. Corção, "Violência e não violência," *O Globo*, 18 July 1968, 2.

54. Corção, "Moscou e o Projeto Rondon II," *O Globo*, 3 October 1968, 2.

55. Ibid.; Corção, "Um rápido inventário," *O Globo*, 2 January 1969, 2.

56. Assumpção, "A ideologia na obra."

57. Pacheco e Silva, *Hippies, drogas, sexo, poluição*, 45.

58. Ibid., 50, 79, 82.

59. Pacheco e Silva, *Reminiscências*, 183, 256.

60. "Resumo dos relatórios da viagem ao estrangeiro realizada em maio, junho, e julho de 1971, por A. C. Pacheco e Silva," AN, Fundo DSI, caixa 40/04174, processo 137, ano 1971, pasta 1, 3.

61. Deutsch, *Las Derechas*, 111; Motta, *Em guarda*, 139. The League struggled to redefine its identity after World War II as anticommunism, temporarily elided by antifascism, became once again paramount.

62. Founding members included Belisário Penna and noted moralist Viveiros de Castro. Deutsch, *Las Derechas*, 108–11.

63. "A Liga de Defesa Nacional e a televisão educativa," *A Defesa Nacional*, December 1962, 71; "A ação da Liga de Defesa Nacional através do rádio," *Boletim do Diretório da Liga de Defesa Nacional* (hereafter *Boletim*), November 1962, 4.

64. Menezes, "A pornodisdascalia," *Boletim*, July/August 1972, 4; Silva, "Cardeal Primaz vê o Brasil em estado desditoso e mísero," *Boletim*, January 1964, 4.

65. "Apelo à mulher brasileira," *Boletim*, October 1962, 3.

66. Breiner, "Causas da decadência" (see introd., n. 1; emphasis added).

67. Ibid. Eric Zolov and Victoria Langland have observed such double standards in attitudes toward Mexican and Brazilian students. Zolov, *Refried Elvis*; Langland, *Speaking of Flowers*, 138.

68. Soares, "Moral e comunismo," *Boletim*, April/May 1969, 3 (emphasis added).

69. Deutsch, *Las Derechas*, 4, 44, 108, 251, 282–85.

70. Avia, "An Archive of Counterinsurgency," 44; Manzano, *Age of Youth*.

71. Corção, "Terrorismo cultural" (see introd., n. 3).

72. Câmara, "A tolerância que acoberta os facinoras favorece a ousadia par o mal, afirma Dom Jaime," *Boletim*, April 1964, 4.

73. Examples include Oswaldo Aranha and General Juarez do Nascimento Fernandes Távora, both onetime presidents of the LDN; prominent intellectual Pedro Calmon; Raimundo Moniz de Aragão; ex-Integralist, IBAD conspirator, and ESG instructor Marshall Ignácio de Freitas Rolim; and Minister of Education and Culture Abgar Renault, sometime president of the League's Brasília chapter.

74. Sylvestre Travassos Soares, "A Liga de Defesa Nacional e sua linha de ação," *Boletim*, March/April 1973, 3; *Boletim*, July/August 1971, 4; Álvaro da Motta e Silva to Augusto do Amaral Peixoto, 31 January 1969, CPDOC, Arquivo Augusto do Amaral Peixoto, AAP c 1969.01.31.

75. SNI, "A propaganda adversa na imprensa—revista 'Nova'" (26 Jun 1979), AN/COREG, BR-AN-RIO-TT-0-MCP-PRO-1693, 8.

76. *Um homem, uma obra*, 47, 96, 102.

77. "Pelé e mais 300 mil assinaram o manifesto contrário ao divórcio," *O Globo*, 13 June 1966, 6; "A TFP e a investida divorcista no Brasil," *Catolicismo*, June 1966, 1.

78. *Um homem, uma obra*, 88, 117; "Presidente recebe d. Sigaud"; A. J. de Paula Couto, "Ladrão que grita: Pega o ladrão," *Zero Hora* (Porto Alegre), 9 May 1975; *A TFP em 30 Dias*, May 1982, 4. According to the United States TFP, Reagan (no stranger to conflating sexuality and subversion) sent a letter of support to national chapter president John R. Spann. "President Reagan Desires 'Continued Growth for the TFP,'" *TFP Newsletter* 4, no. 3 (1984); De Groot, "Ronald Reagan."

79. DPF, Delegacia Regional no Paraná e Santa Catarina, "Tradição Família e Propriedade" (12 October 1970), AN/COREG, Fundo PF, caixa 37-A, DPF 37-A-0536-0537; CISA, "Sociedade Brasileira de Defesa da Tradição Família e Propriedade" (7 October 1975), AN/COREG, Fundo CISA, BRB-AN-BSB-VAZ-009A-008.

80. Guerra, *Memórias*, 126.

81. Buchman, *Remaking the World*, 46.

82. "To Change the World," *Time*, 14 June 1948, 74.

83. *Para a crise mundial*, 38, 82.

84. Dreifuss, *1964*, 370; Motta, *Em guarda*, 240.

85. Alberto Freire Kowarick to Magalhães, 15 April 1966, CPDOC, Arquivo Juracy Magalhães, JM 66.01.14.

86. "Remarks by Ambassador Juracy Magalhães, of Brazil, at the Conference for Tomorrow's America, Moral Re-Armament Center, Mackinac Island," 15 August 1964, CPDOC, Arquivo Juracy Magalhães, JM pi Magalhães, J. 1964.08.15.

87. Examples include Germano Seidl Vidal, Augusto Fragoso, Jorge Boaventura, Moacir de Araujo Lopes, and IPES's Colonel João Paulo Moreira Burnier. Germano Seidl Vidal, "Leitura selecionada," ESG BGCF, LS7-123-71, 3; Augusto Fragoso, "Guerra revolucionária," ESG BCGF, C55-60; Boaventura, Os sofrimentos, 247–50; Moacir de Araújo Lopes, "A educação moral e cívica e o serviço militar" (conference speech, 1982); and Dreifuss, 1964, 370.

88. SNI, Agência Rio de Janeiro, "Hermes Guimarães" (12 November 1981), AN/COREG, Fundo SNIG, C0053510-1981.

89. CNMC: Boletim Informativo da Comissão Nacional de Moral e Cívica, January–June 1984, 4, and July–December 1984, 10. Ironically, by this point, Moral Re-Armament had dwindled almost to irrelevance in the United States.

90. Heinz and Frühling, Gross Human Rights Violations, 133–34.

91. "12° aniversário da Revolução" (1976) and "Brasileiros" (n.d.), CPDOC, Arquivo Cordeiro de Farias, CFa tv 1976.00.00.

92. "Ao povo da Baixada Fluminense" (1976?), CPDOC, Arquivo Cordeiro de Farias, CFa tv 1976.00.00.

93. CISA, "Pichamento de igrejas em Nova Iguaçu" (7 December 1979), AN/COREG, Fundo CISA, BR-AN-BSB-VAZ-077-0119.

94. "Ao povo da Baixada Fluminense."

95. Trevisan, Devassos no paraíso, 346.

96. Comando de Caça aos Comunistas de Santos, "Senhor distribuidor do livreiro" (n.d.), AN/COREG, Fundo CODESP, BR-AN-BSB-PA-001-010.

97. Cowan, "Rules of Disengagement."

98. The Schwarz Report, accessed 5 October 2015, http://www.schwarzreport.org/about.

99. Schwarz, You Can Trust the Communists, 14–15, 28.

100. "Frentes comunistas: O nascimento de uma frente," Boletim, June 1963, 4; "Relatório dos livros da biblioteca do IPES-GB," AN, Fundo IPES, caixa 29, pacote 2; "Livros editados por outros e distribuidos pelo IPES," AN, Fundo IPES, caixa 22, pacote 3.

101. Labin, Hippies, Drugs, and Promiscuity, 252–53.

102. Ibid., 212.

103. Labin, Secret of Democracy, 125.

104. Labin, Em cima da hora, 19.

105. 109 Cong. Rec. 3479–80 (4 March 1963); "Liberty Is a Lady," Time, 27 February 1956, 111.

106. Pacheco e Silva, Hippies, drogas, sexo, poluição, 50.

107. Carlos Lacerda, introduction to Em cima da hora, 15.

108. Dulles, Carlos Lacerda, 158.

109. "Relatório dos livros da biblioteca do IPES-GB"; "Relatórios do IPES, 1962–1963," AN, Fundo IPES, caixa 53, pacote 2; Deifuss, 1964, 409, n. 125.

110. *Ação Democrática*, December 1961, 6.

111. *Um homem, uma obra*, 95.

112. Labin, *Em cima da hora*, 146.

Chapter 4

1. Buzaid, "Em defesa," 34; Decreto-Lei No. 1077, 26 January 1970, Diário Oficial da União, 7 May 1970 (Brazil), 1079 (emphasis added).

2. Buzaid, "Em defesa," 42.

3. Langland, *Speaking of Flowers*, 189.

4. Stepan, "The New Professionalism," 54.

5. Farhat, "Política de comunicação social e a opinião pública brasileira" (speech, ESG, 21 May 1980), ESG BGCF T102-80, 17.

6. Oliveira, "Fortalecimento da família" (1976), ESG BGCF, TE-76, 58.

7. Dario Abranches Viotti, "Analise dos antecedentes e das conseqüências da Revolução de Marco de 1964" (1970), ESG BGCF, TT1-123-70, 41, 67.

8. Arruda, "A Lei de Imprensa e a segurança interna" (speech, ESG, 18 July 1973), ESG BGCF, T139-73, pt. 2, 28.

9. Fico, *Reinventando o otimismo*, 38–43. As Fico affirms, such notions of moral crisis in the 1960s and 1970s extended beyond the military regime itself to zealous ordinary people who, fearing for the country's "moral strength," wrote to censors. Fico, "Prezada censura," 260.

10. Antonio Alves de Almeida, "Política e estratégias, 1976–1985/Campo psicossocial/A família" (1975), ESG BGCF, TE-75.C.PSICOS.T.25B, 98; Oliveira, "Fortalecimento da família," 7, 37; Alfredo Moacyr de Mendonça Uchoa et al., "Terceiro trabalho de grupo (Grupo G)" (1960), ESG BGCF, TG-27-60, 18; Jayme Magrassi de Sá et al., "Quinto trabalho de grupo (Grupo C)" (1955), ESG BGCF, G-28-55, 1–2.

11. David Mussa, "Estudar a evolução social da família brasileira" (1972), ESG BGCF, TT1-58-72, 62, 106; Antonio Joaquim Coelho, "A família brasileira e a conservação de nossos valores" (1978), ESG BCGF, TE-78/C.PSICOSSOCIAL.T.54, 17.

12. Serbin, *Secret Dialogues*, 53.

13. "Editorial," *A Defesa Nacional*, May/June 1969, 5.

14. Tavares, *Segurança nacional*, esp. 121–35.

15. Escola Superior de Guerra, *Manual básico*, 231.

16. Othongildo Rocha, "A Problemática do Divórcio" (1975), ESG BGCF, TE-75/C.PSICOS.25C; Farhat, "Política de comunicação social," 16.

17. Luiz Edmundo Brígido Bittencourt and Paulo César Prado Ferreira da Gama, "A formação do jovem para a liderança como instrumento de segurança política" (1974), ESG BGCF, SP1-74/SUBGRUPO C, 1, 11–12; Jorge Sá Freire de Pinho et al., "Integração da juventude" (1976), ESG BGCF, TE-76/C. PSICOS.T.25, 2; Eugênio José Andrade de Almeida e Silva, "A juventude brasileira e os objetivos nacionais" (1972), ESG BGCF, TT1-70-72, 10–12.

18. Pinho et al., "Integração da juventude," 1.

19. "Grupo 'A' relatório: Participação da juventude na execução da política nacional" (1972), ESG BGCF, SP1-123-72, 3.

20. Author interview with Guilherme Santanna, 13 June 2012, Rio de Janeiro; author interview with Samuel Carvalho, 21 November 2007, Rio de Janeiro; "Grupo 'A' relatório," 3; José Leme Lopes, "Problemática da juventude" (lecture, ESG, 6 September 1973), ESG BGCF, T187-73, 7–9.

21. On counterculture limited to upper- and middle-class consumers, see Dunn, *Brutality Garden*, 44–55; on concerns about promiscuity and white, bourgeois girlhood, see Langland, "Speaking of Flowers," 97–98.

22. Coimbra, *Operação Rio*; Luiz Raul Guimarães, "Estudar a evolução social da família brasileira" (1972), ESG BGCF, TT1-59-72, 55–56.

23. Antônio Ismar Braga, "A participação efetiva da juventude na vida nacional" (1978), ESG BGCF, TE-78/C.PSICOS.T.64, 9, 13.

24. Campos, "Integração da juventude no desenvolvimento comunitário" (1974), ESG BGCF, TEP-74C.PSICOS.A.1, iv, 8.

25. Caulfield, *In Defense of Honor*, 55–56; Besse, *Restructuring Patriarchy*.

26. Pick, *Faces of Degeneration*, 3, 74–75; Foucault, *History of Sexuality*, 123.

27. For analysis on this point, see Cowan, "Sex and the Security State."

28. Ávila, "Ideologia, religião e moral no Brasil" (lecture, ESG, 3 September 1974), ESG BGCF, CE-I/74, 12.

29. Euclides de Faria S.J., "A problemática da juventude" (1975), ESG BGCF, TE-75.C.PSICOS.T.26B, 29.

30. Adams, *Trouble with Normal*; Damousi and Plotkin, *Psychoanalysis and Politics*; Manzano, *"Sexualizing Youth"*; Pensado, *Rebel Mexico*.

31. Priolli, "A tela pequena," 31.

32. See, for example, Nicolau Tuma, "A comunicação social e os objetivos nacionais" (1969), ESG BGCF, TT1-69-72, 9; José A. T. Tavares, "Política e estratégias, 1976–1985—tema: comunicação social" (1975), ESG BGCF, TE-75.C.PSICOS.T.32C, 5; Francisco Hermógenes de Paula, "Propor a política e formular estratégias para o decênio 1978–1987, com relação à comunicação social" (1977), ESG BGCF, TE-77/C.PSICOS.T.19B, 1.

33. Paulo Cavalcanti da Costa Moura, "Características da época contemporânea" (speech, ESG, 30 August 1979), ESG BGCF, T230-79, 8; Nilson Cunha Silva, "Trabalho de turma, tema n°1" (1971), ESG BGCF, TT1-46-71, 42; Antônio Carlos de Seixas Telles, "Integração da juventude" (1976), ESG BGCF, TE-76/C.PSICOS.T.25B, 11.

34. Madeira, "A comunicação social perversa e a segurança pública" (speech, ESG, 6 October 1980), ESG BGCF, CE-III/80.T5.

35. Daltro Miguel Keidann, "Difusão pornográfica e vulnerabilidade social" (1982), ESG BGCF, TE-82.C.PSICOS.TEMA-27.GR.22A, 10–11.

36. I consulted reports whose formal topic included *comunicação social*, catalogued as such in the ESG's institutional archive.

37. Ferreira, "Propor a política e formular estratégias para o decênio 1978–1987, com relação à comunicação social" (1977), ESG BGCF, TE-77/C.

PSICOS.T.19C, 30; Camargo et al., "Comunicação social, opinião pública, e censura" (1981), ESG BGCF, TE-81/C.PSICOS.T.18, 4; Paulo Gurgel de Siqueira, "Propor a política e formular estratégias para o decêncio 1978–1987, com relação à comunicação social" (1977), ESG BGCF, TE-77/C.PSICOS.T.19A, 5.

38. On such concerns about Western popular culture, see Cowan, "Sex and the Security State," 474–75.

39. Renato Horta Lopes, "Poder de polícia nos meios de comunicação social como fator decisivo na preservação dos objetivos nacionais" (1973), ESG BGCF, SP1-73/GR.H, 3.

40. Carlos Alberto de Avellar Werner, "Difusão pornográfica e vulnerabilidade social" (1982), ESG BGCF, TE-82.C.PSICOS.TEMA-27.GR.22B, 25–26 (emphasis added). This quote from Lenin, of doubtful authenticity, suffused ESG intellectual production, having appeared as early as 1965 in U.S. anticommunists' accounts of pornography. Boller and George, *They Never Said It*, 65–66.

41. Farhat, "Política de comunicação social," 16–17.

42. Author interview with Paulo Francisco Junior, 13 June 2012, Rio de Janeiro.

43. Baden, *Muffled Cries*, 54; Soares, "Censura durante o regime autoritário," 34; Kushnir, *Cães de guarda*; Fico, "Prezada censura."

44. The lines would remain blurred throughout the period, but even when prior censorship of certain press outfits gained its own, ostensibly political bureaucracy, the personnel were drawn, tellingly, from the moral and entertainment censorship body. Smith, *Forced Agreement*, 84–85.

45. Joan Dassin's pioneering account of the censorial apparatus dismisses morality censorship as a by-product. Dassin, "Press Censorship," 175. Douglas Marcelino indicates that more radical anticommunists distanced themselves from moral censorship; many, as I argue, did not do so. Marcelino, "Para além da moral," 35, n. 58.

46. Tavares, "Política e estratégias," 88; Cowan, "Rules of Disengagement."

47. Baden, *Muffled Cries*, 54 (emphasis added). As early as 1980, Paolo Marconi's sampling of newspaper pronouncements suggested links, in the minds of select military officers, between moral censorship and countersubversion. Marconi, *A censura política*, 16–19.

48. "Relator é pela censura prévia," *O Estado de S. Paulo*, 20 May 1970, 5.

49. See chap. 5 and 7.

50. Gaspari, *A ditadura envergonhada*, 299; Costa, *Censura, repressão*; Dunn, *Brutality Garden*, 81; Pires, *Zé Celso*.

51. DPF, Gabinete do Ministro, "Peça 'Roda-Viva,'" AN/COREG, Fundo CISA, BR-AN-BSB-VAZ-040-0240.

52. Perelli, "Military's Perception," 95–96; Pion-Berlin, "Security Doctrines," 412–13.

53. Oliveira, "Fortalecimento da família," 66; Giovanni Gargiulo, "Fortalecimento da Família" (1976), ESG BGCF, TE-76/C.PSICOS.T.24A, 31.

54. Altenfelder, "Desajustamento da familia brasileira e o problema do menor" (1966), ESG BGCF, TT1-46-66, 62.

55. Schwartzman, Bomeny, and Costa, *Tempos de Capanema*, esp. 107–40; Deutsch, *Las Derechas*, 44, 282; and Dulles, *Brazilian Communism*, 42.

56. Escola Superior de Guerra, *Manual básico*, 399.

57. Momsen, *Gender and Development*, 196; Alves, "Paradoxos da participação," 15.

58. Telles, "Integração da juventude," 15, 22.

59. Taylor, *Disappearing Acts*, 183–223; May, *Homeward Bound*, 73, 93, 139–40.

60. Keidann, "Difusão pornográfica," 3–4.

61. Coelho, "A família brasileira," 19–20.

62. Schmidlin, "Responsabilidade social do estado na educação. Educacão para a cidadania" (1976), ESG BGCF, TE-76/C.PSICOS.T.27C, 3.

63. The 1930 papal encyclical *Casti connubii*'s pathologizations of women's extradomestic labor formed the backbone of a 1955 ESG speech by Álvaro Negromonte (see chap. 1), who demonized divorce, unmarried cohabitation, and women's legal emancipation. Negromonte, "O problema da recuperação moral do país—a família" (speech, ESG, 12 September 1955), ESG BGCF, C-85-55.

64. Mussa, "Estudar a evolução," 87.

65. See chap. 1; Stepan, *Hour of Eugenics*; Rosemblatt, *Gendered Compromises*, 149–84; Besse, *Restructuring Patriarchy*; and Deutsch, *Las Derechas*, 44.

66. Mussa, "Estudar a evolução," 53, 87, 97.

67. Schneider, *Brazilian Propaganda*, 60.

68. O'Donnell, "Tensions in the Bureaucratic-Authoritarian State and the Question of Democracy," in *The New Authoritarianism in Latin America*, ed. David Collier (Princeton, N.J.: Princeton University Press, 1979), 293.

69. Leopoldo Hugo Frota, Walmor Piccinini, and João Romildo Bueno, "Professor José Leme Lopes: Notas biográficas e breve homenagem," Associação Brasileira de Psiquiatria, accessed 3 May 2010, http://www.abpbrasil.org.br/historia /galeria/Leme_Lopes.pdf.

70. Alves and Nelson José O. de Almeida, "Trabalho especial de pesquisa: Integração da juventude brasileira no desenvolvimento comunitário" (1974), ESG BGCF, TEP/74.A.1.2, 38; Alves, "Juventude brasileira: Integração da juventude no desenvolvimento comunitário" (1974), ESG BGCF, TEP-74-C-PSICOS.A.1.3, 23, 25.

71. Francisco Leme Lopes, "Examinar o problema da infiltração comunista nos meios intelectuais e universitários, tendo em vista o objetivo nacional permanente da democracia representativa" (1967), ESG BGCF, TT1-17-67, 13.

72. Author interview with José de Oliveira Trovão, 20 November 2007, Rio de Janeiro.

73. Padilha, "A contestação política no Brasil—a violência" (speech, ESG, 11 May 1971), ESG BGCF, C2-13-71, 19, 27, 29.

74. Buzaid, "Em defesa," 37, 40–42 (emphasis added).

75. Galvão, "A liberdade de informação" (see chap. 2, n. 36).

76. Buzaid, "Em defesa," 34; Antônio Carlos da Silva Muricy, "Guerra revolucionária" (speech, Natal, 30 May 1963), CPDOC, Arquivo Antonio Carlos Muricy, ACM PM 1963.05.30, 21.

77. Rudolfer, "Problemática da juventude no Brasil. Psicologia e psicopatologia da adolescência," paper presented at ESG, 17 September 1974, ESG BGCF, T241-74, 11. See Cowan, "Sex and the Security State," 467–68.

78. Lopes, "Problemática da juventude," 5–6.

79. Lopes, "Educação e cultura" (1965), ESG BGCF, TT1-48-65, 75, 95.

80. Lopes, "Problemática da juventude," 7.

81. Rudolfer, "Elementos básicos da nacionalidade brasileira: O homem" (speech, ESG, 1965), ESG BGCF, C1-40-65, 1.

82. Rudolfer, *Introducção à psychologia educacional*, 123, 198; Bederman, *Manliness and Civilization*, 95.

83. Rudolfer, "A crise da adolescência moderna" (speech, ESG, 4 July 1970), ESG BGCF, C95-1-70, 9, 15–17.

84. Alves, "Juventude brasileira," 4; Lopes, "Problemática da juventude," 4. Buzaid backed up his warnings of "psycho-sexual" degeneration via citations as far back as 1908, six decades before his call to moralist arms. Buzaid, "Em defesa," 34.

85. See, for example, Luiz Carlos Bastos Hosken, "Informações para o público e propaganda no quadro da comunicação social no Brasil" (1969), ESG BGCF, TT4-03-69, 27; Tavares, *Segurança nacional*, 185; Pacheco e Silva, *A guerra subversiva em marcha*, 32. These citations of Le Bon reiterated long-standing notions of nonwhite and nonelite Brazilians as incorrigibly "emotional," the principal obstacle to national "progress."

86. See, for example, Werner, "Difusão pornográfica"; "Relatório do tema 25," 10 (see introd., n. 35).

87. Rocha, "Problemática do divórcio," 11.

88. Antônio Alves de Almeida, "Política e estratégia," 49–50; Salgado, "Como exterminar um povo," *Diário do Congresso Nacional*, 18 October 1973, 7451. Other such ESG referents from the right-wing past included Father Álvaro Negromonte and Miguel Reale, a cofounder of the Integralist movement (both spoke at the ESG), as well as Pedro Calmon, since the 1930s a proponent of moral/hygienic "militarization" and "regeneration" of Brazil's youth. Negromonte, "O problema"; Miguel Reale, "Cultura política brasileira" (speech, ESG, 14 July 1978), ESG BGCF, T104-79; Guimarães, "Estudar a evolução," 60; Lenharo, *Sacralização da política*, 80.

89. Ignácio de Freitas Rolim, "Caráter nacional e poder militar" (1960), ESG BGCF, TT1-83-60, 51–53; Equipe C, "Estudo conclusivo sôbre as repercussões da conferência tricontinental de Havana no movimento religioso no brasil e sua possível evolução" (1970), ESG BGCF, TG1-3-70/Eq. C, 1, 8–9, 18.

90. Schmidlin, "Responsabilidade social do estado," 2.

91. See, for example, Couto, "Trabalho de turma" (1970), ESG BGCF, TT1-123-70, 79–81; Jorge Boaventura de Souza, "Ação política: Soluções autocráticas" (1970), ESG BGCF, C5-123-70; and Mussa, "Estudar a evolução," 106.

92. See, for example, Couto, "O exército brasileiro" (speech, ESG, 1971), ESG BCGF, C48-123-71. Signaling the durability of hard-liners' adherence to extreme-right sources, Paula Couto's work across two decades (1970s–1990s) relied on the *same* passages from Labin, Hutton, Schwarz, and the like.

93. Couto, *O que é a subversão?*, 18.

94. Moralists at the ESG saw themselves alongside foreign anticommunist allies, facing down a common, countercultural conspiracy. See Cowan, "Sex and the Security State," 475.

95. Cunha, "Características psicossociais da época contemporânea" (speech, ESG, 3 September 1975), ESG BGCF, T220-75, 11, 20.

96. Faria, "A problemática da juventude," bibliography; Telles, "Integração da juventude," 25.

97. Motta Filho, "O papel da comunicação social na cultural nacional" (speech, ESG, 1972), ESG BGCF, C6-12-72, 6. Roszak's seminal *The Making of a Counter Culture* (1969) is credited with coining the term.

98. These included, among others, Geraldo Bezerra de Menezes, Moacir de Araújo Lopes, Carlos de Meira Mattos, Jorge Boaventura de Souza, José Camarinha Netto, Djacir Menezes, and Hélio Fraga.

99. Antonio Rafael de Menezes, "Política e estratégias/1976–1985/Campo psicossocial/Juventude" (1975), ESG BGCF, TE-75 C.PSICOS.T.26C; Alves and Almeida, "Trabalho especial"; Antônio Pedro de Souza Campos, "Integração da juventude no desenvolvimento comunitário" (1974), ESG BGCF, TEP-74C.PSICOS.A.1, 29; Pinho et al., "Integração da juventude," 53; Coronel Osmany Maciel Pillar, "A juventude e o bem comum" (1975), ESG BGCF, TE-75 C. PSICOS.T.26A; Faria, "A problemática da juventude"; Alves, "Juventude brasileira."

100. "Ética moral" (1982), ESG BGCF, LS14-82.

101. See, for example, Pinho et al., "Integração da juventude," 53; Alves and Almeida, "Trabalho especial," 4; Octávio Duval Meyer e Barros, "Integração da juventude" (1976), ESG BGCF, TE-76/C.PSICOS.T.25C, 41; Pillar, "A juventude," 7.

102. Stepan, *Rethinking Military Politics*, 47–52.

103. Coelho, "A família brasileira," 31.

104. Menezes, "Política e estratégias," 16–18.

105. Ibid.

Chapter 5

1. The title of this chapter comes from a letter reportedly sent by a medical student to the Minister of the Air Force. In a 1971 speech at the Ministry of Education, General Antônio Carlos da Silva Muricy used the letter to support his claims about sexual subversion: "With respect to the means by which the moral degradation of youth, especially young women, is accomplished, I refer to the following facts: A medical student from Natal . . . in a letter recently sent to the Minister of the Air Force, reports, 'I have seen young ladies being seduced and induced, by the desperation of their situation, to become part of terrorist groups.'" Muricy, speech to Associação Brasileira de Educação, 11 November 1971, CPDOC, Arquivo Antônio Carlos da Silva Muricy, ACM pm 1964.07.20, reel 1, plate 659, 20.

2. Comando da Quarta Zona Aérea, named report (7 July 1969), AN/COREG, Fundo CISA, BR-AN-BSB-VAZ-035-0055.

3. Ustra, *A verdade sufocada*, 426.

4. A complete list of ESG-linked, influential moralists would overwhelm this chapter but would certainly include the following: Carlos Átila Alvares da Silva, Figueiredo's press secretary; ESG professor Mário Pessoa, handpicked by Justice Minister Armando Falcão for a secret commission to consolidate moral censorship; Joint Brazil-United States Military Commission (JBUSMC) Chief Murillo Vasco do Valle Silva; Ruy Vieira da Cunha, tenant of several influential educational and editorial posts, from Director of Extracurricular Education for the Ministry of Education to member of the National Commission on Morality and Civics to editorial board member for the army's in-house publications; Jorge Boaventura de Souza e Silva, sometime president of MOBRAL (the government literacy project) and of the national Commission to Summarily Investigate Education and Culture, as well as a principal member of the Meira Mattos Commission (convened by President Costa e Silva to "analyze the student crisis" in 1967; named after its reactionary leader and fellow *esguiano* Carlos de Meira Mattos).

5. Historians have tended to divide Brazil's military rulers into two principal factions: the "Sorbonne group," of internationally oriented, pro–United States, developmentalist moderates, epitomized by President Castelo Branco and reinvigorated by Presidents Ernesto Geisel and Figueiredo; and a more hard-line, nationalist faction represented by Presidents Costa e Silva and Médici. Skidmore, *Politics of Military Rule*; Gaspari, *As ilusões armadas*.

6. Figueiredo granted Fanini the rights to a Rio de Janeiro television channel for fifteen years, enabling the birth of a televangelical empire. Cunha, *A explosão gospel*, 60.

7. "Aborto, sexo, temas de Figueiredo," *O Estado de S. Paulo*, 30 April 1980, 17.

8. "Aula inaugural do Presidente Emílio G. Médici" (speech, ESG, Rio de Janeiro, 10 March 1970), 17.

9. "Atas do 48a reunião do Conselho de Segurança Nacional" (29 April 1969), AN/COREG, Fundo Atas, BR-AN-BSB-N8-ATA-005-048, 137; Muricy, *Antônio Carlos Murici I*, 142.

10. Muricy, "A guerra de hoje" (2 September 1968), AN/COREG, Fundo CAMDE, BR-AN-RIO-PE-0-0-120-d.

11. CISA, named report (6 March 1975), AN/COREG, Fundo CISA, BR-AN-BSB-VAZ-067A-0002.

12. Serbin, *Secret Dialogues*, 78.

13. "Murici [*sic*] aponta aliciamento de jovens para o terror," *Diário de Pernambuco*, 28 July 1970, 8.

14. Ibid.

15. Muricy, speech to Associação Brasileira de Educação, 12.

16. Ibid., 9, 17–18.

17. "Estatutos da ADESG," *Segurança e Desenvolvimento*, no. 137 (1970): 2. Records of the ADESG study programs are rather spotty and therefore difficult to gauge. Nevertheless, these courses and conferences seem to have championed

moralism with more discursive variety than the ESG itself. Certainly the organization underwrote forums that *did* take the rote ESG tack—like the 1970 First Course of Study on National Security and Development, which denounced communist warfare as "a new type of sneaky, disguised, clandestine combat" only defeatable via "moral and civic" means. Augusto do Amaral Peixoto et al., "Trabalho de grupo," CPDOC, Arquivo Augusto do Amaral Peixoto, AAP tc 1970.04.06. Nevertheless, there were ADESG series, particularly by the 1980s, that engaged in moral panic (vis-à-vis family structure, youth, drugs, and working women) but did *not* necessarily tie this concern to explicit anticommunism. See Mayan Salomão et al., "Assistência social" (Rio de Janeiro: ADESG, Departamento de Ciclos de Estudos, 1976), ADESG Library.

18. Press release, 27 January 1965, CPDOC, Arquivo Juracy Magalhães, JM c emb 1964.06.12.

19. Ávila, "Elementos básicos da nacionalidade—as instituições" (speech, ESG, 26 May 1971), *Segurança e Desenvolvimento*, no. 145 (1971): 47; Buzaid, "Da conjuntura política nacional," *Segurança e Desenvolvimento*, no. 150 (1972): 8–9, 13, 16.

20. Castro, *O espirito militar*, 12; Stepan, *Military in Politics*, 51; McCann, "Military," 50.

21. Danilo Darcy de Sá da Cunha e Mello, "Tácticas revolucionárias," in *Ação educativa contra a guerra revolucionária*, Estado Maior do Exército (Rio de Janeiro: Imprensa do Exército, 1965), 276; Mário de Assis Nogueira, "Unidade II: Mobilização da opinião pública; Propaganda e boato," in Estado Maior do Exército, *Ação educativa*, 14. Nogueira himself graduated from the ESG in 1975.

22. See, for example, Antônio de Fonseca Sobrinho, "A guerra revolucionária," in Estado Maior do Exército, *Ação educativa*, 187.

23. "ECEME—1963—nota de aula no. 1.1 e 2.1—guerra revolucionária," CPDOC, Arquivo Ulhoa Cintra, UCi g 1959.01.08, reel 3, plate 14, 4.

24. Capistrano, "Operações psicológicas do inimigo interno" (1979), Biblioteca 31 de Março, MO 1336 ECEME 1979, 9, 13, 41.

25. Nascimento, "A revista *A Defesa Nacional*," 5.

26. McCann, "Military," 58; Editorial, *A Defesa Nacional*, March/April, 1973, 3–4.

27. Editorial, *A Defesa Nacional*, March/April 1966, 3.

28. D'Araujo, Soares, and Castro, *Os anos de chumbo*, 73; Vidal, "Projeção dos valores espirituais e morais na atuação das forças armadas brasileiras," in "Leitura selecionada" (1971), ESG BGCF, LS7-123-71, 3. Once again, the list might continue but would exhaust our space constraints. Other moralistic editors included Danilo da Cunha e Mello and Ayrton Salgueiro de Freitas.

29. Cowan, "Rules of Disengagement."

30. Corção, "Liberdade de que?," *A Defesa Nacional*, July/August 1969, 197–98.

31. Jonas Correia Neto, "Carta a um aluno do colégio militar," *A Defesa Nacional*, March/April 1970, 189; Cadete Wanderley da Costa Morães, "A atitude mais adequada do estudante," *A Defesa Nacional*, March/April 1970, 199.

32. Costa, "Compreensão da revolução brasileira," *A Defesa Nacional*, September/October 1964, 61–72.

33. Dantas, "A família e seu reflexo na posição da juventude perante a segurança nacional," *A Defesa Nacional*, July/August 1973, 22, 24.

34. Humberto de Souza Mello, editorial, *A Defesa Nacional*, May/June 1969, 3; Jorge Boaventura, "Revolução mundial?," *A Defesa Nacional*, March/April 1974, 34.

35. Lopes, "Liberdade e democracia," *A Defesa Nacional*, November/December 1968, 5–6 (emphasis in the original).

36. A. de Lannes, "Conhecendo o inimigo interno," *A Defesa Nacional*, September/October 1978, 127–28.

37. Editor's note, *A Defesa Nacional*, January/February 1967, 105.

38. Obino Lacerda Álvares, "Juventude em crise," *A Defesa Nacional*, July/August 1966, 89–97; Hilda Reis Capucci, "Mocidade transviada ou abandonada?," *A Defesa Nacional*, January/February 1967, 105–9; Marília Mariani, "Orientação e formação para a cidadania na escola" (speech, I Congreso Sul-Americano da Mulher em Defesa da Democracia, April 1967), *A Defesa Nacional*, May/June 1967, 86. The conference at which Mariani delivered this speech was the brainchild of CAMDE, the rightist women's organization that advised women elsewhere in Latin America. Simões, *Deus, pátria e família*, 131.

39. Correia Neto, "Carta a um aluno do colégio militar," 187, 189.

40. Luiz Carlos Aliandro, "Carta a um caçula," *A Defesa Nacional*, May/June, 1970, 189–90.

41. Narciso Kalili, "Aquí está o adultério," *Realidade*, March 1968, 142–49.

42. Álvares, "Juventude em crise," 90.

43. Lannes, "Conhecendo o inimigo interno," 130.

44. Matta, *A casa e a rua*, 44, 48, 50.

45. Author interview with Guilherme Santanna, 13 June 2012, Rio de Janeiro.

46. Corção, "Liberdade de que?"; José de Sá Martins, "A estratégia revolucionária no quadro mundial," *A Defesa Nacional*, January 1963, 9; and Ararigboia, "Os filmes 4R," *A Defesa Nacional*, July/August 1970, 91.

47. On Labin's popularity in French military journals, see Dard, "Suzanne Labin," 196.

48. João Perboyre de Vasconcellos Ferreira, "A guerra revolucionária," *A Defesa Nacional*, March 1963, 16; Ferreira, "Guerra insurrecional," *A Defesa Nacional*, July/August 1962, 9, 17; and Hélio Lemos, "Psicopolítica e contrapsicopolítica," *A Defesa Nacional*, November/December 1975, 21–22, 40. *A Defesa Nacional* contributors—like their ESG counterparts—also reached out to more mainstream authorities, notably Arnold Toynbee, Marshall McLuhan, and communication studies pioneer Wilbur Schramm. As at the ESG, citations of these more moderate sources only served to reinforce the moral paranoias of *A Defesa Nacional*. See Edmirson Maranhão Ferreira, "Comunicação e segurança nacional," *A Defesa Nacional*, May/June 1972, 77.

49. Indeed, Carlos Fico's pioneering work with documents from the Ministry of Justice notes the appearance of sexuality in the security correspondence pertinent to that body. Fico posits a post-*abertura* transition from understanding subversion as armed conflict to envisioning it as "ethico-moral" degeneracy.

Working with more limited sources, Fico does not convey the depth and longevity of connections between sex and *guerra revolucionária*. As my evidence shows, this conflation spanned various security agencies, suffused approaches well beyond the Ministry of Justice itself, and dated back at least to the 1960s. Fico, *Como eles agiam*, 102, 133, 175, 213.

50. SNI, "Atividades subversivas—movimentos de massa" (8 October 1976), APERJ, setor DGIE, pasta 237, 235-a.

51. SNI, Agência Central, "Apreciação sumária no. 6/74. Campo interno" (25 June 1974), CPDOC, Arquivo Ernesto Geisel, EG pr 1974.03.00, reel 1, plate 763, 5.

52. CIE, "Proliferação de livros erótico-pornográficos" (10 June 1975), AN/COREG, Fundo DSI/MJ, BR-DF-ANBSB-NS-AGR-COF-ISI-0088-D.

53. CISA, Agência Brasília, "Ação esquerdizante do corpo docente no meio estudantil brasileira" (4 April 1977), AN, Fundo DSI-MJ, caixa 3567/0037, processo 006, ano 1971–82, pasta I.

54. SNI, "Apreciação especial no. 01/19/AC/78" (2 January 1978), CPDOC, Arquivo Ernesto Geisel, EG pr 1974.03.00, reel 2, plate 3; SNI, "Apreciação sumária no. 19/GAB/76" (24 May 1976), CPDOC, Arquivo Ernesto Geisel, EG pr 1974.03.00, reel 1, plate 1308, 7; SNI, "Apreciação sumária no. 27/GAB/76" (19 July 1976), CPDOC, Arquivo Ernesto Geisel, EG pr 1974.03.00, reel 1, plate 1380; SNI, "Retrospecto de 1977," CPDOC, Arquivo Ernesto Geisel, EG pr 1974.03.00, reel 2, plates 1–2.

55. SNI, "Corrupção de costumes por intermédio dos veículos de comunicação no Brasil" (28 December 1972), AN/COREG, Fundo DSI/MJ, BR-RJANRIO-TT-0-MCAP-AVU-0203-D001, 11–13. On this apocryphal citation of Lenin, see chap. 4. Emphasis in original.

56. "Atividades suspeitas de 'Hipies' [*sic*]—contato com elemento russo," APERJ, setor DOPS, pasta 186, 10–11.

57. "Congresso dos 'Hippies' na Bahia" (27 February 1970), APERJ, setor DOPS, pasta 132, 24. Circulated to DOPS hierarchs by federal police, this document shows the importance of information sharing not only between civil police forces but also between ostensibly civilian and military intelligence organizations, since the memorandum attributes its information to an SNI report of 1969.

58. DGIE, "Movimento contracultura," APERJ, setor DGIE, pasta 303, 126–27; CIE, "Assunto: Chico Buarque de Holanda e outros artistas na área estudantil" (11 October 1972), APERJ, setor estudantil, pasta 39, 20–20a; DOPS report, 20 February 1970, APERJ, setor DOPS, pasta 132, 282; CIE, "Ultra secreto," AN/BRB, Fundo CIEX, BR-AN-BSB-IE-007-004, 533.

59. Green, *Beyond Carnival*, 249–59.

60. CIE, Informação n°1676S/102/A11 (29 December 1977), AN/BRB, Fundo DSI-MJ, BR-AN-RIO-TT-0-MCP-PRO-1219; SNI, "Apreciação especial no. 01/19/AC/78" (2 January 1978), CPDOC, Arquivo Ernesto Geisel, EG pr 1974.03.00, reel 2, plate 3, 3.

61. CIE, Informação n°1676S/102/A11; SNI, "Apreciação especial no. 01/19/AC/78," 3 (emphasis in original).

62. DGIE, "Movimento contracultura"; CIE, "Chico Buarque."

63. SNI, "Apreciação sumária no. 29/GAB/76" (2 August 1976), CPDOC, Arquivo Ernesto Geisel, EG pr 1974.03.00, reel 1, plate 1383, 3.

64. CISA, "Caetano Veloso e 'Chico' Buarque de Holanda" (23 November 1972), AN/COREG, Fundo CISA, BR-AN-BSB-VAZ-118A-0020. Dunn, *Brutality Garden*, 146–47; Green, *We Cannot Remain Silent*, 116.

65. Marcelino, "Para além da moral," 56.

66. DCDP, "Parecer no. 6114/75" (3 July 1975), AN/COREG, Fundo DCDP, série Televisão, subsérie Telenovelas, caixa 29.

67. Moacyr Coelho to Edgardo Erichsen, Brasília, 26 August 1975, AN/COREG, Fundo DCDP, série Administração Geral Notado, BR-AN-BSB-NS-AGR-COF-MSC-062.

68. SNI, "Apreciação sumária no. 27/GAB/76"; SNI, "Apreciação sumária (campo interno) no. 2/GAB/75" (1 September 1975), CPDOC, Arquivo Ernesto Geisel, EG pr 1974.03.00, reel 1, plate 894, 5.

69. SNI, "Apreciação sumária no 8/74" (n.d.), CPDOC, Arquivo Ernesto Geisel, EG pr 1974.03.00, reel 1, plate 766, 6. Braga's murder was never solved, though journalists later revealed that suspects included "Rezendinho" (Eurico Rezende Filho) and Alfredo Buzaid Junior, nicknamed "Buzaidinho"—the sons, respectively, of prominent moralists Senator Eurico Rezende and Justice Minister Alfredo Buzaid. See "Ana Lídia," Linha Direta—Justiça, Rede Globo, accessed 2 January 2012, http://redeglobo.globo.com/Linhadireta/0,26665,GIJo-5257-250694,00.html.

70. Ministério da Aeronáutica, Comando da 4a Zona Aérea, DSI, Informe no. 027/A-2/IV COMAR (4 February 1981), AN/COREG, Fundo CISA, BR-AN-BSB-VAZ-048A-0128, 6.

71. See Caulfield, *In Defense of Honor*, 79–104, and chapter 1.

72. DOPS, named report (27 November 1968), APERJ, setor estudantil, pasta 39, 56.

73. Ministério do Trabalho e Previdência Social, Divisão de Segurança e Informações, "Suspeito de Arapuca" (27 October 1970), APERJ, Fundo Polícias Políticas, setor secreto, pasta 79, 83–84.

74. DOPS, Divisão de Informações, "Pedido de busca no. 635/70" (4 November 1970), APERJ, Fundo Polícias Políticas, setor secreto, pasta 79, 154. João Magalhães is also a pseudonym.

75. Ibid., 156; "Suspeita de um grupo de terroristas" (6 July 1966), AN/COREG, Fundo CISA, BR-AN-BSB-VAZ-059-0039.

76. Ministério da Aeronáutica, "Atividades subversivas em São Paulo" (7 July 1969), AN/COREG, Fundo CISA, BR-AN-BSB-VAZ-131A-0005, 5. In a related vein, Jeffrey Lesser has written about the "emasculation" of male militants in press and police accounts. Lesser, *Discontented Diaspora*, 103–4.

77. Tasso Villar de Aquino, "D. Waldyr Calheiro de Novães e outros" (1 December 1969), AN/COREG, Fundo CGI-PM, BR-DFANBSB-AAJ-IPM-0853.

78. DOPS, "Pedido de busca no. 635/70."

79. DSI/MJ, "Informação n° 271/74" (12 July 1974), AN/COREG, Fundo DSI/MJ, BR-AN-RIO-TT-MCP-PRO-0371.

80. CISA, "Ação psicológica" (20 April 1971), AN/COREG, Fundo CISA, BR-AN-BSB-VAZ-053-0152; SNI, Agência São Paulo, "Revista Hora Presente; Revista Permanência" (12 August 1974), AN/COREG, Fundo SNIG, ASP-ACE-6015-81.

81. DPF, "Teste Rorschach aplicado em terroristas" (19 October 1971), AN/COREG, Fundo CISA, BR-AN-BSB-VAZ-008-0174.

82. Giordani, *Brasil sempre*, 101.

83. Ministério do Exército, "Inquérito policial-militar instaurado pelo Exmo. Sr. Gen. Cmt. I Exército, para apurar os responsáveis diretos pelo seqüestro do embaixador Charles Burke Elbrick" (20 January 1970), AN/COREG, Fundo CGI-PM, BR-DF-AJBSB-AAJ-IPM-0899-d, 45–52.

84. Couto, "Defesa da família" (4 February 1980), AN/COREG, Fundo DSI-MJ, BR-AN-RIO-TT-0-MCP-PRO-1684; Couto, "Ofício n. 371/80-CNMC" (27 June 1980), AN/COREG, Fundo DSI-MJ, BR-AN-RIO-TT-0-MCP-PRO-1756; CISA, "Atividades subversivas na AMAN" (26 July 1968), AN/COREG, Fundo CISA, BR-AN-BSB-VAZ-096-0167; CSN, "Lei de Segurança Nacional (diversos)" (n.d.), AN/COREG, Fundo CSN, BR-AN-BSB-N8-005-B.

85. Ministério da Aeronáutica, Quarta Zona Aérea, Quartel-Geral, 2a Seção, "Radicalismo católico brasileiro," AN/COREG, Fundo CISA, BR-AN-BSB-VAZ-026-0107, 6.

86. "São Paulo por dentro: Relatório no. 1325," APERJ, Fundo Polícias Políticas, setor secreto, pasta 52, 135–39 (emphasis added); "Subversão: Informe SP/SAS no. 0714" (16 June 1970), APERJ, Fundo Polícias Políticas, setor secreto, pasta 52, 87.

87. Branco, *Segurança nacional e subversão: Dicionário teórico e prático* (Rio de Janeiro: Secretária de Estado de Segurança Pública, 1977), 1–3, 70.

88. Ibid., 5, 21–22, 31, 106, 341, 348.

89. "São Paulo por dentro: Relatório no. 1325," 139.

90. Lannes, "Conhecendo o inimigo interno," 129.

91. "Morre Brilhante Ustra, ex-chefe do DOI-Codi durante a ditadura," O Globo, 16 October 2015, http://g1.globo.com/distrito-federal/noticia/2015/10/morre-brilhante-ustra-ex-chefe-de-orgao-de-repressao-na-ditadura.html.

92. Ustra, *A verdade sufocada*, 429.

Chapter 6

1. Sources of the epigraphs introducing this chapter: Camargo, *A espada virgem*, 142; DSI/MJ, "Informação n° 371/71/DSI/MJ" (27 October 1971), AN/COREG, Fundo SNIG, AC-ACE-47259-71, 5.

2. Lopes, "Parecer No. 29/71" (25 October 1971), in *Legislação e documentação referentes à Educação Moral e Cívica no Brasil,* edited by Vilmar da Silva Rocha (Goiás: Governo de Goiás, 1972), 50–56.

3. Ibid., 51.

4. Germano, *Estado militar*, 137; Nava, "Pátria and Patriotism," 185; Filgueiras, "O livro didático."

5. Cruz, *Antecedentes e perspectivas*; Cunha and Góes, *O golpe na educação*, 73–74; and Germano, *Estado militar*, 127–35.

6. "Relatório Meira Mattos mostra situação do ensino universitário," special supplement, *Correio da Manhã*, 25 August 1968, 5 (emphasis added).

7. Moacir Araújo Lopes, "Política nacional para a defesa dos valores espirituais, morais e culturais brasileiros face à luta ideológica" (speech, ECEME, 27 August 1974), in *Valores espirituais e morais da nacionalidade: Fortalecimento do homem brasileiro e da democracia brasileira, Lopes et al.* (Rio de Janeiro: *Conferências*, 1975), 46.

8. Menezes, *Educação Moral e Cívica*, 51; Costa, "Parecer" (15 June 1970), in Afro Amaral Fontoura, *Princípios de Educação Moral e Cívica*, (Rio de Janeiro: Editora Aurora, 1972), 17–19.

9. Costa, "Parecer," 18. "Insidious technique" was a catchphrase of theories of *guerra revolucionária*.

10. Paupério, "A preservação," 68.

11. Paupério, "A democracia como estilo de vida" (speech, Academia Militar das Agulhas Negras, August 1974), in Lopes et al., *Valores espirituais*, 171.

12. Ruy Vieira da Cunha, "A importância do professor de Educação Moral e Cívica," in *Anais do VIII Encontro Nacional de Educação Moral e Cívica*, 50–51; Menezes, *Educação Moral e Cívica*, 16, 26, 67.

13. Garcia, *Educação Moral e Cívica*, 165.

14. Grande, *Educação cívica das mulheres*, 56, 67.

15. Lopes, "Política nacional," 37–38.

16. Raymundo Moniz de Aragão et al., "Amplitude e desenvolvimento dos programas de Educação Moral e Cívica em todos os níveis de ensino," in *Educação Moral e Cívica*, Comissão Nacional de Moral e Civismo (hereafter CNMC) (Porto Alegre: Comissão Central de Publicações da UFRGS, 1970), 43.

17. CNMC, *Os centros cívicos*, 4; CNMC, *Educação Moral e Cívica como disciplina obrigatória*, 7–9, 21, 28.

18. Muricy, speech to Associação Brasileira de Educação (see chap. 5, n. 1); Joaquim Etelvino da Cunha, "Educação Moral e Cívica: Exame e sugestões quanto aos princípais problemas decorrentes" (1970), ESG BGCF, TT1-20-70, 1–3, 15.

19. These include Tarcísio Padilha, Ruy Vieira da Cunha, Francisco Leme Lopes, Eloywaldo Chagas de Oliveira, and Raymundo Moniz de Aragão.

20. Lopes, "A Educação Moral e Cívica no Brasil: Perspectivas atuais" (1970), ESG BGCF, C83-1-70, 8–9.

21. Couto, "Trabalho de turma," (see chap. 4, n. 90).

22. *CNMC: Boletim Informativo da Comissão Nacional de Moral e Civismo*, July–December 1984, 7.

23. Mariani, "Orientação e formação," 83, 86 (see chap. 5, n. 38); Nilda Bethlem Bastos, "Currículo e cidadania," *A Defesa Nacional*, March/April 1967, 89–102.

24. Elisabetta Maria Martinelli to "Excelentíssimos Senhores Pais" (see chap. 3, n. 5).

25. Mariani, "Orientação e formação," 86. Interestingly, this discrepancy between anxiety about girls and "solutions" focused on boys was echoed in other national contexts. In Canada, for example, Mary Louise Adams reports that despite hand-wringing about the putative sexual delinquency of young women, girls were "underserved" by the youth services programs designed to assuage moral panic and safeguard national sexuality and security. Adams, *Trouble with Normal*, 66, 76.

26. Lannes, "Conhecendo o inimigo interno," 129, 134 (see chap. 5, n. 36).

27. "Visitas," *CNMC: Boletim Informativo*, January-June 1984, 4. The LDN promoted EMC at least as early as 1962 and celebrated Decree-Law 869 in the *CNMC: Boletim Informativo*. Lúcia de Lemos, "Comportamento cívico," *CNMC: Boletim Informativo*, October 1962, 2; "Educação Moral e Cívica," *CNMC: Boletim Informativo*, October 1969, 2; "Otávio Costa afirma que a educação cívica visa a aperfeiçoar as criaturas," 1° Caderno, *Jornal do Brasil*, 17 February 1970, 3; Passarinho, "A problemática da educação no Brasil," *A Defesa Nacional*, March/April 1970, 77.

28. CISA, "Educação Moral e Cívica" (29 June 1970), AN/COREG, Fundo CISA, BR-AN-BSB-VAZ-004-0082.

29. DSI/MEC, Universidade de Brasília, "Informação n° 040/SICI/1/DSI/MEC/76" (10 May 1976), AN/COREG, Fundo ASI/UNB, BR-AN-BSB-AA1-AJD-059.

30. See, for example, "Aula de Educação Moral e Cívica" (17 November 1970), AN/COREG, Fundo CISA, BR-AN-BSB-VAZ-037A-0091; SNI, " 'Educação Moral e Cívica' e 'Estudos dos [sic] Problemas Brasileiros' " (22 February 1978), AN/COREG, Fundo CISA, BR-AN-BSB-VAZ-077-0020.

31. Caulfield, *In Defense of Honor*; Besse, *Restructuring Patriarchy*.

32. Only one text that I was able to find recommended something of a female service corps, focused on "nursing, social assistance, administrative activities, [and] manual jobs." Anselmo Nogueira Macieira, "Trabalho de turma" (1971), ESG BGCF, TT1-45-71, 54.

33. J. A. Pires Gonçalves, "Subsídios para implantação de uma política nacional de desportos," *A Defesa Nacional*, May/June 1972, 135, 141; July/August 1972, 114–15.

34. Vidal, "Ação cívica das forças armadas," *A Defesa Nacional*, May/June 1967, 42–53.

35. Neves, "O serviço militar e a segurança nacional," *A Defesa Nacional*, September/October 1968, 33–37; Neves, "Tiros de guerra e segurança nacional," *A Defesa Nacional*, January/February 1967, 129–37.

36. Lopes, "Política nacional," 34, 62 (emphasis added).

37. Lenharo, *Sacralização da política*. Besse (*Restructuring Patriarchy*, 110–24) notes 1940s Brazilian reformers' preoccupation with moral-hygienic training to create hale, republican mothers.

38. Tibery, *Fundamentos de segurança*, 46–48, 84–86 (emphasis added).

39. Kelly, *Introdução à Educação Moral e Cívica*, 71. Kelly collaborated with other moralists, including Moral Re-Armament leader Peter Howard, Padre Álvaro

Negromonte, and José Leme Lopes—the latter on issues of sexual education. Magalhães, "Remarks by Ambassador Juracy Magalhães" (see chap. 3, n. 86); Celso Kelly to Gustavo Capanema, [1952?], CPDOC, Arquivo Gustavo Capanema, GC b Kelly, C., reel 3, plate 671/3.

40. Lenharo, *Sacralização da política*, 80.

41. Calmon, "Os grandes fatos," 93.

42. Stepan, *Hour of Eugenics*, 160.

43. Ministério do Exército, "Manual de campanha," 163–66.

44. Ministério do Exército, "Programa-padrão," 11–22.

45. Stepan, *Hour of Eugenics*, 85–90.

46. Neiva, *Educação Moral e Cívica*, 42.

47. Lopes, "Publicações sôbre Educação Moral e Cívica," appendix to Couto, "Trabalho de turma."

48. Moacir de Araújo Lopes, "Relações públicas e civismo," (speech, Centro de Estudos do Pessoal, 28 October 1969), *A Defesa Nacional*, March/April 1970, 93.

49. CNMC, *Os centros cívicos*, 19. IPES and Cardinal Jaime de Barros Câmara were also among the authoritarian proponents of scouting-as-moralism. "Relatório das atividades do IPES-SP em 1963," AN, Fundo IPES, caixa 65, pacote 3; Dreifuss, *1964*, 256–57.

50. Rosenbaum, "Project Rondon," 187, 188.

51. Victoria Langland, e-mail message to author, 15 September 2007; Langland, *Speaking of Flowers*, 180.

52. Nilson Cunha Silva, "Trabalho de turma" (1971), ESG BGCF, TT1-46-71, 5, 28.

53. Almeida e Silva, "A juventude brasileira," 56–58 (see chap. 4, n. 16).

54. Macieira, "Trabalho de turma," 67.

55. Cesar Prinz Salomão, "Brasil jovem," *A Defesa Nacional*, September/October 1971, 129–30; "Otávio Costa afirma."

56. Filgueiras, "A Comissão Nacional," 7.

57. Menezes, *Educação Moral e Cívica*, 35–36; Filgueiras, "O livro didático.".

58. "Extinta a Moral e Cívica" (16 October 1974), AN/COREG, Fundo ASI-UFMG, BR-DFANBSB-AT4-0014-0004-D.

59. Onghero, "O ensino de educação moral e cívica," 96.

60. Ferreira, *Educação Moral e Cívica*, 11, 53, 57.

61. Guimarães et al., *Enciclopédia nacional*, 89.

62. Ferreira, *Curso de Educação Moral e Cívica*, 12; Barbosa, *Educação Moral e Cívica 2*, 39; and Lucci, *Passeio pelo mundo*, 15.

63. Fontoura, *Princípios*, 90; Garcia, *Educação Moral e Cívica*, 16–17.

64. Mariani, *Guia de civismo*, 13.

65. Duarte, *Educação Moral e Cívica*, 60.

66. Fontoura, *Princípios*, 88–89; Ferreira, *Curso de Educação Moral e Cívica*, 108.

67. Fontoura, *Princípios*, 32, 88–89.

68. Ferreira, *Curso de Educação Moral e Cívica*, 107; Andrade, *Juventude verdade*, 78; Duarte, *Educação Moral e Cívica*, 59; and Cotrim, *Educação Moral e Cívica*, 91–92.

69. Silva and Capella, *Educação moral e cívica*, 12.

70. Galache, Zanuy, and Pimentel, *Construindo o Brasil*, 109–17.

71. Grande, *Educação cívica das mulheres*, 71.

72. Ferreira, *Curso de Educação Moral e Cívica*, 107; Mettig and Magalhães, *Educação Moral e Cívica*, 57.

73. Macedo, *Educação Moral e Cívica*, 27.

74. Mariani, *Guia de civismo*, 48–49.

75. Garcia, Sette, and Menezes, *Educação Moral e Cívica*, 77–78; Garcia, *Educação Moral e Cívica*, 77, 165.

76. Torres, *Educação Moral e Cívica*, 18–23; Correa, *Estudo dirigido*, 31; and Duarte, *Educação Moral e Cívica*, 60.

77. Rodrigues, *Ética e civismo*, 4.

78. Torres, *Educação Moral e Cívica*, 21 (emphasis added).

79. After a health crisis, Andrade metamorphosed into the yogi widely known as Professor Hermógenes.

80. José Hermógenes de Andrade, *Educação Moral e Cívica*, 103–104; Lopes, "Publicações."

81. Andrade, *Juventude verdade*, 78, 84.

82. Ibid., 86.

83. Ferreira, *Educação Moral e Cívica*, 39–40.

84. Borges, "Puffy, Ugly, Slothful, and Inert," 250–53; Fontoura, *Princípios*, 90.

85. Moschini, Costa, and Mussumeci, *Educação Moral e Cívica*, 15, 21.

86. Ferreira, *Curso de Educação Moral e Cívica*, 36–37. Reinforcing anachronistic theoretical links, Ferreira relied on Eduard Spranger and eugenicist Nicola Pende (see chap. 4).

87. See, for example, Macedo, *Educação Moral e Cívica*, 24.

88. Caiafa, *Moral e civismo*; Galache, Zanuy, and Pimentel, *Construindo o Brasil*, 169; Conceição, *Educação integrada*, 21–23; and Bortoli, *Educação Moral e Cívica*. For an excellent discussion of EMC textbooks' treatment of race and indigeneity, see Nava, "Pátria and Patriotism," 187–90.

89. See, for example, Benedicto de Andrade, *Educação Moral e Cívica*.

90. Ferreira, *Educação Moral e Cívica*, 112.

91. Guimarães et al., *Enciclopédia nacional*, 86.

92. Fontoura, *Princípios*, 321–22.

93. Pereira, *Educação Moral e Cívica*, 5; Mariani, *Guia de civismo*, 202.

94. Guimarães et al., *Enciclopédia nacional*, 86, 89.

95. Ibid., 38–91.

96. Ibid.

Chapter 7

1. Sources of the epigraphs introducing this chapter: "Censura libera 'Hair' e diz que nem sempre nu tem sentido de erotismo," *Jornal do Brasil*, 17 February 1970, 3; Frota, *Ideais traídos*, 640.

2. See, for example, Priore, *Histórias íntimas*, 187.

3. Gaspari, *A ditadura envergonhada*, 41.

4. Cremilda Medina, "As múltiplas faces da censura," in *Minorias silenciadas: História da censura no Brasil*, ed. Maria Luiza Tucci Carneiro (Campinas: USP, 2001), 426; Maurício Maia, "Censura, um processo de ação e reação," in Carneiro, *Minorias silenciadas*, 490, 492.

5. "JB divulga hoje os verbêtes do Pe. Ávila julgados subversivos," *Jornal do Brasil*, 5 November 1967, 22.

6. Ávila, *Pequena enciclopédia de moral e civismo*.

7. "JB divulga hoje os verbêtes."

8. "Censura libera 'Hair'"; Camargo, *A espada virgem*, 131.

9. Octávio Costa, "A revolução e o militarismo" (2 September 1968), AN/COREG, Fundo CAMDE, BR-AN-RIO-PE-0-0-120-d.

10. "Polícia do Estado do Rio não sabe como censurar," *Jornal do Brasil*, 17 February 1970, 3.

11. DOPS/Guanabara, "Informação no. 834" (20 August 1969), AN/COREG, Fundo CGI-PM, BR-DFANBSB-AAJ-IPM-0527.

12. "Censura será descentralizada," *O Globo*, 17 February 1968, 3.

13. Camargo, *A espada virgem*, 154.

14. DPF, Superintendência Regional no Estado do Paraná, Serviço de Informações, "Divisão de Censura de Diversões Públicas (Sua legislação e atividade operacional)" (24 Oct 1983), AN/COREG, Fundo PF, BR-AN-BSB-ZD-007-017. The CSC had lain dormant for ten years after its legalization in 1968; it diversified the censorial hierarchy, engendering some liberalization. Inimá Ferreira Simões, "A censura cinematográfica no Brasil," in Carneiro, *Minorias silenciadas*, 374.

15. "Polícia federal proíbe exibição de 10 filmes," *O Estado de S. Paulo*, 23 June 1973, 7.

16. "Passarinho é contra a proibição de peças," *O Estado de S. Paulo*, 16 June 1973, 7.

17. "A universidade e a sociedade," *Plataforma Liberdade*, May 1978, 3.

18. Galvão, "A liberdade de informação," 69 (see chap. 2, n. 36).

19. Johnson and Stam, *Brazilian Cinema*, 45; Dennison and Shaw, *Popular Cinema in Brazil*, 171; Martins, "Produzindo no escuro," 42.

20. "Passarinho é contra."

21. Abreu, *O olhar pornô*, 76; Ramos, *Cinema Marginal*, 42, 66; and Freitas, "Pornochanchada," 74.

22. Bernardet, "Pornografia," 107; Freitas, "Pornochanchada," 83.

23. Sales Filho, "Doce sabor," 70. Inimá Ferreira Simões perceptively notes *pornochanchadas*' patriarchal "abasement of women and of minorities," stigmatization of sex, and "machista trickery." Simões, *Roteiro da intolerância*, 208.

24. Jeffrey Lesser has illuminated how *chanchadas* splashed Japanese Brazilians across screens in unprecedented ways, noting the sexual and ethnic stereotyping at the heart of these films. Lesser, *A Discontented Diaspora*, 47–62.

25. Norma Couri, "A pornochanchada no Banco dos Reus," Caderno B, *Jornal do Brasil*, 5 April 1980, 1.

26. Martins, "Produzindo no escuro," 116.

27. Leite, *Cinema brasileiro*, 110.

28. Avellar, "Teoria da relatividade," 71–77.

29. "E a nossa arte?" (see chap. 2, n. 39).

30. "A universidade e a sociedade."

31. Martins, "Produzindo no escuro," 17.

32. SNI, "Serviço Nacional do Teatro" (21 October 1976), AN/COREG, Fundo SNIG, A1014171-1976.

33. Martins, "Produzindo no escuro," 54, 57.

34. Robert Stam, João Luiz Vieira, and Ismail Xavier, "The Shape of Brazilian Cinema in the Postmodern Age," in *Brazilian Cinema, eds.* Randal Johnson and Robert Stam (New York: Columbia University Press, 1995), 405.

35. "Censurado aqui, convidado para festival em Nova Iorque," Caderno B, *Jornal do Brasil*, 25 February 1979, 5.

36. Leonor Souza Pinto, "Guerra tropical contra a censura," Memória da Censura no Cinema Brasileiro 1964–1988, January 2007, accessed 31 October 2012, http://www.memoriacinebr.com.br/Textos/Guerra_tropical_contra_a_censura.pdf.

37. Pinto, "Guerra tropical contra a censura."

38. Diegues, interview in Johnson and Stam, *Brazilian Cinema*, 100.

39. Johnson and Stam, *Brazilian Cinema*, 45; Rui Guerra, interview in Johnson and Stam, *Brazilian Cinema*, 102.

40. "Segue a briga," *Veja*, 15 November 1978, 92; Embrafilme, *I Simpósio Nacional do Cinema Brasileiro* (Brasília: Embrafilme, 1978).

41. IPPF's interventions in Brazil also aroused the ire of feminists (among other progressive groups), who perceived BEMFAM as failing to empower women vis-à-vis their own bodies; instead, the program seemed to focus obsessively and imperialistically on bodily regimentation and population control. Dalsgaard, *Matters of Life and Longing*, 103; Fonseca Sobrinho, *Estado e população*, 109–14.

42. "Natalidade é valor para o país—BEMFAM parte para nova etapa," *O São Paulo*, 19 May 1973, 1.

43. SNI, "ASSUNTO: Sociedade de bem estar familiar no Brasil" (21 November 1973), AN/COREG, Fundo CISA, BR-AN-BSB-VAZ-069-0132.

44. Carmen Barroso and Christina Bruschini, "Building Politics from Personal Lives: Discussions on Sexuality among Poor Women in Brazil," in *Third World Women and the Politics of Feminism, ed.* Chandra Talpade Mohanty and Ann Russo (Bloomington: Indiana University Press, 1991), 155.

45. "Controle familiar não é privilégio," *Folha de S. Paulo*, 6 August 1974, 5.

46. "Risco da gravidez chega a 29%," *O Estado de S. Paulo*, 10 June 1977, 16.

47. "INPS também fará controle familiar," *O Estado de S. Paulo*, 29 July 1977, 14.

48. Ibid.; "Plano para gravidez começa no Nordeste," *O Estado de S. Paulo*, 1 November 1977, 12.

49. DINSAMI, *Analise de desempenho das atividades do Programa de Saúde Materno-Infantil, da Região Norte em 1978* (Ministério da Saúde, 1979).

50. "INPS também fará controle familiar."

51. Ibid.

52. "Saúde controlará risco no uso de anticoncepcional," *O Estado de S. Paulo*, 28 October 1977, 16.

53. Coutinho, "Controle da natalidade," Seção Cultura, *O Estado de S. Paulo*, 12 February 1978, 20.

54. "Saúde controlará risco."

55. "Faltam verbas para programas de saúde," *O Estado de S. Paulo*, 3 March 1979, 16.

56. "PND fixa política de saúde," *O Estado de S. Paulo*, 12 September 1979, 12.

57. "Controle familiar terá clínicas," *O Estado de S. Paulo*, 26 April 1980, 11.

58. Coutinho, "Controle da natalidade"; "Controle familiar terá clínicas."

59. "No planejamento familiar, a doutrina da ESG," *O Estado de S. Paulo*, 30 April 1980, 17. In an ironic twist, BEMFAM president Walter Rodrigues had actually spoken at the ESG in 1978, advocating his organization's more aggressive measures and accusing "leftist elements" of opposing birth control for subversive reasons. Nevertheless, support for the Pill does not seem to have emerged definitively at the ESG. Rodrigues, "Planejamento familiar" (speech, ESG, 5 June 1978).

60. "Aborto, sexo, temas de Figueiredo," *O Estado de S. Paulo*, 30 April 1980, 17.

61. CISA, "Controle da natalidade" (15 January 1981), AN/COREG, BR-AN-BSB-VAZ-131A-0045.

62. Motta, "O anticomunismo," 148. Primary accounts also attest to this sense of marginalization. See, for example, Guerra, *Memórias*, 30, 79.

63. CISA, "Controle da natalidade."

64. "INPS também fará controle familiar."

65. DPF, Serviço de Informações, "Informe no. 003/83" (1983), AN/COREG, Fundo PF, caixa 30-B, 167–70.

66. DPF, Superintendência Regional Estado de Paraná, Serviço de Informações, "Pedido de busca no. 109/80" (17 November 1980), AN/COREG, Fundo PF, caixa 38-A, 66–67.

67. Priore, *Histórias íntimas*, 206.

68. DPF, Centro de Informações, "Informe no. 502/05/80" (9 September 1980), AN/COREG, Fundo PF, caixa 38-A, 60–65.

69. Moura, "O quadro atual da subversão no Brasil" (speech, Chamber of Deputies, Brasília, April 1983), AN/COREG, Fundo PF, caixa 48-A, 1, 3.

70. *Diário do Congresso Nacional*, 27 May 1981, 4394–95.

71. Magdalena da Cunha Coelho, "Carta aberta à censura federal" (1 August 1978), AN/COREG, Fundo DCDP, BR-AN-BSB-NS-AGR-COF-MSC-135.

72. *Diário do Congresso Nacional*, 27 May 1981, 4420.

73. "INPS também fará controle familiar."

74. "INPS também fará controle familiar."

75. Serbin, *Secret Dialogues*, 159–60.

76. Della Cava and Montero, *E o verbo se faz*, 150.

77. "A teoria e os fatos: Veto a revistas," *O São Paulo*, 19 May 1972, 1.

78. "Cinema, aquí, ó!," *Campus*, April 1977, 12.

79. "Pílulas . . . ora, pílulas!," *Brasil Mulher*, December 1975, 6–7; Fonseca Sobrinho, *Estado e população*.

80. DOPS/SP, "Informe no. 379/05/67," AN/COREG, BR-AN-BSB-VAZ-026A-0021, 8–9.

81. Carpeaux, "Convênios monstruosos," *Amanhã*, 27 April 1967, 12.

82. Armando Falcão, interview by Jorge Escosteguy, television program *Roda viva*, 16 October 1989.

83. Falcão, *Tudo a declarar*, 368.

Conclusion

1. DPF/São Paulo, "Organizações clandestinas" (September 1980), AN/COREG, Fundo PF, DPF 46-A-0001-0056, caixa 46-A.

2. Dehesa, *Queering the Public Sphere*, 81–83.

3. DPF/São Paulo, "Campo psicossocial: Movimento-Sindical" (10 July 1980), AN/COREG, Fundo PF, DPF 46-A-0342-0396, caixa 46-A; CIE, "Publicações referentes ao carnaval contrárias à moral e aos bons costumes" (25 March 1982), AN/COREG, Fundo PF, DPF 45-A-0150-0151, caixa 45-A.

4. Falcão, interview in *1964—31 de março: O movimento revolucionário e a sua história*, vol. 1, ed. Aricildes de Morães Motta (Rio de Janeiro: Bibliex Editôra, 2003), 216, 218; Reis, interview in Motta, *1964*, 142. The term "useful innocents" or "useful idiots" developed in midcentury Atlantic anticommunist circles to describe those unwittingly susceptible to subversion by communists.

5. Boaventura, *Os sofrimentos*.

6. Examples abound, too numerous to list. See Rafael Queiroz, "As raízes ideológicas do movimento gay," *Direitistas do Brasil* (blog), 29 June 2009, accessed 30 January 2010, http://direitistasdobrasil.blogspot.com/search/label/Gayzismo; Taiguara Fernandes de Sousa, "O gayzismo tá rolando solto!," *En Garde!* (blog), 10 January 2010, accessed 30 January 2010, http://taiguaraonline.blogspot.com /2010/01/o-gayzismo-ta-rolando-solto.html; and Leonardo Simões Matos, "A ditadura do 'movimento homossexual,'" *Integralismo* (blog), 20 June 2012, accessed 23 August 2013, http://integralismo.blogspot.com/2012/06/ditadura-do -movimento-homossexual.html.

7. Lind, "Dead but Not Gone," *The American Conservative*, 10 October 2005, 33–34.

8. Buchanan, *Death of the West*, 83–90.

9. Charles Scaliger, "Where America?," *The Schwarz Report*, November 2014, 1; Schlafly, "Toying Again with Socialism," *The Schwarz Report*, January 2010, 2–3; Kuhner, "Communism Is Alive and Well," *The Schwarz Report*, January 2010, 3.

10. Schwarz and Noebel, *You Can Still Trust*.

11. Self, *All in the Family*; Moreton, *To Serve God and Wal-Mart*; and McGirr, *Suburban Warriors*.

12. Potent examples of this correspondence include Christian newspapers' coverage, in each country, of evangelical growth, politics, and setbacks in the others. See, for example, "Evangelical Attorneys Unite to Fight Homosexual Movements in Brazil," *The Christian Telegraph*, 5 December 2012, 1; "Aumenta a guerra contra os valores cristãos nos EUA," *Mensageiro da Paz*, June 2012, 1.

13. Viotti, "Analise dos antecedentes," 41, 67 (see chap. 4, n. 6).

14. Mariani, *Guia de civismo*, 13.

15. "Comissão da Verdade quer convocar Ustra," *O Estado de S. Paulo*, 18 August 2012, 13.

16. Huggins, "Urban Violence," 113–14; Sikkink, *Justice Cascade*, 158–62; and Wiebelhaus-Brahm, *Truth Commissions*, 75–76.

17. Maciel and Nascimento, *Orvil*, 827.

18. Armando L. M. de Paiva Chaves, "Retrato do tempo," *Crônica* 61 (September 2010).

19. Paulo Martins, "Ditadura militar?," *Ternuma* (blog), accessed 1 November 2012, http://www.ternuma.com.br/index.php/art/1388-ditadura-militar-paulo -martins.

Works Consulted

Archives

Arquivo Geral da Cidade do Rio de Janeiro (Centro)
Arquivo Histórico do Exército (Rio de Janeiro, Centro)
Arquivo Nacional do Brasil (Rio de Janeiro, Centro)
Arquivo Nacional do Brasil, Coordenação Regional no Distrito Federal
    (Brasília, DF)
Arquivo Público do Estado do Rio de Janeiro (Botafogo)
Biblioteca da Academia Militar das Agulhas Negras (Resende)
Biblioteca da Associação dos Diplomados da Escola Superior de Guerra
    (ADESG) (Rio de Janeiro, Centro)
Biblioteca do Exército (BIBLIEX), Biblioteca Franklin Doria
    (Rio de Janeiro, Centro)
Biblioteca Nacional do Brasil (Rio de Janeiro, Centro)
Escola de Comando e Estado Maior do Exército (ECEME), Biblioteca 31 de
    Março (Urca)
Escola Superior de Guerra (ESG), Biblioteca General Cordeiro de Farias (Urca)
Fundação Getúlio Vargas, Centro de Pesquisa e Documentação de História
    Contemporânea do Brasil (Botafogo)

Periodicals

Ação Democrática
Arquivos Brasileiros de Psicotécnica Aplicada
Boletim do Diretório da Liga de Defesa Nacional
Catolicismo
Claudia
Correio da Manhã (Rio de Janeiro)
Correio Popular (Campinas)
Cultura Política
A Defesa Nacional
O Diário de Minas Gerais (Belo Horizonte)
Diário de Notícias (Rio de Janeiro)
Diário de Pernambuco (Recife)
O Estado de S. Paulo
Estrela do Sul (Porto Alegre)
Folha de S. Paulo
O Globo (Rio de Janeiro)

Jornal do Brasil
O Legionário
Manchete
Military Review
A Offensiva
A Ordem
Paz e Terra
Realidade
Revista ECEME
Revista Militar Brasileira
Revue Militaire Generale
O São Paulo
Schwarz Report
Segurança e Desenvolvimento
Small Wars Journal
A TFP em 30 Dias
Time
Veja
Zero Hora (Porto Alegre)

Interviews

All interview subject names, with the exception of José Pedriali, are
    pseudonyms.
Carvalho, Samuel. Interview by author, 21–22 November 2007. Rio de Janeiro.
Estevão, João. Interview by author, 28 July 2006. Salvador da Bahia.
Junior, Paulo Francisco. Interview by author, 13 June 2012. Rio de Janeiro.
Magalhães, Fred. Interview by author, 19 July 2006. Salvador da Bahia.
Pedriali, José. Interview by author, 16–17 June 2012. Londrina, Paraná.
Santanna, Guilherme. Interview by author, 13 June 2012. Rio de Janeiro.
Trovão, José de Oliveira. Interview by author, 20 November 2007.
    Rio de Janeiro.

Published Sources

Abreu, Nuno César. *O olhar pornô: A representação do obsceno no cinema e no video.*
    Campinas: Mercado de Letras, 1996.
Abreu, Vanessa Kern de, and Geraldo Inácio Filho. "A Educação Moral e
    Cívica—doutrina, disciplina e prática educativa." *Revista HISTEDBR On-line,*
    no. 24 (2006): 125–34.
Adams, Mary Louise. *The Trouble with Normal: Postwar Youth and the Making of
    Heterosexuality.* Toronto: University of Toronto Press, 1997.
Aderaldo, Vanda Maria Costa. *Educação e política no Estado Novo: A reforma do
    ensino secundário em 1942.* Rio de Janeiro: Fundação Getúlio Vargas / CPDOC,
    1982.

Agee, Philip. *Inside the Company: CIA Diary*. Harmondsworth, England: Penguin Books, 1975.

Alvarez, Sonia E. *Engendering Democracy in Brazil: Women's Movements in Transition Politics*. Princeton: Princeton University Press, 1990.

Alves, José Eustáquio Diniz. "Paradoxos da participação política da mulher no Brasil." Rio de Janeiro: Escola Nacional de Ciências Estatísticas/Instituto Brasileiro de Geografia e Estatística, 2007.

Alves, Márcio Moreira. *A Igreja e a política no Brasil*. São Paulo: Editora Brasiliense, 1978.

Alves, Maria Helena Moreira. *State and Opposition in Military Brazil*. Austin: University of Texas Press, 1985.

Anais do VIII Encontro Nacional de Educação Moral e Cívica. Brasília: MEC / CNMC, 1985.

Andrade, Benedicto de. *Educação Moral e Cívica*. 4th ed. São Paulo: Editora Atlas, 1974.

Andrade, José Hermógenes de. *Educação Moral e Cívica*. Rio de Janeiro: Record, 1978.

———. *Juventude verdade: Educação Moral e Cívica*. 2nd ed. Rio de Janeiro: Record, 1975.

Anos 70: Trajetórias. São Paulo: Iluminuras, 2006.

Anshen, Ruth, ed. *The Family: Its Function and Destiny*. New York: Harper, 1949.

Antoine, Charles. *O integrismo brasileiro*. Translated by João Guilherme Linke. Rio de Janeiro: Civilização Brasileira, 1980.

Archdiocese of São Paulo. *Brasil: Nunca mais*. Petrópolis: Vozes, 1985.

———. *Torture in Brazil: A Shocking Report on the Pervasive Use of Torture by Brazilian Military Governments, 1964–1979*. Translated by Jaime Wright. Austin: University of Texas Press, 1998.

Armony, Ariel C. *Argentina, the United States, and the Anti-Communist Crusade in Central America, 1977–1984*. Athens: Ohio University Center for International Studies, 1997.

———. "Transnationalizing the Dirty War: Argentina in Central America." In Joseph and Spenser, *In from the Cold*, 134–71.

Arruda, Waldemar. *Pontos de Educação Moral e Cívica*. 2nd ed. São Paulo: Instituto Brasileiro de Edições Pedagógicas, 1973.

Assis, Denise. *Propaganda e cinema a service do golpe—1962–1964*. Rio de Janeiro: Mauad, 2001.

Assumpção, Francisco B., Jr. "A ideologia na obra de Antônio Carlos Pacheco e Silva." *Revista Latinoamericana de Psicopatologia Fundamental* 6, no. 4 (2003): 39–53.

Avellar, José Carlos. "Teoria da relatividade." In *Anos 70: Cinema*, edited by Jean-Claude Bernardet, José Carlos Avellar, and Ronaldo Monteiro, 71–77. Rio de Janeiro: Europa Editora, 1979.

Avia, Alexander. "An Archive of Counterinsurgency: State Anxieties and Peasant Guerrillas in Cold War Mexico." *Journal of Iberian and Latin American Research* 19, no. 1 (2013): 41–51.

Ávila, Fernando Bastos de. *Pequena enciclopédia de moral e civismo*. Rio de Janeiro: MEC, 1967.

Bacchetta, Paola, and Margaret Power, eds. *Right-Wing Women: From Conservatives to Extremists around the World*. New York: Routledge, 2002.

Backeuser, Everardo, ed. *Enciclopédia do Integralismo*. Vol. 9, *Integralismo e a educação*. Rio de Janeiro: Livraria Clássica Brasileira, 1959.

———. *A sedução do comunismo*. Rio de Janeiro: Centro Dom Vital, 1933.

Baden, Nancy T. *The Muffled Cries: The Writer and Literature in Authoritarian Brazil, 1964–1985*. Lanham, Md.: University Press of America, 1999.

Bailey, Beth. *Sex in the Heartland*. Cambridge, Mass.: Harvard University Press, 1999.

Bandeira, Maria. *A Igreja Católica na virada da questão social (1930–1964)*. Rio de Janeiro: Vozes, 2000.

Barbosa, Nélson. *Educação Moral e Cívica, 2*. São Paulo: Editora Itamaraty, 1971.

Barbosa, Regina Maria. "Mulher e contracepção: Entre o técnico e o político." Ph.D. diss., Universidade Estadual do Rio de Janeiro, 1989.

Barr-Melej, Patrick. "Siloísmo and the Self in Allende's Chile: Youth, 'Total Revolution,' and the Roots of the Humanist Movement." *Hispanic American Historical Review* 86, no. 4 (2006): 747–84.

Barroso, Gustavo. *Espírito do século XX*. Rio de Janeiro: Civilização Brasileira, 1936.

———. *Judaismo, maçonaria e comunismo*. Rio de Janeiro: Civilização Brasileira, 1937.

Beattie, Peter M. "The House, the Street, and the Barracks: Reform and Honorable Masculine Social Space in Brazil, 1864–1945." *Hispanic American Historical Review* 76, no. 3 (1996): 439–73.

———. *The Tribute of Blood: Army, Honor, Race, and Nation in Brazil, 1864–1945*. Durham, N.C.: Duke University Press, 2001.

Bederman, Gail. *Manliness and Civilization: A Cultural History of Gender and Race in the United States, 1880–1917*. Chicago: University of Chicago Press, 1995.

Beichman, Arnold. "Club Dead." *National Review*, 13 December 1985, 45.

Bernardet, Jean Claude. "Pornografia, o sexo dos outros." In *Sexo e poder*, edited by Guido Mantega, 103–8. São Paulo: Brasiliense, 1979.

Bertonha, João Fábio. "A direita radical brasileira no século XX: Do monarquismo e das Ligas Nacionalistas ao fascismo e à ditadura militar (1889–2011)." *Studia Historica. Historia contemporánea* 30 (2012): 133–50.

———. "Plínio Salgado, os integralistas e a ditadura militar. Os herdeiros do fascismo no regime dos generais (1964–1975)." *História & Perspectivas* 24, no. 44 (2011): 427–49.

Besse, Susan K. *Restructuring Patriarchy: The Modernization of Gender Inequality in Brazil, 1914–1940*. Chapel Hill: University of North Carolina Press, 1996.

Betto, Frei [Carlos Alberto Libânio Christo]. *Batismo de sangue: Guerrilha e morte de Carlos Marighella*. Rio de Janeiro: Civilização Brasileira, 1982.

Birtle, Andrew J. *U.S. Army Counterinsurgency and Contingency Operations Doctrine, 1942–1976*. Washington, D.C.: Center for Military History, 2006.

Black, Jan Knippers. *United States Penetration of Brazil*. Philadelphia: University of Pennsylvania Press, 1977.

Blee, Kathleen M., and Sandra McGee Deutsch, eds. *Women of the Right: Comparisons and Interplay across Borders*. University Park: Pennsylvania State University Press, 2012.

Blume, Norman. "Pressure Groups and Decision-Making in Brazil." *Studies in Comparative International Development* 3, no. 11 (November 1967): 205–23.

Boaventura, Jorge. *Os sofrimentos e o caos deste final de século (Suas verdadeiras causas e a restauração, possível, da justiça e da paz)*. Rio de Janeiro: Editora Presença, 1995.

Boller, Paul F., and John H. George. *They Never Said It: A Book of Fake Quotes, Misquotes, and Misleading Attributions*. New York: Oxford University Press, 1989.

Borges, Dain. "'Puffy, Ugly, Slothful, and Inert': Degeneration in Brazilian Social Thought, 1880–1940." *Journal of Latin American Studies* 25, no. 2 (1994): 235–56.

Bortoli, Lurdes de. *Educação Moral e Cívica*. São Paulo: Companhia Editora Nacional, 1978.

Brands, Hal. *Latin America's Cold War*. Cambridge, Mass.: Harvard University Press, 2010.

Brennan, Mary. *Wives, Mothers, and the Red Menace*. Boulder: University of Colorado Press, 2008.

Bruneau, Thomas C. *The Political Transformation of the Brazilian Catholic Church*. Cambridge: Cambridge University Press, 1974.

Buchanan, Patrick. *The Death of the West: How Dying Populations and Immigrant Invasions Imperil Our Country and Civilization*. New York: Thomas Dunne Books / St. Martin's Press, 2002.

Buchman, Frank N. D. *Remaking the World*. London: Blandford Press, 1961.

Buzaid, Alfredo. "Em defesa da moral e dos bons costumes." In *Conferências*, 31–60. Brasília: Imprensa Nacional, 1971.

Caiafa, Maria. *Moral e civismo através de jograis*. Belo Horizonte: Editora Lemi, 1980.

Calil, Gilberto Grassi. *O integralismo no pós-guerra: A formação do PRP (1945–1950)*. Porto Alegre: EDIPUCRS, 2001.

Calmon, Pedro. "Os grandes fatos e os grandes homens na Educação Moral e Cívica." In *O cidadão e o civismo: Educação Moral e Cívica—suas finalidades*, edited by Adonias Filho, 85–94. São Paulo: Instituição Brasileira de Difusão Cultural, 1982.

Camargo, J. M. de Toledo. *A espada virgem (Os passos de um soldado)*. São Paulo: Icone, 1995.

Carey, Elaine. *Plaza of Sacrifices: Gender, Power, and Terror in 1968 Mexico*. Albuquerque: University of New Mexico, 2005.

Carmo, Paulo Sérgio do. *Culturas da rebeldia: A juventude em questão*. São Paulo: Senac, 2003.

Carneiro, Maria Luiza Tucci, ed. *Minorias silenciadas: História da censura no Brasil*. Campinas: USP, 2001.

Carone, Edgar. *Da esquerda à direita*. Belo Horizonte: Oficina de Livros, 1991.

Castro, Celso. *O espirito militar: Um estudo de antropologia na Academia Militar das Agulhas Negras*. Rio de Janeiro: Jorge Zahar, 1990.

Castro, Ruy. *O anjo pornográfico: A vida de Nelson Rodrigues*. São Paulo: Companhia das Letras, 1992.

Caulfield, Sueann. "The Birth of Mangue: Race, Nation, and the Politics of Prostitution in Rio de Janeiro, 1850–1942." In *Sex and Sexuality in Latin America*, edited by Daniel Balderston and Donna J. Guy, 86–101. New York: NYU Press, 1997.

———. *In Defense of Honor: Sexual Morality, Modernity, and Nation in Early-Twentieth-Century Brazil*. Durham, N.C.: Duke University Press, 2000.

Centro Dom Vital de São Paulo. *Algumas sugestões ao plano nacional de educação*. São Paulo: Revista dos Tribunaes, 1936.

Chalmers, Douglas A., Maria do Carmo Campello de Souza, and Atilio A. Boron. *The Right and Democracy in Latin America*. Westport, Conn.: Praeger, 1992.

Charen, Mona. *Useful Idiots: How Liberals Got It Wrong in the Cold War and Still Blame America First*. Washington, D.C.: Regnery, 2003.

Chauí, Marilena. "Apontamentos par uma crítica da Ação Integralista Brasileira." In *Ideologia e mobilização popular*, edited by Marilena Chauí, 17–124. Rio de Janeiro: Paz e Terra, 1978.

Chirio, Maud. *A política nos quartéis: Revoltas e protestos de oficiais na ditadura militar brasileira*. Rio de Janeiro: Zahar, 2012.

Cohen, Stanley. *Folk Devils and Moral Panics: The Creation of the Mods and Rockers*. Oxford: Oxford University Press, 1972.

Coimbra, Cecilia Maria Bouças. *Guardiães da ordem: Uma viagem pelas práticas psi no Brasil do "Milagre."* Rio de Janeiro: Oficina do Autor, 1995.

———. *Operação Rio: O mito das classes perigosas; Um estudo sobre a violência urbana, a mídia impressa e os discursos de segurança pública*. Rio de Janeiro: Oficina do Autor; Niterói: Intertexto, 2001.

Collier, David, ed. *The New Authoritarianism in Latin America*. Princeton, N.J.: Princeton University Press, 1979.

Colling, Ana Maria. *A resistência da mulher à ditadura militar no Brasil*. Rio de Janeiro: Rosa dos Tempos, 1997.

Comblin, José. *The Church and the National Security State*. Maryknoll, N.Y.: Orbis Books, 1979.

Comisión Nacional sobre la Desaparición de Personas. *Nunca más: Informe de la Comisión Nacional sobre la Desparición de Personas*. Buenos Aires: EUDEBA, 1984.

Comissão Nacional da Verdade. *Relatório*. Vol. 3. Brasília: CNV, 2014.

Comissão Nacional de Moral e Civismo. *Os centros cívicos*. Brasília: CNMC, 1975.

———. *Educação Moral e Cívica*. Porto Alegre: Comissão Central de Publicações da UFRGS, 1970.

———. *Educação Moral e Cívica como disciplina obrigatória nos três níveis de ensino: Prescrições sôbre currículos—programas básicos*. Rio de Janeiro: Imprensa do Exército, 1970.

Conceição, Dejanyra Maria da. *Educação integrada: Religião—moral—civismo.* São Paulo: FTD, [1970?].

Corção, Gustavo. *O século do nada.* Rio de Janeiro: Record, n.d.

Cordeiro, Janaina Martins. *Direitas em movimento: a Campanha da Mulher pela Democracia e a ditadura no Brasil.* Rio de Janeiro: Fundação Getúlio Vargas, 2009.

Corradi, Juan E., and Patricia Weiss Fagen. *Fear at the Edge: State Terror and Resistance in Latin America.* Berkeley: University of California Press, 1992.

Correa, Avelino Antônio. *Estudo dirigido de Educação Moral e Cívica.* Vol. 2. São Paulo: Ática, 1978.

Costa, Albertina de Oliveira, Maria Teresa Porciuncula Moraes, Norma Marzola, and Valentina da Rocha Lima. *Memórias das mulheres do exílio.* Rio de Janeiro: Paz e Terra, 1980.

Costa, Maria Cristina Castilho. *Censura, repressão e resistência no teatro brasileiro.* São Paulo: Annablume, 2008.

Cotrim, Gilberto. *Educação Moral e Cívica para uma geração consciente.* São Paulo: Saraiva, 1986.

Couto, Adolpho João de Paula. *O desafio da subversão.* Porto Alegre: Gráfica FLEPLAM, n.d.

———. *O que é a subversão?* Rio de Janeiro: Comissão Nacional de Moral e Civismo, 1984.

Cowan, Benjamin. "Rules of Disengagement: Masculinity, Violence, and the Cold War Remakings of Counterinsurgency in Brazil." *American Quarterly* 66, no. 3 (2014): 691–714.

———. "Sex and the Security State: Gender, Sexuality, and 'Subversion' at Brazil's Escola Superior de Guerra, 1964–1985." *Journal of the History of Sexuality* 16, no. 3 (2008): 459–81.

———. "'Why Hasn't This Teacher Been Shot?': Moral-Sexual Panic, the Repressive Right, and Brazil's National Security State." *Hispanic American Historical Review* 92, no. 3 (2012): 403–36.

Crahan, Margaret E. "National Security Ideology and Human Rights." In *Human Rights and Basic Needs in the Americas,* edited by Margaret E. Crahan, 100–119. Washington, D.C.: Georgetown, 1982.

Cruz, Maury Rodrigues da. *Antecedentes e perspectivas da educação e no Brasil.* Curitiba: Editora da Universidade Federal do Paraná, 1982.

Cunha, Luiz Antônio, and Moacyr de Góes. *O golpe na educação.* Rio de Janeiro: Jorge Zahar, 1985.

Cunha, Magali do Nascimento. *A explosão gospel: Um olhar das ciências humanas sobre o cenário evangélico no Brasil.* Rio de Janeiro: Mauad, 2007.

Cunha, Maria Carneiro da. *Comportamento sexual: A revolução que ficou no caminho.* São Paulo: Livraria Nobel, 1987.

Cytrinowicz, Roney. "Integralismo e anti-semitismo nos textos de Gustavo Barroso na década de 30." M.A. thesis, FFLCH-USP, 1992.

Da Costa, Marcelo Timotheo. *Um itinerário no século: Mudança, diciplina e ação em Alceu Amoroso Lima.* Rio de Janeiro: PUC, 2006.

Dalsgaard, Anne Line. *Matters of Life and Longing: Female Sterilisation in Northeast Brazil*. Copenhagen: Museum Tusculanum Press, 2004.

Damousi, Joy, and Mariano Ben Plotkin. *Psychoanalysis and Politics: Histories of Psychoanalysis under Conditions of Restricted Political Freedom*. Oxford: Oxford University Press, 2012.

D'Araujo, Maria Celina, Gláucio Ary Dillon Soares, and Celso Castro, eds. *Os anos de chumbo: A memória militar sobre a repressão*. Rio de Janeiro: Relume Dumará, 1994.

Dard, Olivier. "Suzanne Labin: Fifty Years of Anticommunist Agitation." In *Transnational Anti-Communism and the Cold War: Agents, Activities, and Networks*, edited by Luc Van Dongen, Stéphanie Roulin, and Giles Scott-Smith. New York: Palgrave Macmillan, 2014.

Dassin, Joan. "Press Censorship and the Military State in Brazil." In *Press Control around the World*, edited by Joan R. Dassin and Jane Leftwich Curry, 149–86. New York: Praeger, 1982.

Dávila, Jerry. *Diploma of Whiteness: Race and Social Policy in Brazil, 1917–1945*. Durham, N.C.: Duke University Press, 2003.

———. *Hotel Trópico: Brazil and the Challenge of African Decolonization, 1950–1980*. Durham, N.C.: Duke University Press, 2010.

Davis, Darien J. "The Arquivos das Polícias Politicais [*sic*] of the State of Rio de Janeiro." *Latin American Research Review* 31, no. 1 (1996): 99–104.

Davis, Sonny B. *A Brotherhood of Arms: Brazil-United States Military Relations, 1945–1977*. Niwot: University Press of Colorado, 1996.

Dean, Robert D. *Imperial Brotherhood: Gender and the Making of Cold War Foreign Policy*. Amherst: University of Massachusetts Press, 2001.

De Groot, Gerard J. "Ronald Reagan and Student Unrest in California, 1966–1970." *Pacific Historical Review* 65, no. 1 (1996): 107–29.

Dehesa, Rafael. *Queering the Public Sphere in Mexico and Brazil: Sexual Rights Movements in Emerging Democracies*. Durham, N.C.: Duke University Press, 2010.

D'Elboux, Luiz Gonzaga da Silveira. *O Padre Leonel Franca S. J.* Rio de Janeiro: Agir, 1953.

Della Cava, Ralph. *A igreja em flagrante: Catolicismo e sociedade na imprensa brasileira 1964–1980*. Rio de Janeiro: Zero, 1985.

Della Cava, Ralph, and Paula Montero. *E o verbo se faz imagem: Igreja Católica e os meios de comunicação no Brasil, 1962–1989*. Petrópolis: Vozes, 1991.

D'Emilio, John. *Sexual Politics, Sexual Communities: The Making of a Homosexual Minority in the United States, 1940–1970*. Chicago: University of Chicago Press, 1983.

D'Emilio, John, and Estelle Freedman. *Intimate Matters: A History of Sexuality in America*. Chicago: University of Chicago Press, 1998.

Dennison, Stephanie, and Lisa Shaw. *Popular Cinema in Brazil: 1930–2001*. Manchester: Manchester University Press, 2004.

Deutsch, Sandra McGee. *Las Derechas: The Extreme Right in Argentina, Brazil, and Chile, 1890–1939*. Stanford, Calif.: Stanford University Press, 1999.

Dias, Lucy. *Anos 70: Enquanto corria a barca*. São Paulo: Senac, 2003.

Dockhorn, Gilvan Veiga. *Quando a ordem é segurança e o progresso é desenvolvimento, 1964–1974*. Porto Alegre: EDIPUCRS, 2001.

Dreifuss, René Armand. *1964: A conquista do estado. Ação política, poder, e golpe de classe*. Petrópolis: Vozes, 1981.

Duarte, Gleus Damasceno. *Educação Moral e Cívica, manual do professor*. Belo Horizonte: Editora Lê, 1979.

Dulles, John W. F. *Brazilian Communism, 1935–1945: Repression during World Upheaval*. Austin: University of Texas Press, 1983.

———. *Carlos Lacerda, Brazilian Crusader*. Vol. 1, *The Years 1914–1960*. Austin: University of Texas Press, 1996.

———. *Resisting Brazil's Military Regime: An Account of the Battles of Sobral Pinto*. Austin: University of Texas Press, 2007.

———. *Sobral Pinto, the "Conscience of Brazil": Leading the Attack against Vargas (1930–1945)*. Austin: University of Texas Press, 2002.

Dunn, Christopher. *Brutality Garden: Tropicália and the Emergence of a Brazilian Counterculture*. Chapel Hill: University of North Carolina Press, 2001.

———. "Desbunde and Its Discontents: Counterculture and Authoritarian Modernization in Brazil, 1968–1974." *The Americas* 70, no. 3 (2014): 429–58.

———. "'Experimentar o Experimental': Avant-garde, Cultura Marginal, and Counterculture in Brazil, 1968–72." *Luso-Brazilian Review* 50, no. 1 (2013): 229–52.

Durham, Martin, and Margaret Power, eds. *New Perspectives on the Transnational Right*. New York: Palgrave Macmillan, 2010.

Eidelman, Ariel. "Pornografía y censura estatal en Buenos Aires en la década del 60." Paper presented at XIV Jornadas Interescuelas/Departamentos de Historia, Mendoza, Argentina, October 2003.

Escola Superior de Guerra. *Manual básico*. Rio de Janeiro: Escola Superior de Guerra, Departamento de Estudos, 1975.

Estado Maior do Exército. *Ação educativa contra a guerra revolucionária*. Rio de Janeiro: Imprensa do Exército, 1965.

Falcão, Armando. *Tudo a declarar*. Rio de Janeiro: Editora Nova Fronteira, 1989.

Faria, Octávio de. *Machiavel e o Brasil*. 2nd ed. Rio de Janeiro: Civilização Brasileira, 1933.

Ferreira, Ebenézer Soares. *Educação Moral e Cívica*. 4th ed. Rio de Janeiro: Junta de Educação Religiosa e Publicações, 1978.

Ferreira, Luís Pinto. *Curso de Educação Moral e Cívica*. Rio de Janeiro: José Konfino Editor, 1972.

Fico, Carlos. *Como eles agiam: Os subterrâneos da Ditadura Militar; Espionagem e polícia política*. Rio de Janeiro: Record, 2001.

———. "'Prezada censura': Cartas ao regime militar." *Revista Topoi*, no. 5 (2002): 251–86.

———. *Reinventando o otimismo: Ditadura, propaganda e imaginário social no Brasil*. Rio de Janeiro: Fundação Getúlio Vargas, 1997.

Figueiredo, Federico de Lima. *Os militares e a democracia: Análise estrutural da ideologia do Pres. Castelo Branco*. Rio de Janeiro: Edições Graal, 1980.

Filgueiras, Juliana Miranda. "A Comissão Nacional de Moral e Civismo: 1969–1986." Paper presented at IV Brazilian Congress of the History of Education, Goiânia, Brazil, November 2006.

———. "O livro didático de Educação Moral e Cívica na ditadura militar de 1964: A construção de uma disciplina." In *Anais do VI Congresso Luso-Brasileiro de História da Educação*. Uberlândia: COLUBHE, 2006.

Finchelstein, Federico. *The Ideological Origins of the Dirty War: Fascism, Populism, and Dictatorship in Twentieth Century Argentina*. New York: Oxford University Press, 2014.

———. *Transatlantic Fascism: Ideology, Violence, and the Sacred in Argentina and Italy, 1919–1945*. Durham, N.C.: Duke University Press, 2009.

Fischer, Brodwyn M. *A Poverty of Rights: Citizenship and Inequality in Twentieth-Century Rio de Janeiro*. Stanford, Calif.: Stanford University Press, 2008.

Fitzpatrick, Edward A. "Manpower and Atomic War." *Annals of the American Academy of Political and Social Science*, no. 278 (November 1951): 126–36.

Fonseca, Selva Guimarães. "O ensino de história e o golpe militar de 1964." In *1964–2004: 40 anos do golpe; Ditadura militar e resistência no Brasil*, edited by Carlos Fico and Maria Celina d'Araujo, 364–80. Rio de Janeiro: 7Letras, 2004.

Fonseca Sobrinho, Délcio da. *Estado e população: Uma história do planejamento familiar no Brasil*. Rio de Janeiro: FNUAP, 1993.

Fontes, Lourival. *Homens e multidões*. Rio de Janeiro: José Olympio, 1950.

Fontoura, Afro Amaral. *Princípios de Educação Moral e Cívica*. Rio de Janeiro: Editora Aurora, 1972.

Foucault, Michel. *The History of Sexuality*. Vol. 1, *An Introduction*. Translated by Robert Hurley. New York: Vintage Books, 1990.

Franca, Leonel, S.J. *A crise do mundo moderno*. 4th ed. Rio de Janeiro: Agir, 1955.

———. *A formação da personalidade*. 2nd ed. Rio de Janeiro: Agir, 1958.

Freitas, Marcel de Almeida. "Pornochanchada: Capítulo estilizado e estigmatizado da história do cinema nacional." *Comunicação e Política* 11, no. 1 (2004): 57–105.

Friedman, Andrea. "The Smearing of Joe McCarthy: The Lavender Scare, Gossip and Cold War Politics." *American Quarterly* 57, no. 4 (2005): 1105–29.

Frota, Sylvio. *Ideais traídos*. Rio de Janeiro: Jorge Zahar, 2006.

Gabeira, Fernando. *O crepúsculo do macho*. Rio de Janeiro: Codecri, 1980.

Gaiarsa, José Ângelo. *A juventude diante do sexo*. São Paulo: Editora Brasiliense, 1967.

Galache, G., F. Zanuy, and M. T. Pimentel. *Construindo o Brasil: Educação moral, cívica, e política*. São Paulo: Edições Loyola, 1971.

Garcia, Edília Coelho. *Educação Moral e Cívica*. São Paulo: Livros Irradiantes, 1973.

Garcia, Edília Coelho, Thamar Sette, and Maurício Bret de Menezes. *Educação Moral e Cívica*. São Paulo: Livro Irradiantes, 1980.

Gaspari, Elio. *As ilusões armadas*. Vol. 1, *A ditadura envergonhada*. Vol. 2, *A ditadura escancarada*. São Paulo: Companhia das Letras, 2002.

Gauvreau, Michael. *The Catholic Origins of Quebec's Quiet Revolution, 1931–1970*. Montreal: McGill-Queen's University Press, 2005.

Germano, José Willington. *Estado militar e educação no Brasil (1964–1985).* São Paulo: Cortez / Unicamp, 1992.

Gilbert, James. *Men in the Middle: Searching for Masculinity in the 1950s.* Chicago: University of Chicago Press, 2005.

Gill, Lesley. *The School of the Americas: Military Training and Political Violence in the Americas.* Durham, N.C.: Duke University Press, 2004.

Giordani, Marco Pollo. *Brasil sempre.* Porto Alegre: Tchê!, 1986.

Goldenberg, Mirian. *Toda mulher é meio Leila Diniz.* Rio de Janeiro: Record, 1995.

Gomes, Ângela Maria de Castro. "A construção do homem novo: O trabalhador brasileiro." In Oliveira, Velloso, and Gomes, *Estado Novo,* 151–66.

Goode, Erich, and Nachman Ben-Yehuda. *Moral Panics: The Social Construction of Deviance.* Oxford: Oxford University Press, 1994.

Grande, Humberto. *Educação cívica das mulheres.* Rio de Janeiro: Reper Editora, 1967.

Grandin, Greg. *The Last Colonial Massacre: Latin America in the Cold War.* Chicago: University of Chicago Press, 2004.

Green, James N. *Beyond Carnival: Male Homosexuality in Twentieth-Century Brazil.* Chicago: University of Chicago Press, 1999.

———. "(Homo)sexuality, Human Rights, and Revolution in Latin America." In *Human Rights and Revolutions,* edited by Jeffrey N. Wasserstrom, Lynn Hunt, Marilyn B. Young, and Gregory Grandin, 139–54. Lanham, Md.: Rowman & Littlefield, 2007.

———. *We Cannot Remain Silent: Opposition to the Brazilian Military Dictatorship in the United States.* Durham, N.C.: Duke University Press, 2010.

———. " 'Who Is the Macho Who Wants to Kill Me?': Male Homosexuality, Revolutionary Masculinity, and the Brazilian Armed Struggle of the 1960s and 70s." *Hispanic American Historical Review* 92, no. 3 (2012): 437–69.

Grendon, Alexander, et al. " 'Crisis at Berkeley': Readers Comment on the Recent Science Articles." *Science* 148, no. 3675 (1965): 1273–74.

Grünspun, Haim, and Feiga Grünspun. *Assuntos de família.* São Paulo: Almed, n.d.

Guerra, Cláudio. *Memórias de uma guerra suja.* Rio de Janeiro: Topbooks, 2012.

Guimarães, Carmen Dora. *O homossexual visto por entendidos.* Rio de Janeiro: Garamond, 2004.

Guimarães, Décio Gonçalves Ribeiro, et al., eds. *Enciclopédia nacional de Educação Moral e Cívica.* São Paulo: Formar, [1982?].

Guy, Donna J. *Sex and Danger in Buenos Aires: Prostitution, Family, and Nation in Argentina.* Lincoln: University of Nebraska Press, 1991.

Hahner, June E. *Emancipating the Female Sex: The Struggle for Women's Rights in Brazil, 1850–1940.* Durham, N.C.: Duke University Press, 1990.

Harmer, Tanya. *Allende's Chile and the Inter-American Cold War.* Chapel Hill: University of North Carolina Press, 2011.

Heinz, Wolfgang S., and Hugo Frühling. *Determinants of Gross Human Rights Violations by State and State-Sponsored Actors in Brazil, Uruguay, Chile, and Argentina, 1960–1990.* N.p.: Martinus Nijhoff, 1999.

Herzog, Dagmar. *Sex after Fascism: Memory and Morality in Twentieth-Century Germany.* Princeton, N.J.: Princeton University Press, 2005.

Hilton, Stanley E. *Brazil and the Soviet challenge, 1917–1947.* Austin: University of Texas Press, 1991.

Höffner, Joseph. *Fundamentals of Christian Sociology.* Translated by Geoffrey Stevens. Westminster, Md.: Newman Press, 1962.

Htun, Mala. *Sex and the State: Abortion, Divorce, and the Family under Latin American Dictatorships and Democracies.* Cambridge: Cambridge University Press, 2003.

Huggins, Martha K. *Political Policing: The United States and Latin America.* Durham, N.C.: Duke University Press, 1998.

———. "Urban Violence and Police Privatization in Brazil: Blended Invisibility." *Social Justice* 27, no. 2 (2000): 113–34.

Huggins, Martha K., Mika Haritos-Fatouros, and Philip G. Zimbardo. *Violence Workers: Police Torturers and Murderers Reconstruct Brazilian Atrocities.* Berkeley: University of California Press, 2002.

Imbiriba, Mário Fernandes. *Breviário da instrução moral e cívica do soldado.* Rio de Janeiro: Ministério da Guerra / Biblioteca Militar, 1939.

Isaia, Artur Cesar. *Catolicismo e autoritarismo no Rio Grande do Sul.* Porto Alegre: EDIPUCRS, 1998.

Johnson, David K. *The Lavender Scare: Cold War Persecution of Gays and Lesbians in the Federal Government.* Chicago: University of Chicago Press, 2004.

Johnson, Randal. "The Nova Republica and the Crisis in Brazilian Cinema." *Latin American Research Review* 24, no. 1 (1989): 124–39.

———. "Regarding the Philanthropic Ogre: Cultural Policy in Brazil, 1930–45/1964–90." In *Constructing Culture and Power in Latin America*, edited by Daniel H. Levine, 311–56. Ann Arbor: University of Michigan Press, 1993.

Johnson, Randal, and Robert Stam, eds. *Brazilian Cinema.* New York: Columbia University Press, 1995.

Joseph, Gilbert M. "What We Know Now and Should Know: Bringing Latin America More Meaningfully into Cold War Studies." In Joseph and Spenser, *In from the Cold*, 3–46.

Joseph, Gilbert M., and Daniela Spenser, eds. *In from the Cold: Latin America's New Encounter with the Cold War.* Durham, N.C.: Duke University Press, 2008.

Kelly, Celso. *Introdução à Educação Moral e Cívica.* Rio de Janeiro: Reper Editora / Editora Renes, 1970.

Kimmel, Michael S., ed. *The History of Men: Essays in the History of American and British Masculinities.* Albany: State University of New York Press, 2005.

Kinsman, Gary. "'Character Weaknesses' and 'Fruit Machines': Toward an Analysis of the Anti-Homosexual Security Campaign in the Canadian Civil Service." *Labour/Le Travail*, no. 35 (Spring, 1995): 133–61.

Kohli, Atul. *State-Directed Development: Political Power and Industrialization in the Global Periphery.* Cambridge: Cambridge University Press, 2004.

Kon, Igor Semenovich. *The Sexual Revolution in Russia: From the Age of the Czars to Today.* New York: Simon & Schuster, 1995.

Koutzii, Flávio, and José Corrêa Leite. *Che: 20 anos depois; Ensaios e testemunhos.* São Paulo: Busca Vida, 1987.

Kuklick, Bruce. *Blind Oracles: Intellectuals and War from Kennan to Kissinger.* Princeton, N.J.: Princeton University Press, 2006.

Kuri, Ariel Rodríguez. "El lado oscuro de la luna. El momento conservador en 1968." In *Conservadurismo y derechas en la história de México*, vol. 2, edited by Erika Pani. Mexico City: Fondo de Cultura Económico, 2009.

Kushnir, Beatriz. *Cães de guarda: Jornalistas e censores, do AI-5 à constituição de 1988.* São Paulo: Boitempo, 2004.

Labin, Suzanne. *Em cima da hora.* Translated by Carlos Lacerda. Rio de Janeiro: Distribuidora Record, 1963.

———. *Hippies, Drugs, and Promiscuity.* Translated by Stephanie Winston. New Rochelle, N.Y.: Arlington House, 1972.

———. *The Secret of Democracy.* Translated by Otto E. Albrecht. New York: Vanguard, 1955.

Landau, Saul. *The Dangerous Doctrine: National Security and U.S. Foreign Policy.* Boulder, Colo.: Westview Press, 1988.

Langland, Victoria Ann. "Birth Control Pills and Molotov Cocktails: Reading Sex and Revolution in 1968 Brazil." In Joseph and Spenser, *In from the Cold*, 308–49.

———. "Speaking of Flowers: Student Movements and Collective Memory in Authoritarian Brazil." Ph.D. diss., Yale University, 2004.

———. *Speaking of Flowers: Student Movements and the Making and Remembering of 1968 in Military Brazil.* Durham, N.C.: Duke University Press, 2013.

Lazreg, Marnia. *Torture and the Twilight of Empire: From Algiers to Baghdad.* Princeton, N.J.: Princeton University Press, 2007.

Leacock, Ruth. *Requiem for a Revolution: The United States and Brazil, 1961–1969.* Kent, Ohio: Kent State University Press, 1990.

Leite, Sidney Ferreira. *Cinema brasileiro: das origens à retomada.* São Paulo: Perseu Abramo, 2005.

Lemos, Renato. "Filinto Müller." In *Dicionário histórico-biográfico brasileiro: Pós-1930.* 2nd ed. Rio de Janeiro: Fundação Getúlio Vargas, 2001.

Lenharo, Alcir. *Sacralização da política.* Campinas: Editora Unicamp / Papirus, 1986.

Lesser, Jeff. *A Discontented Diaspora: Japanese Brazilians and the Meanings of Ethnic Militancy, 1960–1980.* Durham, N.C.: Duke University Press, 2007.

———. *Welcoming the Undesirables: Brazil and the Jewish Question.* Berkeley: University of California Press, 1995.

Levine, Robert M. *Father of the Poor? Vargas and His Era.* Cambridge: Cambridge University Press, 1998.

Lewis, Tom. "Legislating Morality: Victorian and Modern Legal Responses to Pornography." In *Behaving Badly: Social Panic and Moral Outrage—Victorian and Modern Parallels,* edited by Judith Rowbotham and Kim Stevenson, 143–58. Hampshire, England: Ashgate, 2003.

Lima, Délcio Monteiro de. *Os homoeróticos.* Rio de Janeiro: Francisco Alves, 1983.

——. *Os senhores da direita*. Rio de Janeiro: Antares, 1980.

Linz, Juan J. *Totalitarian and Authoritarian Regimes*. London: Lynne Rienner Publishers, 2000.

Lopes, Moacir de Araújo, Arthur Machado Paupério, and Geraldo Montedônio Bezerra de Menezes. *Valores espirituais e morais da nacionalidade: Fortalecimento do homem brasileiro e da democracia brasileira*. Rio de Janeiro: 1975.

Lopez, George A. "National Security Ideology as an Impetus to State Violence and State Terror." In *Government Violence and Repression: An Agenda for Research*, edited by George A. Lopez and Michael Stohl, 73–95. Westport, Conn.: Greenwood Press, 1986.

Lucci, Elian Alabi. *Passeio pelo mundo de moral e civismo*. São Paulo: Saraiva, 1981.

Lumsden, Ian. *Machos, Maricones, y Gays: Cuba and Homosexuality*. Philadelphia, Pa.: Temple University Press, 1996.

Lustosa, Oscar de Figueiredo. "A igreja e o integralismo no Brasil, 1932–1939." *Revista de História* 54, no. 108 (1976): 503–33.

Macedo, Sérgio D. T. *Educação Moral e Cívica*. São Paulo: Livros Irradiantes, 1973.

Maciel, Licio, and José Conegundes Nascimento. *Orvil: Tentativas de tomada do poder*. São Paulo: Editora Schoba, 2012.

Maes, Cari Williams. "Progeny of Progress: Child-Centered Policymaking and National Identity Construction in Brazil, 1922–1954." Ph.D. diss., Emory University, 2011.

Mainwaring, Scott. *The Catholic Church and Politics in Brazil, 1916–1985*. Stanford, Calif.: Stanford University Press, 1986.

Maio, Marcos Chor. *"Nem Rothschild nem Trotsky": O pensamento anti-semita de Gustavo Barroso*. Rio de Janeiro: Imago, 1992.

Mallon, Florencia E. "Barbudos, Warriors, and Rotos: The MIR, Masculinity, and Power in the Chilean Agrarian Reform 1965–74." In *Changing Men and Masculinities in Latin America*, edited by Matthew C. Gutmann, 179–215. Durham, N.C.: Duke University Press, 2003.

Manzano, Valeria. *The Age of Youth in Argentina: Culture, Politics, and Sexuality from Perón to Videla*. Chapel Hill: University of North Carolina Press, 2014.

——. "The Making of Youth in Argentina: Culture, Politics, and Sexuality, 1956–1976." Ph.D. diss., Indiana University, 2009.

——. "Sexualizing Youth: Morality Campaigns and Representations of Youth in Early 1960s Buenos Aires." *Journal of the History of Sexuality* 14, no. 4 (2005): 433–61.

Marcelino, Douglas Attila. "Para além da moral e dos bons costumes: A DCDP e a censura televisiva no regime militar." Baccalaureate thesis, Universidade Federal do Rio de Janeiro, 2004.

Marconi, Paolo. *A censura política na imprensa brasileira (1968–1978)*. São Paulo: Global, 1980.

Mariani, Marília. *Guia de civismo, nivel médio*. Rio de Janeiro: Editora Paulo de Azevedo, 1970.

Martins, Rui. *A rebelião romântica da Jovem Guarda*. Rio de Janeiro: Fulgor, 1966.

Martins, William de Souza Nunes. "Produzindo no escuro: Políticas para a indústria cinematográfica brasileira e o papel da censura (1964–1988)." Ph.D. thesis, Universidade Federal do Rio de Janeiro, 2009.

Marwick, Arthur. *The Sixties: Cultural Revolution in Britain, France, Italy, and the United States, c.1958–c.1974.* New York: Bloomsbury, 2012.

Mathias, Suzeley Kalil. *A militarização da burocracia: A participação militar na administração federal das comunicações e da educação, 1963–1990.* São Paulo: UNESP, 2003.

Matta, Roberto da. *A casa e a rua: Espaço, cidadania, mulher e morte no Brasil.* São Paulo: Editora Brasiliense, 1985.

May, Elaine Tyler. *Homeward Bound: American Families in the Cold War Era.* New York: Basic Books, 1988.

McCann, Frank D. "The Military." In *Modern Brazil: Elites and Masses in Historical Perspective*, edited by Frank D. McCann and Michael L. Coniff, 47–82. Lincoln: University of Nebraska Press, 1989.

McGirr, Lisa. *Suburban Warriors: The Origins of the New American Right.* Princeton, N.J.: Princeton University Press, 2001.

McSherry, J. Patrice. *Predatory States: Operation Condor and Covert Warfare in Latin America.* Lanham, Md.: Rowman & Littlefield, 2005.

Medeiros, Umberto Augusto de. *Estudo dirigido de Educação Moral e Cívica.* Goiânia: P. D. Araujo, 1974.

Mehlman, Natalia. "Sex Ed . . . and the Reds? Reconsidering the Anaheim Battle over Sex Education, 1962–1969." *History of Education Quarterly* 47, no. 2 (2007): 203–32.

Menezes, Geraldo Bezerra de. *Educação Moral e Cívica.* Rio de Janeiro: Livraria Editora Cátedra / MEC Instituto Nacional do Livro, 1980.

Mettig, Olga Pereira, and Maria Lígia Lordello de Magalhães. *Educação Moral e Cívica: Curso primário.* São Paulo: Editora do Brasil, 1972.

Miller, Francesca. *Latin American Women and the Search for Social Justice.* Hanover, N.H.: University Press of New England, 1991.

Ministério do Exército. *Manual de campanha: Guerra revolucionária.* 2nd ed. Rio de Janeiro: Biblioteca do Exército, 1971.

———. *Programa-padrão de instrução. Período básico de selva.* 1st ed. Rio de Janeiro: Biblioteca do Exército, 1972.

Miyamoto, Shiguenoli. "Escola Superior de Guerra: Mito e realidade." *Política e Estratégia* 5, no. 1 (1987): 78–92.

Mohanty, Chandra Talpade, and Ann Russo. *Third World Women and the Politics of Feminism.* Bloomington: Indiana University Press, 1991.

Momsen, Janet Henshall. *Gender and Development.* London: Routledge, 2004.

Moreton, Bethany. *To Serve God and Wal-Mart: The Making of Christian Free Enterprise.* Cambridge, Mass.: Harvard University Press, 2009.

Morris, Michael F. "Al-Qa'ida as Insurgency: The Quest for Islamic Revolution." In *Strategic Challenges for Counterinsurgency and the Global War on Terrorism*, edited by Williamson Murray, 277–302. Washington, D.C.: United States Army Strategic Studies Institute, 2006.

Moschini, Felipe N., Otto Costa, and Víctor Mussumeci. *Educação Moral e Cívica*. São Paulo: Editora do Brasil, S.A., [1972?].

Mosse, George L. *The Image of Man: The Creation of Modern Masculinity*. New York: Oxford University Press, 1996.

Motta, Aricildes de Morães, ed. *1964—31 de março: O movimento revolucionário e a sua história*. Vol. 1. Rio de Janeiro: Bibliex Editora, 2003.

Motta, Rodrigo Patto Sá. "O anticomunismo e os órgãos de informação da ditadura nas universidades brasileiras." *Contemporánea: Historia y Problemas del Siglo XX* 3, no. 3 (2012): 133–48.

———. *Em guarda contra o "perigo vermelho": O anticomunismo no Brasil*. São Paulo: Editora Perspectiva, 2002.

Muricy, Antônio Carlos. *Antônio Carlos Murici I*. Interview with Aspásia Alcântara de Camargo, Ignez Cordeiro de Farias, and Lucia Hippolito, 26 February 1981. Rio de Janeiro: Fundação Getúlio Vargas, 1993.

Nascimento, Fernanda de Santos. "A revista *A Defesa Nacional* e o projeto de modernização do exército brasileiro (1931–1937)." Paper presented at ANPUH, São Paulo, July 2011.

Nava, Carmen. "Pátria and Patriotism: Nationalism and National Identity in Brazilian Public Schools, 1937–1974." Ph.D. diss., University of California, Los Angeles, 1995.

Needell, Jeffrey D. "Identity, Race, Gender, and Modernity in the Origins of Gilberto Freyre's Oeuvre." *American Historical Review* 100, no. 1 (1995): 51–77.

Neiva, Álvaro. *Educação Moral e Cívica e as instituições extraclasse*. Rio de Janeiro: José Olympio, 1972.

Netto, Henrique Coelho. *Breviário cívico (Publicação da Liga de Defesa Nacional)*. Rio de Janeiro: Norte, 1921.

Nixon, Richard. *Six Crises*. Garden City, N.Y.: Doubleday, 1962.

O'Donnell, Guillermo. *Modernization and Bureaucratic-Authoritarianism: Studies in South American Politics*. Berkeley: Institute of International Studies, University of California, 1979.

Oliveira, Eliézer Rizzo de. *Militares: Pensamento e ação política*. Campinas: Papirus, 1987.

Oliveira, Hermes de Araújo. *Guerra revolucionária*. Rio de Janeiro: Biblioteca do Exército, 1965.

Oliveira, Lúcia Lippi. "Autoridade e política: O pensamento de Azevedo Amaral." In Oliveira, Velloso, and Gomes, *Estado Novo*, 48–70.

———. "Tradição e política: O pensamento de Almir de Andrade." In Oliveira, Velloso, and Gomes, *Estado Novo*, 31–47.

Oliveira, Lúcia Lippi, Mônica Pimenta Velloso, and Ângela Maria de Castro Gomes. *Estado Novo: Ideologia e poder*. Rio de Janeiro: Zahar, 1982.

O'Neill, Bard E. *Insurgency & Terrorism: Inside Modern Revolutionary Warfare*. Washington, D.C.: Brassey's, 1990.

Onghero, Andre Luiz. "O ensino de educação moral e cívica: Memórias de professores do Oeste de Santa Catarina (1969–1993)." *Horizontes* 26, no. 1 (2008): 107–17.

Pacheco e Silva, Antônio Carlos. *A guerra subversiva em marcha*. São Paulo: Centro das Indústrias do Estado de São Paulo, Coleção Forum Roberto Simonsen, 1959.

———. *Hippies, drogas, sexo, poluição*. São Paulo: Martins, 1973.

———. *Reminiscências*. São Paulo: União Cultural Brasil Estados Unidos, 1995.

Pani, Erika, ed. *Conservadurismo y derechas en la historia de México*. 2 vols. Mexico City: Fondo de Cultura Económico, 2009.

Para a crise mundial: Uma resposta; Rearmamento Moral na concepção de Frank Buchman. Rio de Janeiro: Edições Rearmamento Moral, [1975?].

Paula, Christiane Jalles de. "Combatendo o bom combate: Política e religião nas crônicas jornalísticas de Gustavo Corção (1953–1976)." Ph.D. diss., Instituto Universitário de Pesquisas do Rio de Janeiro, 2007.

Paupério, Arthur Machado. "A preservação, o fortalecimento e a projeção dos valores espirituais e éticos da nacionalidade." In *O cidadão e o civismo: Educação Moral e Cívica—suas finalidades*, edited by Adonias Filho, 31–46. São Paulo: Instituição Brasileira de Difusão Cultural, 1982.

Pedro, Joana Maria. "A experiência com contraceptivos no Brasil: Uma questão de geração." *Revista Brasileira de História* 23, no. 45 (2003): 239–60.

Peña, Susana. *¡Oye Loca! From the Mariel Boatlift to Gay Cuban Miami*. Minneapolis: University of Minnesota Press, 2013.

Pensado, Jaime M. *Rebel Mexico: Student Unrest and Authoritarian Political Culture during the Long Sixties*. Stanford, Calif.: Stanford University Press, 2013.

Pereira, Flávio A. *Educação Moral e Cívica*. Rio de Janeiro: José Olympio, 1970.

Perelli, Carina. "The Military's Perception of Threat in the Southern Cone of South America." In *The Military and Democracy: The Future of Civil-Military Relations in Latin America*, edited by Louis W. Goodman and Johanna S. R. Mendelson, 93–105. Lexington, Mass.: Lexington Books, 1990.

Perlstein, Rick. *Before the Storm: Barry Goldwater and the Unmaking of the American Consensus*. New York: Nation Books, 2009.

Pick, Daniel. *Faces of Degeneration: A European Disorder, c. 1848–1918*. Cambridge: Cambridge University Press, 1989.

Pimentel, Layana Karine. "*Paz e terra*: O pensamento da esquerda cristã expresso nos debates da revista (1966 a 1969)." *Revista Brasileira da História das Religiões* 1, no. 3 (2009).

Pion-Berlin, David. *The Ideology of State Terror: Economic Doctrine and Political Repression in Argentina and Peru*. Boulder, Colo.: Lynne Rienner Publishers, 1989.

———. "Latin American National Security Doctrines: Hard and Softline Themes." *Armed Forces & Society* 15, no. 3 (1989): 411–29.

Pires, Ericson. *Zé Celso e a Oficina-Uzyna de Corpos*. São Paulo: Annablume, 2005.

Pittman, David J. "Mass Media and Juvenile Delinquency." In *Juvenile Delinquency*, edited by Joseph S. Roucek, 230–47. Freeport, N.Y.: Books for Libraries Press, 1970.

Plotke, David. "The Success and Anger of the Modern American Right." In *The Radical Right*, 3rd ed., edited by Daniel Bell, xiv–lxxvi. New Brunswick, N.J.: Transaction Publishers, 2002.

Porter, James E. *Audience and Rhetoric: An Archaeological Composition of the Discourse Community.* Englewood Cliffs, N.J.: Prentice Hall, 1992.

Power, Margaret. *Right-Wing Women in Chile: Feminine Power and the Struggle Against Allende in Chile, 1964–1973.* University Park: Pennsylvania State University Press, 2002.

————. "Transnational Connections among Right-Wing Women: Brazil, Chile, and the United States." In Blee and Deutsch, *Women of the Right.*

Priolli, Gabriel. "A tela pequena no Brasil grande." In *Televisão e vídeo,* edited by Fernando Lima Barbosa, Gabriel Priolli, and Arlindo Machado, 20–43. Rio de Janeiro: Zahar, 1985.

Priore, Mary del. *Histórias íntimas: Sexualidade e erotismo na história do Brasil.* São Paulo: Planeta, 2011.

Ramiro Ramírez, Hernán. "Os institutos de estudos econômicos de organizações empresariais e sua relação com o estado em perspectiva comparada: Argentina e Brasil, 1961–1996." Ph.D. diss., Universidade Federal do Rio Grande do Sul, 2005.

Ramos, Fernão. *Cinema Marginal (1968–1973): A representação em seu limite.* São Paulo: Editora Brasiliense/EMBRAFILME, 1987.

Realizações 1: Panorama da educação nacional: Discursos do presidente Getúlio Vargas e do ministro Gustavo Capanema. Rio de Janeiro: Ministério de Educação e Saúde, 1947.

Ribeiro, Ivete, and Ana Clara Torres Ribeiro. *Família e desafios na sociedade brasileira: Valores como ângulo de análise.* Rio de Janeiro: Centro João XXIII, 1993.

Ridenti, Marcelo. *Em busca do povo brasileiro: Artista da revolução, do CPC à era da TV.* Rio de Janeiro: Record, 2000.

Rocha, Vilmar da Silva, ed. *Legislação e documentação referentes à Educação Moral e Cívica no Brasil.* Goiás: Governo de Goiás, 1972.

Rodrigues, Afonso. *Ética e civismo para professores e curso fundamental.* Rio de Janeiro: Livraria José Olympio Editora, 1972.

Rogin, Michael Paul. *Ronald Reagan, the Movie, and Other Episodes in Political Demonology.* Berkeley: University of California Press, 1987.

Rosemblatt, Karin Alejandra. *Gendered Compromises: Political Cultures and the State in Chile, 1920–1950.* Chapel Hill: University of North Carolina Press, 2000.

Rosenbaum, H. Jon. "Project Rondon, a Brazilian Experiment in Economic and Political Development." *American Journal of Economics and Sociology* 30, no. 2 (1971): 187–202.

Roszak, Theodore. *The Making of a Counter Culture: Reflections on the Technocratic Society and Its Youthful Opposition.* Garden City, N.Y.: Doubleday, 1969.

Rotundo, E. Anthony. *American Manhood: Transformations in Masculinity from the Revolution to the Modern Era.* New York: Basic Books, 1994.

Rouquié, Alain. *The Military and the State in Latin America.* Translated by Paul E. Sigmund. Berkeley: University of California Press, 1987.

Rubenstein, Anne. "The War on 'Las Pelonas': Modern Women and Their Enemies, Mexico City, 1924." In *Sex in Revolution: Gender, Politics, and Power* in *Modern Mexico*, edited by Jocelyn Olcott, Mary Kay Vaughan, and Gabriela Cano, 57–80. Durham, N.C.: Duke University Press, 2006.

Rudolfer, Noemy da Silveira. *Introducção à psychologia educacional*. São Paulo: Companhia Editora Nacional, 1938.

Ruggiero, Kristin. *Modernity in the Flesh: Medicine, Law, and Society in Turn-of-the-Century Argentina*. Stanford, Calif.: Stanford University Press, 2004.

Sack, Daniel. *Moral Re-Armament: The Reinventions of an American Religious Movement*. New York: Palgrave, 2009.

Sadek, Maria Tereza Aina. *Machiavel, Machiavéis: A tragédia Octaviana*. Rio de Janeiro: Edições Símbolo, 1978.

Saldaña-Portillo, Maria Josefina. *The Revolutionary Imagination in the Americas and the Age of Development*. Durham, N.C.: Duke University Press, 2003.

Salem, Tania. "Do Centro Dom Vital à Universidade católica." In *Universidades e instituições científicas no Rio de Janeiro*, edited by Simon Schwartzman, 97–134. Brasília: CNPq, 1982.

Sales Filho, Valter Vicente. "Pornochanchada: Doce sabor da transgressão." *Comunicação e Educação*, May–August 1995, 67–70.

Santos, Rubens Ribeiro dos, and Marly Ribeiro dos Santos. *Compêndio da Educação Moral e Cívica: Problemas brasileiros*. Rio de Janeiro: Símbolo, 1973.

Schneider, Nina. *Brazilian Propaganda: Legitimizing an Authoritarian Regime*. Gainesville: University Press of Florida, 2014.

Schwartzman, Simon. "A Igreja e o Estado Novo: O Estatuto da Família." *Cadernos de Pesquisa*, no. 37 (1981): 71–77.

Schwartzman, Simon, Helena Maria Bousquet Bomeny, and Vanda Maria Ribeiro Costa. *Tempos de Capanema*. Rio de Janeiro: Paz e Terra, 1984.

Schwarz, Frederick. *You Can Trust the Communists (. . . to Do Exactly as They Say!)*. Englewood Cliffs, N.J.: Prentice Hall, 1960.

Schwarz, Frederick, and David A. Noebel. *You Can Still Trust the Communists to be Communists (Socialists and Progressives, Too)*. 2nd ed. Manitou Springs, Colo.: Schwarz Report Press, 2011.

Seganfreddo, Sonia. *UNE: Instrumento de subversão*. Rio de Janeiro: Edições GRD, 1963.

Self, Robert O. *All in the Family: The Realignment of American Politics since the 1960s*. New York: Hill and Wang, 2011.

Serbin, Kenneth P. *Needs of the Heart: A Social and Cultural History of Brazil's Clergy and Seminaries*. South Bend, Ind.: University of Notre Dame Press, 2006.

———. *Secret Dialogues: Church-State Relations, Torture, and Social Justice in Authoritarian Brazil*. Pittsburgh, Pa.: University of Pittsburgh Press, 2000.

Shafer, D. Michael. *Deadly Paradigms: The Failure of U.S. Counterinsurgency Policy*. Princeton, N.J.: Princeton University Press, 1988.

Sigaud, Geraldo de Proença. *Catecismo anticomunista*. 5th ed. São Paulo: Vera Cruz, 1963.

Sikkink, Kathryn. *The Justice Cascade: How Human Rights Prosecutions Are Changing World Politics*. New York: W. W. Norton, 2011.

Silva, Carla Luciana. *Onda vermelha: Imaginários anticomunistas brasileiros (1931–1934)*. Porto Alegre: EDIPUCRS, 2001.

Silva, Jaldyr Bhering Faustino da, and Ayrton Capella. *Educação moral e cívica para as 1a e 2a séries dos ginásios*. Rio de Janeiro: Laudes, 1971.

Silva, José Luiz Werneck da. *A deformação da história ou para não esquecer*. Rio de Janeiro: Zahar, 1985.

Silva, Paulo Julião da. "A Igreja Católica e as relações políticas com o estado na era Vargas." *Anais dos Simpósios da ABHR* 13, no. 10 (2012).

Simões, Inimá Ferreira. *Roteiro da intolerância: A censura cinematográfica no Brasil*. São Paulo: Senac, 1999.

Simões, Solange de Deus. *Deus, pátria e família: As mulheres no golpe de 1964*. Petrópolis: Vozes, 1985.

Skidmore, Thomas E. *Black into White: Race and Nationality in Brazilian Thought*. Durham, N.C.: Duke University Press, 1993.

———. *The Politics of Military Rule in Brazil, 1964–85*. New York: Oxford University Press, 1988.

Smith, Anne-Marie. *A Forced Agreement: Press Acquiescence to Censorship in Brazil*. Pittsburgh, Pa.: University of Pittsburgh Press, 1997.

Soares, Gláucio Ary Dillon. "Censura durante o regime autoritário." *Revista Brasileira de Ciências Sociais* 4, no. 10 (1989): 21–43.

Sodre, Muniz. *O monopólio da fala (função e linguagem da televisão no Brasil)*. Petrópolis: Vozes, 1977.

Springhall, John. *Youth, Popular Culture and Moral Panics: Penny Gaffs to Gangsta-Rap, 1830–1996*. New York: St. Martin's Press, 1998.

Stepan, Alfred. *The Military in Politics: Changing Patterns in Brazil*. Princeton, N.J.: Princeton University Press, 1971.

———. "The New Professionalism of Internal Warfare and Military Role Expansion." In *Authoritarian Brazil: Origins, Policies, and Future*, edited by Alfred Stepan, 47–68. New Haven and London: Yale University Press, 1973.

———. *Rethinking Military Politics: Brazil and the Southern Cone*. Princeton, N.J.: Princeton University Press, 1988.

Stepan, Nancy Leys. *The Hour of Eugenics: Race, Gender, and Nation in Latin America*. Ithaca, N.Y.: Cornell University Press, 1991.

Sternberg, Hilgard. *Escotismo e a educação: Educação extra-escolar e de adultos. Concurso para inspetor regional de ensino*. Rio de Janeiro, 1939.

Strub, Whitney. *Perversion for Profit: The Politics of Pornography and the Rise of the New Right*. New York: Columbia University Press, 2011.

Sutter, Gavin. "Penny Dreadfuls and Perverse Domains: Victorian and Modern Moral Panics." In *Behaving Badly: Social Panic and Moral Outrage—Victorian and Modern Parallels*, edited by Judith Rowbotham and Kim Stevenson, 159–76. Hampshire, England: Ashgate, 2003.

Tavares, Aurélio de Lyra. *Segurança nacional: Problemas atuais*. Rio de Janeiro: Ministério de Educação e Cultura, 1965.

Taylor, Diana. *Disappearing Acts: Spectacles of Gender and Nationalism in Argentina's 'Dirty War'*. Durham and London: Duke University Press, 1997.

Thornton, Bruce S. "The Chorus of Useful Idiots." *Front Page Magazine*, 1 November 2002, http://archive.frontpagemag.com/readArticle.aspx ?ARTID=21386.

Tibery, Hécio de Magalhães. *Fundamentos de segurança e desenvolvimento: Educação moral e cívica*. Rio de Janeiro: Freitas Bastos, 1972.

Torres, João Camillo de Oliveira. *Educação Moral e Cívica*. Vol. 2. Belo Horizonte: Edições Jupiter, 1971.

Trevisan, João Silvério. *Devassos no paraíso: A homossexualidade no Brasil, da colônia à atualidade*. Rio de Janeiro: Record, 2000.

Trindade, Hélgio Henrique. *Integralismo: O fascismo brasileiro na década de 30*. São Paulo: Difel, 1974.

———. "O radicalismo militar em 64 e a nova tentação fascista." In *21 anos de regime militar: Balanços e perspectivas*, edited by Gláucio Ary Dillon Soares and Maria Celina d'Araujo, 123–41. Rio de Janeiro: Fundação Getúlio Vargas, 1994.

Tsipursky, Gleb. "Citizenship, Deviance, and Identity: Soviet Youth Newspapers as Agents of Social Control in the Thaw-Era Leisure Campaign." *Cahiers du Monde Russe* 49, no. 4 (2008): 629–50.

Um homem, uma obra, uma gesta. Homenagem das TFPs a Plínio Corrêa de Oliveira. São Paulo: Edições Brasil de Amanhã, 1989.

Ustra, Carlos Alberto Brilhante. *Rompendo o silêncio: OBAN DOI/CODI, 29 set 70-23 jan 74*. Brasília: Editerra, 1987.

———. *A verdade sufocada: A história que a esquerda não quer que o Brasil conheça*. Brasília: Ser, 2006.

Vasconcellos, Gilberto. *Ideologia Curupira: Análise do discurso integralista*. São Paulo: Editora Brasiliense, 1979.

Vaughan, Mary K. *Cultural Politics in Revolution: Teachers, Peasants, and Schools in Mexico, 1930–1940*. Tucson: University of Arizona Press, 1997.

Velho, Gilberto, and Luiz Antônio Machado. "Organização social do meio urbano." *Anuário antropológico* 76 (1977): 71–82.

Velloso, Mônica Pimenta. "Cultura e poder político: Uma configuração do campo intellectual." In Oliveira, Velloso, and Gomes, *Estado Novo*, 71–108.

———. "A Ordem: Uma revista de doutrina, política, e cultura católica." *Revista de Ciência Política* 21, no. 3 (1978): 117–60.

Ventura, Zuenir. *1968: O ano que não terminou*. Rio de Janeiro: Editora Nova Fronteira, 1988.

Vieira de Sousa, Jessie Jane. *Círculos operários: A Igreja Católica e o mundo do trabalho no Brasil*. Rio de Janeiro: Universidade Federal do Rio de Janeiro, 2002.

Walker, Louise E. *Waking from the Dream: Mexico's Middle Classes after 1968*. Stanford, Calif.: Stanford University Press, 2013.

Weinbaum, Alys Eve, Lynn M. Thomas, Priti Ramamurthy, Uta G. Poiger, Madeleine Y. Dong, and Tani E. Barlow, eds. *Modern Girl around the World: Consumption, Modernity, and Globalization*. Durham, N.C.: Duke University Press, 2008.

Wiebelhaus-Brahm, Eric. *Truth Commissions and Transitional Societies: The Impact on Human Rights and Democracy.* New York: Routledge, 2010.

Williams, Margaret Todaro. "Church and State in Vargas's Brazil: The Politics of Cooperation." *Journal of Church and State* 18, no. 3 (1976): 443–62.

———. "Integralism and the Brazilian Catholic Church." *Hispanic American Historical Review* 54, no. 3 (1974): 431–52.

Wolfe, Joel. *Autos and Progress: The Brazilian Search for Modernity.* New York: Oxford University Press, 2010.

———. *Working Women, Working Men: São Paulo and the Rise of Brazil's Industrial Working Class, 1900–1955.* Durham, N.C.: Duke University Press, 1993.

Wolff, Christina Scheibe. "Feminismo e configurações de gênero na guerrilha: Perspectivas comparativas no Cone Sul, 1968–1985." *Revista Brasileira de História* 27, no. 54 (2007): 19–38.

Zolov, Eric. *Refried Elvis: The Rise of the Mexican Counterculture.* Berkeley: University of California Press, 1999.

Index

Capanema on, 33; celibacy and, 172; Corção and, 85–86, 89–90; education and, 44; Escola Superior de Guerra (ESG) and, 116–17; fascism and, 34; gender and, 29; liberalism and, 31, 46; Lima and, 255 (n. 32); Moral and Civic Education (EMC) and, 182; moralism and, 29–30; Muricy and, 116–17; sexuality and, 57, 85; sexual liberalization and, 66; two currents in, 33; Vargas and, 21, 253 (n. 3); women and, 87, *88. See also* Centro Dom Vital; Religion

Catholic Electoral League, 42

Catolicismo (magazine), 80, 87, *88*

Caulfield, Sueann, 28, 32, 256 (n. 53)

"Causes of Decadence" (Breiner), 95

Cavalcanti, Cláudio, 222

CCC (Command for Hunting Communists), 104, 127, 177

Celibacy, of priests, 172

CENIMAR (Naval Intelligence Service), 162

Censorship, 126–28, 211–19, 221

Center for Internal Defense Operations (CODI), 174

Central Intelligence Agency (CIA), 76, 109

Centro Dom Vital, 29, 43–44, 79, 87, 133. *See also* Catholic Church

Cesar, Maria Luiza, 57

CFC (Federal Council on Culture), 83, 89, 95

CFE (Federal Education Council), 187, 196–97

Children, anticommunism and, 80–83, *82. See also* Youth

Chile, 166

Christian Anticommunist Crusade, 105, 242

Christian Family Movement, 68

CIA (Central Intelligence Agency), 76, 109

CIE (Army Intelligence Service), 162, 166–67, 215

Cinema Novo, 224

CISA. *See* Air Force Intelligence Service

Claudia (magazine), 57–58

CNMC. *See* National Commission on Morality and Civics

CNV (National Truth Commission), 247–48

CODI (Center for Internal Defense Operations), 174

Côdo, Ruy, 234

Coelho, Antônio Joaquim, 130

Coelho, Moacyr, 168–69, 214

Coelho, Henrique, Neto, 208

Coimbra, Cecilia, 120

Coimbra, Cyro, 228

Coitus interruptus, 230

Command and General Staff College (ECEME), 152–53

Command for Hunting Communists (CCC), 104, 127, 177

Communism, 1, 11–12; anti-, 24–31; family and, 80, 92–93; in Penna, 25; psychological warfare and, 124–25; in Salgado, 26; sexuality and, 64; in textbooks, 205–8, *206. See also* Anticommunism; International Communist Movement; Marxism

Conservatism, 12

"Conservative modernization," 252 (n. 20)

Contos eróticos (*Erotic Tales*; Andrade), 222

Contraception, 9, 52, 54, 66, 92, 224–31, 286 (n. 59)

Corção, Gustavo, 2, 12, 70, 80, 83–91, 95; birth control and, 232, 235; Capanema and, 48; *A Defesa Nacional* and, 155–56; Escola Superior de Guerra (ESG) and, 138; influence of, 109–10; Institute for Social Research and Study (IPES) and, 79; intelligence agencies and, 174; Liga de Defesa Nacional (LDN) and, 97; Lima and, 68;

DPF (Department of Federal Police), 162

Dreifuss, René, 252 (n. 20)

Drucker, Peter, 140

Duarte, Gleus Damasceno, 199

Duarte, Luciano José Cabral, 242, 247

Dunn, Christopher, 252 (n. 24)

Dutra, Eurico Gaspar, 42

Dutra, Tarso, 183, 214

ECEME (Command and General Staff College), 152–53

Echeverría, Luis, 97

"Economic Miracle," 9, 52

ECOSOC (United Nations Economic and Social Council), 224–25

Education, 33–34, 39–40, 43–45, 56–58, 85–86, 122, 196–208, 203–4, 206. See also Escola Superior de Guerra; Moral and Civic Education

Educative Action against Revolutionary Warfare (Army General Staff), 153

Ele Ela (magazine), 67

Elbrick, Charles Burke, 174–75

Embrafilme (government film corporation), 219–24

EMC. See Moral and Civic Education

Em cima da hora (Labin), 108–9

EME (Army General Staff), 153

Encyclopedia of Integralism (Penna), 25

Eros and Civilization (Marcuse), 51

Eroticism, 17, 63, 67, 117, 123–24, 138, 140, 142, 220, 232–33. See also Sexuality

EsAO (Officers' Finishing School), 241

Escobar, Ruth, 168

Escola Superior de Guerra (ESG), 13, 16–17, 63; abroad, 147–51; anticommunism and, 74, 115–31; authoritarianism and, 113–14; Catholic Church and, 116–17; Corção at, 84; countersubversion and, 113; *A Defesa Nacional* and, 156–57; Marxism and, 138–39; mass media and, 122–24, 139; modernity and,

128–31; Moral and Civic Education (EMC) and, 187–88, 207–8; moral crisis categories of, 117; pseudoscience and, 114; Schwarz and, 107; sexuality and, 135–37; sexual revolution and, 134; Muricy and, 116–17; technocracy and, 113, 132–35; women and, 129–31; "Youth Problem" and, 118–22. See also Association of ESG Alumni

Estado de S. Paulo, O, 61, 63, 89, 101, 218, 226

Estado Novo, 21–22, 24, 31–37, 35

Eugenics, 22, 25–27, 36, 38, 93, 137, 192–93

Eva, the Principle of Sex (film), 217

Falcão, Armando, 241

Family: birth control and, 228–31; Catholic Church and, 33–34, 37, 67–68; communism and, 80, 92–93, 152; Escola Superior de Guerra (ESG) and, 114–17, 129–32; gender roles and, 255 (n. 29); Moral and Civic Education (EMC) and, 183; moralism and, 148; Pacheco y Silva and, 92–93; sexuality and, 70, 150–51; threat to, 27–28, 159–60; Vargas and, 32, 256 (n. 53); women's rights and, 157. See also Tradition, Family, and Property

Family code, 38, 256 (n. 53)

Fanini, Nilson, 148, 230

Farhat, Said, 114, 125, 133, 148

Faria, Octávio de, 29–30, 36, 48, 74, 84

Farias, Roberto, 224

Fascism, 5, 21; Barroso and, 27; Catholic Church and, 34; Federal Council on Culture (CFC) and, 84; Integralists and, 28, 31, 130; Muricy and, 149; Penna and, 28; Salgado and, 26; Vargas and, 22

Fashion, 10, 52, 69, 96, 124

Federal Council on Culture (CFC), 83, 89, 95

Federal Education Council (CFE), 187, 196–97

Federal police (DPF), 162

Feminine Civic Union (UCF), 234

Feminism, 64, 130, 168, 232, 236, 285 (n. 41)

Ferreira, Darley de Lima, 124

Ferreira, Ebenézer Soares, 204

Ferreira, Oliveiros S., 63

Fertility, 226–27

Fico, Carlos, 116, 251 (n. 9), 276 (n. 49)

Figueiredo, João Baptista de Oliveira, 11, 148, 230–31, 274 (n. 5)

Figueiredo, Jackson de, 27

Film, 24, 77, 219–24. *See also* Mass media

Fischer, Brodwyn, 32

FJD (Democratic Youth Front), 79

Floridi, Alessio Ulisses, 175

FNFi (National College of Philosophy), 78–79, 159, 171

Forrachi, Marialice, 60

Fraga, Hélio, 84

Franca, Leonel, 30, 38, 43, 74, 138, 152, 237, 259 (n. 105)

Franco, Francisco, 88

"Free Love," 24, 111, 130, 138, 156. *See also* Sexual revolution

Freitas, Euridice, 56, 70

French Revolution, 30, 152

Freud, Anna, 137, 141

Frota, Sylvio, 211

Gabeira, Fernando, 64–65

Gabriela (novela), 168–69

Gaiarsa, José Ângelo, 56, 58, 70

GALF (Lesbian Feminist Action Group), 232

Galton, Francis, 137, 143

Galvão, Flávio, 63, 71, 218–19

Galvão, Patrícia, 24

Gambling, 45–46

GAP (Patriotic Action Group), 79

Garcia, Edília Coelho, 201

Gaspari, Elio, 212

Gays. *See* Homosexuality

Gazeta do Povo, A, 89

Geisel, Ernesto, 73, 102, 274 (n. 5)

Gender: in Barroso, 28; Catholic Church and, 29; citizenship and, 41; in Estado Novo, 31–37, 35; inversion, 186; Moral and Civic Education (EMC) and, 182, 185–86; in Penna, 25; in Salgado, 26; sexual revolution and, 95–96; textbooks and, 200–201; unorthodoxy, 59–60. *See also* Masculinity; Women

Gil, Gilberto, 125, 168

Girl Guides, 194

Gismonti, Egberto, 168

"Global village," 122–28, 139

Globo, O, 89, 168, 216

Globo (media corporation), 168

Góes Monteiro, Pedro de, 31–32, 37

Goulart, João, 9, 62, 75–78, 99

Grande, Humberto, 184, 186, 200

Green, James N., 167, 261 (n. 43)

Grünspum, Haim, 60

Guarany, Lúcia de Noronha, 82–83

Guerra, Cláudio, 100

Guerra, Ruy, 224

Guerra conjugal (*Conjugal Warfare;* Andrade), 222

Guerra revolucionária, 52, 115–30, 141, 149, 153–61, 169, 181–86, 190–94, 205, 211, 241, 277 (n. 49), 280 (n. 9)

Guevara, Che, 51, 65

Guide to Civics (Mariani), 198

Guimarães, Hermes, 102

Hair (musical), 59, 211–12, 215

Hall, G. Stanley, 27, 43, 48, 137–38, 141, 143

Harari, Ronaldo, 58

Health, 35, 41, 56, 114, 130–31, 158, 204, 227, 229

Hernandes, Maria Teixeira, 217

Higher War College. *See* Escola Superior de Guerra

Hipólito, Dom Adriano, 102–3

CPSIA information can be obtained
at www.ICGtesting.com
Printed in the USA
LVOW07s0809161217
559968LV00005B/414/P

Securing Sex